The Genesis and Geometry of the

LABYRINTH

The Genesis and Geometry of the
LABYRINTH

Architecture,
Hidden Language,
Myths, and Rituals

PATRICK CONTY

with the assistance of

ARIANNE CONTY

Inner Traditions
Rochester, Vermont

Inner Traditions International
One Park Street
Rochester, Vermont 05767
www.InnerTraditions.com

Library of Congress Cataloging-in-Publication Data
Conty, Patrick.
The genesis and geometry of the labyrinth ; architecture, hidden
language, myths, and rituals / Patrick Conty.
p. cm.
Includes bibliographical references and index.
ISBN 0-89281-922-7 (pbk.)
1. Labyrinths—Religious aspects. I. Title.
BL325.L3 C66 2002
291.3'7—dc21
2002015054

10 9 8 7 6 5 4 3 2 1

Printed and bound in the United States at Capital City Press

Text design and layout by Priscilla Baker

This book was typeset in Goudy, with Albertus used as a display typeface

CONTENTS

PART 4: THE MAZE

PART 5: IMAGES OF THE LABYRINTH

PART 6: MYTH AND MEANING

PREFACE

I have been three times resident
in the castle of Arianrhod . . .
I have been in an uneasy chair
above Caer Sidin
and the whirling round without motion
between three elements.

—TALIESIN

Graspings: wholes and not wholes
convergent divergent, consonant dissonant
from all things one and from one thing all.

—HERACLITUS

. . . or with it or with his hammer or with his stick
or with his fist or in thought in dream,
I mean never he will never or with his pencil with his stick
or light, light I mean.

—SAMUEL BECKETT, *MALONE DIES*

The labyrinth, that most ancient and fundamental symbol of our human condition, remains an enigma that has still not been explained in a complete and coherent way. This shortcoming represents a missing link in our knowledge of ancient wisdom and in our methods of interpreting and elucidating myths and rituals. Semiology and the science of interpretation, or hermeneutics, appear from this point of view to be limited and incomplete, and their methods must be reconsidered.

This claim, however, will not meet with ready acceptance. There is, in fact, an imposing body of knowledge about the labyrinth, and this has led many to consider the subject a closed chapter of our cultural history. Yet each interpretation takes up only a single facet of the symbol, leaving us with a tangle of contradictory conclusions, demonstrating once again that understanding is not equivalent to knowledge. Surely there must be some way to weave these various threads into a coherent fabric!

As a symbol, the labyrinth was supposed to contain the secrets of freedom and ancient wisdom. But modern science has surreptitiously been trying to convince us that such a complete understanding of the human condition is bound to be vain or illusory. More circumspect philosophers extricate themselves by concluding that "we are the sum of everything we don't understand." The labyrinth, with its ever-changing hermeneutical contours, can be seen as representing this sum. Other philosophers claim that ancient and modern knowledge are incompatible. Yet quantum physics, for example, leads to paradoxes, new paradigms, and a new conception of reality strongly resembling those found in the older Eastern religions and myths. Many books associated with the New Age movement[1] have explored this parallel, but the question remains: Upon what is this similarity based?

This investigation of the labyrinth will attempt to show that the geometry—or, to be more precise, the topology—that explains the construction of this ancient symbol is the same as that underlying quantum physics. Thus, the most recent developments in Western geometry will be shown to correspond to the most ancient. The old science and the new, that of the East and the West, rest on a common foundation, meeting like the two sides of a Möbius strip; they are continuous even though they appear opposed. Working from this common base, we shall explore the ways in which these two systems complement each other. Up until now, the New Age movement has based its comparisons on apparent similarities, thus succumbing to a certain superficiality. My ambition in this work is to offer a more solid foundation.

Given the nature of the labyrinth, this book will analyze its subject from three different perspectives. First, we shall outline the problems that arise when one attempts to determine the meaning of the labyrinth. Second, we shall elaborate a method of interpretation capable of forming a more complete explanation. Finally, a geometrical exploration will reveal a method of transforming different diagrams that will allow us to understand the correspondences between many abstract geometrical drawings in ancient and primitive art. In this way we shall also discover a unity hidden behind the diversity of primitive art, a unity parallel to that which unites the different myths. The geometrical demonstrations will constitute a first attempt to introduce topology into what is known as sacred or symbolic geometry. This study will progress hand in hand with the elucidation of the symbol of the labyrinth, which also represents a path leading to unity.

I am convinced that the demonstration of the validity of an idea is less important than the retracing of its origin and growth. This work is thus more of a labyrinthine path leading to the formation and elucidation of certain ideas than a typical thesis based on those ideas. Examples of this are the Cretan seals appearing throughout the text and serving as an introduction to the last chapter, where I venture a theory on the nature of this unique art. It is thought that these seals correspond somehow to the view obtained on and from a labyrinth that changes shape as we progress into it, or to the images a pilgrim receives of his world as he is progressively transformed by the labyrinth. We could also say that the seals are related to the labyrinth in the same indefinable way as they are to the chapters in which they appear. They offer to the text of modern analysis the counterpoint of a silent and very ancient context. The suggested interpretations of the seals do not constitute in any case a definitive interpretation, but instead are there to expose the difficulty of such an interpretation.

This book is the result of thirty years of investigation. My earliest notes on the subject were informal ones intended for personal use. For this reason, I did not always record the exact location and page number of certain quotes. I have made attempts to retrace my research and identify sources in as exacting a manner as possible. I ask forgiveness from the inquisitive reader for any remaining gaps in the citations.

I would like to thank my daughter Arianne for her patient work in translating my original text from French into English, and for her invaluable support as an endless resource for documentation. Also, the erudite suggestions and challenging questions of the conscientious editor Cannon Labrie were very useful at a time when I needed some feedback as he prodded me to add weight to the original manuscript.

1
The Enigma

1

The Götland Labyrinth

Once, while walking on the island of Götland in Sweden, I discovered a rudimentary arrangement of stones placed not far from the shore—a labyrinth. I was intrigued by the archaic character of the formation, which somehow seemed familiar to me, and so, after briefly contemplating its construction, I ventured in. When I completed the circuit, I was perplexed by the path I had discovered and by the strange sensation of having been duped. So I entered again, this time at a run, remembering how as a child, when playing with my cousin, we would spin round and round like badly trained dervishes until we fell to the ground, dizzy, elated, and somehow closer to each other, as if in communion with one another. As I advanced, looking straight ahead and following the ever-narrowing circles, the tide breaking on the shore was indistinguishable from the movement of the clouds, which in turn was one with the rock formations on the hill. The four different landscapes surrounding the labyrinth communicated and merged so that a narrow path leading to a chapel seemed to surge out of a slow maelstrom, indicating, as it rose, the presence of an unknown longing. At this moment, time stood still. The hidden face of the land unveiled itself, revealing the essential meaning of the entire island. Perhaps it was this disorientation that I had sought, that I had hoped to find in its ancient runes, or in a landscape capable of reviving childhood memories that somehow seemed to hold a secret.

How could a rock formation, so simple that it could not even be qualified as architecture, be so suggestive as to evoke the most intimate and elusive of experiences? The labyrinth was certainly worth a third try. I hesitated, perhaps out of a desire to preserve the freshness of my first impressions, and then I walked away, forgetting about it.

Fig. 1.1. The labyrinth at Troy Castle on the island of Götland

Fig. 1.2. A similar labyrinth on St. Agnes, an island off the coast of Cornwall, England.
Photo courtesy Thomas Wiewandt Telegraph Colour Library.

2

The Enigma

These things never happened, but always are.
—SALUST

The story of how Ariadne fell in love with the brave and daring Theseus is well known. Betraying her father, King Minos, and her half brother, the Minotaur, Ariadne gave Theseus a ball of thread that unwound before him, showing him the way through the labyrinth built by Daedalus to imprison the Minotaur. Thus equipped, Theseus escaped from the inextricable labyrinth, and after having killed the Minotaur and liberated his companions, he set sail for Athens with Ariadne, whom, for reasons that remain obscure, he abandoned along the way on the island of Naxos.

The myth presents us, as it did Theseus, with a specific problem: how to find the path from the entrance to the center of the maze. Theseus certainly did not just let the thread unroll behind him as he advanced, like Tom Thumb leaving behind a trail of pebbles to find his way home. Rather, he used the thread to find the center. This task is linked to a geometric and topological problem epitomized by the Gordian knot, which had to be unraveled without one's knowing the location of the ends of the rope.

Gordius, legendary king of Phrygia, used this knot to attach a yoke to the shaft of his chariot. It was later preserved in Zeus's temple at Gordium. The legend held that whoever could untie the knot would become master of the world. Alexander the Great, far too impatient for this endeavor, cut it in half with his sword.

If the rope of the Gordian knot were untied and rolled into a ball to avoid its getting tangled, would it not be similar to Ariadne's ball of thread? It could then be seen as representing the complex path of the rope in the knot, at once untangled and arranged in a new manner, but as if preserved in memory. The image of the ball of thread that indicates the way as it unwinds can also be seen as the backward projection of a film capturing the movement of the knot being unraveled and of the rope being progressively rolled into a ball. Ariadne's thread seems to be a subtle link between two similar topological problems.

Even though the quest for a solution should be less burdensome for us than it was for Theseus, seeing that we no longer have to fear a confrontation with the Minotaur, the problem seems nonetheless impossible to solve, since no one agrees about what the labyrinth really was or where it was located. Some suggest that it was the palace of Knossos itself, built as a replica of the famous Egyptian labyrinth that disappeared without a trace, or else that it was simply one courtyard of this palace where ritual bullfights took place. Others state that it refers to neighboring quarries, or to those of Crotone, in Calabria. Still others suggest that the myth corresponds to a ritual that is represented in one of the frescoes in the palace of Knossos that represents a bullfighting game

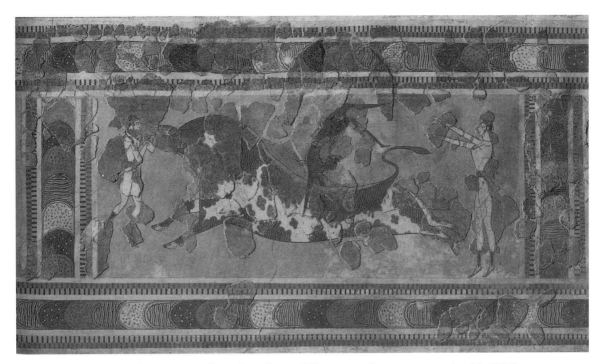

Fig. 2.1. This fresco comes from the palace of Knossos and represents a ritual bullfight. The circles in the border represent the phases of the moon.

(see fig. 2.1). According to Herbinger, this fresco can be interpreted as a ritual calendar in which the circles in the border represent the lunar months.[1]

There are a multitude of mazes, labyrinths, and drawings depicting them from all over the world, but their solutions are too obvious or too simple to entirely justify the "inescapable" character of the labyrinth referred to in the myth. What is more, the classical geometrical labyrinths can be construed from a fret wound in upon itself (fig. 2.2).

Thus any sinuous path, any fortress or fortified enclosure, can eventually represent or evoke a labyrinth. When its angles are rounded, the fret can also take on the form of a series of waves that represent the sea or the element of water and thus, by extension, all of life. Without being able to formulate the problem we are confronted with explicitly, it is difficult, if not impossible, to find a strategy capable of bringing us nearer to a solution.

Should we then see the labyrinth in the same way as Kafka's castle or court? Should we see it as a simple metaphor or as a way of evoking those "things [that] never happened, but always are"? Does this mean that the myth is speaking to us about "Being"?

Fig. 2.2. The labyrinth transformed into a fret

In any case, the myths and legends in which all civilizations since the beginning of history have presented different versions of the labyrinth raise this question: What is the meaning of the myth? Here again, a precise answer is difficult to formulate, as many myths present different versions, each one offering many different possibilities for interpretation. Like Proteus, the labyrinth eludes all attempts to lay hold of it by constantly presenting itself in new forms. Where the Greek myth presents the labyrinth as a prison from which escape is impossible, the *Aeneid* suggests that it hides the entrance to Hades. The Mahabharata describes it as a lethal formation used in the battle of Kurukshetra, but in the Ramayana it is an impregnable fortified castle, lair of the demon Ravana. In tantric art the labyrinth is a yantra symbolizing *citta*, or the mind. The Native Americans see it as the point of emergence and path along which their distant ancestors entered this world. In certain parts of Africa the labyrinth takes the form of a strategic duel. For medieval man it is the Road to Jerusalem, the path that led the pilgrim to a total reorientation. But it can also represent the siege and storming of Troy, and for the Jews, it represented the capture of Jericho. In each case, the meaning given to the labyrinth is different, which makes for great flexibility in its interpretation. This variety can indicate that the labyrinth's original or fundamental significance is either lost or very broad. Thus the ancient Egyptian labyrinth located near Lake Moeris was known to be a sort of matrix, reflecting the structure of the universe. In Korea, there is a labyrinth called the Ocean Seal (fig. 2.3), conceived by the first patriarch of Hua-yen Buddhism to contain a fundamental metaphysical text, called the "round" or "all-embracing" view, and whose profound meaning it seems to reflect. Finally, the very ancient Tihuanaco calendar, like the one at Knossos previously mentioned, seems to link the structure of the labyrinth to the passage of time.

Any attempt to synthesize these different versions and the interpretations they suggest comes up against some major problems. Karl Kerenyi, classical mythographer and author of *Eleusis*, warns us against this difficulty. "The study of the problem of the labyrinth has the strange characteristic, common to the major part of the problems which surge among mythological research when they are examined seriously, that there does not exist a solution which eliminates them." Kerenyi concludes by saying that the labyrinth must remain a "mystery," which seems more than a bit evasive! If we can legitimately suppose that the labyrinth is connected to ancient mysteries, it remains to be seen how this is so, and to which mysteries.

In fact, interpretations of the labyrinth do exist, but as we shall see, they do not resolve the problem mentioned by Kerenyi. Western tradition generally represents the labyrinth as a world that holds us captive, with Ariadne's thread being the symbol of liberation. If this liberation is that promised by all religions, the key to attaining it is to be found precisely in the ancient mysteries. The image of the labyrinth seems to echo the question—"Where are you?"—that God asked Adam after he had committed the transgression that excluded him from paradise. Here again, in yet another form, we are faced with a complex topological situation (*topos* in Greek means "place" or "location"). If the labyrinth is the path of all seeking, it must also hold the answer to the Sphinx's questions: "Who are you? Where do you come from? Where are you going?" Or to the *Quo vadis* heard by Paul on the road to Damascus. But it can also become the symbol for the center or the primordial castle spoken of by mystics and known as the home of the spirit, such as that described by Meister Eckhart: "There is within the soul a fortified castle where even God's eye, in its three manifestations, cannot penetrate because it is the abode of pure unity." This notion of an impregnable castle seems to contradict that of an inescapable prison, but when the path leading out of the labyrinth appears, it need only be reversed to become the path leading from the exit to the center. To find the path leading to liberation one must have already traveled the path leading to the

Text of the Ocean Seal of Hua-yen Buddhism [2]

1. Since dharma nature is round and interpenetrating, it is without any sign of duality.
2. All dharmas are unmoving, and originally calm.
3. No name, no form, all (distinctions) are abolished.
4. It is known through the wisdom of enlightenment, not by any other level.
5. The true nature is extremely profound, exceedingly subtle, and sublime.
6. It does not attach to self-nature but manifests following (causal) conditions.
7. In one is All, in Many is One.
8. One is identical to All, Many is identical to One.
9. In one particle of dust is contained the ten directions.
10. And so it is, with all particles of dust.
11. Incalculable long eons are identical to a single thought-instant.
12. And a single thought-instant is identical to incalculably long eons.
13. The nine times and the ten times are mutually identical.
14. Yet are not confused or mixed, but function separately.
15. The moment one begins to aspire with one's heart, instantly perfect enlightenment (is attained).
16. Samsara and nirvana are always harmonized together.
17. Particular phenomena and the Universal principle are completely merged without distinction.
18. This is the world of the Bodhisattva Samanthabhadra, and the ten Buddhas.
19. In Buddha's Ocean Seal—*samadhi*.
20. Many unimaginable (miracles) are produced according to one's wishes.
21. This shower of jewels benefiting all sentient beings fills all empty space.
22. All sentient beings receive this wealth according to their capacities.
23. Therefore he who practices returns to the primordial realm.
24. Without stopping ignorance it cannot be obtained.
25. By unconditional expedient means, one attains complete freedom.
26. Returning home (the primordial realm), you obtain riches according to your capacity.
27. By means of the law (of dependent origination), an inexhaustible treasure.
28. One adorns the *dharmadatu* like a real palace of jewels.
29. Finally, one reposes in the real world, the bed of the Middle Way.
30. That which is originally without motion is called Buddha.

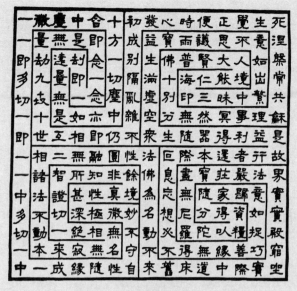

Fig. 2.3. Uisang's Ocean Seal with text and commentary

From Uisang's Commentary on the Ocean Seal

Question: Why do you depend upon (the form of) a seal?

Answer: Because I wish to express that three kinds of worlds included in Sakya Tathagata's teaching system are produced from ocean seal *samadhi*. These so-called three worlds are the material world, the world of sentient beings, and the world of perfectly enlightened wisdom. Those who have perfectly enlightened wisdom are buddhas and bodhisattvas. These three kinds of worlds include and exhaust all dharmas. . . .

Question: Why does the seal have only one path?

Answer: Because it expresses the One sound of Tathagata, the so-called expedient means.

Question: Why does it have so many meanderings?

Answer: To follow (all the) sentient beings whose capacities and desires are various. This is the teaching of the three vehicles.

Question: For what reason does the One Way have no beginning and end?

Answer: To manifest that (Tathagata's) expedient means has no (fixed) method but should correspond to the world of dharma so that the ten (spatial and temporal) worlds are mutually corresponding and completely interpenetrating. This means the round teaching (of Hwaom).

Question: Why are there four sides and four angles?

Answer: To express the four inclusives (or the four means of conversion—that is, *dana*, or giving; *priyavadita*, or kind words; *arthacarya*, or helpfulness; and *samanarthata*, or consistency (between words and deeds)—and the four immeasurables (or four infinite minds—that is, *maitri*, or friendliness; *karuna*, or compassion; *mudita*, or sympathetic joy; and *upeksa*, or equanimity). This means that by depending on the three vehicles, the text manifests the one vehicle. . . .

center, symbol of pure unity, for it is only this knowledge that is capable of bringing about final liberation. In other words: "Everything that appears to be without is in fact within." As if written on an obscure palimpsest, these two images with inverse meanings are juxtaposed, with one of them coming to the fore depending on the direction of the traveler.

The traditional Western interpretation applies to medieval labyrinths, those called the Road to Jerusalem, which were laid into the floors of churches and basilicas. Jerusalem here designates the celestial city—that is, paradise recovered.

If not suspect, this interpretation is at least incomplete. It presents a single meaning for a polysemous myth that offers a constellation of interwoven meanings. In this medieval tradition one of the many implicit meanings of the myth becomes explicit, and thus finds itself separated from its context in order to justify the dogmas and mysteries of the Christian faith. Ariadne's thread becomes simply a symbol of grace or even the string of a rosary. But we never really understand the importance of the thread or how it is supposed to guide the pilgrim. The concrete topological problem of the myth—how to get out of the maze—fades and becomes unsolvable. The relationship between geometry and metaphysics remains obscure.

The exegetical method used by the Western tradition to interpret the myth is in itself mysterious and obscure, as it springs from an intimate contact with a revelation that transmits, or rather translates or transposes, an old message into a new context. This revelation can be achieved from arduous studies, but it can also be the fruit of uncommon experiences, accidents, or a destiny or a pathway that more often than not can only be described in singularly subjective terms. This destiny is precisely one of the themes interwoven with that of the labyrinth in Jorge Luis Borges's short stories. We can also find it in one of the inscriptions that accompanies a labyrinth from the Renaissance, FATA VIAM INVENIENT, "All destinies find their path." As it reveals itself, the meaning of

the labyrinth is transformed, taking on yet another disguise.

Yet by the very fact that these images handed down from tradition are incomplete and yet explicit, they speak to us more directly than the myth. Sometimes, when we try to think about our life and to understand its ultimate meaning, it does effectively seem to stretch before us devoid of all purpose, to follow a somewhat random path across a tangle of other paths, with all of them leading nowhere. And when we try to avoid dead ends, to find an exit or a reason for living, to get to the bottom of it or to establish a more satisfying itinerary, we find only new twists and loops in a Gordian knot; the more we struggle, the more it seems to confine us. If, finally, we recognize the past, like our reflection in a mirror, we discover a sort of Minotaur staring back at us, half man, half beast. And so, if we tend to drift, to go around in circles, to follow goals that ultimately lead us away from our most essential desire, to which no compass can direct us, we can easily suspect that we are living, like the character in Robert Pirsig's *Zen and the Art of Motorcycle Maintenance*, in an inextricable maze:

> They talk once in a while in as few pained words as possible about "it" or "it all" as in the sentence "There is just no escape from it." And if I asked, "From what?" the answer might be "The whole thing," or "The whole organized bit," or even "The system." Sylvia once said defensively, "Well, *you* know how to *cope* with it," which puffed me so much at the time I was embarrassed to ask what "it" was, and so remained somewhat perplexed.[3]

It is remarkable that in our age, when the idea of the Fates unwinding the thread of our destiny seems old-fashioned and makes us smile, the labyrinth is still linked to the problem of the meaning of our existence and even haunts our consciousness with renewed vigor as the symbol of a quest that has become ever more obscure. The most subtle writers of our time, Kafka, Joyce, Roussel, Borges, Robbe-Grillet, Eco, have all found in the maze an effective image to represent our world, and have each proposed his own version, which he presents as a castle, a court, the city of Dublin, an immense library, a secret garden, or even a strategy. Perhaps this can be attributed to the fact that with the arrival of the scientific revolution, language itself has become a kind of maze:

> The social subject itself seems to dissolve in this dissemination of language games. The social bond is linguistic, but it is not woven with a single thread. It is a fabric formed by the intersection of at least two (and in reality an indeterminate number of) language games, obeying different rules. Wittgenstein writes: "Our language can be seen as an ancient city; a maze of little streets and squares, of old and new houses with additions from recent periods; and this surrounded by a multitude of new boroughs with straight streets and uniform houses.[4]

Scientists themselves use these images to describe the inconclusive or indeterminate character of knowledge that modern science leads to. Rudy Rucker gives us an example when he describes Gödel's incompleteness theorem: "Mathematicians can never formulate a correct and complete description of the set of ordinary whole numbers (0, 1, 2, 3 . . .). They are thus left like Kafka's K. in *The Castle*, unable to escape from the imprisoning passageways. Endlessly they hurry up and down corridors, meeting people, knocking on doors, conducting their investigations. But nowhere in the castle of science is there a final exit onto absolute truth."[5]

Even the new scientific method, which seemed to have cleared itself a straight path, is now described as a labyrinth:

> It is now less a path than a multitude of tracks, a map: the labyrinthine forest of the intellect's wanderings . . .
>
> The scientific problem is an interrogation of intersubjectivity. . . . It is enclosed within the complex graph of the encyclopedic labyrinth. So that if

the labyrinth itself torments and is problematic, in and of itself and by the complication of its intersections, it is nonetheless both causing the problems and solving them precisely by the very power of its intersections. The object of science grows, correlatively in power, and its problem in generalities. The scientific problem raises itself suddenly to universalizing dignities, recognized of late, by the philosophical question: less the facing of an obstacle than the confrontation of a community to a global complication that concerns it and that it concerns.[6]

But when we speak about a labyrinth today, are we trying to analyze or chart a structure in order to find an exit or a center, or is it more in order to survive within it and adapt like intelligent laboratory rats? Today, Ariadne's thread is ignored, and it seems that only the negative aspect of the labyrinth has been maintained. As for its positive aspect, which evokes a final liberation, a threshold, a chiasmus where a radical transformation is brought about, or a *metamorphosis* (evoked, for example, by Kafka, though in the opposite direction in his novel of the same name)—it remains suspicious and foreign. This positive aspect lives on at most as a truth of historical value, a possibility that departed with the gods, a secret that must remain shut away, like the Minotaur, in the domain of the fantastic. It is as if reality, like the lowlands of Holland, needed a carefully maintained dike to protect it against the myth.

Like the protagonists of *Waiting for Godot*, the man who enters the modern labyrinth has resigned himself to endure and to adapt to his new environment. Or else, taking the opposite stance, he is resolved, come what may, to sever the Gordian knot. Modern man can identify himself with Daedalus: He admires a "cunning craftsman" who advocates artificial intelligence and genetic engineering, but who seems little concerned with assuming responsibility for his inventions. He can identify himself with the Minotaur, also called Asterius, the man marked with a star, but much less so with Theseus, whom he converts into a Don Quixote. He has abandoned the search for a center and an exit and given up the conquest of death, so that instead of being opposed to birth it has become opposed to life, thereby determining its absurd meaning. He follows Heidegger's "paths leading nowhere" without ever understanding what this nowhere might mean. As Borges has pointed out in his book *Labyrinths,* "it is absurd that such a long corridor should lead to such a small room."

The modern labyrinth is a realm of the mind where an irremediable divorce has separated two worlds—the visible and the invisible. This broken bond has condemned us to a definitive exile. As if its interpretation were obeying the swinging of a pendulum, the modern labyrinth presents a flaw exactly inverse to that of the medieval tradition.

Fig. 2.4. Meanders on Cretan seals

3

The Labyrinth Is Not a Maze

If I were untied, it would be easy. How to undo this knot, how not to want any more,
or to want to be, or else to want to be the water that can be placed in all vases . . .
. . . Me, I am nothing but knotted knots, I am made of nothing but knots that
resist, that want to be knots. I cannot, I do not want, I cannot, I do not want . . .

—EUGÈNE IONESCO, *JOURNAL EN MIETTES*

If the key to understanding the problem of the meaning of the labyrinth is the link between metaphysics and geometry, we should pay particular attention to the geometrical drawings of the labyrinth. Just as there exist many myths and interpretations of the labyrinth, there are a great variety of labyrinths as well as numerous more ambiguous diagrams such as interlacings related to the labyrinth. To avoid getting lost in a field that remains undefined because its contours are indistinct, we must first delimit a smaller terri-tory. If there is no original maze that can be identi-fied in Crete, there is nonetheless a diagram specifi-cally representing the Cretan labyrinth (fig. 3.1). We shall try to establish that this labyrinth is a classic and universal pattern that can be considered a prototype.

The Cretan labyrinth in figure 3.2A, C, and E was engraved on coins and Cretan seals and incorpo-rated into Greek paintings whose inscriptions identify it as precisely the maze described by the myth. It can be found in Roman mosaics and was later integrated

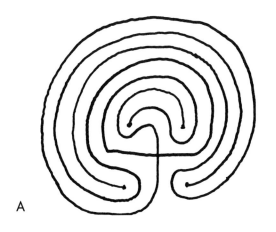

A

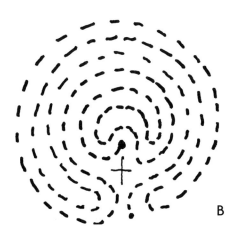

B

Fig. 3.1
(A) The Cretan labyrinth. (B) The path in the Cretan labyrinth.

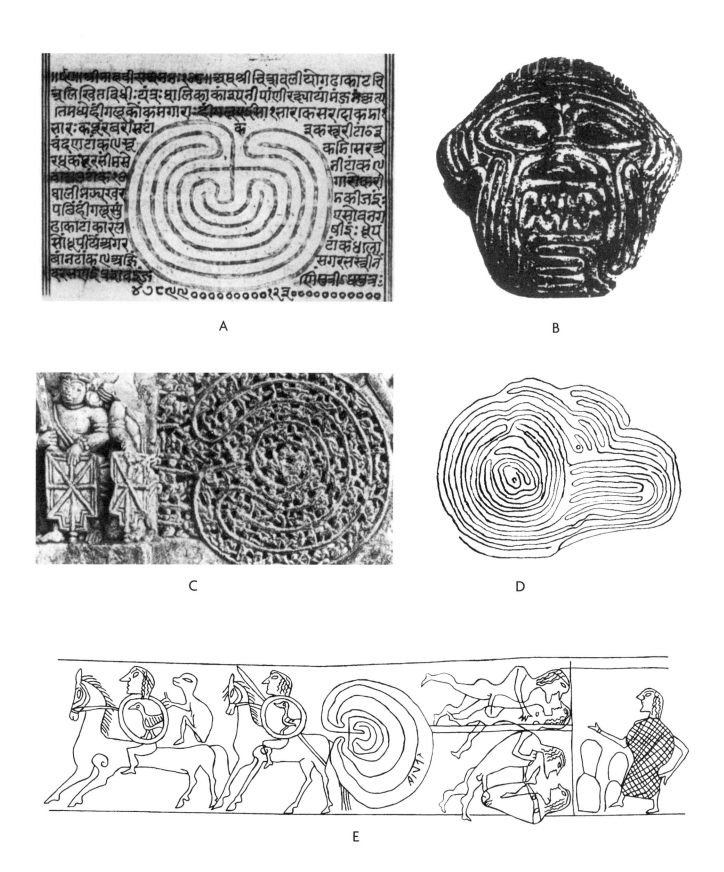

Fig. 3.2

(A) Chakra Manas, Rajasthan, eighteenth century. (B) Mask of Humbaba (Babylonian): "He guards the large labyrinthine forest with his sevenfold terror." (C) Temple of Halebib, Mysore. War scene of the battle of Kurukshetra with Chakra-Vyuha. (D) A Zulu labyrinth. (E) Painting on a Greek jar, Traglia Tella.

Fig. 3.3. The labyrinth in Chartres

into medieval architecture. Although many of these mosaics were destroyed, it is likely that most Western basilicas and cathedrals had this type of labyrinth, or one similar to it, built into their ornamental tiling or pavement. The most famous is the one at Chartres (fig. 3.3).

But the labyrinth is also a Celtic and Scandinavian motif. We find it intact as well among Native Americans, primarily in their basketwork, representing the point of emergence (see fig. 3.4). Among the Hopi, it represents the house of the sun, and among the Pima it is the house of Siuhii, a mythic hero who lived far away in the mountains and whose tracks were so confusing that no one could follow them. Finally, all the important myths that explicitly describe a labyrinth associate it with this same diagram. In India, it is this model that is used as the tantric yantra representing *citta*, the mind considered as the source of images that we project and by which we perceive the world. This same diagram of the labyrinth is sculpted on a wall of the Halebib temple in Mysore. It illustrates the lethal strategic formation used by the ma-

gician Drona in the Kurukshetra battle described in the Mahabharata (see fig. 3.5).

Abhimanyu, the youngest of the Pandava warriors and the most virtuous, is chosen to break this formation at the head of his warriors. He is confident, as he has learned the secret of how to penetrate the formation from his father, Arjuna: "I will penetrate this array like an insect filled with rage entering a blazing fire. . . . Before I was born while in my mother's womb I heard my father describe how to penetrate this array." But he had learned only how to enter the war machine, not how to find his way back out. The formation works like a slipknot, and once trapped in the middle, isolated from his men, he is killed by the surrounding Kauravas. In this story, a principle of exclusion and selection is clearly developed. It seems that Abhimanyu's perfection leads to his downfall because he is but a sum, an accumulation of qualities that have not been integrated into a synthesis. Compared to Abhimanyu, Theseus seems closer to the hero described by Robert Musil in *The Man Without Qualities*.

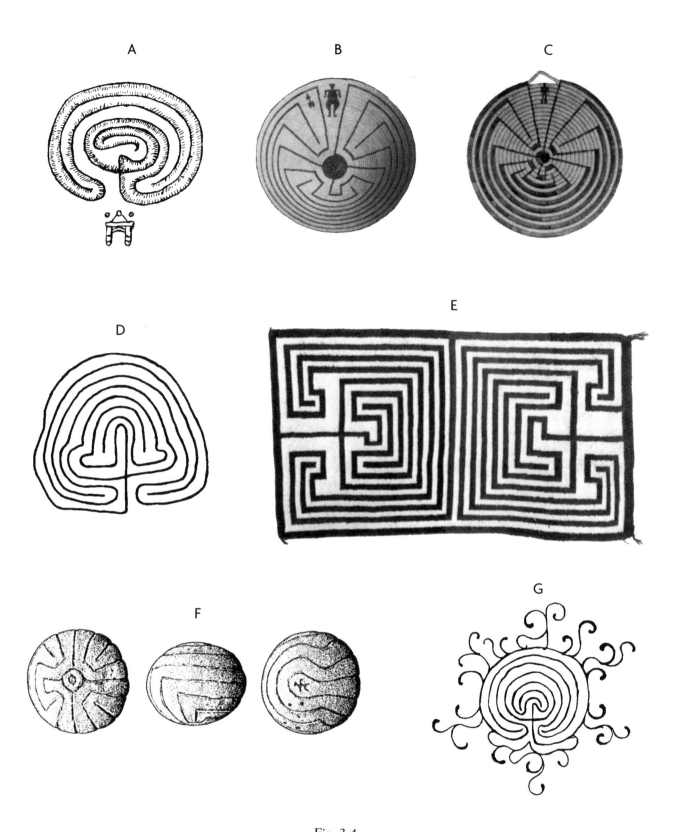

Fig. 3.4

(A) Reproduction of a Pima drawing in sand. (B) Pima basket. Tcuhu is depicted at the entrance.
(C) Papago mat. (D) Hopi Mother Earth symbol. (E) Navajo saddle. (F) Engraved spheric labyrinth found in the Superstition
Mountains of Arizona. (G) Amazonian Caduveo drawing from the collection of Lévi-Strauss.

Fig. 3.5. Illustration of the battle of Kurukshetra, which accompanies a Persian translation of the Mahabharata and Ramayana dating from A.D. *1582*

The same diagram can also be found on ancient petroglyphs (fig. 27.1) and on a tablet that dates from 1200 B.C. All these examples seem to show that this diagram is indeed the original drawing that corresponds to the Greek myth. The other diagrams can be seen as derivations emphasizing particular aspects of a rite, such as those found on Egyptian seals, where schematic designs demonstrating the structure of tombs and sanctuaries take the form of a labyrinth that was intended to protect the dead. There are also later patterns, which were probably made more complex in an attempt to make the diagrams coincide more precisely with the description in the Greek myth.

The universality of this particular drawing is enigmatic in and of itself, as it is difficult to conceive of an organized exchange between ancient cultures that were so different and located so far apart. It is also difficult to decide whether these cultures could have shared the memory of a common origin or whether such an elaborate drawing could spring—complete—from the collective unconscious. These three hypotheses are not, in any case, necessarily contradictory.

This universality of the labyrinth shows that there exists something common, shared by all ancient cultural systems, and, what is more, there exists something fundamental and central, seeing as it is the symbol of our origin and ultimate destination. Given this universality, we should be entitled to seek the meaning of the labyrinth by finding common elements shared by these cultural systems and the myths belonging to them. In other words, we shall allow ourselves to seek further than what might be authorized by the comparative-religion approach, taking care, however, to avoid syncretism.

When we finally examine the diagram of the Cretan labyrinth, we see that it is unicursal, that it contains a single path, making it impossible to get lost. It cannot, therefore, represent the complex maze described by the myth, nor does it coincide with the metaphor of life seen as a maze. The labyrinth is not a maze! It must represent instead the way through the maze, the correct path to the exit as revealed by Ariadne's thread. The problem of finding a way in the maze raised by the Greek myth is thus reversed. We are given the solution, which we must then use to work our way back to the initial problem. To use the key represented by Ariadne's thread we must also find in which lock it fits. The path through the maze is useless unless we can identify the maze and represent it geometrically. The unknown element is thus not the path in the maze, but rather the maze itself and its connection to Ariadne's thread.

From now on we shall therefore distinguish between a geometric labyrinth presenting a single path and a maze presented by the Greek myth as having a number of misleading paths. We are now in a position to understand more fully the difference between the medieval interpretation and the modern one. The former, confident in a divine benevolence, refers to the labyrinth, while the latter refers to the maze and seeks to reevaluate the existential nature of the problem posed by the myth. What is missing, then, is what links these two systems. We have yet to discover how the evasive question of the myth corresponds to the precise though silent answer of the diagram.

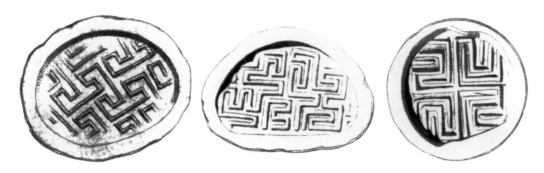

Fig. 3.6. Frets or parts of labyrinths on Cretan seals

4

The Trace of the Ritual

Go toward the obscure and unknown by what is even more obscure and unknown.
—Marguerite Yourcenar

Rather than seeking the hidden meaning of Ariadne's thread in an unlearned tradition, it should be sought directly in the myth itself, by means of a special reading. According to the structuralist approach, a myth's implicit meaning can be decoded and elucidated by comparing different myths and different themes, or "mythemes," interwoven in the myths such as to suggest, in a relative manner, a meaning otherwise ineffable. Each myth is a variation on one or several subjects that are combined differently in other myths; thus the rapprochement between complementary myths will give a more complete picture of the meaning that would be conveyed by all the different variations combined together.

Since structuralism sees all myths as being indirectly linked, however, and since new comparisons with other myths will always bring new complementary information, the work of comparing myths never ends. The structuralist method is one of an infinite, or rather indefinite, exploration. As an endless search, it can lead us to feel as if we are lost, reduced to studying the form and structure of the maze in which the myth dooms us to lose our way. The implicit meaning revealed by this method cannot then be complete; it is either derived from a partial study or assumed by an endless inquiry. Both of these approaches ignore the center and the way out of the maze.

In other words, the myth is presented as being self-referential; the problem the myth explicitly raises is the search for an exit from an inextricable maze, which is the same as the one involved in decoding its message. Its description of the maze simultaneously evokes its own structure and the structure that unites the entire mythological corpus.

This semantic problem appears more and more complex, as the maze described by the myth represents not only our universe but also the structure of the myth describing this universe and constituting a part of it. How can we find our way out of this hermeneutic circle, where the container is in its turn contained by its own contents? We need the help of Ariadne's thread to escape, because the ultimate meaning of the myth is not of the same nature as the concrete nonconceptual logic with which it is built. In other words, only Ariadne's thread can ultimately lead to a hidden meaning found both outside the myth and inaccessibly within it, at a place comparable to that of the soul or the spirit within the body. Just as we can dissect and analyze every inch of the body without ever finding the soul, so the formal structuralist method can never unveil more than an immanent and partial meaning of the myth. As Roland Barthes has pointed out, the subject comes undone "like a spider dissolving itself in the constructive secretions of its web."[1]

Let it be added at this point that the structuralist method still proves to be a precious tool, as we must somehow recognize the structure of the maze in order to find where and how to introduce the thread. What is more, the diagram of the labyrinth belongs to ritual.

Ritual both depends on myth and is often its source, reuniting it with diagrams, dances, incantations, offerings, and actions. It is through ritual that a secret and perhaps unformulable meaning or initiatic thread is transmitted. In rituals, the limits of the word are defined by what the poet priest does with them. Thus, because myth is inseparable from the rites that accompany it, it possesses an aura, a dimension that transcends the corpus of the myth itself. Since ritual can contribute to the origin of myth, its hidden meaning is situated both within and without its hidden recesses. It is in ritual that we must first look for the meaning of Ariadne's thread.

Here, however, we encounter yet another obstacle: The meaning of ancient rituals seems even more difficult to understand today than that of myths. As the prophet Merlin announced to King Vortigern, the secret meaning of ritual has been buried: "After this, Janus shall never have priests again, his door will be shut and remain concealed in the crannies of Ariadne's castle."[2]

As the ancient Greek rites linked to the labyrinth have all but disappeared, we are reduced to seeking its traces in various forms of gnosis or in ancient philosophical systems that attempted to interpret the role played by ritual and that proposed a discipline and a pathway reminiscent of the one traced by Ariadne's thread. Thus we must return to tradition, but to a more learned one and from a different perspective.

The hidden meaning that this sort of tradition gives to Ariadne's thread corresponds to the positive aspect of the labyrinth, which has been lost. It will indicate the whereabouts of a semantic content that might otherwise remain obscure when we examine the formal and structural aspect of the myth. But the hidden meaning we shall encounter outside the myth may itself appear enigmatic or hermetic. Without always offering an explicit interpretation, forms of the gnosis and philosophical systems will present us with an analogous image that we must recognize as such. Jung, after Freud, already exposed this dilemma: "A meaning of the myth which would suit us is suspicious because as a rule, the standpoint of the subconscious is complementary or compensatory to consciousness and thus unexpectedly different."[3]

The meaning thus obtained will not offer a definitive, completely satisfactory interpretation, but it will serve as a guiding thread leading us to the myths relevant to our study. It will allow a fusion to be made among several meanings that have grown obscure over time, and help us discover a network of meanings that may coincide with the complex network of the maze, or at least inform us about its constitution. An interpretation of the myth should be considered satisfactory not if it produces a meaning that is particularly accessible to our modern mentality, but more important if it allows us to discover a junction between a mythic container and its contents—in other words, between an inextricable maze and a thread capable of revealing the path to the center.

In order to reach a possible interpretation of Ariadne's thread, we shall begin by studying alchemy. According to Geber, in alchemy, "to each genesis corresponds an exegesis"; we thus find a confirmation that this kind of gnosis corresponds to an interpretation. Alchemy contains numerous allusions to the labyrinth—for instance, in the analogous form of the *athanor*, the adepts' furnace. In the terms of the Great Work, this alchemical oven represented the human body in the image of the cosmos; or to be more precise, it was the etheric body, conceived of as a fabric of the soul's powers and using the physical body as a support.

According to Fulcanelli, it is knowledge of matter, prepared in the center, that secures one's entrance into the labyrinth. The mutation by fire of this prepared matter represents the exit: "The most impenetrable mystery hides the progress of this admirable metamorphosis."[4] The philosophers recommend the use of Ariadne's thread to the alchemist in order to find his way from the start without getting lost. A treatise written by Batsdorff is thus consecrated to teaching initiates how to use Ariadne's thread. We can find in the middle of a labyrinth or of a double swastika representing it, a marguerite with white petals—symbols of death, and a gold center—symbol of gold as the final fruit of the alchemical work. The correspondence, however, between alchemical and mythical terms is anything but clear, and hermetic alchemical discourse in its evasiveness presents its own problems of interpretation that are as complex as those encountered in the myth. For example, "Daedalus and Icarus personify the stable part of the magistery which is volatilized. Daedalus is the first Sulphur, in which is born the second, which, after being sublimated on top of the vase, falls back into the philosopher's sea. The labyrinth in which they were enclosed is in this case the symbol of matter in putrefaction."[5] Similarly inscrutable is this passage from the *Tractatus Aureus*: "Circumambulation is the circulation of spirits or circular distillation, that is, the outside to the inside, the inside to the outside and likewise the highest and the lowest, and when they meet together in a circle you can no longer recognize what was outside or inside or at the top or the bottom but all would be one thing in one circle or vessel. For this vessel is the true philosophical 'pelican' and no other is to be sought for in all the universe."[6]

The first quote suggests that, instead of corresponding to a path in an immutable maze, the path leading to the exit is created by the transformation or mutation of a maze conceived of as both container and contained. If this aspect of transformation is what is being alluded to in the war strategy described in the Mahabharata, where the formation changes and closes itself on Abimayu, it is not as immediately evident in the Greek myth. Although the second quote's reference to the labyrinth is at first less obvious, again it is a vase or a matrix in which a transformation is brought about that is being designated. The passage also alludes to the way a structure can make one feel lost or confused, becoming mazelike through its constantly being modified and transformed. Instead of a pilgrim turning this way and that in the labyrinth, we find the contents of the labyrinth whirled about, which is the same as saying that the pilgrim is himself whirled about by the labyrinth. If we are dealing here essentially with an upheaval in the pilgrim's psyche, the two descriptions complement each other nicely. Finally, the more we examine this concept of circumambulation—literally meaning to walk in a circle—the more it will appear as a definition of travel through a labyrinth leading to a center where all becomes suddenly different. In fact, this circumambulation also corresponds to a specific behavior, which, according to the apostle Peter, leads to a transformation of knowledge or of psyche: "Unless you make the things of the right hand as those of the left and those of the left as those of the right, and those that are behind as those that are before, ye shall not have knowledge of the kingdom."

What is more, this description of circumambulation seems appropriate to describe the Vedic myth of the churning of the ocean to obtain soma, the nectar of the gods and the spiritual sustenance par excellence. In this last myth, we are no longer directly dealing with the transformation of man finding his way in a world maze, but rather with the concoction of an elixir of immortality, extracted from the world, but which also can transform man. The final result is the same. Thus the connection among different but complementary points of view offers a more complete picture of a single phenomenon presented by myths having no apparent connection. We shall return to this notion of circumambulation often, as it is of particular significance in that it establishes a link between an alchemical transformation (psychological or spiritual) and a curious geometry that is reminiscent of the one found in Eastern mandalas.

From this first approach we can conclude that *the maze can represent man as an aggregate of matter and spirit*. Ariadne's thread leads to the transformation from unconscious man to real man.

As already mentioned, the motif of the labyrinth is also present in tantrism in the form of a yantra representing the mind. This system can also help us find the implicit meaning of Ariadne's thread. The word *tantra* can be translated as "loom" or as either "ribbon" or "warp"—that is, whatever guides the yarn in the loom. It thus designates the continuous thread, complementary to that of a woof constituted by the (thread) of the sutras (*sutra*, from the same root as *suture*, means "thread").

According to Chögyam Trungpa Rinpoche, Tibetan Buddhist, artist, and scholar, this tantric thread is what leads—through a teaching correctly followed by one of healthy mind—to ultimate reality. It is the thread that suddenly links a disciplined mind with the exterior world in all its complexity. Like a powerful and terrifying wave of energy, it connects unused spiritual resources with the outside world to create extremely precise situations. In this way the coincidence of mutually exclusive truths is brought about. Not without a certain sense of humor, Trungpa describes the experience that tantrism (also called "the sudden way" or "crazy wisdom") leads to as "the sky falling on our heads like a blue pancake."

Renowned mythologist Heinrich Zimmer's description of tantric yoga brings to mind the construction of a maze and a method of finding the exit:

> The important thing is to find the right mode of association with ourselves and with God; this is one and the same thing. . . . The spider in its web is to the Indian a metaphor for the divine principle which out of itself brings forth the world of substance and form. But this divine principle Brahma is our deep

unconscious, we, all of us sit in the web of our world which we have wrought with the protection of our *shakti*; it is the maya in which we are caught.

> To overcome this nature given imprisonment, the yogi learns to develop out of himself, in inner visualization a structure corresponding to the spider web; he himself is its center and source. He weaves it into a circular design of the world filled with figures (mandala) or into a linear diagram full of symbols, representing the world of divine forces, which unfold into macrocosm and microcosm. This structure he develops out of himself in inner vision, he holds it fast as his reality and by degrees takes it back into himself. Thus he learns to understand the genesis and passing away of the world as a process of which he himself is the source and center.[7]

In the mandala, the yogi then successively takes on the role of Daedalus, who conceived and constructed the maze, and of Theseus, who deconstructed it or pulled it back within himself to escape his maya. In the mandala, the purely geometric drawings of yantras are replaced by a grouping of figures embedded one within the other. The yantra of the labyrinth can be seen, then, as the substructure of the mandala. It represents, in a certain sense, the energy of the mantra made visible. It is like a subtle path, hidden in the mandala, that leads to the divine principle, like the path indicated by Ariadne's thread. Finally, it seems that the mandala may be related to the yantra in a similar way as the myth is related to the labyrinth. The myth itself could be compared to a mandala where the grouping of figures is replaced by that of narratives. From this second approach we can conclude that *the maze can also represent the world or the image of the world as we perceive or project it*.

This tantric thread that connects and elucidates things can also be considered analogous to the Logos as it is described by Heraclitus when he said that "[t]he thunder-bolt steers the universe."[8] This is not the logical and rational Logos of Aristotle, but a Logos that corresponds to a pre-ontological notion that, like a bolt of lightning, joins heaven and earth, illuminating and revealing a path in a dazzling flash. This is a Logos that is opposed to discursive language and should rather be equated with the Word or the spirit, since "the letter kills while the spirit revives." As R. A. Schwaller de Lubicz reveals to us,

> It (the logos) is generally (and especially in literature) taken to mean "word" (*verbum*), but it would be more exact to relate it to the term "weaving" in its traditional symbolic sense. It stands for the intersection of complementary notions, as in the craft of weaving where intersection gives form to two threads, which by themselves cannot be situated. Taken in this acceptation of "weaving" the term *Logos* in the Gospel of John actually contains in itself the significance of that "circuit-phase": "the manifestation of diverse work of creation as well as the immanence of the creator of this work." The word is not to be considered as magical, but the action it implies is magical action par excellence.[9]

It is a Logos that presents itself, like the path in the maze, as an enigma, an escape route from a world that remains misunderstood.

> *The logos is eternal,*
> *but men have not heard it,*
> *and men have heard it and not understood.*
>
> *Through the logos all things are understood,*
> *yet men do not understand,*
> *as you shall see when you put acts and words to the test.*
> *I am going to propose:*
>
> *One must talk about each thing according to its nature,*
> *how it comes to be and how it grows.*
> *Men have talked about the world without paying*
> *attention to the world and to their own minds,*
> *as if they were asleep or absent-minded.*

> *Man who is an organic continuation of the logos,*
> *thinks he can sever that continuity and exist apart from it.*[10]

In Heraclitus's second fragment we can easily recognize the theme of the legend of Alexander the Great cutting the Gordian knot. Cutting the knot and the continuity of the thread can also be seen as separating existence from Being. Ariadne's thread, on the other hand, like the Logos, suggests an uninterrupted pathway joining the visible to the invisible, the world of things to the world of soul or spirit. In the myth, the hidden meaning of this pathway is brought out by a verbal alchemy that offers an alternative to the discursive logic that analyzes, cuts, and separates. Contrary to the analytical decomposition of discourse, the language of myth is akin to the alchemical decomposition that "kills the lively and enlivens the dead"; the "dead" here stands for the Logos, or profound unconscious, that is as if forgotten, asleep, or dead within us.

As Heraclitus put it, "You would not reach the limits of the soul, even by traveling along every path—so deep is its Logos."[11] If the world is misunderstood, it is because the soul, that "fabric of power," is an unfathomable and integral part of the universe, and for this reason it is similar to a maze that we can never fully explore. The realm of the soul is not only intangible, it is also diffuse, penetrating the body and the world as well as carrying the potential of the spirit, like a matrix nurturing an embryo before it develops. The soul becomes the path or the vessel leading from matter to spirit, and as such it is inseparable from the path of the Logos, but also inseparable from the maze of the world that is gradually transformed along with it.

To be deaf to the Logos, then, is to ignore the dimension and depth of the soul as well, and thus to be separated from continuity. Even if we explore every path, if we ignore our inner world because it appears inaccessible, elusive, or unfathomable, we remain as if asleep or forgetful, lost in a maze, incapable of understanding the outside world.

Finally, if Ariadne's thread is analogous to the path of the Logos, *the maze can represent the world of language as well as the outside world and the world of soul*. In fact, the drawing of the labyrinth that we find on Cretan seals or coins is the mark or logo of Daedalus. Like the Egyptian god Ptah, who is a demiurge and (consequently) the creator of language, and the Celtic magician Merlin, who interprets and reads signs as well as evokes them, so Daedalus, archarchitect, archinventor and blacksmith, master of molds and forms, and one capable of giving life to his creations, can also be considered the master of language and the guardian of the Logos. In the mythic realm, speech is an act, and the creative act always manifests itself as a power of the Word. Objects appear when they are called by their names. The cosmos and Logos are inseparable, the Logos being the order of the cosmos. Language is also inseparable from the invention of technique. Without the path of the Logos, the most inventive technique, like the most skillful language and the most radical logic, would only lead one further astray.

Paradoxically, the maze seems simultaneously to symbolize the world, the human being as the aggregate of matter and spirit, and language. Everything is connected in a continuity that alone can enable us to hear and understand. In fact, a more subtle and complete study of the systems of thought we have mentioned would show that these diverse interpretations of the maze complete each other and belong together, representing different perspectives on the whole. For the alchemist, the observation that everything observable is symbolic leads to the affirmation that everything symbolic is observable and, in consequence, that "the man who is true to himself can contemplate the incarnation of logos in matter."[12]

Reciprocally, the revealed word or the voice of the Logos corresponds to a vision where everything observable takes on a symbolic character.

Hence the maze represents a whole, the sum of all visible and invisible aspects of the universe that are mysteriously woven together with Ariadne's thread. It could then correspond to a system like the one exposed in the "round teaching" of Hua-yen Buddhism, or even to an idealist or "mind only" philosophy that affirms that the world we know is created by the very constitution of our mind.

We still don't understand, however, how this thread becomes a precise path in the labyrinth and a simple diagram. Even if we endorse the point of view of the esoteric doctrines, we seem, from this point of view, to be at a standstill. To understand the diagrams and their source, we must return to the myths with the new information we have gained from gnosis. This information consists in the existence of three models corresponding to both the maze and the labyrinth. We can assume that these models are borrowed from the myths and rituals. They are expressed in the myths through metaphor and are expressed in rituals through symbolic objects, schemas, and diagrams. In gnosis there is the translation of a mixture of heterogeneous languages presented in new terms. This is one reason why a secret meaning conveyed through ritual remains obscure and incomprehensible in gnosis to the uninitiated.

In gnosis there is a mixture of heterogeneous languages. In order to find the connection between geometry and meaning, we must now seek out in myths the images or models they propose to explain the nature and structure of all that the maze was said to represent—namely, the world, language, mankind, and the whole. We can then search further for diagrams of rituals that correspond to these models and expect that to the metaphysical connection between the models found in gnosis will correspond a geometrical connection. Our strategy will be to weave continuously among myth, ritual, and gnosis. Finally, it is geometry that will present the key to the intricacy of meaning and to the structure of myth. The images offered by the myths are the mean terms that will permit the joining of the geometry of rituals with the meaning of gnosis.

But before we return to the myths, we should ask ourselves whether this excursion into the esoteric has clarified the meaning of the labyrinth or made it more obscure. Do we find ourselves in a centrifugal bend of the labyrinth or in a centripetal one? It seems at this stage that the path and the Logos remain as enigmatic as ever. We have found no formula or concept that can lead us to a clear understanding of what they are. It seems that, aside from being incarnated in some messenger, they can only be suggested by an intangible bond or a flash of lightning or a tongue of fire like the one that descended upon the apostles. Thus Ariadne might have uttered, as the root of her name indicates, "I am light," as well as "I am the way and the life." To continue in this vein, we can suppose that had Christ been a Cretan, he might have said, "I am the word, the way, and the thread." It is probably because we have lost the meaning and use of the ancient concept of a center and origin that we are startled by an apparent interchangeability among words like *way, truth, light, life,* and *word,* which today belong to distinct semantic fields. We cannot decide whether this equivalence is the product of a "deconstruction" that has dislodged the precise meaning of words or a "circumambulation" that unites them by making them indistinguishable.

Of course these remarks are made tongue in cheek to avoid contradicting yet another of Heraclitus's aphorisms: "The mysteries that men commonly share initiate them to impiety" (fragment 14). Such a tone can also illustrate how, when we make a serious attempt at understanding the myth, the solution always appears too vague or too cramped, always below or above the mark. It is also necessary for unmasking a superficial or nonintegrated understanding and to keep a momentum. For the sake of finding a comprehensive solution, we might be tempted to adopt the inspired and prophetic voice of Edgar Allan Poe in *Eureka,* but here the solution's validity depends solely on a path that would make its discovery possible.

Without limiting ourselves to a comparative-religions approach or subscribing to a form of syncretism (an approach that boils down to washing down one good wine with another), it is preferable, when in a foreign land, to stammer or adopt the disparate discourse of a Pangloss than to remain silent. Well-trodden paths exist if one has a mind to lecture about the esoteric or the exoteric, but we are easily lost in the mesoteric, where a forked tongue or at least a constantly hedging discourse is necessary. The ethnologist Gregory Bateson noticed this phenomenon and made the following comment: "The first step away from false analytic distinctions such as that presented by Cartesian dualism toward some sort of monism is to get matters that had been separated in the past into the same conversation, and then to establish some formal rules for working with them—what I had planned to call a syntax of consciousness."[13]

The discovery of a formal rule will depend precisely on how we shall go about choosing, combining, and churning all the necessary parts into a satisfactory synthesis. While constructing that rule, playing dumb or adopting an ironic tone can accommodate a rambling discourse or the delirium that takes control when intellectual vertigo grips us and drags us into the vortex of the labyrinth. The ironic tone corresponds to a deconstruction (a demolition of ready-made ideas and preconceptions), but a deconstruction that is not an end in itself, but rather one that is linked to a new construction. The rambling discourse corresponds to the search for a method of circumambulation that represents the ultimate holistic approach. The delirium can be seen as an intermediary phase between a total stupor and the utterance of "crazy wisdom." It can be translated by a stuttering and crisscrossing diction that winds in circles and could throw itself back into a circumambulation. It expresses a contagious disorder, an entropy of language, a chaos from which a new order emerges. This delirium that we emulate and attempt to decipher is the one present in myth, where a profound level of information is reached by the transformation of metaphors and analogies, creating monsters and extraordinary episodes that reveal elusive connections and a hidden continuity. The maelstrom throws up strange wreckage.

But perhaps it is also a matter of falling into step with the dismay or irony of a reader who has noticed an attempt on the part of the author to leave nothing out, to explore a multitude of dead ends and strange circuits in order to re-create the semblance of a maze or to present an enigma in such a way as to have the decipherer—the detective!—gain further merit for solving it. Or perhaps the attempt is to transform an inquest into a quest, so that the path leading to a solution merges with the one that leads, in myths and tales, to marvelous conquests.

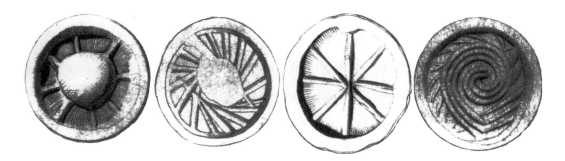

Fig. 4.1. Cretan seals suggesting a sun, or the search for an absolute center, or the striving for a complete union

5

The Equation and Its Solution

The lord whose oracle is at Delphi neither declares nor disguises but gives a sign.
—Heraclitus, fragment 93

Our next step will be to seek models in myths that correspond to structures and geometrical patterns and which suggest the meaning of the maze—that is to say, the structure of the world, of language, of mankind, and of the whole. Often the structure of these models will simply be alluded to, as was the case with the maze and the Gordian knot, but a study of ritual can reveal the geometrical diagrams that correspond to them. Even if myth deals principally with meaning and ritual with the use of diagrams, they must both contain information about what brings myth and ritual together.

Here, then, is the crux of the matter: What is the relationship between the geometric pattern of the labyrinth and the structure of the myth? Or, what is the relationship between the sequence of pathways and turns presented by the diagram and the combination of tropes (figures or turns of language) that constitute the structure of the myth?

Also, precisely what kind of geometry are we talking about? The diagram of the labyrinth seems to be a topological pattern that we should be able to class among others, such as Klein's bottle and the Möbius strip. These patterns can serve as models for linguistic structures, since topology is precisely the branch of mathematics that deals with continuity and corre-

spondences. In *The Jealous Potter*, Lévi-Strauss already used the model of Klein's bottle to represent the structure of a particular group of myths.

This question is crucial when seeking the meaning of a "way" that the ancient mysteries led to, because geometry has always been traditionally integrated with the esoteric tradition. The inscription above the gate of Pythagoras's school—"No one may enter here who does not know geometry"—is a sort of complement to that other dictum—"Know thyself"—and Pythagoras himself was carrying on a more ancient Egyptian tradition. Even in Plato we find this correspondence between the search for truth and the study of geometry; and later philosophers such as Leibniz, Pascal, and Descartes were inspired by mathematical and geometrical models. Just as without geometry we cannot conceive of physics and modern cosmology, it is likewise impossible to conceive of the ancients' way of ordering the universe without knowing the latent or implicit geometry upon which it was founded. But even if a modern mathematical theory exists for finding one's way in a maze, no mathematical solution has been proposed to identify the diagram of the labyrinth or to explain its construction. Thus the problem remains intact, and the quantity of books that bring together an imposing amount of information about the labyrinth only makes it all the more astonishing that none of them has realized the importance of this intriguing fact. As Heraclitus pointed out long ago, men talk "about the world without paying attention to the world and to their own minds."

Is our progress stopped by an incomplete knowledge of what ancient geometry was? Are we following a false lead by seeking a geometry that can transform a maze into a labyrinth? Could a labyrinth simply represent a perfectly fortuitous but harmonious combination of spirals?

To the question, "What is a labyrinth?" the tantric master Chögyam Trungpa answered, "It's a divine doodle." Could this also be Heraclitus's answer when he said (fragment 124) that "the most beautiful order in the world is a pile of sweepings assembled by chance"? Trungpa adds: "It is perfectly useless to enter the labyrinth as Mickey Mouse." The Indian yogi Ramamurti offered an even more laconic answer: "It will kill you . . . inside it you will meet death." Thus, even if we ask for the help of masters who can speak with authority about the symbols and pitfalls that present themselves along the spiritual path, they seem more concerned with the use of the symbols than with their origin, and their answers reflect, more often than not, a deeper level of perplexity hidden in our question.

If we cannot identify this geometric figure, it is probably because we do not recognize in it the schematization of natural objects that the labyrinth is nonetheless connected to and that the myths indirectly present as a rebus: a spider's web, a shell, entrails, a matrix, the convolutions of the brain, or the passages of the inner ear. Even if the labyrinth is an abstract symbol, its structure can be understood only by finding the substratum of an object or a family of objects and a particular way to represent or transform them in order to help the image take on meaning. The geometric form, if it is something, must be based on something else, this thing being the first available symbol of its existence. There is no symbol without

the support of an object, or in the words of Aristotle, "there is no concept in our mind that is not first given by the senses." Inversely, as William Carlos Williams has pointed out, in myths as in poetry, there are "no ideas but in things." Without an initial connection to a clearly defined concrete object or a precise map of the maze, the labyrinth will remain an enigma: an enigma that, like the Sphinx's riddle or the Gordian knot or a Zen koan, describes a closed circuit, a maze with no apparent exit.

Instead of perplexing or paralyzing us, this enigma should encourage us, for the contradiction between the explicit meaning of the myth and the geometric diagram reflects the paradox presented by its implicit meaning, that of an absolute liberation obtained through an inescapable imprisonment. If the labyrinth tends to represent the spirit or even a threshold opened by the mind, we can be satisfied that the myth and the diagram associate the point of view of a confused mind with that of an enlightened mind. It can also reflect the bicameral or Janus-like aspect of the brain. The presentation of the subject is true to its nature. It is marvelous that the myth juxtaposes two complementary crossing codes, one corresponding to a semantic aspect and an enunciation, the other to a gestalt, a structure, and a visual aspect. Thus the intellect cannot separate and appropriate a single aspect of a complete meaning that addresses man in a complete way:

> Habitually one opposes that which can be said to that which is ineffable, the rational to the irrational, by confusing the rational with what can be said and the irrational with the ineffable. The depth of thinking opened by Wittgenstein is to get out of this opposition by contrasting the visible with that which can be said. Thus, what is said, hides. From here the link between that which can be uttered and the invisible can be drawn. Inversely, what is seen is silent; hence the link between the visible and the ineffable.[1]

The drawing of the labyrinth thus becomes a sign, a sign that leads to an unknown path: "There is always the violence of a sign that forces us to seek, that makes peace impossible."[2] If the labyrinth is the symbol of a path of the spirit or of Logos that we no longer recognize and are no longer able to understand, we need a sign that can guide us toward it in an incomprehensible and disturbing way, a sign that fulfills Heraclitus's definition of the word: "The lord whose oracle is at Delphi neither declares nor disguises but gives a sign."

The pathway indicated by the sign is there to lead us to an adventure and an experience that is the only way to measure the truth combined in the symbol. It is itself also the meaning of the symbol. But since we can no longer participate in the ancient rituals, it will first represent a path leading to other images, to other diagrams, and to the way they are linked or transformed. If, as linguist and writer Umberto Eco proposes, "the final function of myth is to signify signification," the drawing of the labyrinth must present itself as the archetype of the sign; it is there to indicate how meaning is born from an assemblage of signs that correspond and are transformed into one another.

It appears, finally, that we are faced with two inseparable problems: that of understanding the message of the Greek myth and that of understanding the structure of the diagram; the solution to these two problems must also be interdependent. We have to solve an equation with two unknowns, and, as we know, this requires two equations. We must therefore find another, complementary myth linked in a similar manner to another diagram.

As it is difficult to find this complementary diagram directly, since we do not know exactly how they are connected, first we must study the relationship between complementary myths and complementary models presented by the myths. This relationship will in turn lead us to the key diagram. In this way, the search for the meaning of the labyrinth can be seen as a game of hopscotch or of snakes and ladders, where we progress toward a center or a "sky" along a spiral, moving forward and backward in a series of jumps. These games are in fact traditionally considered equivalent to the labyrinth. Each circuit and each turn in the labyrinth can be seen as corresponding to a particular symbol, and the grouping of these symbols then constitutes a sort of mandala. Typically, circularity meant an unlimited potential, but when instead of being circular the labyrinth is square, triangular, or octagonal, the angles correspond to concepts that are associated with specific symbols.

Fig. 5.1. Cretan seals
These represent a movement from geometry to chaos, or perhaps
Heraclitus's "pile of sweepings assembled by chance."

6

The Bound Universe
and the Eternal Return

Nothing is created, nothing is lost, everything is transformed.
—Lavoisier

We shall begin our search for an image or model that represents the universe as a maze by looking at an Orphic myth that describes the structure of the world. According to this myth, Zeus, while putting each thing in its place, paused to consult the night, and asked: "How could all things be both united and divided?" He was instructed that he should surround the world in ether and bind the package with a golden cord."[1]

In this myth, the way in which the package of "all things" is tied—that is, the knot that ties the ether to the world—replaces the way things are linked by the Logos. The tying of the cord can represent the structure of space as well as that which links matter to spirit, represented by Zeus. But the myth deals more specifically with the spirit of the night or the spirit in the night, which is to say, the light that shines in the darkness, or the knowledge that lies dormant in the unconscious and that is meant to guide us. Plato also mentioned the golden cord in his *Laws*, saying that we must keep hold of it if we want to be well governed and not be distracted by our passions. According to Homer, it is with this same golden cord that Zeus could pull all things to himself (*Iliad* 8.18).[2] Zeus is thus like the spider in its web that, after spewing

forth the cord of its web, is able to pull it back into itself. The cord thus becomes equivalent to Ariadne's thread, but with an inverse function. The golden cord with which Zeus pulls all things to himself is necessarily—if taken in the opposite way—the cord that leads men to Zeus and the divine, just as it reveals the path uniting the whole.

Since the envelope is made of ether and thus of space, it must also penetrate the interior and the smallest corners of the package. The enveloping path of the cord becomes the path penetrating the most secret interior, like the path of the Logos that intrinsically links all things. A verbal description of this way of enveloping and tying up would quickly become impossible or incomprehensible. The mystery that it evokes can be better rendered by juxtaposing Ariadne's thread with Zeus's golden cord. The combination of these two images brings to mind the secret meaning of the Gordian knot, which can also represent the world structure. The structure of the universe is thus represented by a collection of several kinds of knots. These knots, or similar interlacings, can be found everywhere in primitive art, and particularly in Celtic art.

The turning of Zeus's cord into Ariadne's thread

indicates that the rule that links these myths together obeys a geometric or topological transformation where we find, as with the Möbius strip, a continuity between what is without and what is within. The branch of modern topology that deals with the science of knots also studies the relations among different kinds of knots and complementary networks representing the space both embedded in these knots and surrounding it. In myths, as in topology, there is not only a passage from the inside to the outside, but also a passage from the knot to the structure of space. By rendering the invisible concrete and by extending the concrete into the realm of the invisible, the myth accomplishes one of its tasks, which is to evoke abstract concepts with concrete models. This transformation suggests that the diagram of the labyrinth is the result of a similar topological transformation applied to another diagram representing all things both united and divided, or a structure of the cosmos similar to a tying process or a knot.

The image of a universe held together by a cord can seem ludicrous, yet most of the cosmologists studying dark matter conclude, as does Yannic Mellier, that "[t]he universe is a sort of net—essentially, visible matter is concentrated in the knots of this stitching. We have discovered that dark matter is localized in the long filaments that join together these knots."[3] Superstring theory, which proposes to unify the theories of relativity and quantum physics, presents also a strikingly similar image of the cosmos. According to this theory, elementary particles are composed of infinitely thin dancing filaments, comparable to rubber bands that oscillate. The properties of each kind of particle are a reflection of the way the strings vibrate. As formulated by the physicist Brian Greene: "If string theory is right, the microscopic fabric of our universe is a richly intertwined multidimensional labyrinth within which the strings of the universe endlessly twist and vibrate, rhythmically beating out the laws of the cosmos."[4] But there are also infinitely long cosmic strings, immense continuous threads that are intertwined in such a way as to form complex knots:

Just after the Big Bang . . . the Higgs field, trying to align itself, ties microscopic knots in space. Point-like knots turn out to be magnetic monopoles; inflation dilutes them and scatters them through the supercosmos of bubble universes. The Higgs field can tie space into more complex and exotic structures which are equally rare . . . like strings with the thickness of only one elementary particle but millions of light-years long and having the mass of a few galaxies or "walls" of energy dividing the universe into different domains. . . . Says Guth, "one of the great virtues of the theory is its forgetfulness. The universe erases its own history.[5]

Superstrings vibrate; from a certain point of view, these vibrations could also constitute the primordial sound, or an inaudible sound, that penetrates and supports the universe, a sound from which, according to Hindu philosophy, all things originate. What is more, as they represent particles in their most elementary state, they give birth not only to matter, but also to photons and thus to light.

Here once again, it is knot topology that provides the structure for the superstring theory:

Last July, Michael Atiyah, a mathematician at Oxford University in England, startled mathematicians and physicists by asserting that the mathematics of the Jones polynomial is exactly the mathematics of elementary particle physics. . . .

A few years ago, almost by accident, Vaughn Jones, a knot theorist and topologist at the University of California at Berkeley, found a polynomial equation that could be used to tell knots apart. . . .

Dr. Jones said that the physics connections are also enhancing knot theory. Previously, he said, the Jones polynomial only worked for knots in ordinary three-dimensional space. In order to calculate a Jones polynomial for a knot, mathematicians first had to look at its shadow as it is projected onto a flat plane. But mathematicians also study other spaces, with additional dimensions and with strange twists and turns in the spaces themselves. Projections were useless for such spaces.

But the language used in quantum gauge theory is independent of ordinary three-dimensional space and allows mathematicians to calculate Jones polynomials for knots in other spaces.

Even better, Dr. Jones said, [recent studies by a leading physicist] mean that the knot theory results can apply even when there is no knot at all. The space itself can be twisted.[6]

The mathematics used in quantum mechanics proves to be the same as that used in knot theory. We must ask ourselves if it is not the topological model that in the end colors the theory by creating the image used by physicists to perceive reality. The tool that makes conception possible creates in its own image. A Polish physicist has recently discovered that just like matter and energy knots are quantized. Pieransky calculated "the 3D writhes of all ideal, alternating prime knots with up to nine crossings" and, to his surprise, found that knots seem to have their own quantum theory.[7]

It is the tool's origin that becomes intriguing and that myth speaks to us about. As for modern physicists, even if they sometimes insinuate that God is a mathematician, it is inconceivable to them that physics occupies itself with a thread that would connect matter to Zeus, spirit, or the unconscious mind. The scientific model thus remains purely materialistic, and the essence and effect of the mathematical tool remain obscure. Physicists do not explore in depth the link between their theories and the spirit of geometry. They study matter with audacity, but become timorous with the matter of thought.

With the union of physics and topology, the knot becomes an abstraction, a third term that links the structure of matter to that of space, the visible to the invisible, and multiple universes to each other. We can add that this transition that leads from a knot to a twisted and folded space can also be observed in Minoan and Sumerian seals. In these seals no longer

do we recognize an explicit geometry of skillfully elaborated interlacing that sometimes represents serpents, dragons, or even human figures as in Celtic or archaic Chinese art, but rather figures that seem distorted and knotted or even dislocated by the space that envelops them. This twisting brings to mind an overturning or a course imposed by destiny, which reveals the essential nature of the entity thus represented.

In physics, just as in myths, the aspect and the nature of the world that is described depend upon a particular point of view; it is the way the mathematical tool is used that gives rise to the form of the model and the object described. Thus, by using knot theory in a different way, physicists like Abhay Ashtekar and Lee Smolin were able to formulate a theory that rivals the superstring theory by describing space itself as being a net or a carpet woven with ultrafine loops. In this way it is space and not matter that becomes structured. The model they conceived was so concrete that Ashtekar took weaving lessons to sharpen his intuition.

Stephen Hawking is also a proponent of a unified theory in the domain of quantum cosmology. Replacing the word *particle* with *universe*, his studies led him to a model where an infinity of possible universes are linked together by a network of tunnels called "worm holes." According to this theory, a universe no longer represents the sum of what actually exists, but rather the sum of what can possibly exist. In his development of this theory, Sidney Coleman explains that these worm holes, by permitting communication with other possible universes, keep our universe from bursting or dying out. These linkages bring to mind the path of the labyrinth, which also leads to another world and is necessary for survival. But, of course, in Hawking's cosmology, it is not humanly possible to enter the tunnel and survive the passing through; there is no specific universe for souls and for the spirit. There is likewise no theory describing how these possible universes are also potentially contained within man.

The physicist Paul Davies describes the promises that a unified theory offers in terms that are reminiscent of the alchemists' dream, at least those who truly believed they could create gold: "We could change the structure of space and time, tie our own knots in nothingness and build matter to order. Controlling the superforce would enable us to construct and transmute particles at will, thus generating exotic forms of matter. We might even be able to manipulate the dimensionality of space itself, creating bizarre artificial worlds with unimaginable properties. Truly we should be lord of the universe."[8] Again, there is no mention made of the fact that to become a master of the universe necessarily entails becoming master of oneself. The reign in question is that of Alexander the Great rather than of Theseus. The physicists are speaking about a maze rather than a labyrinth.

Is it because modern science has discovered knot topology that it offers a new approach to study myth? Or are we witnessing, with the development of topology, the return of an ancient science expressed in a new language and seen from a new angle?

If, as is suggested in *Hamlet's Mill*, what we call myth is in fact ancient science, we can ask ourselves what kind of myth is disguised behind modern science and how this science can help us elucidate ancient myths.[9]

> We are playing against myth; and we mustn't think that myth, which reaches us from so far back in time and space, has nothing to offer us but an outdated game. Myths do not consist in a game played once and for all. They are tireless, they begin a new game every time they are told or read. . . .
>
> Some will ask what is the point of struggling to pierce, analyze and foil a strategy that myths have been repeating with no variation for perhaps tens, even hundreds of millennia, when for rational thought, they have been definitively supplanted by scientific method and techniques? Didn't myth lose the match a long time ago? This is not certain, or at least it is no longer certain. We have every reason to doubt that such a great distance separates the forms of mythic thought and the famous paradoxes that, without hope of being able to make themselves un-

derstood otherwise, the masters of contemporary science propose to us, ignorant public that we are: Schrödinger's "cat", Wigner's "friend"; or else the apologies invented to make the EPR (and now GHZ) paradox accessible to us . . .

> In other words, between the scholar who gains access through numbers to an unimaginable reality, and the public, impatient to grasp something of this reality that is based on mathematical evidence that goes against all the dictates of common sense, mythic thought becomes once again an intermediary; it is the only way for physicists to communicate with non-physicists.[10]

Instead of simply opposing ancient with modern science, we can consider how, within a vast cycle, a series of reversals and upheavals can bring them into correspondence with each other. The primordial unity that the myths speak about implies precisely that all polarities and all diversity are the product of a reversal; reciprocally, the discovery of a reversal and the way it is accomplished could guide us toward a new union.

Myth speaks about an evolution and a transformation in many different ways—for example, in the Sphinx's riddle: "Who has four legs in the morning, two at noon, and three in the evening?" By describing where we come from and where we are going, the myth also speaks about its own evolution, about its transformation and the way it disguises and reveals itself over time and across different cultures, among which we must include our own. As the myth of Osiris suggests, the mythic way lives on even when it is buried. It manifests itself in a reversal.

Even when the meaning of myth is buried or becomes hermetic, it manages to find a mirror or an exterior path to perpetuate itself, like that of Heraclitus or even that of Saint John the Evangelist: "In it (the Logos) was life, and life was the light of men" (John 1:4). In the field of topology, it is the concrete substance of the myth that is resurfacing.

From a purely scientific point of view, the superstring theory presents a major inconvenience: Because of the minuscule dimension of the strings, it cannot be experimentally verified. According to Feynman's definition, science has become a system that, using concrete data, attempts to create a harmony and a symmetry among all laws; but it seems that it must progress by following this concept of harmony as it evolves beyond the given data. It is this aspect that we discover in myth without being able to discern precisely a system of laws upon which the harmony of myths might rest.

The farther science penetrates into the cosmos, the more it discovers thought or the mind and the end of the reductionist theory. As Niels Bohr stated, "It is false to think that the task of physics is to discover how nature is. Physics is only concerned with *what we can say* about nature."[11] When, in its turn, philosophy studies the mind and thought, it also discovers language and "the end of philosophy." Finally, the more the language of myth is unveiled to us, the more the universe appears as a whole that any particular subjective interpretation is incapable of rendering. This circle seems to indicate and protect a central zone where ancient and modern science could meet.

Another objection to the superstring theory is that it doesn't lead to a concrete representation of the cosmos. Since it implies seven—or even ten—dimensions, and since it is made possible only through algebra, it is impossible to produce images that correspond directly to geometry. In turn, we must admit that we don't really know how to interpret the interlacings of primitive art either, or how they correspond to a complex notion of space-time. The connection that we have tried to establish between the new models of physics and the motifs of ancient art appears to be founded on nothing but a vague resemblance, but it is precisely this superficiality that has driven our backs to the wall, revealing how badly equipped we are to discover a science behind myth and the art that is associated with it. If myth also presents a system of seven or more dimensions, it seems evident that to accomplish this it must combine and

Fig. 6.1. A woodcut by Albrecht Dürer (1471–1528) showing seven interwoven lines

interconnect multiple two-dimensional images in a complex and precise manner (fig. 6.1).

Emile Malle saw medieval art as "simultaneously a script, a calculus, and a symbolic code"; a fortiori, we can apply this interpretation to more ancient, primitive art. But these words remain vague or even devoid of meaning if we cannot understand the relationship among the script, the code, and the calculus, or even what calculation is involved. In fact, it is largely thanks to the advances in cosmology and modern mathematics as well as the abstract diagrams that they present that we see ancient art in a new light and suspect a complex meaning that escapes our understanding. It used to be theology's role to explore this complexity, but science offers us a new approach precisely because the models that it proposes need to be interpreted.

The active locus of science, portrayed in the past by stressing its two extremities, the Mind and the World, has shifted to the middle, to the humble instruments, tools, visualizations skills, writing practices, focusing techniques, and what has been called representation. Through all these efforts, the mediation has eaten up the two extremities: the representing mind and the represented world . . .

When science began to be seen as a mediating visual activity, then the visual arts offered a fabulous resource.[12]

We must discover if, besides modern mathematics, myths and rituals themselves offer the possibility of discovering an ancient knot topology or a geometry governing the code and the calculus. We shall see later that this is the case. Topology's progress, which has invaded and influenced all the sciences, seems to have marked our time and suggests the closing of a circle or a cycle achieved through a reversal. In this reversal, the ancient and the modern, the East and the West, appear like the two sides of a Möbius strip, or like thesis and antithesis, that together allow us to imagine the possibility of a future synthesis or even, in a utopian vision, a unified theory of the mind and the cosmos.

Fig. 6.2. Cretan seals
These may represent strings, nets, or the structure of matter or space

7

The Woven Myth

A discourse on life-death must occupy a certain space between
logos and grammé, analogy and program.
—J. DERRIDA, *THE EAR OF THE OTHER*

We have been following a trail that should lead from one model to another, so how shall we find the next one? Since we have suggested that the maze represents not only the structure of the universe but also the structure of language, and in particular that of mythic language, we must now inquire as to whether ancient models or images describing the structure of language exist. What is more, if today there is a return and a reversal of ancient science, will we discover a corresponding reversal of modern concepts or models of language? One of the problems immediately encountered is that this structure has several levels. Does the structure we are seeking link only sounds and words that together make sense or does it more generally and more essentially link mythos and logos, confabulation and reason?

It should be well established by now that if we wish to reach the truth about myth, we cannot limit ourselves to a logical explanation of its meaning. We can no longer oppose mythos and logos as was once done, for they are mutually dependent. The myth is like the cosmos it presents, a manifestation of the path and life of the Logos.* When Logos becomes

logic and the signifier, the myth becomes absurd and insignificant.

The *difference* established by Jacques Derrida between logos and *grammé* seems more appropriate and fertile. The *grammé* is the letter or the script, the written trace, the graph. Between these two terms we find the gap between the utterance of the myth and the sign presented by the mazelike diagram that has preoccupied us. The concept of the *grammé* presents a connection between geometry and language. The pitfalls of *grammé* and logos seem to be the Scylla and Charybdis between which we must navigate to find our way, struggling all the while against a perfidious current. To reach the open sea, we must direct ourselves toward these traps one after the other, changing course only at the last minute.

It seems certain that Derrida's *grammé* is borrowed from the Hebraic tradition and derives from the word *tetragrammaton*—that is, YHWH, the name of God. Already in the thirteenth century, one finds in the works of Abulafia and his disciples formulations very similar to those of the structuralists:

Know that these letters, which are sacred letters, can be called *signs* or (means) of transmission, the exterior form of which, by prophecy and by the Holy

---

*This concept will be further discussed in chapter 35.

Spirit, will reveal itself to the prophet; and this when the concave form, by a reversal, will become a convex exterior form. . . . The internal concave form is nothing other than the intellect, while the external convex form is the imaginary form. . . .

And if it is in its power to push and continue further (the combination of letters), its interiority will project itself outside, and it will take, thanks to the power of its limpid and clear imagination, the form of a clear vision, and this is what is called the reversal of the sword flash (Gen: 3:24), which is to say, that the other (the exterior form), by a reversal effect becomes internal, leading him thus to the knowledge of his interiority's essence.[1]

Hence, in some manner, Derrida's project is to laicize a method that was applied to sacred names and that aimed to reach unity or a mystic union by applying itself to common language. By the same token, however, the goal Derrida arrives at becomes opposite to the ancient one.

I shall thus try to give a succinct overview of what I understand by *grammé*. Saussure already established that there was no direct correspondence between the signifier (the word or the language sign) and the thing signified (the object or the concept referred to by language). The language sign derives its meaning from the place it holds in the structure holding together all the signs. It finds its meaning in relation to other signs. In this way, the structure of language replaces the structure that connects all things, the structure of the cosmos. As Michel Foucault has put it, "words find their place in a tropological space."[2] In the same way, Jacques Derrida speaks of a turn of writing:

Language is a structure . . . a system of oppositions of places and values . . . and an oriented structure—let us rather say, half in jest, that its orientation is a disorientation. One will be able to call it a polarization. Orientation gives direction to movement by relating it to its origin as to its dawning. And it is starting from the light of origin that one thinks of

the West; the end and the fall, cadence and check, death and night. According to Rousseau, who appropriates here a most banal opposition from the seventeenth century, language turns, so to speak, as the earth turns.

There will be neither a historical line nor an immobile picture of languages—there will be a turn (trope) of language. And this movement of culture will be both ordered and rhythmed according to the most natural thing in nature: the earth and the seasons. Languages are sown.[3]

The *grammé* is thus the written sign, the letter, or the mark that evokes a line, a connection with other signs, a chain of signs, or a network that brings about meaning. While the spoken word is naturally limited by a particular context and by the intention expressed in the tone of voice, the line of the written word leaves room for an unlimited number of possible connections. In writing, each sign holds the trace of other possible meanings and other connections with other signs within language. This chain or net of possible interrelations constitutes, then, a structure of language. But seeing as the global structure of language and the way each sign is connected with the whole remains undetermined, it is impossible to reach an absolute meaning. The Logos, the Word, the ultimate meaning or absolute content, remains elusive or incomprehensible. The meaning thus reached relies on a subjective interpretation, on complicity or compromise. It can or must be "deconstructed," and deconstruction consists, in a certain sense, in discovering and elaborating a structure that defines and reveals the relativity of meaning, or that of comprehension and communication. In other words, since the whole structure is undefined, it has no center. It seems formless, like the structure of space or time, and we can even conclude with Umberto Eco that it is as if "absent." To describe this structure wholly and completely, we are forced to use analogous images that are as vague as those of the maze presented by the myth, or as those of a network produced by chance and always in movement. A precise definition corresponds only to a closed and limited region of the maze, and it eliminates all chances of finding the center and the exit. Like that of the myth, the meaning found depends on an indeterminate number of relations.

A few comments seem appropriate at this point. If relative meaning is defined by a relation and by a chain or a network of signs, it is also dynamically defined by the movement leading indefinitely from one sign to another that constantly modifies it, and thus by impermanence. The language theory that affirms that words have no inherent meaning and that an absolute meaning is analytically impossible to find appears finally like a theory of "interdependence." In this way, without its adherents even being aware of it, this modern language theory shares a good deal with the Buddhist theory of interdependence, or dependent origination, which denies the inherent or even substantial existence of phenomena, as well as of names and forms. Finally, if we accept the validity of the Buddhist doctrine, there would be, contrary to Saussure's formulation, a link between the subtle nature of words and the subtle nature of things, which is emptiness, but an emptiness that is a far cry from nihilism and that, possessing an infinite potential, unites with the primordial clarity for which it is the condition. In a similar way, the quantum void is a unique backdrop of potentialities, a reservoir of energetic and material fluctuations. This diversion is relevant because we are dealing with an esoteric concept of the labyrinth, and the concept of the void is more or less explicit in ancient religions.

Myths present a surprisingly similar distinction to the one developed by Derrida. In ancient Egypt, language, or the structure of language, is represented by a net (see fig. 7.1). This net has the same relationship to language that Zeus's golden cord had to the cosmos; where the golden cord united the things themselves, the net unites words and the names of things, which are analogous to the knots of the net. It can also present a particular image of the maze that is sometimes represented by a hoop net or by the movement of waves forming a hoop net (fig. 7.2). The net is used to catch fish, birds, and other game in a field of reeds and papyrus that is also the "field of transformation," an allusion to the alchemical theater (fig. 7.1). The net catches all that lives, evolves, and interacts in the field of transformation. Symbolically, the net holds meaning fast. But the pattern of the net also brings to mind the structure linking ideograms and hieroglyphs (ideas in things and things as ideas; the articulation of axes within things and the delineation of things). This symbolism, I might add, lives on in the gospel, where after having miraculously obtained fish by throwing their net into the deep, the apostles must learn to fish for men's souls with a net symbolizing God's word.

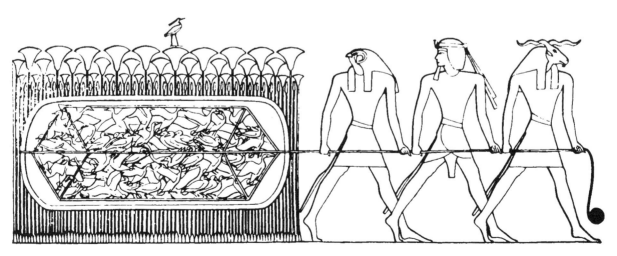

Fig. 7.1. The Egyptian net of language

Fig. 7.2. Athenian frying pan representing a hoop net

When the net is loose and tangled the structure becomes indeterminate. But there also exists a symbol for the word or Logos linked to the net. It is represented by a peg or a stake that keeps the net tight (fig. 7.3). This stake, which stands like the number one, can be seen as keeping Osiris's place, which represents the unity linking all things or even the place kept by the scribe and demiurge Ptah, who invented and spread language. Planted firmly in the ground, it holds the net steady. But to keep the net tight and avoid its becoming entangled, two stakes are necessary. The second stake is represented by a stump upon which Horus's head flowers (which represents Osiris's soul). It is as if the first stake had grown roots that were flowering farther off. In the earth, the dead wood begins a new life, fertilizing the earth at the same time. The first stake stands as a witness to Osiris's death and to his retreat into the chthonic world. The underground path joining the two stakes brings to mind both the path of Logos and that of the transformation and transfiguration of Osiris after his withdrawal into the Underworld.

In carpentry the peg is a sort of stake that joins the tongue to the groove. Thus it is also the symbol of that which joins the tongue to the mouth, the abyss to the flame of the spirit, the cave where Ptah is enclosed to the devouring flame of Sekhmet, his wife and liberator. The Word becomes the symbol of an axis that joins, or a universal hinge. In the ancient system, there is therefore a very clear distinction between the path that links words and constitutes the structure of language and the path of Logos, which somehow keeps the net tight in order to capture living beings, and thus allows language to capture correctly the meaning of beings and things. This is different from the modern model of language, where

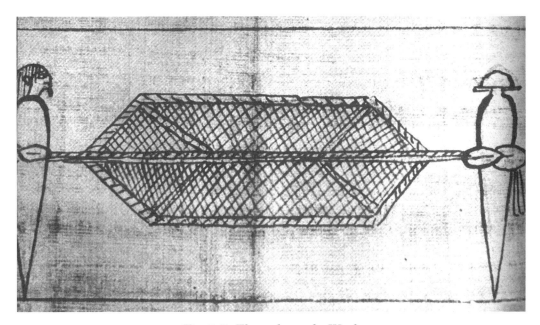

Fig. 7.3. The stake as the Word

the Logos as it is defined by Heraclitus is ignored or denied.

The Logos is also represented by a "super" stake, the pillar of Osiris. The dismembered body of Osiris was assembled in a tree that was felled to serve as a pillar in a temple. Although Osiris later followed the path of his destiny in the chthonic world, his power is manifested in his son Horus, the rising sun, who incarnates the transcendent Osiris. As Osiris transcends himself, the trunk or pillar that lay on the ground is erected, corresponding to the rising of Horus. Just as the pillar supports the roof of the temple, the pillar of Osiris (the *djed* column) holds up the vault of the sky (see fig. 7.4). It plays the same role as Shu, space (but also the intellect), and becomes the axis of the world (see fig. 16.14C). We find here a new complement to the golden cord.

The interdependence between the two orthogonal planes (the underground horizontal plane joining the two stakes and the vertical plane joining the earth to the sky) can also be seen in a diagram representing the net that, according to R. A. Schwaller de Lubicz, was used to demonstrate Pythagoras' theories (fig. 7.5). Originally, then, the Pythagorean system could have served to demonstrate a connection between Logos and language.

Fig. 7.4. Djed column or pillar of Osiris

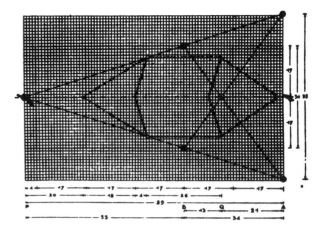

Fig. 7.5. This diagram represents the net that was used to demonstrate Pythagoras's theories.

But the image of the net and peg remains an archetypal figure. To represent how language proceeds within myth, we must find other images that correspond to a state where there is no longer a simple stake or word but a language composed of a multitude of words. In *The Raw and the Cooked*, Lévi-Strauss reminds us that for primitive societies, cat's cradles are analogous to myths (see fig. 7.6). These primitive peoples often accompany the narration of the myth with the making of a cat's cradle, recognizing in the pattern formed by the crossing of the string the images corresponding to the events told about in the myth.

This has always appeared natural to me, as when I was a child, a nanny, to whom I am grateful to this day, taught me how to tie my shoelaces and my tie and to remember the different steps by telling me a story about a fox whose tail was still showing after he entered his hole located beneath a tree that was represented by the loop. Much later, I saw in each knot a possible story and in nature an invisible bond mysteriously uniting traces and forms.

In a cat's cradle, one's ten fingers function as stakes to keep the cord tight, allowing an image to emerge. Since ten can represent a very large number, the ten fingers can be seen as replacing words, or the divided and scattered Word. In Greece, the symbolism of the fingers finds its expression in the dactyls. In the throes

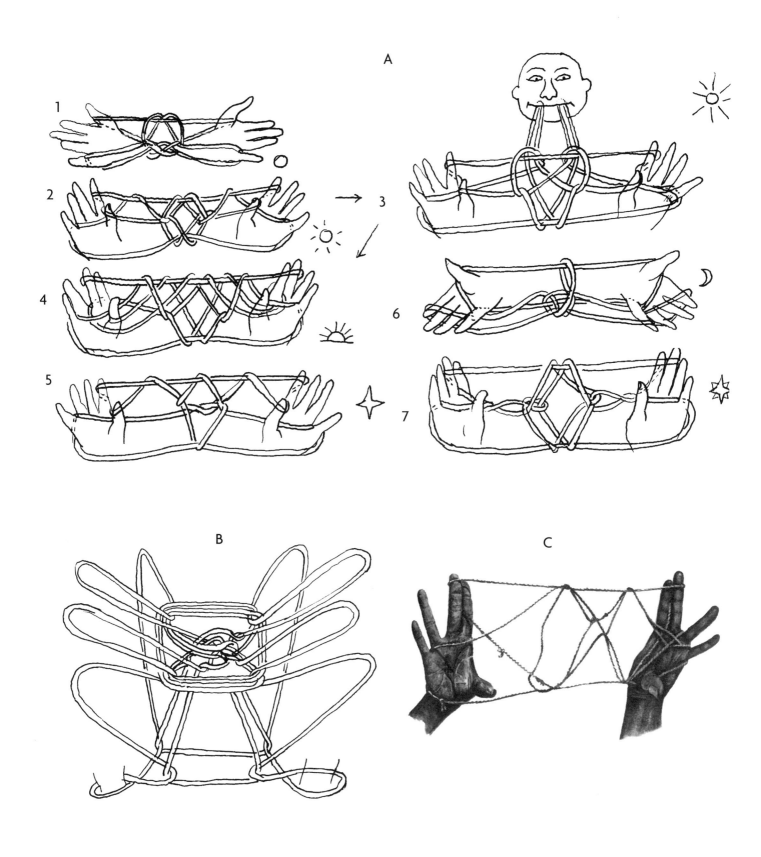

Fig. 7.6. Cat's cradles

(A) 1. Sun clouded over; 2. Sun with full rays; 3. Sun at zenith; 4. Sun setting; 5. Moon crescent; 6. Star; 7. Star.
(B) Bombaceus tree, Warrau Indians, from Lévi-Strauss, *Du Miel aux cendres*. (C) Canoe, Arnhem Land, northeast Australia.

of giving birth to Zeus, Rhea dug her fingers in the earth. It is from this gesture that the dactyls were born: five men who would become blacksmiths for the right hand and five women who would hold the secrets of the Orphic teachings for the left. The dactyls are linked to words in yet another way, as in the Orphic religion the fingers represent different trees but also the letters of the alphabet.

Sometimes the cat's cradle is held between the teeth as if it were an image of words streaming out of the mouth. We no longer have a net taut in order to hold things and their meaning in place, but a network that presents rudimentary images of things as they emerge, thereby representing their creation. The segments of the thread are ambiguously reminiscent of either an axis or a contour. The cat's cradle technique that transforms and links images by pulling the string and weaving the loops together can be seen as representing the way in which myths weave meaning with the thread of a plot by creating and transforming metaphors and analogies. The image is modified by a finger poking through the woof to grab and pull the thread. The finger becoming like the beak or claw of the falcon Horus manifests the power of the word. The movement of the fingers is captured by the weaving of the thread, which suggests, like hands joined in prayer, how words come together to evoke but also to invoke. The cat's cradle that begins with a single ring, similar to a zero, an image of emptiness or of a mandorla like the one surrounding Christ with glory (and which is also a cosmic womb when it surrounds the whole body of Christ), normally ends in the same way, but it can also become a false knot when the fingers are not pulled out correctly at the last moment. The original ring suggests that the structure of language, like the structure of the cat's cradle, can be reduced like the image of the Word or that of the void to a circle or a perfect sphere held by a virtual path of the Logos joining the fingers.

This simple game thus shows how the pathway of the Word creates meaning and new words or a new language and how the path of Logos or the path joining the fingers is integrated into this new language. Rediscovering the path followed by the fingers (or by words) in a game of cat's cradle that can continue indefinitely may remind us of the problem encountered when seeking the path of Ariadne's thread in the maze. The models of the net of language and of the cat's cradle (formed by the pathway of the fingers) complete each other in a way similar to how the models of the golden cord (tying up the cosmos) and the path of Ariadne's thread in the labyrinth complete each other.

In Buddhism, name and form (which represent the fourth link of interdependence or dependent origination) are symbolized by a collection of upright posts that come together in a form similar to a tepee and are tied together at the top by a rope; if the knot is undone, all the posts collapse, showing that the inherent existence of this aggregate is illusory or dependent on exterior factors. This new image with a complementary meaning is thus consistent with those

Fig. 7.7. This fresco at Çatal Hüyük (6000 B.C.), which must certainly correspond to an important ritualistic or symbolic activity, can represent the making of a kind of net, but more probably it represents a cat's cradle. Thus we can assume that before they became simple games, cat's cradles were part of rituals.

that have been presented already, halfway between that of the posts holding the net tight and the fingers bound and united by the cat's cradle.

The theme of a net or string game representing language as a fundamental human or social structure has also inspired some modern writers, for example, Italo Calvino in *Invisible Cities*.

> In Ersilia, to establish the relationships that sustain the city's life, the inhabitants stretch strings from the corners of the houses, white or black or gray or black and white according to whether they mark a relationship of blood, trade, authority, agency. When the strings become so numerous that you can no longer pass among them, the inhabitants leave: the houses are dismantled; only the strings and their supports remain.
>
> From a mountainside, camping with their household goods, Ersilia's refugees look at the labyrinth of taut strings and poles that rise in the plain. That is the city of Ersilia still, and they are nothing.
>
> Thus when traveling in the territory of Ersilia, you come upon the ruins of the abandoned cities, . . . spider web of intricate relationships seeking a form.[4]

In myths and rites, images of all kinds of knots, including false knots and interlacings, replace abstract or obscure notions presented later by other systems of thought. A topological puzzle replaces the skein of ancient mysteries, and a topological problem presents itself alongside a fantastic or mystic quest. It is as if each loose knot or netting also represented the exotic vibration of a string and the task consisted in liberating its harmonics, making other fibers within us vibrate by resonance. As Lévi-Strauss often remarked, myth is very similar to musical composition. Myth is built not upon concepts but rather on what the philosopher George Ivanoff Gurdjieff called "thought through form." According to Gurdjieff, it is this kind of thought that must "be used to perceive the exact meaning of all writing, and to assimilate it, after consciously confronting it with information acquired beforehand." Thinking through form is thus opposed to "mental thought," which operates by association and can only be expressed by words having a relative meaning.

Fig. 7.8. Cretan seals, from net to knot

2
The Solution

8

The Malekulan Ritual
and the Story of Aeneas

*At the summit of the distant sky
Is the word, enveloping everything.*
—Rig Veda

I can imagine this text being read by two different types of readers. The first includes those impatient to arrive at the solution; for them it is the validity of the solution that will indicate the validity of the approach I have chosen to pursue, and I shall try to satisfy them. The second type is more curious and perhaps more critical of the method being used; I refer these readers to chapters 35, 36, and 37 which, after some hesitation, I have placed in part 6. After reading these chapters this second group will perhaps better understand what I have in mind when I speak of the structure of myths.

So far, we have discovered only a vague relationship between myths and patterns—between the meaning of Ariadne's thread and different knot patterns. We still haven't found a specific diagram representing the maze that can be transformed into a labyrinth. To solve the equation with two unknowns presented by the juxtaposition of the Greek myth and the diagram of the labyrinth, we must follow the myth's transformations and pursue the evolution of themes and relationships until we chance upon a particularly revealing new connection between a complementary myth and a new diagram.

We could suggest, as others have before us, that the maze is also represented by the siege of Troy, Ulysses' voyage, Jason's quest for the Golden Fleece, the magic forest in the myths of the Round Table, or the one in the Babylonian myth of Gilgamesh that provides shelter for the monster Humbaba (fig. 3.2B). We even find this theme outside of myth—for example, in the Indian tale "The King and the Corpse,"[1] which represents a transition between myth and a more literary story where the enigma is transferred from the geometric level to the level of language. Here, instead of wandering in an inextricable world or around an impenetrable citadel, we find a series of interminable comings and goings, provoked by a series of riddles. A king is given the task of untying a hanged man and bringing him to a magician who needs the corpse to accomplish a sacrifice. But each time the king heaves the corpse on his back, its ghost asks him a riddle. If the king refuses to answer, his head will burst, but each time he finds an answer, the corpse returns to its initial place, hanging from the tree. The king's answers show that he cannot escape his intellect, and if he is finally liberated from this exhausting repetition, it is by a perfectly balanced last riddle, which leaves him speechless.

The riddle is as follows. A widower and his son follow the charming footprints left on a path by two women whom they decide to marry. The father decides to marry the owner of the larger footprints and the son the owner of the smaller ones. But the prints belong to a widow and her daughter, who owns the larger feet. The father thus marries the daughter and the son the mother. Both women give birth to a son and the ghost asks the king to explain the relation between the two children. "Precisely what was each to the other, and precisely what were they not? . . . The children would be living paradoxes of interrelationship, both this and that: uncle and nephew, nephew and uncle, at once on the father's side and on the mother's. But is it not always so—with all things—in some secret respect? Is not everything, in some deep way, its own opposite?" The paradoxical and inexpressible relationship between the children seems to indicate how a particular meaning, just as paradoxical and inexpressible, is produced by the crossing of mythic codes.

This sort of investigation could lead us indefinitely to the exploration of a complex maze linking all myths. But here we are going to take a shortcut directly to a strategic crossroads where we shall find a polar relationship to the one existing between the myth of the maze and the diagram of the labyrinth. This crossroads is situated antipodal to Greece, on the island of Malekula in Vanuatu. The myth of Malekula was discovered by John Layard, but its correspondences to the Greek myth were also described by Jackson Knight, who believes that it represents one of the most universal archetypes, "a scheme of ritual initiation which seems to have begun as an inhumation rite."[2] As an introduction, and to establish a link between the Greek and Malekulan myths, Knight summarizes a passage from the sixth book of Virgil's *Aeneid:*

The story of Virgil's Cumae is this. Aeneas with his Trojans sailed westward after the fall of Troy, and after several visits, including one to Carthage and two to Sicily, landed at Cumae in Campagia. Near Cumae was the supposed access to the world of the dead, controlled by a priestess of Apollo and Diana, the sibyl who guarded a temple of Apollo and a cave. Aeneas went to the temple and stayed reading the picture of the Cretan labyrinth on the gates. Then the sibyl appeared and told him not to waste time, but to offer sacrifices. He obeys; she prophesies his future to him; and he asks to be shown how to visit his father Anchises in the world of the Dead. The sibyl tells him that there are difficulties, especially in returning; that he must find and pick a "golden bough" as a passport; and that he must bury a dead friend, whose death is unknown to him. He obeys and with the bough he is guided through the cave by the sibyl. . . . Eventually he finds Anchises in Elyseum, open country bounded by "walls built by the cyclops." Anchises shows him a vision of Roman history and explains the moral government of the universe; at last Aeneas returns to his ships, coming through the ivory gate, one of the twin gates of sleep; the gate by which , as it seems, untrue dreams come. After this great experience, there is a change in Aeneas; he is firmer with a stronger faith.[3]

This story (or should we say history?) has a lot in common with the Cretan myth. After his return from Crete, Theseus, like Aeneas, establishes a new democratic government in Athens. Later on, he also descends into Hades (the kingdom of the dead) though his motive is to help his friend Pirithoüs, who is courting Persephone's favors. After remaining prisoner of the "chair of oblivion," an enchanted rock from which Heracles delivers him, he returns safe and sound to the world of the living, but alone.*

---

* This last theme is a fairly frequent one. The reader will remember that Gilgamesh also descended to hell to rescue his friend Enkidu.

The variations between these two stories are clues to a polarity that draws them together. When we later include the Malekulan myth, the comparison of these three myths will lead us to a new interpretation of the labyrinth. Furthermore, by discovering how these myths are interconnected, we shall obtain information about the way the symbolic diagrams that accompany them are also connected.

In the Aeneas version, the Sibyl tells him not to lose time contemplating the sign or *schema* of the labyrinth. Rather, it is the ritual accompanying this sign that is important in order to accomplish a project or *scheme*. And a serious scheme it is, for if Aeneas wants to penetrate Hades, it is so he can learn the secret of the order of the universe, told to him by his father's ghost (in other words, his father in the next world). On the other hand, Theseus's descent to hell is presented more as a prank, which could, nevertheless, lead to the upheaval of the established order, since he intends to kidnap Persephone, who represents a cycle of nature.

Before descending to Hades, Theseus does not make a sacrifice and he does not need a passport. It appears that his previous conquest of the maze is what gives him the right to visit Hades. It is as if his experience in the maze has supplied him with a map of the Underworld, as if Ariadne's thread were somehow equivalent to the entry-procuring golden bough. *The maze is also the domain of death, similar to Hades, except that it is situated in this world rather than in the hereafter.* This reasoning reveals an interesting doubling of the world of the dead, which counters the existence of a simple duality opposing two distinct worlds, one here and the other hereafter (or in this case, "here-under").

The only thing that Theseus has to gain from this adventure is an experience of forgetfulness on the enchanted rock, which can be equated with *a* loss of time, or *the* loss of time that leaves him as if dead. Along with the duplication of Hades we now have a second doubling, that of forgetfulness as an analogy of death. But as Aeneas's encounter with Anchises reveals, death can also contain the secret of an ancient memory and a universal order. There are thus two kinds of death, one that corresponds with total forgetfulness and emptiness and the other with a rupture, a letting go that allows one to gain access to a vital memory and an essential truth. The former corresponds to getting lost in a maze, the latter to the path of the labyrinth leading to an exit and an existence on another plane.

The fact that Aeneas, once awakened, brings a truer vision of reality back through the gate of untrue dreams seems to signify that for the men of this world, who are as if asleep and forgetful, the message of the unconscious or of the hereafter is meaningless. This message seems to be nothing but a deception, like a dream or like a myth to modern man. Down here (or rather here at the surface, since Hades is below), the real is perceived as an illusion produced by untrue dreams. Thus the labyrinth, like the kingdom of Hades, can be seen as also representing the domain of the deep unconscious, which constitutes true consciousness. The relationship between these two myths seems to show that the discovery of the unconscious is equivalent to a journey to the next world in this lifetime. The forgetfulness that must be feared and struggled against is the one that makes us forget the unconscious and the Logos. Just as there are two kinds of death, there are also two kinds of forgetfulness.

The myth specifies that the ivory gate through which deceptive dreams pass and through which Aeneas returns is in fact a twin gate. The other side must be the gate of horn through which the dead enter Hades. This naturally brings to mind the "gate of horn" that designates the entrance to the labyrinth as being a passage between the horns of a bull (see figs. 16.11A and 16.20B).[4] The doublings repeat and cross each other in many ways, showing how the world can present itself to a man who passes from sleep to awakening. We shall discover later that this doubling and symmetry is also a main feature of the geometry of the labyrinth and must originate from it.

Other comparisons confirm our initial deductions:

If Aeneas, like a shaman, finds his father by descending into the depths of Hades, Theseus, forgetting to change his black sail for a white one, loses his father, who in despair plunges to the depths of the Aegean Sea. The black sail is a sign that he is as if dead or dead to this world. Aegeus's fall separates him from Theseus in the world of the living, but draws them closer to each other in the world of the dead. The fall of Aegeus seems to answer the implicit descent of Theseus into the kingdom of the dead, and thus to a sort of rupture with his living descendents. This is in fact a double rupture, since, as an abandoned child, he had already lost his father once before, and it is revealing, since, in truth, he is said to be the son of Poseidon. As he lives simultaneously in two worlds, Theseus must have two fathers. We can even say that he has two mothers, since he was, in a certain sense, reborn in the labyrinth thanks to Ariadne's thread, which becomes like a second mother. It was possibly to avoid a form of incest that Theseus abandoned Ariadne instead of marrying her. We can also surmise that by plunging into the sea, Aegeus joins Poseidon, thereby unifying Theseus's divided origins. We can observe a sort of reciprocal exchange between the two myths; the way that Theseus's father descends to join his son mirrors Aeneas's descent to join his father.

Theseus is also a reversed Oedipus, since by provoking his natural father's death and penetrating the labyrinth, the cosmic womb, he encounters his otherworldly father and is united with a universal mother. When Oedipus discovers, at a crossroads, that he has married his natural mother and killed his father, he suddenly finds himself lost in the maze of life, and abandons his kingship instead of finding it. It is by blinding himself and forgetting this world that he hopes to discover a guiding thread.

Let us return, however, to Jackson Knight, who describes a similar myth from the island of Malekula:

The inhabitants of Malekula believe in a future life to be attained through a complicated series of rites during a lifetime. These rites are mainly concerned with the erection of monoliths representing ancestors; and with a journey said to be undertaken after death, whereby the ghost of a dead man reaches the land of the dead. . . . Ghosts of the dead of the Semiang district pass along a "road" to Wies, the land of the dead. At a certain point on their way they come to a rock called Lembwell Song. . . . Always sitting by the rock is a female ghost, Temes Savsap, and on the ground in front of her is drawn *the complete geometrical figure known as Nahal.* The path which the ghost must traverse lies between the two halves of the figure. . . . As each ghost comes along the road, the guardian ghost hurriedly rubs out one half of the figure. The ghost now comes up, but loses his track and cannot find it. He wanders about searching for a way to get past the Temes of the rock, but in vain. Only a knowledge of the completed geometric figure can release him from the impasse. If he knows this figure, he at once completes the half which Temes Savsap rubbed out and passes down the track in the middle of the figure. If, however, he does not know the figure, the Temes, seeing he will never find the road, eats him, and he never reaches the abode of the dead.[5]

The half-erased *nahal* thus becomes a maze and the axis of the completed figure a path of liberation like the one indicated by Ariadne's thread. Some versions of this myth tell how this road, called "the path of fire," can lead to two different places: to a cave where the ancestors dwell (and where the ghost is also identified as a flying fox, a kind of bat) and to an "island of fire" (presided over by a volcano), which is the final destination for the souls of heroes. There is also a third possible destination, reached if a ghost is devoured by the guardian. In this case he is considered as if joined to his pig or boar (his double or corpse). For a Malekulan native, the boar is a very dear life companion. It is raised with care, and can be offered to Temes as a replacement for the dead man's spirit. During breeding, the boar is mutilated so that its lower tusk pierces through its upper lip, forming a

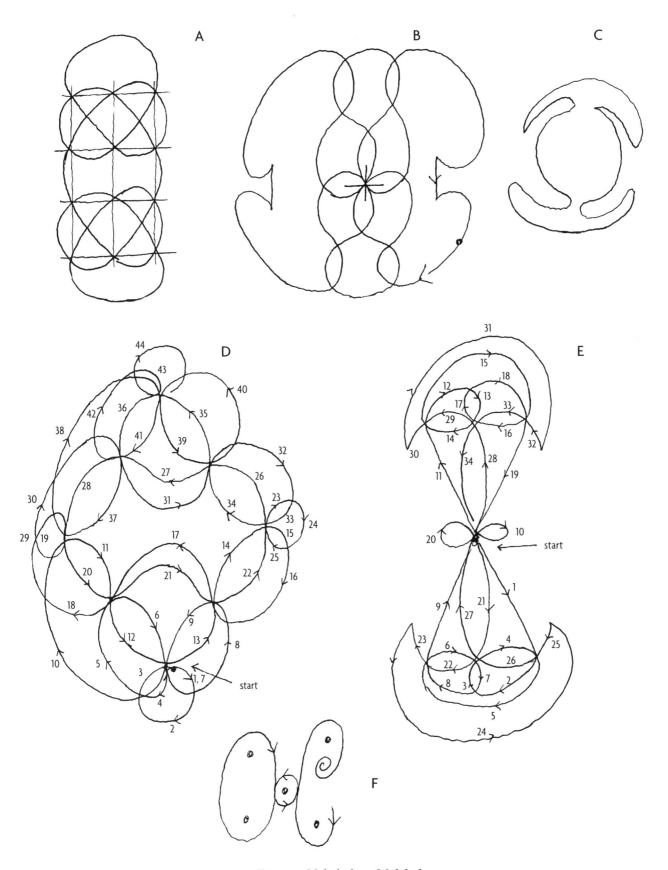

Fig. 8.1. *Nahals from Malekula*

(A) Path of the ghost toward Wies. (B) Road of the ghost or Stone of Tambi. (C) Temes Sevsap, the guardian ghost.
(D) Nautilus. (E) Old and new moon. (F) Snake wound around the bodies of four pigeons. The numbers in
(D) and (E) demonstrate how to follow the pattern.

circle, or even a double circle or a spiral. These tusks are considered important ornaments and are symbolized by torches, representing both the road of the dead and "the path of fire."

Besides a vast collection of *nahal* tracings (figs. 8.1 and 8.3), there are also dances (fig. 8.4) in which the dancers represent mythological figures and form patterns similar to those depicted in the *nahals* by circling between rows of other participants. The *nahal* tracings thus suggest, like myths and dances, ways of existing, of behaving, and of communing.

In the Malekulan ritual we can recognize a transposition of several elements from the Cretan myth. In the ghost world, for example, the boar replaces the bull and the tusks replace the horns. What is more, there is a Malekulan myth that tells how, long ago, a hero killed Temes Savsap and overturned her rock. This hero corresponds to Theseus killing the Minotaur and to a time when Temes existed in this world, before being relegated to the world of ghosts.

The symmetry between the two myths reveals a double equation that can help us find an implicit meaning for the Greek myth. In Malekula a kind of puzzle is completed to attain life after death and to avoid a second, quite irremediable death. Now, if there are two deaths, there must also be two births. This is precisely one of the Greek myth's implicit meanings. Ariadne's thread can easily be seen as an umbilical cord; entering the labyrinth and returning to the "emergence point" is a return to the original womb for a second birth that offers a guarantee against a second dreadful and everlasting death. But this second birth cannot come about without a necessary and intended death, a letting go that is equivalent to a death or to a journey to the Underworld.

We have discovered in the Malekulan myth a new connection between myth and geometric pattern and a complementarity between Greek and Malekulan myths. Instead of a myth about the living that describes the abode of the dead, we find a myth about the dead connected to a multiplicity of *nahal* tracings that represent ways of living.

In the first case, the solution to the complex labyrinth created by the art and science of Daedalus lies in the magic or secret capacities of a ball of thread. In the second case, it is the wandering of the ghost in an incomplete, half-erased, and invisible maze that seems produced by magic, while the discovery of the road corresponds to a perfectly explicit art or science. The Malekulan myth shows us a precise method to find our way out of the maze.

We shall first examine the meaning brought to light by comparing the two myths, and then look at how a similar comparison of geometric patterns reveals a method that can be used to find the unique path of the labyrinth. The way the two myths complement each other will indicate how the two sorts of diagrams are linked.

Fig. 8.2. Cretan seals

These depict boats and rings similar to suns and moons that can represent the passing of time or waves.

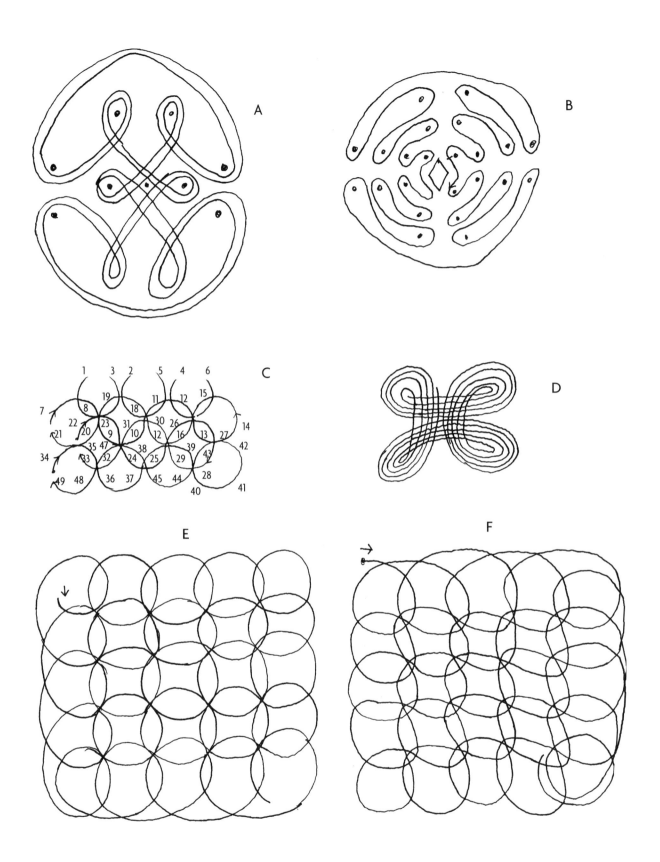

Fig. 8.3. Other nahals

(A) Nimbé ei: two secret societies of Semiang. (B) Hambut sharpening a stone adze on the beach and being driven off in successive stages by the high tides. (C) Roots of the mimumang tree. (D) Nest of the Tarang pigeon. (E) Path of the Grandmother. (F) Octopus, or food of the ghost.

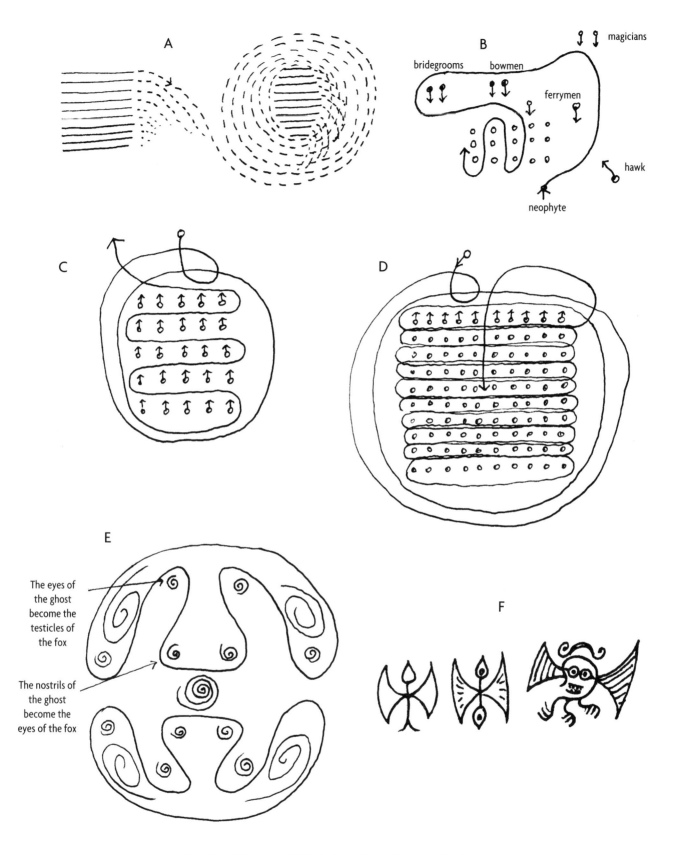

Fig. 8.4. Dances of Malekula and the "eyes of the ghost"

(A) Ten lines of dancers. (B) Course of the neophytes. (C) Other choreography. (D) Other choreography with course of the hawk. (E) Nahal *representing in an ambiguous manner either the ghost or two flying foxes (a sort of bat). Note: There is an interesting similarity between (E) and the designs from Cretan seals that represent the double ax becoming a winged goblin (F).*

9

The Living and the Dead

Ultimately, we rest in the real world,
The bed of the middle way.
—UISANG

If taken literally, the visit of the living Aeneas to the Underworld is even more difficult to accept than the concept of absolute liberty, or that of a path that souls must discover, or the existence of an inextricable maze. Yet this idea of a link between the living and the dead is what allows the connection to be made between a Greek myth that presents two births and a Malekulan myth that presents two deaths. The structure of the two myths is built on this connection. To find its implicit meaning, we shall again turn to Heraclitus, who in his enigmatic way seems to echo the enigmas of the myths and at the same time lead us through the maze.

> Man, in his sleep, touches the dead; waking he touches the sleeper.

> [The souls in Hades] arise, and become the watchful guardians of the living and the dead.

> Immortals mortals, mortals immortals: living each other's death, dying each other's life.[1]

In his sleep, man forgets and "touches the dead." Even when awake, he behaves like a sleepwalker as he is disconnected from the Logos, from his soul, and from a memory that lies in the unconscious. He goes, in Rilke's words, "from a misunderstood sleep to an inattentive awakening." He addresses his self as an "other," a stranger or a double, and his soul as a ghost. Only the soul is in contact with the Logos; it is its ever-watchful guardian, its true custodian. Life is a kind of death and death a kind of life. The unconscious is true consciousness, and what we normally call the conscious state is like sleep.

Heraclitus not only establishes a reversal of values, but he also sets in place a balance and an equilibrium. Inattentive man, who ignores the dimension of the spirit, lives at the expense of his soul, which remains hidden, inaccessible, and as if imprisoned in Hades, undeveloped in Limbo, or forgotten in Lethe. Mortals live the death of immortals, who alone are united with their souls and as if dead to this world, who must act like the dead and withdraw into the unconscious or Hades, to help mortals by delivering their souls.

Man's life thus corresponds to the insularity of a hidden realm that has the name of Hades. It is so structured that certain space-time dimensions have become hidden, disconnected, separated, or isolated from common experience. There is thus a connection between modes of being and the dimensions of space-time. By qualifying these dimensions, the myth anticipates the transition to the topology governing the diagrams of ritual, a topology dealing with dimensions of space. In myth, "Every form of existence takes place in a space appropriate to its nature. Whether a being is eternal, invisible, or mortal, it is co-involved with its own space in such a way that the two realities reveal one another's character. The space of the universe is not vague and undefined but structured and knowable. . . . Each culture identifies several kinds of space, all of which have come into existence since the demise of the primordium or since the withdrawal of the full manifestation of primordial beings."[2]

In Hades an exchange takes place, and it is this place, this *topos* that the myth tries to situate in order to characterize the exchange. The invisible soul is equally difficult to define. Like space, it appears empty, an extension or hidden dimension of the body or an animated field of subtle energy, produced by we don't know what. The ghost of the dead is also an ephemeral ectoplasm that can adopt and remember the form of the body, but we don't understand how it lasts. It will thus be indirectly described by the relative place it occupies or by the path it follows.

The Malekulan myth indicates that the soul becomes immortal when the ghost of the dead man defines an axis by reestablishing the symmetry of the *nahal* pattern. To make this axis apparent, the pattern, which essentially represents life or a way of living, must be quickly rebuilt and thus perfectly understood from the inside during one's lifetime. This *nahal* drawing represents a way of existing that allows one to remain connected to the invisible and to the whole. The second half of the pattern is a perfectly symmetrical copy of the first half but traced the other way

around, or, we could say, with a different spin. The two halves bring to mind the way antimatter is described in physics as being the inverse reflection of matter, as if thrown back by a mirror.

In the Malekulan myth, the nature of the soul is analogous to that of the path followed by the ghost. It is like the axis of a figure that is real without being concrete, and its existence depends on the symmetrical configuration that determines it. The soul and the path it follows become one. The soul joins life to death, the visible to the invisible, just as the axis joins and separates two inverse and symmetrical parts of a single pattern. But like the axis of the *nahal* tracing, the soul can be identified only by a realm that defines and clothes its dimension. Otherwise it is indistinguishable, like the path leading out of the Greek maze. The soul can become actualized and immortal only when its realm is completely revealed. The soul and God cannot be isolated and defined independently; they must be recognized in relation to the forms through which they choose to manifest themselves. As Heraclitus put it: "The God . . . day night, winter summer, satiety hunger . . . He undergoes alteration in the way fire, when it is mixed with different incense, is named according to the scent of each" (fragment 67).

The doubling, the exchange, and the mutually illuminating balance between life and death that Heraclitus speaks about reveal the way that the two myths cross and shed light on each other. But this exchange also corresponds to a transformation, to a circumambulation and a code supported by topological and tropological notions. We can thus infer that the correspondence between the different diagrams will also reveal a topology that constitutes the missing link between myth and ritual.

Fig. 9.1. Cretan seals depicting bucrania and their doubling

10

A Puzzle of Myths

Even a drink decomposes if it is not stirred up.
—HERACLITUS, FRAGMENT 125

It is not only the soul that is hidden, but the Logos as well, as they are interdependent. Just as man becomes hardened, developing incompletely and without harmony and producing, as it were, a shell that imprisons his soul, so myth—which *is* language—captures and fetters its Logos. Conversely, as Olivier Clément has stated, "the transcendent only remains within language by consuming it," thereby transforming it.[1] These processes have their own momentum and evolution. The conflict between these two processes produces something! (Something rather than nothing, or, if you will, a force that animates and structures a space, a silence, an interval, or an emptiness that spreads between myths and between the words used to create them.) One could say that by juxtaposing opposites or symmetrical points of view, the language of myth completes a structure and designates yet again an intangible axis. This axis, like the pillar of Osiris or the *axis mundi,* stands for the Logos and for the path of the souls.

Like all sacred scriptures, myths express a mentality that makes connections and reunites, and thus they are linked more or less explicitly to a religion (from the Latin *religare,* meaning "to tie back," "to reunite"), which serves as a structure for a social order and seeks to reunite all things—both the visible

and the invisible. Once put into the context of an ethnic group, religion and tradition become institutionalized, fossilized, dogmatic, and the property of an elite or a caste. Egyptian religion becomes alienating for the Cretans, just as Cretan religion alienates the Athenians. In a reversal, that which connects and reunites becomes that which excludes and separates. The myth's contents must be translated into other languages, seen from new perspectives, and adapted to a new ethnic context. It must disguise itself beneath new myths that link the history of societies and of men to the history of the Logos. It is in this way that the order of Cretan symbols is displaced or reversed by that of the Greeks, though the latter nonetheless suggests the path of the Logos by enriching the puzzle that is composed of all myths in such a way as to ensure that the complete system of interrelations suggests an essential unity. The life-death crossing or chiasmus, is accompanied by a similar crossing of truth with fiction, reality with illusion, and speech with sign. In order to reveal a symmetry from a new angle, the language of myth ceaselessly produces new metaphors and marvelous or fantastic images, which correspond to a transformation of the geometric images.

This process of reversal is described and analyzed

within the Greek myth itself. Poseidon offers Minos the gift of a marvelous bull that surges out of the sea. But this gift is also a gage, as Minos is supposed to sacrifice the bull. Minos, however, becomes greedy and covets the magnificent bull instead of remaining faithful to what it represents. To punish him, Poseidon makes Minos' wife, Pasiphaë, fall prey to an irresistible lust for the creature. With the help of Daedalus, who creates an imitation cow out of wood and leather for her to hide in, Pasiphaë manages to seduce the bull and to copulate with it, conceiving the monstrous Minotaur.

Thus all begins with an alliance and a pact between the gods and men, and with a mandate given to Minos, "confidant of the great Zeus."[2] The bull is the symbol and the sign of a vital force springing from the depths of the sea—again, from a hidden unconscious realm (Poseidon's kingdom is in this sense similar to the kingdom of Hades). Life must be enhanced by the sacrifice of the bull. It is perhaps the role of sacrifice to unveil the meaning behind symbols, saving them from degenerating into idols. But with Minos's attachment to the bull and the outcome of Pasiphaë's lust, everything is turned upside down. By enclosing herself in an inanimate trap, a lure, she reduces herself to being an object of desire; her world, her entourage, is reduced to the environment of the artificial cow. The cow, which symbolizes the celestial vault in Egypt, becomes a constrictive shell, a Trojan horse with an inverse function. The hybrid bastard known as the Minotaur can be seen as a reversed Ptah, who, as creator of language, is also represented as having a bull's head. The path of fire becomes a path to callousness. The labyrinth, which should be a shrine of life dedicated to Zeus, becomes a maze, an inextricable prison and a temple of death. Instead of being a shelter for the Logos, it becomes the cave of the subconscious, like an immense inner ear ceaselessly interpreting possible intentions hidden in the voice of the "other."

An aside seems called for at this point: Perhaps Freud was right when he interpreted the myth of the labyrinth as symbolizing an anal birth, where the sinuous path represents the intestines and Ariadne's thread the umbilical cord. But this is an interpretation of only one of the reversals hinted at by the myth, the displacement of one of the messages by which the subconscious sets off the alarm. Symbols are the product of a coalescence and a synthesis of multiple meanings. Their role is ultimately to reveal affinities and correspondences that take on meaning only in an "uninterrupted whole." They reveal valences for signs, but they are also indirectly the result of a completely inclusive combination. We will propose an alternative to Freud's interpretation.

To find a more inclusive implied meaning for the Greek myth, another myth is not always necessary. We can also combine the myth's major themes with minor and apparently marginal episodes that are associated with them. First, the myth welds the meaning of the maze, which is like an extension of Pasiphaë's womb, to that of the shell made of cowhide she hides in to seduce the bull. Another shell, this one secreted by a mollusk to avoid revealing itself, appears in a related episode. After the death of the Minotaur and Theseus's flight, King Minos avenges himself on Daedalus, sealing him inside the labyrinth. Daedalus manages to escape thanks to a pair of artificial wings, but Minos seeks him out even in exile by means of a ruse. Minos offers a prize to the person capable of solving a problem that he knows only Daedalus can solve. The problem entails passing a thread through a snail shell. Daedalus does in fact solve it by attaching the thread to an ant that he passes through the pierced top of the shell. This episode reveals a correspondence between the shell and the maze. In both cases, a thread reveals the way out. Structurally, in these different episodes, the maze becomes a combination of Pasiphaë's womb and the shell in which she hides herself, the combination of the inside and the outside. But this shell also takes on a protective connotation.

The theme of the shell as a means of protection is again echoed and accentuated when the myth describes a sack made of goatskin that Procris, Minos's mistress, uses as a condom to protect herself from the scorpions that he ejaculates. This sack covers and protects the inside of her womb, contrary to the cowhide that covers Pasiphaë, which exposes her womb by disguising it. Thus this sack gives to the shell, and by the same token to the maze, a protecting role. These two objects, the shell and Procris's pouch, transform the image of Pasiphaë's womb and its covering by assigning them a more limited meaning. They thus lead us to a new interpretation of the maze.

The coalescence of all of these images brings to mind a cocoon, a sort of new, secreted womb, within which a selection, a decomposition, and a digestion take place. This transformation brings forth something "born anew" instead of newborn. The labyrinth is thus not exactly a womb. For Theseus, entering the maze is not, as for Oedipus, a regression or a repossession of the mother. Rather, it is a way of rediscovering the physical and etheric dimensions of his own body. This is perhaps what Montaigne had in mind when he said we should "espouse" our bodies. The body is used as an alchemical athanor. It resembles a cocoon in which the soul is transformed from a caterpillar into a larva and finally into a butterfly (already a symbol of the soul). This interpretation corresponds to the one we discovered when we discussed the alchemical tradition, which sees the maze as a representation of man considered as an aggregate of matter and spirit; and the model of the cocoon, similar to Ariadne's ball of thread, is also consistent with that of a tying process, a net, or even a hoop net. Thus the information obtained from analyzing the components of one myth is consistent with the result obtained by comparing two myths. If we were more familiar with the margins of the Malekulan myth, we could probably find there a complementary constellation of images.

If this reading presents Theseus as being transformed, another reading can portray him as transformer and translator. Like Alexander confronting the Gordian knot, Theseus enters the maze as a stranger. But where Alexander arrives as a conqueror and cuts the knot (in equal and symmetrical halves, somewhat like the guardian ghost in the Malekulan myth), Theseus arrives as a prisoner, and with a subtler approach. As he wanders through the labyrinth, instead of destroying it, he "deconstructs" it in order to transform it. As he charts it, pulling the thread, he seems to transform a spider's web into a ball of thread or the cocoon of a silkworm, transforming himself in the process. He transforms the maze into a labyrinth, liberates the Athenians from a tyrannical subjugation, and by his action transforms an old myth into a new one. His action resembles more that of the Malekulan ghost, who reconstructs the invisible half of a pattern in order to find its axis.

As the myth is itself a sort of maze hiding an ultimate meaning, Theseus is the decipherer and transformer of the myth as well as of his own world. But to transform the myth he must understand the Logos, which entails a self-transformation and an upheaval of his former relationship to his soul. These two actions are interdependent. The connection with the soul and the Logos are polar aspects of a single whole and are both represented by the same path in the labyrinth.

Theseus's transformation is again hinted at in the margins of the myth, where we discover his protagonists' destinies. The changing situations of the different characters are correlative, and their relationship brings to mind a man divided within himself who becomes whole and complete. The myth contains a polyphony of the subject. Theseus's relationship to his soul can be represented by his relationship with Ariadne, who plays the role of his soul mate. Only she can share the secret of the Logos, but only he can put it into practice. When Theseus kills the Minotaur and sets sail for Athens, Ariadne is abandoned and forgotten on the deserted island of Naxos, where she pines away. Thus the birth of the soul in this dark, ignorant, opaque world is also the dark night of the soul. Theseus's descent into Hades corresponds with the union of Ariadne and Dionysus and the locking of Daedalus into the prison of his own making. Daedalus can correspond to Theseus's spirit. When Theseus is liberated from the chair of oblivion by Heracles, Ariadne is transformed into a star, thus revealing her true nature of pure light. With the wings he has invented, Daedalus, in his turn, escapes from the labyrinth by flying at just the right altitude between heaven and earth, between the unfathomable sea and the ruthless sun, representing a junction or a middle way between spirit and matter. Daedalus is thus the antithesis of Pasiphaë. The demiurge and creator no longer touches the ground; he follows a path in space. The work of creation falls back into the hands of the transformed—in other words, Theseus. After having vanquished Procrustes in an early adventure, thereby proving his mastery of dimension on the horizontal plane, he is initiated into a vertical dimension and to a relationship with all dimensions.* Once in the center of the labyrinth, he seems to have gained a comprehensive view of space-time, or of space-time-energy-spirit, which is perhaps the same view that Anchises and Aeneas share in the depths of Hades.

When we see the protagonists as different aspects of the psyche, we can see Hades and Dionysus as two parts of the same whole. The excesses and distortions created by figures of language in the myth, like those exhibited in ancient Dionysian ritual practice, reveal the meaning of life by celebrating death. Here is Heraclitus on this theme: "If it were not in honor of Dionysus that they conducted the procession, and sang the phallic hymn, their activity would be completely shameless. But Hades is Dionysos, in whose honor they rave and perform the Bacchic revels" (fragment 15).

With each new dimension explored in the myth,

language changes meaning. The life-death crossing announced by Heraclitus cannot be taken literally if we use the ordinary meaning of these two words. It is there to indicate a point of view situated outside of three-dimensional space-time and familiar language. An invisible thread maintains a connection between the psychological dimensions of the plot and those of the space in which it unfolds. Like in a game of snakes and ladders, where the dice decide the rhythm of one's progression, multiple readings allow one to discover simultaneously the structure of the myth and the structure of a complex space. As Theseus deconstructs, transforms, and charts the maze, the myth appears as a complex Gordian knot in several dimensions, each particular reading corresponding to a different cross section or projection of the knot. At the same time, in a circumambulation, a complete transformation and upheaval of meaning is brought about.

Different readings speak to different centers in man, before they have been harmoniously united. If we take the protagonists as distinct individuals, we can hear other, less subtle versions and perceive the unfolding of a different story that has inspired many an opera plot. When Theseus leaves the labyrinth he is not yet a realized being, not yet totally free. As he discovers the power of his longing and how he can change the world, perhaps he recognizes in himself the power of a daimon. But his power is still limited, his actions followed by painful consequences, and his quest not yet free from adversity; he is still forgetful and subject to the whims of destiny. When he abandons Ariadne and causes his father's death by forgetting to change sails, we can almost hear him whisper, *"Why hast thou abandoned me?"* or *"Why have I abandoned thee?"* or *"Why did I have to abandon thee?"* These three questions form a knot and raise other questions: What is the price of freedom? What kind of equilibrium demands such sacrifices? The answer can be reached only through experience. Later on, he is himself explicitly betrayed by his wife Phaedra, Ariadne's sister, and he is deceived into indirectly causing the

---

*Procrustes cut or stretched his victims to the same size. One could say he knew only one interpretation of man's condition.

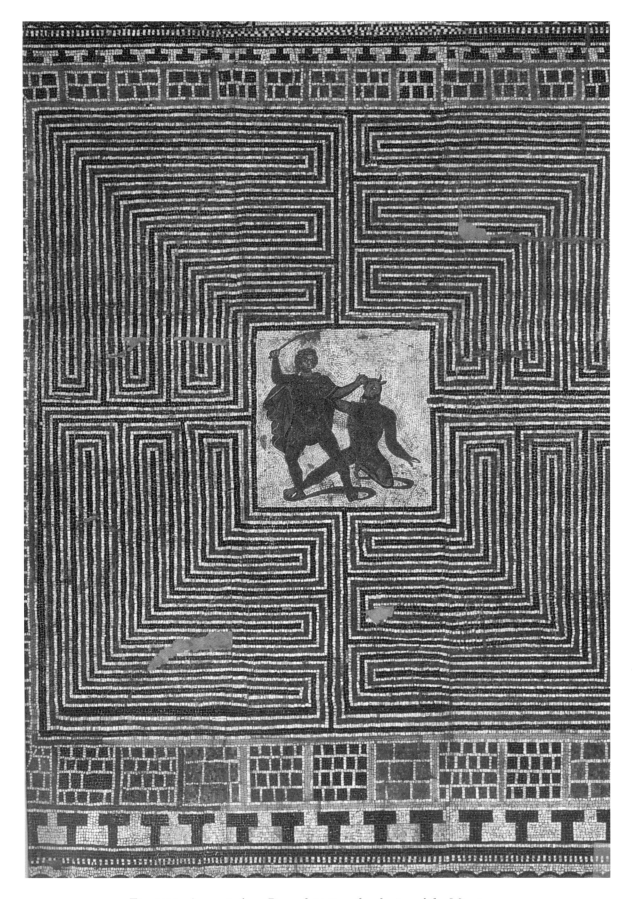

Fig. 10.1. A mosaic from Rome depicting the slaying of the Minotaur

death of his son when he banishes him for something he did not do. After vanquishing the Minotaur in single combat, it is as if he continues to project its shadow behind him, as if the beast's ghost continues to haunt him. Theseus, who finds the meaning of life in death and suffering, learns to integrate the laws and paths corresponding to the structure of the *nahal* tracings, by which, according to the Malekulan myth, he may obtain immortality. By becoming immortal, he lives the death of mortals. Yet by following this path he becomes more truly human. In *Thus Spake Zarathustra* Nietzsche wrote, "But I never believed the people when they spoke of great men; and I maintained my belief that it was an inverse cripple who had too little of everything and too much of one thing."[3]

The sum and unity of all possible interwoven readings, which analysis cannot take into account, can be understood only by a whole person, one whose unconscious has become truly conscious. The interpretation of the Greek myth that we have sketched is thus necessarily incomplete, subjective, and partial.* In developing this interpretation I have tried to chart several axes connected to transformations—in other words, I have tried to elucidate a structure that will correspond to a geometric model. When Theseus transforms a maze into a labyrinth, he reassembles a code, but he also rediscovers the geometry elaborated and used by Daedalus. This geometry alone can support a coherent structure of myth, revealing a secret meaning that is expressed no longer in mathematical terms but by the intermediary of symbols and concrete images.

---

*One can find many interpretations based on scholarly documentation in Jean Canteins, *Dédale et ses oeuvres*.

Fig. 10.2. Cretan seals showing a shell, a swirl, and a frog or scorpion appear on the same steatite three-sided prism. Might they suggest a new birth?

11

The Malekulan *Nahals*

The *nahal* tracings shown in figures 8.1 and 8.3 are drawn on the ground in one even movement. First a simple partitioned frame is drawn, then a continuous line joins the intersections of the frame. The art of producing a complex symmetrical drawing without lifting one's finger off the ground is difficult. John Layard noticed that if the line is drawn loosely, it gives the illusion of a thread woven on the warp represented by the frame. These tracings are, in an ambiguous way, like the shadow projected by a relaxed knot, or a macramé, or a cat's cradle. The choice remains indeterminate and depends on the superimposed order of the line, which is hardly detectable on the image projected by the tracing. Once again, we find the pattern of a false knot that can suggest many kinds of real knots.

These *nahals* that the Malekulan natives must memorize to gain access to a second life represent different beings, whether human beings, spirits, animals, plants, or other familiar objects, all of which are imbued with presence. Rather than representing the appearance of these things, the patterns suggest a pathway along which these things manifest their es-

sence or by which they reach the plane of existence. This mode of representation is radically opposed to what we find today in a portrait or a still life. Thus we have found a figure that corresponds to the third model we were seeking, and which can evoke man or a being seen as a combination of subtle psychic energy and matter. We can recall that the first two models to which different kinds of knots corresponded were the structure of language and that of the universe.

In the same way that to understand one myth it is useful to compare it to others, we can better understand the meaning of the *nahals* if we compare them to other similar diagrams. We can compare them, for example, to the "God's eye" weavings that can be found in the South and Central American indigenous cultures, and also in Tibet, where these figures are called *namkas* (fig. 11.1). Instead of being traced on the ground, a *namka* is composed of threads dyed the colors of the rainbow that are rolled and pulled taut between two sticks in the form of a cross, which replaces the *nahal* frame. The drawing obtained is very similar to certain *nahal* tracings—for example, the one depicting a pigeon's nest in figure 8.3D.

Fig. 11.1. A sample of a Tibetan namka

Namkas *represent the first contact between a spiritual presence and matter in the womb. In this*
image, we see the character Naram Tseku, who removes the mental darkness of living beings.
In front of him is a structure called a dö, which forms a complex namka.

If, among primitive peoples, the meaning of such drawings can only be surmised, the coherent systems of Tibet clearly exhibit the meaning of the *namkas* (a meaning that originally came from shamanism and has been handed down with the adaptation of Bön rites). The *namkas* represent the first contact of a spiritual presence with matter in the womb. Built differently for each individual according to his horoscope, they are used as propitiatory offerings to harmonize the elements of the individual and the various forms of energy related to him. In Tibetan *namka* means "space as the base and support of everything that exists," and as such it represents our real identity. The underlying principle is that our essential being is determined by its relation to the world and to other beings. In more mythic terms, we can be said to be defined by the way we are connected to a particular entanglement of the golden cord that Zeus used to tie up the universe. But, still according to myths, we can also be defined by the way we assemble and actualize potentialities, which is to say by a kind of individual knot. In this way the Egyptians thought that the human being was defined by a knot formed on the continuous cord of his destiny, a knot that also represented his name. It seems to be this last aspect that is associated with the *nahal* tracings. Once more, rather than a rational explanation of a system and the way it functions, we are faced with an assemblage of points of view representing an otherwise indescribable multidimensional universe.

In Castaneda's *The Art of Dreaming*, the sorcerer Don Juan describes a world that corresponds to this particular vision. Even though Castaneda's sources may be partly imaginary and are subject to doubt, they corroborate the models offered by the myths in a way that is reminiscent of scientific vulgarization or science fiction. According to Don Juan, the most significant act of the ancient sorcerers was to see the essence of the universe:

> They said that the essence of the universe resembles incandescent threads stretched into infinity in every conceivable direction, luminous filaments that are conscious of themselves in ways impossible for the human mind to comprehend. . . . Notice that when I talk about *seeing*, I always say "having the appearance of" or "seemed like," Don Juan warned me. "Everything one sees is so unique that there is no way to talk about it except by comparing it to something known to us. . . . From seeing the essence of the universe, the sorcerers went on to see the energy essence of human beings."[1]

We are immediately reminded here of the superstrings, or matter that has itself become conscious. In the human body the ancient sorcerers distinguished, similar to an egg of light, another luminous sphere that made perception possible and that they named the assemblage point, because numerous filaments crossed paths there.

> "How are those filaments you talk about assembled into a steady perception of the world?" I asked. "No one can possibly know that," he emphatically replied. "Sorcerers *see* the movement of energy, but just *seeing* the movement of energy cannot tell them how or why energy moves." Don Juan stated that, seeing that millions of conscious energy filaments pass through the assemblage point, the old sorcerers postulated that in passing through it they come together amassed by the glow that surrounds it. . . . They were convinced that the glow is awareness."[2]

The ancient sorcerers also discovered that it was possible not only to modify the assemblage point within its own sphere but also to displace it to an outside position:

> Since the shifts of the assemblage points are displacements within the luminous ball, the worlds engendered by them, no matter how bizarre or wondrous or unbelievable they might be, are still worlds within the human domain. The human domain is the energy filaments that pass through the entire luminous ball. By contrast, movements of the assemblage points, since they are displacements to positions outside the luminous ball, engage filaments of energy that are beyond the human realm. Perceiving such filaments engenders worlds that are beyond comprehension, inconceivable worlds with no trace of human antecedents in them.[3]

The *namkas* and *nahals* present images that correspond to such an interior vision of a luminous and radiant body connected to the structure of the world.

To understand the *nahals* better we can also compare them to the cat's cradle, which, as we have said, can represent a language process that produces images in myths. The construction of the cat's cradle is based on a movement of loops rather than the movement of a thread, which is to say, it is based on content, since the loops are like containers. The nature of this content can be illustrated by the Egyptian cartouches that consist of a loop closed with a knot and that contain the name of the pharaoh, believed to ensure universal order (see fig. 11.2). But from the start, this content is first represented by the ring with which the cat's cradle begins. It must correspond to an indeterminate and ineffable fundamental meaning that the totality of language, in its premythic state, expressed. This content can be understood as a void, but its nature can also be suggested by traditional teachings that explain how revealed texts like the Torah and the Vedas are but the process of extreme amplification and extension of a single letter, or more exactly of a single unutterable name, the name of God. (The incomprehensible void, the primal cause, and the unnameable God could all be reduced to the same thing.) According to the model of the cat's cradle, it is also by bending, dividing, and crossing this content that a relative meaning can appear.

The *nahal* tracings present another path that leads

Fig. 11.2. Egyptian cartouche, or ren

to similar patterns. This time we are dealing with the movement of a thread that can symbolize life or breath. But if, as the myths affirm, things appear from a primordial unity with their names, these tracings represent not only the essence and the path of a thing or a being, but also its name. Thus the *nahal*, like the Egyptian net, also represents elements of language; it is similar to the names captured in the net, which are themselves equivalent to the interwoven stitching forming the knots of the net. According to these models, the structure of language would then be produced by combining two different processes: the motion of the loops in the cat's cradle and the motion of the thread necessary to form a knot. One process can represent the breath creating sound that captures a content or offers a container to the intangible; the other represents the descent, incarnation, and dispersion of the spirit whose nature is the void in this container. Just as the universe, if it evolved from the big bang, developed from other processes of involution and evolution, so language cannot solely depend on the unutterable name of God; there must also be a phase where the energies or sounds derived from it may react among themselves and reassemble to form and assemble other names. In the structure of language, there is thus a constant exchange between a container, represented by a thread, and its contents, delimited by the moving and turning loops; there is an exchange between a place in a tropological space and what takes place in it. Myths and rites present

once again a harmonious symmetry, an assemblage of different points of view and different models joined together to represent a more complete model that is impossible to describe in its own terms.

The ultimate meaning of the name or the "thing in itself" cannot be expressed directly. It is evoked conjointly by the *nahal* tracing and the path of fire, or *nahal* axis. In their intertwining and coming undone, names and things, being transitory, capture and liberate a complete meaning only by the path they follow. The *nahal* axis is also equivalent to the underground path connecting the stakes that hold the net in place, and to Osiris's pillar that holds up the universe. Thus through the intermediary of space structured by an axis, all models of language, the world, and of being meet. The maze of language can be seen as a knot that is constantly changing shape and that is represented by various projections. This image brings to mind the French expression that describes life as being like a "sack of knots."

It should be noted that by passing from the *nahal* to the cat's cradle, the order of superimposition as well as the crossing of the cord constantly changes. The process is thus comparable to the way a strand of DNA is braided or unbraided and knotted (see fig. 11.3). The strand of genetic code, which is a blueprint of life, must be replicated, transcribed, and recombined to accomplish its genetic function. This manipulation is accomplished by way of enzymes that cut and connect the strands back together, knotting and unknotting, crossing and uncrossing them. The process language uses to create meaning is thus analogous to that which produces organic life.

We must now come back to our principal aim. We have yet to discover precisely how a knot can be transformed into a labyrinth. The polarity between the Greek and Malekulan myths should offer a solution to the geometric problem posed by Ariadne's thread. The way the ghost of Malekula resolves the problem put before him must correspond to a symmetrical and polar method for using Ariadne's thread or discovering its pathway in a maze. We must therefore analyze the method proposed by the Malekulan myth, after which we shall attempt to formulate a complementary technique.

With the *nahals,* we see that net, weaving, macramé, and cat's cradle all belong to the category of the knot. What is more, we must remember that this knot is projected in such a way as to present a symmetry. This "fearful symmetry" (fearful to the ghosts of Malekula) that Lévi-Strauss saw as being the keystone of mythic structure must be restored in order to discover the exit from the maze created by the female ghost and ogre. Once again, we shall not be able to use the given information directly, as it is the result of a language game that must correspond to a geometry but that no longer shares the rational nature of the geometric demonstration. The language game amalgamates and transforms geometric notions in the same way as dreams amalgamate impressions.

The elements that will be useful for our research are as follows:

◎◎ The path of the labyrinth is indicated by an axis around which is folded the drawing of a false knot.

◎◎ The axis is defined by the configuration of a cord folded into a knot.

◎◎ The maze corresponds to the projection of a knot cut into two equal parts.

By reversing this information so that it corresponds to a polar myth, we can deduce that:

◎◎ The path of the labyrinth will be folded around an axis representing the cord of the knot.

◎◎ The axis will be obtained by redressing and thus in a certain sense unfolding the thread forming a knot.

◎◎ The path of the labyrinth will be discovered by the knot being doubled instead of divided.

The form of the solution adopted by Theseus can then be arrived at if the threads that form the knot were taken as an axis, which would allow the knot to be doubled and undone by a projection; or else the knot must be projected in such a way as to appear symmetrically doubled, which would then reveal the path of Ariadne's thread as being bent or rolled around an axis.

Of course, this rather contrived approach to how to proceed resembles a particularly obscure rebus, perhaps even more obscure than the procedures of alchemy. At this stage of investigation we cannot yet put its directives into practice, but we shall see later on that it describes a precise geometric process. For

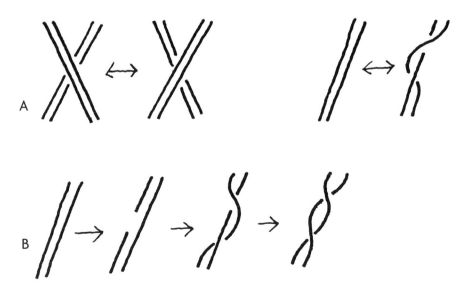

Fig. 11.3
(A) Two actions of an enzyme on DNA. (B) One enzyme can add a complete twist to a DNA molecule.

the moment we need only remember the proposition that *the maze is a kind of knot*. The hypothesis we shall begin with is that the thing or object we are looking for that can serve as the basis of a geometrical transformation leading to the labyrinth is a knot, which is simple enough to serve as a common denominator and an archetype, and represents a basic concept from which other models can be elaborated. From the start, everything seems to point in this direction. The maze is like a Gordian knot that binds and strangles us, and the labyrinth presents the solution to undo it and to escape. Here is, then, the first hypothesis that we must verify. We shall then discover how, in effect, it leads to a solution.

The hypothesis that the labyrinth corresponds to a knot is first corroborated by the fact that some of the *nahals* are composed of a line that does not cross itself. These *nahals* present a meander that brings to mind the path in the labyrinth (in particular, the one in figure 8.3B that describes Hambut sharpening a stone adze at the seashore and being driven back in stages by the incoming tide). Thus there probably exists a transition between knotlike patterns and meanders evoking a labyrinth. John Layard classified the Malekulan tracings into three categories: The first includes only those tracings presenting a symmetry corresponding to the myth of the Temes; the second includes continuous meanders that do not intersect; the last includes drawings whose lines are not necessarily continuous, and tattoo patterns used as protection against evil spirits.

This transition can lead us on an endless trail. Layard describes how overwhelmed he felt when a friend presented him with a collection of tattoos and threshold designs from southern India bearing a strong resemblance to the Malekulan tracings. Somehow the designs of the tattoos (or, rather, scarifications) also represent radiations, the path of rays of light, which could cause stigmatization, such as the signature of a god who, like Zeus, writes simultaneously with visible or invisible lightning, is the light, and is the signature. Thus we can be reminded again of Zeus's golden

cord, itself similar to Castaneda's strings or rays composing the assemblage of the sorcerer. These Indian designs, called *kolams* (fig. 11.4), are used to protect the gate or door of individual dwellings. They are traditionally considered to be mazes, since they represent an interlacing or an entanglement that traps or ties up the evil spirits who attempt to enter the house. Thus the *kolam* and the *nahal* are in a complementary relationship: The *kolam* is a trap set to avoid the intrusion of evil spirits and to protect the home of the living; the *nahal* is a trap erased by an evil spirit to choose those among the dead who can pass a threshold. The Greek maze was built to imprison a monster and it is a trap that only a hero can escape from alive. This complementarity exists between the designs as well. While the *nahal* is composed of a single line, cut in half by the guardian, the *kolam* is composed of a thread divided into several interlocked rings.*

Strangely enough, the interlacing of these rings also corresponds to a modern diagram representing both the structure of language and of the unconscious. What the psychoanalyst Jacques Lacan discovered is that "the unconscious is structured like a language." He presented this common structure in the form of a Borromean knot composed of three interlocked rings representing, respectively, the symbolic, the real, and the imaginary (see fig. 15.4). Each ring is disconnected from its neighbor, but the knot as a whole cannot be undone. Each realm needs the others to fulfill its role, but as we confuse their nature, we find ourselves lost and thus the Borromean knot becomes a sort of symbol of the maze.

The name of the most typical *kolams* are *pavitrams* (rings) and *Brahma mudi* (Brahma's knots). This last is a reference to the knot that joins the three strands

---

*"According to computer scientists, the *kolam* figures illustrate languages which describe pictures starting from a suit of basic elements and formal rules which apply to these elements. These languages stem from the formal language theory elaborated in the sixties by Noam Chomsky." Marcia Ascher in *Pour la science*, April 2002 (author translation)

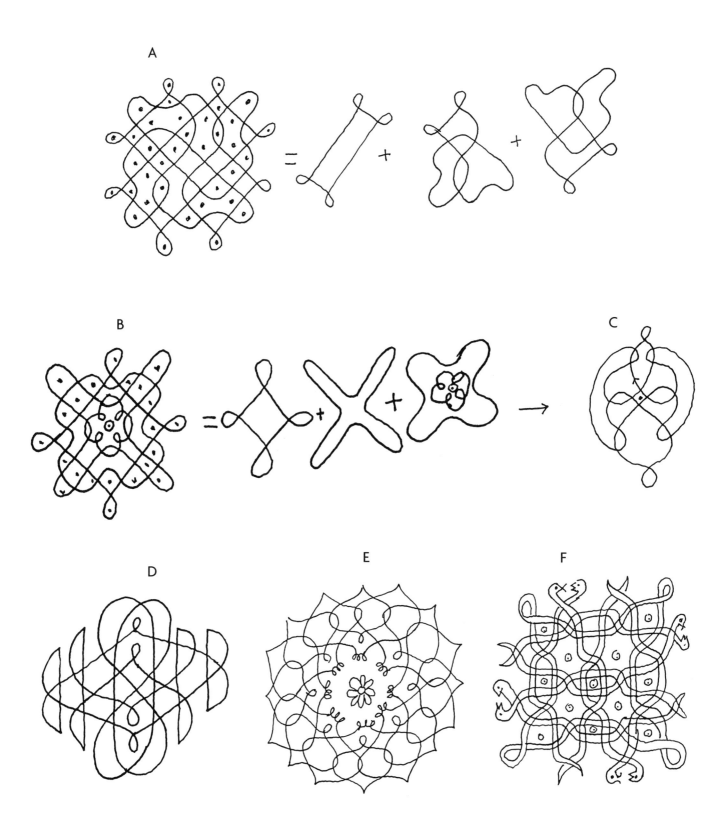

Fig. 11.4. Kolams

(A) Pavitram, *or rings, and its composition.* (B) *Brahma knot and its composition compared to nahals of* (C) *a conch,* (D) *Pavitram,* (E) *Lotus, and* (F) *Snakes.*

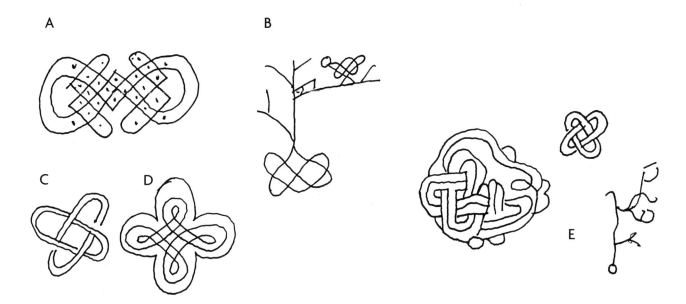

A

B

C

D

E

Fig. 11.5. Somas and related ancient rock paintings from Angola.
(A) Mythic animal. (B) Tree and bird. (C) Limit. (D) A divine symbol called tree with beehive.
(E) Diverse rock paintings demonstrating complex interlacings.

of the sacred cord that all Brahmans wear, a knot tied in such a way that the ends remain invisible. (Here again we are faced with a Gordian knot whose ends are indistinguishable.) There are a great variety of *kolams*, and as they become more complex, their patterns begin to resemble the "tangled threads" of Scotland and even the traditional Indian and Tibetan mandalas. In Angola one finds also designs called *somas* which are like *kolams*. They are somewhat related to complex interlacings or knots of the ancient local cave and wall art (see fig. 11.5). The chain of connections seems endless.

Hidden behind each link in the chain there are rules of transformation or equivalency, and a geometry that still eludes us. To each kind of pattern corresponds a particular symbolic meaning and a different point of view offered by the myth. It is as if the link between the diverse meanings of the symbols corresponded to an algebra that replaces a geometry that is capable of connecting all the patterns.

Fig. 11.6. Cretan seals
These knots and folds, or twists, suggest a recombining of knots

12

The Temple as a Knot

By breaking the silence, language accomplishes
What the silence wanted and was unable to attain.
Silence continues to envelop language;
The silence of absolute language, of thinking language.
—MERLEAU-PONTY

The validity of the hypothesis according to which the maze, or the origin of the drawing of the labyrinth, is a knot can be verified by following another route. Although archaeologists agree that there was no real labyrinth built in Greece or in Crete, we have reliable sources that indicate that the great Egyptian labyrinth truly existed. It was probably built prior to 2000 B.C. Herodotus, Strabo, Diodorus, and Pliny all visited it. Herodotus reported: "I found it greater than words could tell, for although the temples of Ephesus and that of Samos are celebrated works yet all the works and buildings of the Greeks put together would certainly be inferior to that labyrinth as regards labor and expense."[1]

According to Strabo, the labyrinth had three levels and it sheltered sacred crocodiles in an underground crypt. The entire structure was linked to a pyramid and to Lake Moeris. Strabo mentions how this temple united all the nomes (provinces) of Egypt. A section of the temple was attributed to each, and the entire temple was consecrated to the indissolubility of the nomes taken together. This labyrinth thus united all of Egypt, all the aspects of Egyptian reli-

gion, and all the world, as Egypt was organized in the image of the heavens. As Hermes Trismegistus said to Asclepius: "Do you not know, Asclepius, that Egypt is an image of heaven, or rather, the place where here below are mediated and projected all operations that govern and actuate the heavenly forces? Even more than that, if the whole truth is to be told, our land is the temple of the entire world."[2]

Egypt was divided into forty-two nomes, and in each one, just as in each temple, a particular aspect of the cosmogony was exalted. "Each part of an Egyptian myth is developed in connection with one place and each cult exalted at a certain moment. . . . There is a continual transition, but the study of all those changes together reveals a well-defined system and a pattern which must have been planned before."[3] Uniting all the nomes and orchestrating all cosmogonical dimensions, the Egyptian labyrinth was the temple of all of Egypt, or the "world temple," a matrix in which everything was planned and organized. This maze, used during rituals and processions, corresponded not only to the totality of its hallways, but also to the totality of gates that opened and closed according to a perfectly orchestrated tempo, like the connections linking the circuits of a computer. It is the rhythm of time articulated according to a sacred calendar that governed the complexity of this constantly changing maze.

If the ancient temple of everything was a labyrinth, it was also a knot, a knot that linked the myths with the parts or regions or the gods to a residence, and the creator to the creature. In India, in the Ramayana, the theme of a complex and gigantic labyrinthine temple is combined with that of a knot in an explicit manner. "Varuna asked the divine architect Vishvakarma to build a castle made of a hundred sections to contain Surya, a solar woman. To catch Surya on her path, the castle is built on the mountain Ashta where the sun, as it sets, comes nearest to the earth. It was believed that the setting sun could be caught with a rope, which explains why Varuna is called the 'rope thrower,' Pacahasta." *

Varuna's rope is obviously a lasso—in other words, a rope knotted in such a way as to form a slipknot. But why is this lasso necessary? The castle that is placed where the sun sets also represents the Underworld, where the sun disappears each night to regenerate itself and be reborn each morning. The setting sun should then penetrate the castle anyway, making the lasso unnecessary. But since it is placed on the earth, this castle is like a threshold or a coffer where the three realms, the sky, the earth, and the Underworld, meet and form a model of the entire universe. A unifying symbol or a knot is needed to link these diverse realms together. The slipknot of the lasso, which imprisons the sun, also comes to represent the castle and its exceptional structure. At the same time, Varuna's rope is like Ariadne's thread in that it leads to the sun or the center that it represents. The path of the cord is also like the path of the sun that it follows along its course. Thus, paradoxically, the rope of the lasso simultaneously represents the trajectory of

the knot thrown in pursuit of the sun (or the path of the sun) and the pattern of the knot that, like the castle, captures and imprisons the sun. Instead of a path for the sun in the castle, an amalgam of three images is thus created: the sun and its path, the universe, and a knot in movement.†

As is indicated in the following diagram, the relationship between pattern and function, between the structure of the knot and its power to bind, is in itself problematic.

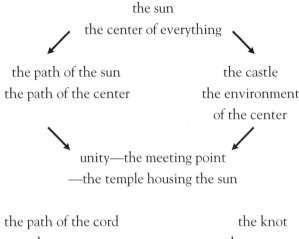
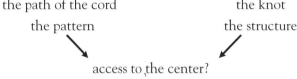

We thus find in the Ramayana an intermediary arrangement between that of Ariadne's thread leading to a center and that of the golden cord with which Zeus ties up the universe but also pulls all things back to himself. This time, instead of having Zeus envelop the universe with a golden thread similar to a ray of sun, it is Varuna who envelops the sun with the universe and renders it accessible in the center of a knot. Myths meet by suggesting a continuous whole through inverse yet equivalent processes.

The underlying problem that must be resolved is how exactly to conceptualize and signify "relation." There can be no "whole" without relation, just as

---

* Varuna represents the spirit of the night, the same spirit who advised Zeus to tie up the universe. From Georges Dumezil, *Apollon Sonore* (Paris: Gallimard, 1982).

† This union occurs in a vision that could be that of a geometer like Daedalus. In Tibetan texts the eye is called "the gate of water leading to the distant lasso."

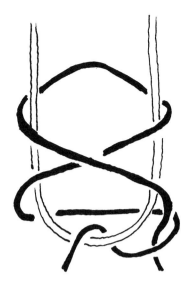

Fig. 12.1 Big Amma knot
"The arch was suspended from a copper or iron chain, whose links symbolized the ancestors holding hands. This support is also compared to a tie made of twin ropes spaced with a series of knots called [big Amma knots]. By itself, each knot represents at the same time the arch and the rope used 'to never forget the descent of the arch,' which is the tight, almost indissoluble tie established by Amma between the ancestors and their descendents . . . when he shaped the world, Amma made four knots anticipating the arch rope, each of them constituting one of the universe seats."[4]

reciprocally all relations find their ultimate value only when there is an uninterrupted whole. The concept of relation depends on that which links and assembles and thus on a visible or invisible knot, a knot that can be made of cord or energy or space. Without a knot whose structure is enigmatic both by definition (the root of the word *enigma* is, in effect, "knot") and due to its presentation, relation loses its deeper meaning.

A similar arrangement to that of the Ramayana can be found in Africa in a Dogon myth. Here, instead of capturing, the knot is used to deliver. The god Amma sends an arch of the covenant (a temple) to men on earth by lowering it from a cord (fig. 12.1).

The knot gives concrete expression to the fundamental principle of primitive mentality that recognizes a participation between a power, its realm or abode, and the path leading to it.

In *The Gate of Horn*, Gertrude Rachel Levy shows

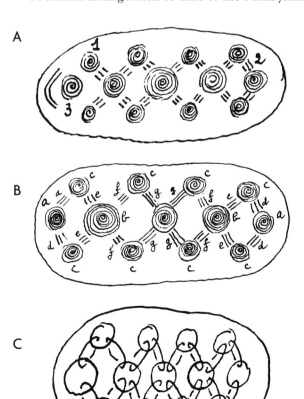

Fig. 12.2. Australian churingas
(A) Mala men decorating themselves for a ceremony:
1. Spirals representing the men; 2. Triple bars representing decorations they paint on their bodies or scarification on their chests; 3. Isolated circles representing the noninitiated young men sleeping behind a shelter.

(B) Rape of a Mala woman: a. Body of Liru man; b. Body of Mala woman; c. Traces left in the sand by the knees of the young Liru man during the rape; d. Legs of the man; e. Arms of the man; f. Legs of the woman; g. Arms of the woman.

(C) The triple bars seen in images (A) and (B) can also be perceived as links or as a system of connected rings, as shown here.

how this characteristic is illustrated by the *churingas* (or *kulpidjis*) made by Australian aborigines (fig. 12.2). *Churingas* are slabs of wood or stone on which circles and meanders are carved and in which "the spiritual body of the eternal . . . ancestor was distributed when he touched the earth."[5] They simultaneously represent the ancestor, his wandering until he reaches the entrance to this world, and the totem where his power is incorporated. The movements of the sinuous path are of a causal nature. The different pathways taken by divine power are themselves currents of energy, similar in this way to the biblical affirmation "I am the way and the life."

The renewal of the union with the totem being perpetuated in a cave, which is the burial place of the ancestors, the *churinga* drawings can also represent the path leading to the cave and the cave itself. The cave is the symbol of a point of emergence and a universal womb where the initiate is reborn and to which he returns. Just as there is an identification between the cave, the path leading to it, and the *churinga*, there is likewise an identification among the temple, the path leading to it or out of it, and the knot. In the same manner, the labyrinth represents a path, an abode, and an abiding spirit. The knot represents that which links them and contains them in an ambiguous manner.

The *churingas* called *kulpidjis* are the most condensed sacred objects of the Pitjanyara tribe. Each *kulpidji* is a concentrated mass representing the essence of life, the Kurumba.

Figures 12.2A and 12.2B are related to the following incident: After the destruction of the harmless carpet snakes by the venemous Liru snake men, Kuma, a young Liru man, preoccupied with making more trouble, traveled to the camp of the Mala women and raped one of them. Figure 12.2B illustrates this last action.

There is no precise, fixed code since the bars can represent either painted marks linking the men (fig. 12.2A) or, in figure 12.2B, the members as links between the bodies and marks left on the ground.

In 12.2B the different parts of the bodies are doubled. There is thus a picture suggesting a knot made of bodies that can be split in some way similar to the *nahals*. Since the three bars are like links, one could also compare the picture to a system of connected rings, as in 12.2C. The spirals with three bars is also comparable to the Egyptian sign *ren* (fig. 11.2) surrounding the name of the pharaohs, made up of a circle barred three times.

Sometimes the *churinga* is attached to a cord and used as a "bull-roarer." The humming as well as the circle made by the cord bring to mind a whirlwind that symbolizes a threshold between two worlds. The whirling, circular movement of the *churinga* restores an equivocal third dimension and a mazelike pattern to the drawing engraved upon it (a knot created by a

Fig. 12.3. In this drawing from an ancient medieval manuscript we see the Cretan labyrinth next to a Solomon's knot (on right). This indicates that medieval texts recognized a link between the labyrinth and the knot.

circulation instead of a knot that circles in pursuit of the sun, as in the Ramayana). The bull-roarer thus indicates the type of door that separates different worlds. Today, children still play jump rope, discovering a rhythm that allows them to cross a threshold without getting caught.

In the Ramayana, the cord follows the path of the sun from the heavens to the earth, thus representing a path of involution. But in other myths the cord can just as easily follow an upward path of evolution. This aspect is important because the labyrinth, as if composed from two opposing spirals, seems to present a synthesis between these two movements. "This is illustrated in the dog totem of northern Australia where the winding path is cut through the bush for a processional march, which represents at the same time the floundering of the ancestral beast through the primeval mud, but also

the rope by which it was drawn onto dry land by its human companions."[6]

The ancient Egyptian labyrinth was thus both a knot and a complex maze. By reuniting all the other Egyptian temples, themselves equivalent to knots, it revealed how several spliced and intertwined knots could come together like pieces of a puzzle to form a new knot. Since each Egyptian temple corresponded to a particular myth or to a particular combination of myths, the labyrinth also represented the way in which all the myths were embedded and woven together (see fig. 12.3).

It is this sort of maze that Theseus had to unravel. As the Egyptian myths were opposed to Cretan and later Greek myths, the entire system of combinations had to be decoded and deconstructed in order to be translated and recombined in Greek terms.

Fig. 12.4. Cretan seals.
A shrine or temple with moon and star designs suggesting a precise date or the passage of time

13

About Knots

Lord Buddha said, "I have tried this way and that way to untie the knots. How would you loosen them, Ananda?"
My lord Ananda replied: "I would first study the knot and find out how it was tied, then it could easily be untied."
Lord Buddha said, "Right you are, Ananda. If you wish to untie a knot you must first know how it was tied."

—The Sayings of Buddha

If the labyrinth is transformed from a knot, its ultimate meaning must reflect its origin. At this stage, the other symbolic meanings attached to the knot become intriguing.

In Egypt, the name *ren*, which revealed the true nature of things, was also represented by a loop closed with a knot or by a cartouche (fig. 11.2) within which the pharaoh's name was inscribed. "The idea of a name—*ren*—is linked to the idea of cyclical rhythm, or the idea of a knot tied with the continuous cord of a destiny and determining one of its episodes. . . . A name is considered to be the determination of a vital rhythm characteristic of a stage in personal genesis,

and its symbol is the cord to which the name is "tied" . . . heaven and earth, gods and men, pharaoh and kingdom are bound inseparably by threads of Neith's weaving."[1]

In Egypt, as well as in Crete, the knot is an important symbol. The ankh, or cross of life, is a knot with three widespread loops, two of which can be seen in profile. In some cases it can look like a loose necktie (fig. 13.1).

> This *ankh* is presented as a loop crossed by a horizontal bar, but the two elements are not truly knotted. . . . This symbol is to be regarded as the potentiality of a

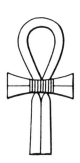

Fig. 13.1. Ankh

Fig. 13.2. The sma: *the heart and tracheal column with the ligature of the two lands*

ligature. This "crux ansata" is not really a *cross*, but a symbol of the intention to knot together two elements without having truly done so.

Although an actual mirror in the usual shape of the *ankh* has never been found, the latter is sometimes seen represented in the form of a mirror. This can be a guide to research, as can the fact that the casing containing the ordinary mirror is called *house* (or container) *of life (ankh)*. . . .

The *ankh* is not life, but it is the *ankh* that gives life once the two principles, spirit and body, exist. . . .

If the *ankh* is not really a knot, the ligature *sma* is (see fig. 13.2).

The ligature [is] represented by the tube of the tracheal artery ending at the heart and the lungs, the complex of the *haty*. This is the center of respiration, the ligature of "spirit" (here symbolized by air capable of animation) with the living and nourishing fluid of the blood. This symbol *sma* is often seen depicted on the base of the throne on which the king is seated. . . .

This ligature can also be made by Horus, master of the North, and by Seth, master of the South, who is often replaced in this function by Thoth.[2]

One must bring attention to the fact that the ligature is made of two strings instead of one, a fact we shall encounter again when we explore the geometry. While most of the knots made with one string

represent a natural or lawful bond, this ligature made of two strings is the symbol of an achieved union.

Pharaonic myth shows Seth and Horus as enemies; the one and the other, Plato's "same" and "other" the fundamental scission of what Lao-tse calls *Tao ko Tao*, "what is and is not" being and nonbeing, all these in one single state which becomes accessible only through the initial scission. . . . The final union of the elements which were originally opposed is what Hermetism calls "the Sone," "the Thing" which acts as a ground for the universal edifice: this is the king par excellence, it is the son of Ra who is like Ra, the son of Heaven generally speaking. *In this sole-singular king, the two crowns are unified,* the silvery white crown of the South (Seth) and the golden red crown of the North (Horus).[3]

The position of the mysterious Isis knot called Tit, which envelops the pillar of Osiris (figs. 13.3B and 13.7) can remind us of the Malekula tracing (which is itself similar to the shadow of a knot enveloping the axis of the path of fire crossing it). The sacred knot, worn at the neck of the Cretan priestess, is represented on many Cretan seals and seems to have come from the Isis knot. If this Cretan knot is made into a bun that rests on the nape of the neck of the priestess, against her ears, one might be led to think that, symbolically, it has to do, like the cerebellum or the inner ear, with a capacity to listen and with a sense of balance and of direction. But one also finds, as in figures 13.3 and 13.4 images of the priestess with a snake knot on the abdomen, in the same place that the knot of Isis appears on the pillar of Osiris. As in certain tantric drawings (fig. 13.5), perhaps this knot represents one aspect of the sleeping psychic energy of the *kundalini*, or serpent power.

The coiled or knotted serpent placed at the base of the spine is not only a metaphor, it is also part of a coded language. On the one hand, the picture of the coiled snake, which sometimes has a sexual connotation, can be linked as it uncoils to a cosmic snake or even to the Ourobouros. It can represent

Fig. 13.3
(A) Knotted-snake girdle on figure of snake goddess, temple repository, Knossos. (B) Djed column with Osiris knot.

that which links or unites different kinds of energies belonging to different scales and spheres. On the other hand, the tantric knot itself, more geometric than figurative, can evoke interpenetrating spheres as well as a bound or a winding movement that connects or reunites all sorts of domains. The liberation of hidden energy opens the doors to all kind of domains. With a symbolic knotted snake, many different or even antinomic notions are brought together.*

Untying the Bonds

In India, the secret technique for undoing these symbolic knots is called the art or science of *nagrantha*. Fulfillment yoga is supposed to loosen the knots at the chakras. These knots, which are said to strangle the psychic nerve channels of ordinary people, must be opened in order to allow the vital winds to enter the central channel . . . The yogin endeavors to activate the chakras by visualizing special mantric letters that are imagined to abide there. Thus letters are associated with the yogic loosening of the knots. A similar technique, probably inspired by the Indian art, also exists in the Kabbalah and was discussed by Abraham Abulafia and his disciples. With Abulafia, the process called "untying the bonds" or "undoing the knots" concerns the mating or coupling of the human intellect with the active intellect, or God, and it can lead to prophecy. It occurs when the human consciousness cuts itself off from natural things and binds itself to the spiritual. The process is thus described as one of untying knots in order to establish a superior bond:

> The individual is bound to the knots of the world, the year, and the soul (to space, time, and the individual's being), and through them is linked to

---

* One can still find on many early Italian crucifixes of the Byzantine style an elaborate knot holding the loincloth of Christ, which seems to have an older symbolic significance. On a crucifix at Pisa, I have observed above this knot an accentuated rendering of the abdominal muscles that leaves the impression of a huge, erect internal or interiorized phallus.

the world of nature; and if he unties these ties that bind him, he will unite with the one who is above them and who watches over his soul like he does with those who call the name of YHWH. . . . And he will know how to unify the name.[4]

Even if the knot is presented as what binds us to our lower nature, untying the knot does not consist in a physical or ascetic discipline. Rather, it involves the simultaneous unraveling of the imbroglios of existence with those presented by the Torah. Thus the symbols that we have already met in other traditions and the correspondences between their abstract and concrete, or transcendent and immanent aspects or connotations are constantly reexamined and reinterpreted.

The cosmic axis is nothing other than the knot of the spheres, and there is no doubt that it is that which secures their existence, and it is to be brought near to the image of the articulations that in man link his limbs; and the "knots" (where are articulated) the limbs of the human body are also called the "axis" in man. . . . And when this knot will untie itself, the meaning of what this knot is witness to will be revealed.[5]

The untying described by Abulafia occurs thanks to the practice of repetition and permutation of the sacred letters of the tetragrammaton or of other sacred names. From this exercise, and the new understanding it brings, a new freedom and rule of conduct will result. Using Buddhist terminology, one would say that it is through the word and the form that the

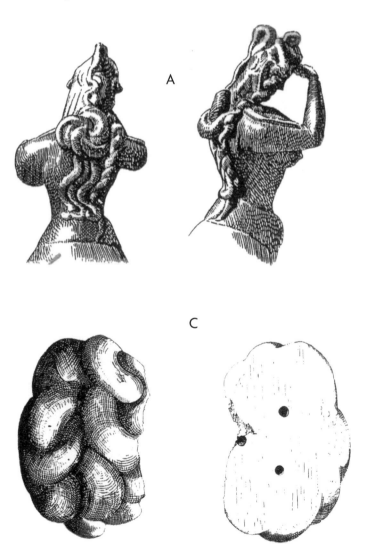

Fig. 13.4
(A) This bronze statue demonstrates the sacred knot as worn by a Cretan priestess. (B) Illustration of a woman wearing the sacred knot. (C) Votive affix made of steatite, Mycenae. These locks of hair probably belonged to a sphinx.

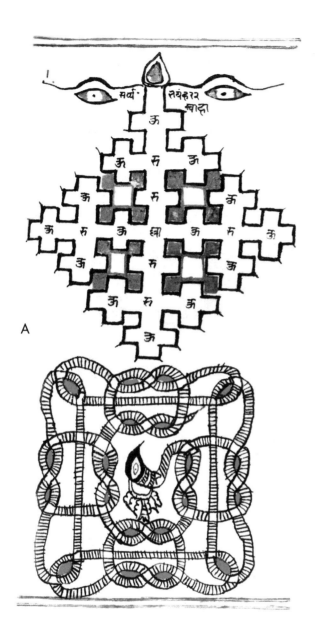

Fig. 13.5
(A) Tantric drawings of sleeping kundalini, *Rajasthan, nineteenth century. (B) Tantric drawing of* naga-bandha, *which is unmanifested psychic energy or sleeping* kundalini.

dependent origination of illusion and attachment occurs. Thus in Abulafia's system, it is also the word that is the instrument of tying and untying. The letter and word must be liberated from the structure of language and act on their own through the adept. "One must bind and invert one name with the other and renew a problem, bind what is united and dissociate what is bound with the well-known names, by making them turn and correspond with the twelve signs [of the zodiac], with the seven planets, and with the three elements, until the one who ties and unties frees himself from the categories of interdiction and

permission, and in that establishes a new form of the forbidden and allowable."[6]

It is indirectly through analogies, symbols, and visionary images that a topological structure like that of a knot is evoked. The obscurely described sacred combinations of letters (the *urims* and *tummims*) are sometimes compared to luminous and dark mirrors. The letters themselves are compared to the rungs of a ladder, but a peculiar spherical ladder that moves in strange ways. Thus the letters appear as simulacra of the molecules combining in the double helix of a strand of DNA (fig. 13.6). "Know that as far as this

Figure 13.6. Crossed exigraphic bands suggesting something like DNA at the Madrasa ince Minare at Ronya, Turkey

ladder is concerned, its circle must be drawn in front of man's eyes, as a full globe turning backward and forward in front of him. . . . Such is the circular ladder which possesses a double circular line with narrow rungs between the two lines, numbering 360."[7]

As the combinations of letters produce complex results, one must keep from drowning in the flux of information or becoming lost in the contemplation of a sort of Gordian knot, which becomes a complex maze.

> And (on the mount and contemplating the horizon), that is what the soul and intellect of Moses our master saw, all around him, and saw from above, the whole Torah, from the Bereshit (first letter of the word of the Torah), until the Lamed, last letter of the word "Israel" (last word of the Torah), written in full circle, all the letters near to each other . . . (made of black fire against white fire). . . . The soul of Moses contemplated them, here and there, trying to locate the beginning of the circle, its end or its middle, but he found nothing, for there does not exist a precise place where one enters the Torah, for it constitutes

one whole, and while he contemplated this circle, it (the Torah) was combining itself unceasingly and was producing all sorts of difficult incomprehensible combinations.[8]

In the recitation of the combinations of letters, the name in effect becomes like the silhouette or the face of the named, which itself is as if present. The letters becoming a face can be illustrated in the art of calligraphy (see fig. 13.7). The recitations also provoke visions of motions and forms that take definite meanings and organize themselves in surprising and disconcerting ways. The names become chaotic script, with chains of strange interlaced shapes, in lines that become knotted and shaped in geometric forms with symbolic meanings. Thus the name becomes a sort of archetype of the modern *grammé*, and to explore this structure efficiently, it seems that a specific topology is needed.

> And the vision he contemplates is in fact YHWH, . . . and that is the meaning of the verse: "That is the

Fig. 13.7. A face illustrated by calligraphy

picture of YHWH that he contemplates," in other words, he was looking at the letters of this name and at their mode of being, and they told him all that was still hidden. . . . The letters are the roots of all wisdom and of all comprehension, without any doubt, and they are by essence the matter of prophecy, they are seen during the prophetic vision like bodies (with a certain) thickness speaking to man mouth to mouth. . . .

And they are perceived as if pure and living angels activated their motion, and taught them to the man who permutes them in rotation, in the form of ethereal angels . . . drawing circular (forms), with their wings, as they fly, and they are nothing else than the breath of the breath.[9]

Finally, in the same way as some tantric designs suggest an implicit connection between a science of knots and a science of yoga that aims to liberate an energy sleeping in man, it seems that Abulafia explores or discovers a crucial link between, on the one hand, a very ancient science of knots and, on the other hand, a kabbalistic science of sacred names that also provokes an influx of energy emanating from the

active intellect or divine principle, but which is investing man as from above instead of surging from his core. Perhaps Abulafia ignored the secrets of the ancient geometry of knots, perhaps he was careful to hide them, or perhaps his purpose was also to uncover, in a subtle way, a hidden meaning in the sacred or symbolic geometry of knots.

In order to make sense of Abulafia's mystic vision, we might venture the hypothesis that the cord of Abulafia's knot is made of connected letters and movements of sequences of letters. In the same way as the molecules in DNA are represented by letters (for example, CGCGAATTCGCG), the knot undoes itself and then recombines and replicates itself under the influence of new combinations of letters, acting like enzymes do on DNA. The letters are bound together, but they can also appear, as in some styles of calligraphy, as knots (see fig. 13.8). The image is of DNA, but the meaning is the structure of the human being as a body, mind, soul complex still linked to its

Fig. 13.8. Letters shown as knots

process of formation. As Nietzsche said: "The amazing is the body." But, obviously, the letters are not going to fly and dance by themselves like a witch's broom; there is no black magic here. We must assume that the exercise with the words and letters is done with an intention, or as a help for a inner exercise perhaps too subtle to be described. As the words are decomposed in parts, so is the identification with the body and the ego; a distance, an in-between is created between an "I" and an "it" where the person can appear in a new relation with the world and the word.

In Abulafia's scheme, as the developing intellect discovers together a knot and a new meaning, transformation of the thought pattern occurs: "While meditating on your thoughts, combine them and you also will be purified." Instead of being produced by chains of associations delimiting the domain of reason, the thoughts organize themselves like crystals or petals in organic symmetrical patterns leading to the heart of things or to the reasons of the heart. As Pascal says, "The heart has its reasons that reason does not know."

Even if Abulafia does not help us concretely or topologically to undo a substantial Gordian knot, he informs us about the possible meaning of such a symbolic knot. We discover that, like the labyrinth, this knot concerns language, the world, the soul, and the whole constituted by their relations. Abulafia does not indicate the knot as a symbol or a model, but how to loosen *the knot that matters*, the invisible knot that keeps us in bondage. The undoing of the visible model cannot liberate us, but it can inform us in a different way of what occurs when we try to loosen the bond. Once again it is the connection between the objective and the subjective, the geometric symbol and its meaning, that will indicate where is reality.

Abulafia's knot corresponds to the labyrinth design of the sixteenth-century kabbalist Moses Cordovero shown in figure 13.9. This labyrinth made of Hebrew letters appears as broken or discontinuous but is in fact completed by the invisible relation uniting the letters and the Sephirot.

Fig. 13.9. Kabbalistic diagram from Moses Cordovero (1522–70)

This is an image of the world using the initials of the ten Sephirot, or emanations of God. From the outside to the center: Keter (supreme crown); Chokhmah (vision); Binah (intelligence); Chesed (love); Gevuvah (might); Tiferet (beauty); Netzach (eternity); Hod (majesty); Yesod (foundation); and, at the very center, Malkuth (kingdom).

Let us now investigate the nature of the Isis knot. In the myth of Osiris, Seth binds Osiris in order to immobilize him, kill him, and dismember him, afterward dispersing (we could say sowing) the pieces across the country. The process is thus the opposite of that used by Zeus, who bound together the disparate elements of the universe in order to unite them. A second binding or connecting action is carried out by Isis. She reconstitutes Osiris's body after having gathered together the scattered pieces. Although she is unable to locate his penis (eaten by a fish), she nonetheless conceives a son, Horus. She thus enacts a reunion (or a doubled union) and a sort of immaculate conception. It is precisely Isis's power to unite and bind that is represented by the *tit*, the Isis knot, which is said to symbolize a great mystery. Since we are seeking to decode or undo a knot, this mystery can also contain the secret of the method symbolized by Ariadne's thread, as he who can knot must also know how to unknot. Isis's power to reconnect and conceive a son from Osiris, and thus to set the *djed*, or pillar of Osiris, upright again (fig. 13.10) also comes from her knowledge of secret names, which she used as magical incantations.

She obtained them by guile, managing to bind the sun god Ra, who exchanged his knowledge of secret names for his freedom. There is thus a connection between the Isis knot and the power of names; the gathered, reassembled, or reanimated Osiris is still in a certain sense a name or a word made flesh. As Isha Schwaller de Lubicz mentions, there is even a double connection in the Egyptian system depending on whether the word is *djed* or *djet*.

> Your bodily form is an illusory solid, perishable: what caused it is a real solid, the *djed*, word of Amon-Ra-Ptah, established in you and become your own. This *djed*, word [of the] pillar of Osiris, is the base of relative stability, principle of whatever is durable in the Osirian world, the world of becoming and return. It is for you to make it eternal, your own *djet* [protects] against agents of destruction.
>
> . . . The *djet* is the inborn Word, shut up in the lowest depths of mortality, awakened, freed and become your essential, incorruptible body. This awakening is the mystery of mysteries, the secret of resurrection, and I shall only speak of it because it is a link without which the chain would be incomplete. But if the rights of Osiris teach men how to form the immortal body, we teach also that the *djet* remains prisoner of earth and Osiris unless Ra comes to deliver it, "unties the ropes" and "undoes the knots."[10]

It seems that the Isis knot can be tied only with the help of magic names forced from a bound sun; but as in the Ramayana, we can think that the Isis knot was first used to capture the sun. This knot can thus suggest a structure like that of language enclos-

Figure 13.10. Djed or Pillar of Osiris

ing magical names tied and knotted together. The Isis knot establishes a link among the word, the spirit, and life. Since Isis's action allowed and announced the erection of the *djed*, one could say that she helps Osiris to reincarnate. After this episode, we find Osiris in the chthonic world, where he is enveloped or knotted in the coils of a giant serpent; the latter binds him in a positive way, as it dissipates the darkness before him. Though he remains in the Underworld like the sun during the night, Osiris is also present in his son, the falcon-sun Horus, and is considered one with Ra, or as representing the soul of Ra. Ra is the transcendent sun, Horus the rising sun, and Osiris the setting sun. Osiris is called "Horus on the horizon" (in other words, Ra) and Horus is called "Osiris on the island of fire," which is to say, Osiris elevated to the mythic center of the world.[11]

Osiris seems to be all things—the Nile, its source and estuary, the languid earth, and the fertilizing power of the sun. He is the living tree in which the pieces of his body are reunited, but also the cut tree that becomes the pillar of the temple and that maintains its structure, the correct distance, and the correct relationship among all things. Finally, he is also the *djed* pillar, uniting heaven and earth, resembling in this way Shu, or space, which plays the same role (see fig. 16.14C). In the being of Osiris, a concept of union, light, and energy is linked to a concept of space and to the geometry that defines it. He is the earth-sun relation, the energy absorbed by the earth bringing forth life. He is the potential that unfolds and becomes manifest, maintaining a unity within multiplicity. He represents all and everything. And the secret to Osiris's omnipresence is the Isis knot.

If the Isis knot remains a secret in the myth, its essential nature and its symbolic meaning must be sought in the way it is made and used and in what it is used to reconstitute or create. As Osiris is all things, both linking and linked to all, the knot that reconstitutes him is also the symbol of this whole. *The knot symbolizes simultaneously the whole, the path leading to unity, and the link binding all things together.* With the knot symbol, the whole defined as the totality of all things or as a sum is replaced by a combination of relations that connect the parts of the whole. The whole becomes the combination of all things infinitely divisible in parts and of "the in-between" parts and things, or the void. It expresses the relation of the objective and the subjective that Schopenhauer called the "world knot." This knot includes within itself words as well as things because, as we have seen, it also represents the means to obtain and link together the secret and sacred names that give life. The knot thus becomes the foundation of all symbols in that they are all related and in that each symbol suggests the essence of a thing by bringing out what is common in all things, thereby revealing a fundamental unity. It can even be considered the archetype of the symbol in that its root is the Greek verb *symballein,* "to bind together."

When we juxtapose the Hindu and Egyptian myths, we discover that the bound sun gives up its magical names to gain its freedom and to escape from a knot-castle-maze, but also does this implicitly in order to be reborn, surging out of the Underworld. The path of magical names that leads to the birth of the falcon-sun Horus is, in the end, similar to that of the sun. There is thus an equivalence among:

- ◉ The path of the labyrinth (leading out of the maze or the Underworld by offering life and freedom)

- ◉ The path of names and of the word, or Logos

(that, once delivered from a knot-maze of language, regenerates life and the sun)

- ◉ The path of the sun that represents the spirit, or the path of Osiris-Ra completed by that of Horus

Ra, the transcendent sun, frees himself by leaving sacred words behind him, but at the same time, in the form of Horus, he is reborn, thanks to the power of those words. The pattern that we find here can help us understand the image of an underground path linking the two stakes representing Osiris and Horus that hold the net of language in place. For the word to have a meaning, it must incarnate or incorporate itself in language, but to reach back to its creative or "magical" power, it must be freed from the maze of language.

The Isis knot also links Osiris and Horus, the path of the father and that of the son; it unites two paths, or the path of Osiris split in two. "He who has seen me, has seen the father," we read in the *Gospel of John.*

Each symbol can be reversed or turned to expose new sides and a complex group of interwoven concepts. While elaborating a model for a whole man or incarnated God, the myth connects the knot, considered as an object, to an absolute meaning. It elaborates a symbolique of the knot that presents itself as a concatenation, a puzzle of different points of view, a knot of interrelations, as it were. Strangely enough, the meaning of the "thing in itself" appears only in relation to other things.

By establishing the centrality of the notion of connection between things and relations, and between the whole and that which links all things, have we simply added a new sophism to those (as, for example, the life-death crossing) that are already scattered across this book? We might first remark that this concept of interdependency is prevalent in Buddhist philosophy. It also exists in quantum physics, where it poses a major problem ("the nature of a particle is defined by its relation"). "The atom is to thought what the sensible object is to the senses.[12] It even corresponds to the notion of space-time. The paradoxes thus obtained simply offer another example of an impossible translation; they correspond to the antinomics produced when one tries to translate the language of myth into concepts or when one projects a space of several dimensions into a space of three dimensions.

As the mosaics of the prieuré of Ganagobie show (fig. 13.11), under the mozarabic influence the symbol of the knot lives in medieval France. We must go back to the fifth century to find similar huge knots on mosaic pavements at Ravenna (on the via D'Azeglio and at the palace of Theodoric) or in Cyprus. These abstract motifs probably corresponded to the iconoclastic period, when the reproduction of the human figure of Christ was forbidden, leading to a search to bring into Christianity some more ancient symbolism. These Byzantine designs later influenced Islamic art.

The relationship between the knot and the word and the two aspects of the imprisoning and liberating knot are also found in the Hindu tradition. The initiation ritual of Tatua-Diksha consists of tying three threads into twenty-seven knots—representing all of the cosmic elements in the body—and offering them in oblation to the sacred fire. There is a knot that mysteriously holds the word, connecting everything and taking on all forms (even that of science), and a knot "that makes one say me, mine," that makes us believe in the ego, and that separates parts from the whole.

> "Where does the world come from?" From him alone, from the Brahma called word, where all succession is reabsorbed, who, at the moment when all phenomena disappear, includes all without being informed, who, beforehand, remains indescribable *in the form of knots of phenomena.* From him come the phenomena that we call "world.". . . It is him, the universal self, who escapes the falseness of all representations. . . . "Even if we localize Brahman, he does not lose his nature, which is to have all forms, and he cannot be contained in concepts."

> . . . "All points of view (express) him completely, and, as if dressed in concepts, he who is beyond all concepts, such do we consider to be the interior man.". . . He is the source of the appearance and disappearance of all points of view, he holds all contradictory meanings; everywhere he is the Brahman who allows and the Brahman who forbids, but the essence of his activity (in reality) doesn't choose between what is permitted and what is forbidden. The Vedas are nothing other than the *pranava* (the OM), this latter is in fact the original form of all words and all objects. From this point of view, the different sciences, inasmuch as they are of the essence of the *pranava,* lose none of their identity with the Veda. . . .

> To reach Brahman is simply to go beyond the *knot of individuality* that makes one say "mine, me. . . ." For others, it is the way phenomena are reduced to their original form . . . the retreat from the senses.[13] (emphasis added)

If Brahman, the word, is first and foremost a sound, we also find in the Hindu system a similarity between the sonic energy of the word and a visual energy that is not that of the senses. "The power that resides in words is the only support of this universe. It is [like] the visual organ, thanks to which the being of intuition is known in a divided form."[14] The power of words would then correspond to an intuition or a revelation that accompanies a vision. This visual power can be seen as that which engenders writing, symbolic diagrams, and geometry. Thus, by finding in the maze a path of Logos described visually, we should be able to retrace a path similar to that of Brahman, or the word described in such fine detail by the Sanskrit grammarians.

Incidentally, the knot is in fact also the fundamental element of the first writing system. In ancient China at the time when the *I Ching* and the *Tao te Ching* were compiled, reference is made to a system of knots used to compute the laws of conduct and government.

Fig. 13.11. Mosaics of the prieuré of Ganagobie, 12th century
(A) *Under the Mozarabic influence, the symbol of the knot lives in Western medieval iconography.*
(B) *Ganagobie south, absidal chapel*

The creation of this writing system, which precedes ideograms, is attributed to Fu-hsi, the first ancestor who established the fundamental laws and who was considered to be a demiurge. Confucius laments the loss of this form of writing and language and considers that its replacement by the ideograms constitutes a regrettable decadence. The time when only knots existed is considered a more essential period, when men participated more actively in the world.

Africans and Incas possessed a similar system, and shepherds in Peru still use a *quipu*, a cord of knots, to count their herds. This system left such a deep mark on the knotted and convoluted figures of Mayan and Aztec hieroglyphs that it seems to have been entirely integrated into them. The Celtic ogam alphabet, which consisted of bars crossing a line, could also share this common origin, in which case only the crossing of the cord forming the knot would remain.

Are we dealing with a more essential alphabet or with the first faltering attempts at writing? Are these simple systems of memorization or are they for computation and divination like the trigrams and hexagrams of the *I Ching*—in other words, a mathematical system embedded within a linguistic code? Are we dealing with a sublanguage, a metalanguage, or both at the same time? The *juthig*, an ancient system of divination based on combinations of knots thrown together, still exists today in Tibet. It comprises 360 main types of knots and innumerable further combi-

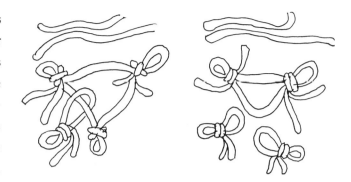

Fig. 13.12. Two examples of knots used in the juthig

nations (fig. 13.12). These numbers and their sophisticated interpretations indicate that the knot writing was more than a means of counting or a memory tool.

Traditional techniques like that of gematria, which seek the hidden meaning of sacred texts by adding together the numerical values of letters, indicate that the problem is complex, and that at a time when writing was reserved for initiates and was used, for example, to consign the cosmic order on "tables of destiny," there existed a recognized connection between language and numbers.

A knot also presents a combination of numbers. Each knot as a unit is constituted by the union of different numbers of crosses, spaces, and loops. It could be that the Chinese binary system and the symbolic arithmetic of the Pythagoreans, which is linked to geometry and meaning, originated from meditating on symbolic knots.

Fig. 13.13. Cretan seals
These show different representations of a double ax or labrys—a symbol of double action or division and double aspect similar to that of Janus with two faces. The seal on the left recalls a hoop net, and hence a connection with a maze.

14

The Origin of Language in Dogon Myth

Language is a symbol of the incommunicable.
—WALTER BENJAMIN

The first system of writing was made out of knots, the structure of language is similar to a knot (a net and a cat's cradle), and, according to Hindu philosophy, the word—Brahma—is contained in "a knot of phenomena." Although this new tangle seems difficult to unravel, myth again can guide us, decoding itself by disclosing the nature of its language. Dogon myths detail a complete theory of language associated with a knot technique, which seems to have retained numerous traits from Egyptian symbology. Dogon civilization, as described by Marcel Griaule in his work, *Dieu D'eau*, appears to be a civilization of the word.

Dogon myths tell how, in the beginning, there existed only a few signs or traces that Amma contemplated deep within himself, and with which he created all things.[1] These signs preceded all things and were called "the invisible Amma" (see fig. 14.1). Combining among themselves, the signs evolved in a complex manner to become marks, then rudimentary plans, and finally designs reproducing the familiar aspects of things. This transformation of signs toward more complete forms finally brought about the existence of things or beings. In a subtle manner, these myths seem to suggest the preexistence of writing, or at least the simultaneous creation of writing and language.

As the world is progressively created, three stages or strata of language appear successively. Braiding, followed by weaving, and finally the cat's cradle are the techniques used by genies or ancestors to reveal and grant language to men.[2] Language first appears as a more or less vague sound that gradually develops by inserting itself into the mold of an implicit system of writing made out of knots.

The first language is revealed with the making of a skirt by the first genie, or Nommo (the perfect union of twins), to cover his mother, the earth, naked and thus without language. The indistinct speech of the Nommo is interlaced with the fibers of the skirt and is given to men with braiding and rope-making techniques.

The Nommo, when he speaks, emits, like all beings, a lukewarm vapor carrying the word, itself the word. And this vapor, like all water, moves in a helicoidal line. The coils of the dress were thus a pathway of predilection for the words that the genie wanted to

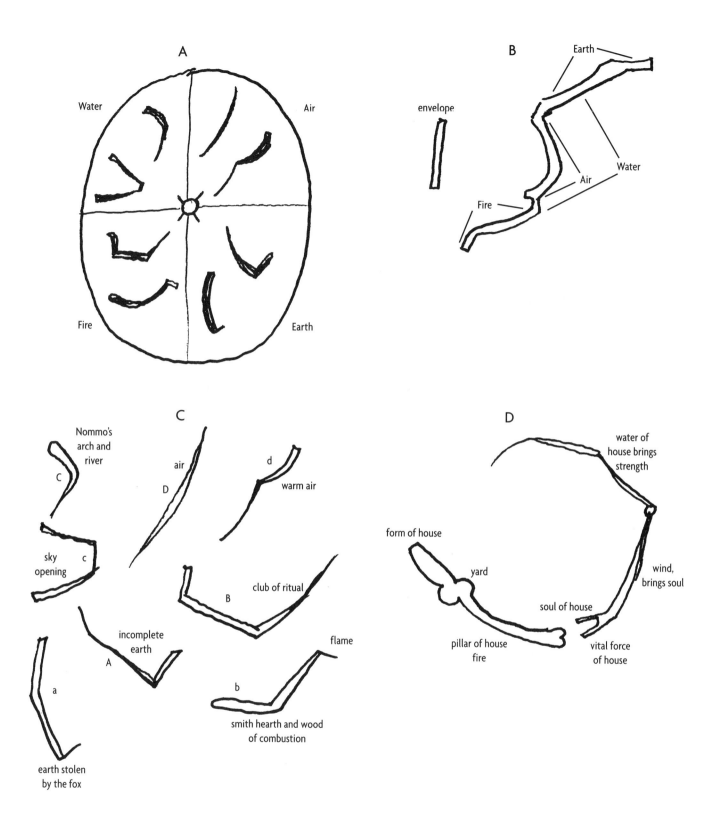

Fig. 14.1. Signs of "the invisible Amma"

(A) "Belly of the world's signs," or table of Amma—the four pairs of complete signs in the primordial egg. (B) The two "guide signs." (C) Pairs of "master signs." (D) Sign of the house. Note: *Altogether there are 266 signs.*

reveal to earth. . . . His humid words coiled themselves into the humid braids. The spiritual revelation penetrated the technical teachings. . . .

Thus dressed, earth had a language, the first of this world. . . . Words were breaths barely differentiated, but carrying strength. As such, this language without nuances was fitting for the great work of the beginning.[3]

The second language is revealed by the seventh ancestor of the second generation. He has the status of master, and thus a perfect knowledge of a language destined for all men. An obscure instinct leads him to reenter mother earth, whose vulva is an anthill (the same action Theseus implicitly makes in penetrating the labyrinth). From the inside, he weaves with his mouth.

> This efficient speech developed the power of its new carrier; for him, the regeneration in the womb of the earth transformed, little by little, into an investment in this womb; he slowly occupied the entire volume of the organism, disposing himself as was required of his work: his lips merged with the side of the anthill, which became a mouth and blossomed. Sharp teeth surged . . . and with his mouth the genie started to weave. . . .
>
> By opening and closing his jaws the genie started to weave with his mouth as with a loom. The genie was speaking. Like the Nommo had done with the first divulgence, he granted his word through a technique in order that it could be reached by men. Thus he demonstrated the identity of material gestures and spiritual forces, or rather the necessity of their cooperation. . . .
>
> The genie spoke and his words were filling all the interstices of the material. They were woven in the threads and became an integral part of the stripe. They were the material itself, and the material was the word. That is why material is said "to be," which signifies: this is the word, and this word also means seven, the rank of the one who spoke as he wove.

A new teaching became the heritage of men and was transmitted from generation to generation by the weavers with the clack of the shuttle and the shrill noise of the pulley, called the "creaking of the word."[4]

The third language appears to correspond to symbols, "speech of this lower world," and to discourse. It is given in a third complex phase that involves a fall or an exile from the celestial home of the genies and the voluntary sacrifice of an ancestor, the *lebe*, which brings about a redemption. His body is eaten, transformed, and finally vomited and reabsorbed into the earth.

With this language the system of the world is complete. For the first time, language becomes articulate, as does the human body, the articulations being represented by the *lebe*'s bones. This third language is represented by the arch of grain that came down from the sky (the latter was brought down with the help of a chain made of knots as shown in fig. 12.1). It corresponds to agriculture, "the language that came from the heart and the lips of the earth has once again been planted. Fecundation is also an activity of discourse."[5] This third language is taught through the making of drums and through the cat's cradle technique, because the skins placed at the two ends of the drum are held tight by certain cat's cradle configurations, which are themselves interwoven with Nommo's words. "To strike the drum is also to weave. The sound under the blow of the stick rebounds from one skin to another within the cylinder, like the shuttle and its thread slide from hand to hand between the crossed planes of the heddles."[6]

> "The most important drum is the underarm drum," he said. "It is the Nommo who made it. . . . He gave its image with his fingers, just as children do with the cat's cradle today. Spreading his hands, he passed the thread ten times around each of his four fingers, the thumbs not being used. . . . The palms of his hands represented the hides at the ends. Symbolically, to hit the drum is to hit the Nommo's hands. . . ."

Ogotommely reminded us that the genie had no ears, only auditory holes: "He used his hands as ears," he said. "To hear, he would always place them on each side of his head. Beating the drum is to beat the palmed hands of the Nommo, to beat his ears. . . ."

During all this work, he spoke as he had when he had taught weaving. But his speech was new, it was the third he had revealed to man. . . . The drum-making technique was similar to that of weaving and, in the hand of the craftsman, the awl used to pierce the border of the hides and to string the tension cord is the symbol of the shuttle and of the genie's tongue. . . .

"The loom," concluded Ogotommely, "is the tomb of the resurrection, the bedroom of the married couple and the prolific matrix. Speech finds its way between the threads, filling the spaces of the fabric . . . the words of the seven ancestors fill the empty spaces and form the eighth."[7]

The Dogon myth clearly demonstrates the mythic mode wherein different strata of language are superimposed and crossed. The division of languages is compared to different techniques and skills that interpenetrate one another, and language is taught together with other crafts. The speech of the genie fills the interstices of a braid, a weaving, a cat's cradle, and reciprocally, in the myths, the implicit message can be found between the words and the mythemes (or mythic elements), braided and woven together. Thus the unspoken message or silent voice of the myth can be heard only by understanding the structure that links the different layers of language as if they were different layers of knots. The message being delivered is finally the technique that weaves the world.

The space surrounding the knot, which, for the Dogon represents the space occupied by language, is also, in topology, the space that allows a knot to be distinguished. Mathematicians seek to determine if two knots are equivalent by observing if one of them can be obtained from the other through bending and twisting the space that surrounds them without cutting or tearing it. Strangely enough, the place held by the word or the humid breath of the genies is similar to the space defined by the equations of modern topological algebra, which, in its turn, is used to describe the structure of matter in quantum physics. To discover dimensions of space we need objects, but the space that precedes, penetrates, and reunites all prevails; it is space that makes the formation of knots possible and it is knotted space that connects words as well as objects and parts of objects in motion or in formation. The following paraphrase of Lao-tzu's aphorism underlines the essential point being made: "A knot is preferable without a cord." The myth describes not only a topology, a relation to and through space, but also how dimensions of space can be discovered only by following a leading thread.

Dogon myths meticulously describe the structure of language and how that structure is found nestled within all objects and all activities, but it remains difficult to visualize this structure in its entirety since the way the different techniques are connected remains ambiguous. Once again, however, a complementary system, this time illustrated in the Shoowa textiles from the Kuba of Zaire, presents us with a satisfactory and even astonishing image. This image will no longer be decoded in the texture of the fabric, but rather will present itself on its surface (see fig. 14.2 and plates 1 and 2).

The designs on these fabrics present a script by which all the stages of development of a complex weaving system are represented with symbolic motifs, such as crossings, twists, loops, and knots. As with the *kolams*, these motifs were derived from older patterns used for scarification, whose symbolic meaning is found in the myths. Here is the description that G. Meurant gives us of these fabrics: "The drawing is complex and multiform, it seems impenetrable, yet it possesses such coherence that one feels there must be an Ariadne's thread to reveal the way the pattern has evolved."[8]

As with the *nahals*, the principal motifs are superimposed on a partitioned frame that can represent

Fig. 14.2. Similarity between Shoowa and Cuna textiles
*The designs show similar interest in patterns, yarns, and weaving technique. (A), (C), and (E) are Shoowa designs.
(B), (D), and (F) are Cuna designs.*

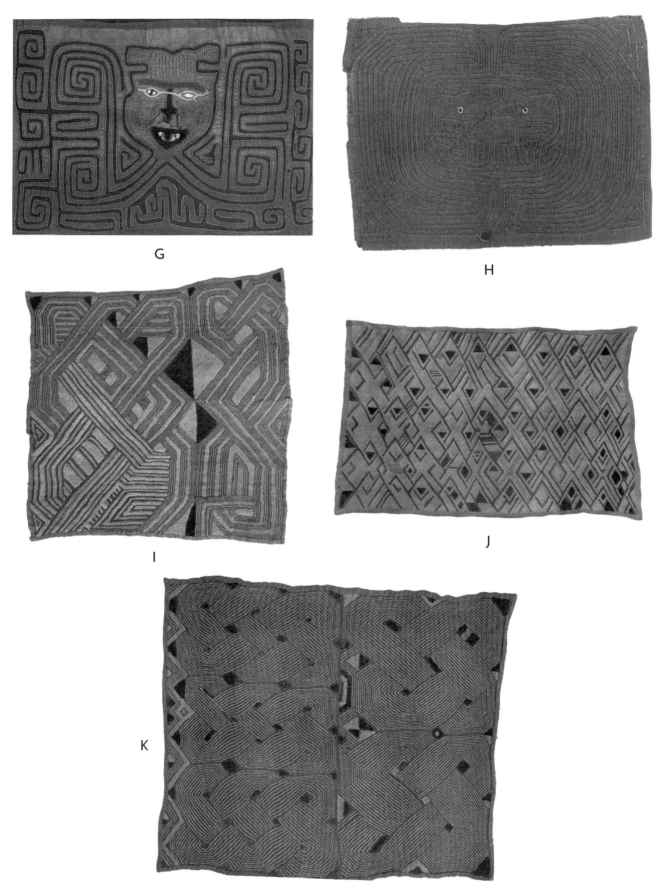

(G) and (H) Cuna textiles (molas) with labyrinthine designs. (I) and (J) Shoowa textiles. I contains modified knots.
(K) Shoowa textile with knots and torus knots.

the warp through which they are woven. But the pattern that depicts the pathway of the woof is accompanied or replaced and modified by the simultaneous representation of either a torsion, a shifting movement, a folding, or an inversion of the pattern of the warp. It is precisely in this manner that the weaving is accomplished on the loom. As the movement of the warp is merely suggested by a change of color or a shifting line, the design of the weaving process can no longer be recognized and becomes incomprehensible. It corresponds more to a vision of weaving obtained in a dream than to a systematic representation of its development. One could also surmise that in a complex process of weaving a pattern, the threads were braided or plaited and pulled as in a cat's cradle instead of being simply pulled back and forth. One would then obtain an image corresponding more completely to the Dogon myth.

As if rising from the deep, these patterns, represented on pieces of cloth, give us concrete images of the maze of language that, according to Dogon myth, is embedded in the fabric. We find a topological connection between knots or twists and the bent and twisted space in which they are embedded. Ultimately what these fabrics represent is yet another Gordian knot-maze, this time in the process of being formed. The maze is inextricable because one can no longer recognize the pathways that led to its completion. It presents itself as a complex four-dimensional knot, or as a knot formation slowly being transformed in the dimension of space-time. This kind of knot can be represented on a flat surface only by juxtaposing cross sections that correspond to different phases of the process and to different dimensions and points of view.

Comparing the designs of the Shoowa textiles with other textile designs will help us understand their conception and how the mazes hide a labyrinthine path. Other images, sometimes strikingly similar in motif, can be found in the fabrics of the Cuna Indians of Panama, though they are created using very different means (see fig. 14.2 and plates 3 and 4).[9]

These textiles are composed of layers of fabric, cut out, and then superimposed so as to cover the entire surface. The fabric is thus a kind of copy of the world described in Cuna myth, which is composed of eight layers or dimensions that only spirits and certain shamans can penetrate entirely. The patterns on the traditional fabrics, called *molas*, represent these spirits taking on diverse forms, or even animals, plants, or objects capable of being invested by these spirits. But they also depict labyrinthine pathways that ambiguously represent either the body of the spirit or the pathway it has followed. They no longer represent an incomprehensible maze, but rather a path followed within the maze. The joined layers of fabric can be seen as representing a flat projection of a path folded within a multidimensional knot-maze.

The pathways of the spirits subtly suggested are not fundamentally different from the path of the word described in Dogon myth. For both the Cuna and the Dogon, ways of doing, acting, and transmigrating are also ways of saying. Instead of the representation of a process culminating in the texture of language and of the world, in the Cuna designs we find the representation of a labyrinthine pathway that crosses its length. It seems that it is only by a jump between different pieces of textile joined end to end and representing separate layers that this pathway can appear as if unfolded (see fig. 14.2 for a comparison of Shoowa and Cuna textiles).

An inverted aspect of the same schema can be found in what Henry Stierlin used to explain the origin of Nazca geoglyphs (fig. 14.3) located in the desert of Peru.[10] These geoglyphs are composed of immense trapezoidal fields joined by long trails, and they depict astonishing animal designs that often can be assimilated to labyrinth paths (see fig. 14.4). According to Stierlin, the geoglyphs were used to make the double-stranded string for the warp of Nazca fabrics, as well as to fold the warp that was held by stakes without having to move the long fragile thread, which would risk its breaking. For magic or symbolic reasons, the thread had to be of one piece, and it was

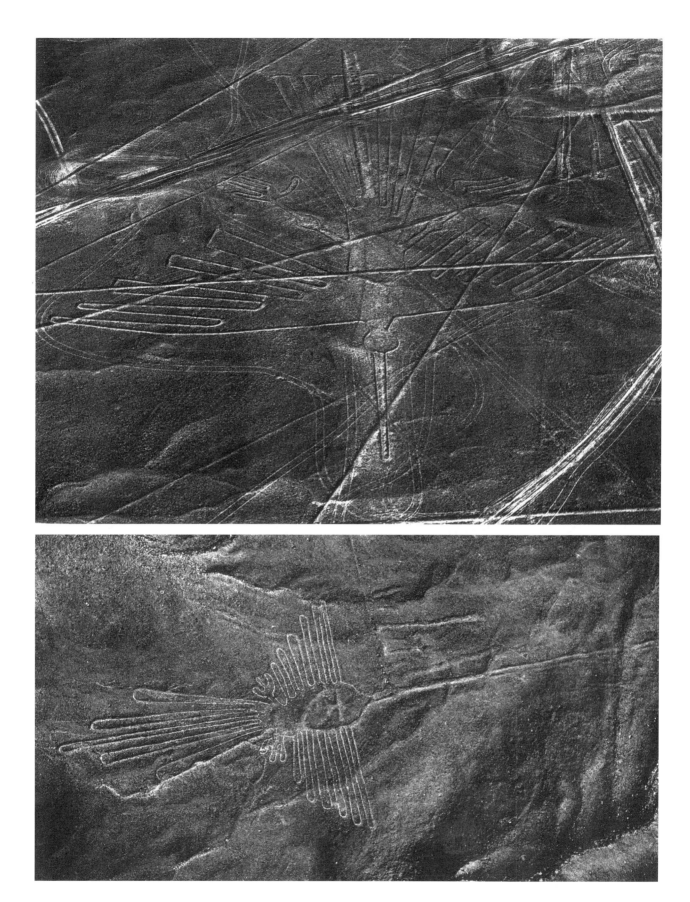

Fig. 14.3. Aerial photos of the Nazca geoglyphs

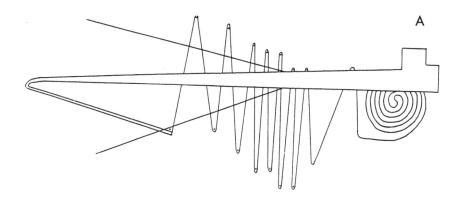

Fig. 14.4. Designs from Nazca geoglyphs located in the Peruvian desert

(A) Thread and needle with the same eight zigzags and spiral as on B. The length of the geoglyph is approximately 650 meters. (B) Monkey with eight zigzags, which reproduce how the thread for weaving was kept or stored without being broken. Length approximately 170 meters. (C) Condor, approximately 135 meters. (D) Sperm whale, approximately 65 meters. (E) Pelican, height approximately 105 meters.

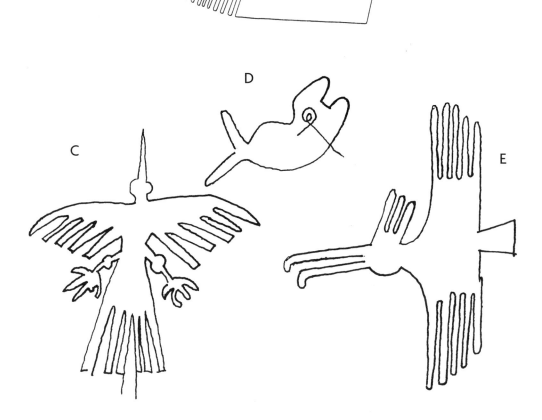

used to make canvases up to 140 yards long with a 115-mile-long thread. Produced with this thread, the canvas called "Fardo" had an immense symbolic value, as it was used to envelop the dead in many layers as a sort of conical cocoon. It represented "more than a viaticum, because it was the place where the afterlife was magically elaborated."[11] This technique of making rope by twisting its strands in long fields was also used by Europeans and this is what inspired Stierlen's hypothesis. Thus, prior to the actual weaving, labyrinthine designs representing different entities were marked out with the thread so as to capture a humid force emanating from the neighboring mountains where clouds accumulated. Instead of appearing in the textile designs, they could be found implicitly captured and dissolved in the textiles, being as if immanent in the new motifs woven on the warp. Their invisible presence brought a living character to these fabrics. There is thus a kind of symmetry and family resemblance between the Nazca designs existing prior to the weaving of the warp and the Cuna designs obtained "after" by cutting and sewing together pieces of cloth, as if resurfacing between the layers of the fabric.

We find again an image similar to that of Osiris entering the earth or the net of language at one end, fecundating it, and reappearing, reincarnated as Horus at the other end. In the Nazca and Cuna designs, instead of the path of a word spoken by a genie, one finds the path followed by the genie himself. In various forms, he invests the textile with life and then finds his way back to reappear between its cut-out pieces. But like his breath or first spoken word, the genie is first and foremost energy; it is by giving speech to man and by investing breath into structure and form that the genie can assume a form to man's eye.

The drawings on the Shoowa fabrics are mainly related to weaving, the Nazca drawings to making rope or braiding, and those of the Cuna to cat's cradle (since they suggest a folding and unfolding process). According to the Dogon, the structure of language can be totally represented only by taking all these different techniques and their interaction into account. Oddly enough, in order to understand completely the symbolic meaning of each textile art, we had to use other complementary designs and techniques belonging to extremely foreign cultures. In the three kind of designs we have mentioned, we find different aspects of the different generations of genies and ancestors that correspond to the different layers of language. Sometimes they are immaterial or only potentially present, sometimes they are invisible or replaced by a texture that can represent their energy, and sometimes they are manifest under a definite form—a form that lends a loaded meaning to a sound or to a language sign.

In the Dogon myth the role of both language and technique is to bind, weave, and knot things together. It is in this way that symbols appear that themselves bind objects to an absolute and inexpressible meaning of life. But as is the case with symbols, a bond is not the same as the object that represents it; it represents a whole that is more than the sum of its parts. When the bond is confused with the knotted thread, or the symbol confused with the object it represents, it becomes an opaque Gordian knot or an inextricable maze.

This subtle distinction between the bond and the thread is expressed in Hindu philosophy:

> The concept of liberty, in Vedic contexts, is repeatedly stated positively in terms of "motion and will" and negatively in those of release from bonds, knots, or nooses (*bandha, granthi, pasa,* etc.). In Sanskrit also, to be independent ("on one's own hook") is expressed by the significant term, *sva tantra,* "being one's own thread, string, or wire"; we are not then, if we "know ourself" the knot, but the thread on which the knot is tied or on which beads are strung, the meaning of which will be clear from the oft-repeated simile of the threaded beads. The knots are many, but the thread is one. Indra, the great hero (Mahavira), is said to have "found out the secret knot of Susna," and it is significant that the followers of the later

Mahavira are known as the Nirgrantha, "whose knot is undone." There is a prayer addressed to Soma to "untie, as it were a knot, the entangled (*granthitam*, knotted) straight and tortuous path," that is, almost literally, to guide us through the labyrinth in which these ways are indeed confused. The spirit is in bonds only where and when the knots of individuality are tied; its and our true self is the continuity of the thread on which the individualized entities are strung.[12]

In this tradition as well the knot's unifying aspects are given priority over its constraining aspects. We are here dealing not simply with the untying of a knot, but with "the appearance of a knot," which, according to the Hindu notion, means to get rid of an illusion created by maya. But this involves discovering a dimension in which the thread is liberated from the knot and where the knot is deconstructed rather than unknotted. In the fourth dimension the bonds are different, and, were we to live there, we would be able to walk through walls. "The hardest rocks become soft and fluid on a geological scale of a million years."[13]

The threefold aspect of the thread, the knot, and the bond remains puzzling. When we try to decipher the myth, we perceive only its mythic content or the structure of language, an image on a rug, or a weaving technique. To uncover the link between the two we must once again use language, thereby finding ourselves in a vicious circle. The enigma is not so much of a secret language as it is a language secret. The medium of the myth, whether word, sign, or breath, becomes a mystery. The medium is the message and it eludes us. It eludes man because he is himself similar to clay or fiber, animated and spirited by breath. He is himself the medium.

In language, the medium is the word or the breath that has become a proper name. In the words of Walter Benjamin, the creative word has become receptive, and, "thus fertilized, it tends to give birth to the language of things themselves." In language, what is communicated is man revealing himself as a mental entity guarding the Logos: "There is no such thing as a meaning of language; as communication, language communicates a mental entity, i.e., something communicable in and of itself. Language is a symbol of the incommunicable." It is only *through* language that "the word communicates something other than itself," but through language, it is only common servitude and fetters that are communicated, for "signs must become confused when things become tangled."[14] Language finds its source and finality only within man.

Man must use his language, techniques, relationships, and behavior as an extension of himself in a search for self-discovery. A language or a technique that is no longer an extension of man's quest for himself becomes alienating, rendering the maze even more complicated.

The fact that such a science of knots linked to language can be conceived explains how these elements constituted the original terms of an essential primitive writing, the traces of which can be seen in the art decorating ancient temples (whether Mayan, Aztec, or Egyptian), which are themselves assimilated to knots in myths. The architecture and decoration of the temple are woven together and wedded to rites and dances tracing knot patterns in such a way that the temple represents a complete language. Concomitantly, in myth, language ties and unties complex knots, thus becoming a temple. In Heidegger's words, "language is the home of Being."

Figure 14.5. Cretan seals with designs comparable to those on Cuna Indian molas

15

The Hidden Language of Nature

We are suspended in language.

—Niels Bohr

Until now, it has been through myths and rituals that we have explored the symbol of the knot. We can ask ourselves why the knot has been privileged as a symbol. Is it merely because it represents the most ancient and primitive technique in human history? In yet another reversal, modern science has rediscovered the knot as the language of genesis and of evolution, and as the newest and most efficient mathematical tool used to decode the secrets of nature. The whole manifests itself in many ways as a knot.

DNA is a knot. The electron microscope reveals that DNA strands are most often knotted. Moreover, when the two ends of a strand of DNA are joined, its double helix structure constitutes a knot (a simple knot when the number of crossings or coilings is odd and an interlaced or torus knot when the number is even, as illustrated in figure 15.1).

Fig. 15.1. Knotted DNA strand
(A) Torus knot, made of two strings. (B) Normal knot, made of one string.

Topological knot theory has become the leading instrument in biology, but biologists are as perplexed about this new language as we have been about myth.

Knot theory allowed molecular biologists at the university of California at Berkeley to make sense of an assortment of DNA strands. "When we first looked at them," said S. A. Wasserman, "it was very confusing how one could generate such a variety of molecules. It wasn't clear that there was a single mechanism that could generate them all." But when they ordered the molecules using a mathematical sequence of knots and links, the "pathway" stood out. . . .

As powerful as the new techniques are, they are also tantalizingly enigmatic: so far knot theorists cannot quite explain why they work as well as they do. Somehow the process of turning a physical structure into an abstract algebraic expression must capture some essence of the knot, but no one knows exactly what. In a sense, the mathematicians understand the algebra behind the new discoveries, but not the geometry. "They're magic," Dr. Birman said. "It's magic that we're doing. This polynomial [the Jones polynomial] catches hold of something, but it's terribly hard to say what it is."[1]

Knot theory is also used to resolve polymer coding problems, and chemists have created knotted molecules possessing new properties. To be active and to function adequately, the long chains of amino acids forming proteins must be folded correctly. They form either loops, helixes, or stacked leaves; thus, they are folded like false knots. It has been discovered, however, that the weaker secondary interactions between the proteins are what that govern this formation. Thus, curiously, fundamental laws similar to those by which DNA originally governs forms are found anew at another level, but this time provoked by a holistic interaction between terminal products.

Modern topology is a useful scientific tool, but it cannot yet explain the relation between the production of a knot, which is a form, and that of a function. Nevertheless, a simple knitted sock or hat can demonstrate that it exists. The form of the sock is created by knitting in a particular pattern. It seems that ancient topology saw and resolved this problem from a different perspective.

Knots can also be discovered in the macro- and microcosmos. Planets orbiting a sun that is itself moving follow a pattern of tangled knots. In superstring theory, the monopoles that are the source of the strings are microscopic knots, and the superstrings themselves are interlaced and form knots. As we have already seen, knot theory has become the prevalent tool in quantum physics and in cosmology.

We can find knots or at least their traces in much of cutting-edge scientific research. For example, the strange attractors in chaos theory are knots. The catastrophe theory elaborated by René Thom, which he also used to sketch a theory of language, is also topological and indirectly associated with knots. We can even mention that computers have their origin in the system of perforated cards used with Jacquard looms, and thus that there is a connection that is more than historically meaningful between the technique of computer language (where "strange loops" can occur) and that of weaving.

In science as well as in the language described in Dogon myth, there is recurrent mention of knots and related diagrams or techniques that are linked with-

out us being able to define precisely the characteristics of this link. The project of science also becomes that of exploring and interpreting a network or a knot that it creates as it develops and that becomes as intriguing as the one presented by the universe.

The sciences have reached a state described by Leibniz: they form or tend to form a "body as continuous as an ocean," which is arbitrarily divided into Ethiopian, Caledonian, etc., seas. This continuum is the seat of movement and exchange: methods, models and results circulate freely within it, exported and imported from and to all places, incessantly, often following regulated pathways, often capricious ones: *a network or net in the sea*. The new spirit was absorbed in a philosophy of negation; the new, new spirit is developing into a philosophy of transport: intersection, intervention, interception. . . .

If each region is an intersection, a knot of interrelations, it ends up containing, at least blindly, an interpretation of the realms it mobilizes, from one bias or another.[2]

The tangled network of knots that we find in myths to explain both the universe and language suggests an ineffable meaning that has been displaced. It is now part of a scientific language that still describes the universe, but that can no longer be translated into everyday language.

The topology that studies the structure of knots can also, as we have seen, be applied to space and to ordinary objects. We can visualize the structure of the volume brought about by the knot's rotation or by that of its loops. We would obtain shapes made of membranes, or "*m*-branes," as they are called in the recent development of string theory in physics. We can imagine the kind of surface that can be supported by a knot used as a frame, for example, the kind of bubble or veil that is produced when a loose knot made of wire is plunged into soapy water. One can also visualize different kinds of immaterial electromagnetic knots. Complex surfaces can also be created by membranes joining different knots. Knot topology is integrated into manifold topology, which is useful in embryology and biology. The play of amino acid chains that spontaneously roll up like knots and govern the development of the cells is later followed by a sort of kaleidoscopic movement when the development of the embryo unfolds like a game of origami, where the folded leaf is torn, pierced, and glued, thus resembling a game of cat's cradle practiced with a wide, uneven, sticky ribbon. All organic forms can be associated in several different ways to the science of knots. Thus the circulatory system presents itself as a knot, and when the interaction among different digestive, respiratory, nervous, and other systems is considered, the whole organism appears as a complex knot. As existential philosopher Merleau-Ponty saw it, "the body, in its pre-conscious, dialectical, non-causal relationship to its environment or given world, is like a knot of living meaning."[3] It is perhaps to remind us of this or of the bonds of the flesh that a curious old custom, still practiced in central France, evolved. It consists in knotting strips of flesh cut out from between pork ribs. Once cooked, these knots, which are served as a meal, can no longer be undone without being torn or sliced.

As Jacques Lacan and René Thom have recognized, topology is also an efficient instrument to grasp certain ambiguous concepts regarding the dynamics of psychology and linguistics. Logic, with its principles of inclusion, exclusion, and connection, also becomes dependent on topology. As we have already emphasized, the essence of the knot resides in the relation between the cord and the space it defines. The loops mark intersecting domains; when a loop shifts, its meaning changes and the relations between the domains also shift. Thus the meaning of the whole knot changes. For example, figure 15.2 indicates how the association among several myths expressing some aspect of a maze can create a complex meaning that cannot be expressed clearly by one myth alone. When *The Odyssey* replaces *The Iliad*, the theater of action changes. The circumambulation around the walls of Troy, which represented the world reduced to principles, becomes the circumambulation of Odysseus across the whole world, a world extended so as to include strange realms connected to the Underworld or the world above. With this shift, Helen, who was easily abducted, and whose thread of destiny seems to be untied, is replaced by Penelope, who keeps at bay a crowd of pretenders by undoing each night what she wove during the day, and who protects the hearth of her home. The trick of the Trojan horse that penetrated Troy is replaced by the guile of Odysseus, who,

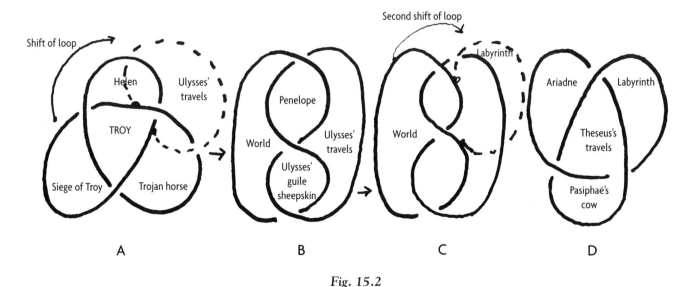

Fig. 15.2
(A) Iliad, *a labyrinth surrounding a fortress.* (B) Odysseus, *the world as labyrinth.* (C) *The shift to the myth of Theseus and the labyrinth.* (D) *Myth of the labyrinth, which becomes between two worlds*

for example, uses a sheepskin to escape the Cyclops's cave. When with the myth of Theseus the loops are shifted once again, the world becomes the labyrinth or the Underworld on earth and Penelope is replaced by Ariadne, who is a liberator and who knows a different secret about weaving and undoing, this time represented by the ball of thread. The Trojan horse and the sheepskin disguise of Odysseus are replaced by Pasiphaë's cow, which attracts and invites a penetration. There is finally a sort of osmosis between the changing terms that become charged with new meaning. As the womb of the different women involved become assimilated to the world, or to the places besieged, or are circumambulated by the heroes, a universal or cosmic feminine principle or matrix emerges.

From a different angle, if, for example, we were to replace the rings of Boolean algebra, used to illustrate a syllogism, with the loops of a knot (fig. 15.3), we would end up with a double relation between the words, placed as if in an Egyptian cartouche, and there would be a place in the center for the verb *to be*. Thus introduced, the verb to be can be used to undermine the syllogism that affirms that Socrates is mortal* and convey the double meaning given to life and death in myths. Being is no longer subjugated to the noth-

---

* Socrates is a man; all men are mortal; therefore Socrates is mortal.

ingness of a total death, and the verb *to be* can be an end in itself. It takes on the double meaning that we find in the Buddhist "I am that: I am," or the "I am he who is" of Christ. In these statements "to be" means to be united with the spirit or to an actualized soul; it is to become immortal. An antinomy is thus included in the logic. Man is presented as double, and from a binary (yes and no) system we pass to a ternary logic.

The psychoanalyst Jacques Lacan used many figures of knot topology. He illustrates the structure of language, as it exists within the unconscious and as it affects our psyche, in the form of a Borromean knot. This knot is composed of three overlapping circles, representing respectively the real, the imaginary, and the symbolic (fig. 15.4); the thesis held by Lacan to be a faithful interpretation of Freud's teaching is that "the unconscious is structured like a language"; the Borromean knot thus simultaneously represents the structure of the unconscious and that of language. From this point of view the unconscious would consist of a grouping of representations associated with words and things that do not necessarily coincide with those of current language or lexicons.[4]

One of the most interesting aspects of the model presented by Lacan is that it clearly expresses how difficult it is to attain the real; in truth, the real should be found at the intersection of the three circles, because truth is defined as the harmonized relation be-

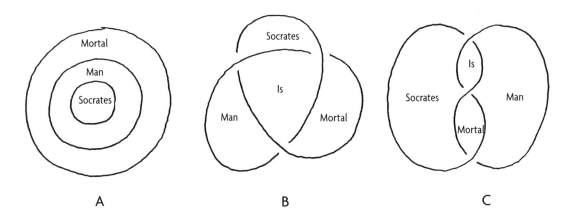

Figure 15.3. The logic of the knot
(A) Boolean logic. (B) Knot logic. (C) Reversal of a loop.

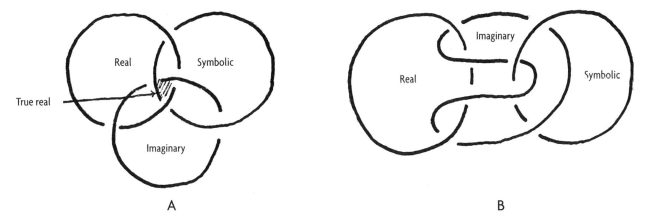

Fig. 15.4. Borromean knot
(A) *The place of true reality.* (B) *The real as we perceive it. Here the knot can represent three links in a chain.*

tween subject and object. But the reality that we recognize usually appears only as that which is opposed to the imaginary and the symbolic. Usually we live in a fantasy world; just as we take an imaginary "I" for the real "I," we only recognize an imaginary real and imaginary symbols to which the imaginary circle gives "consistency." To this effect, science attempts to produce an image of reality by eliminating the subjective and the symbolic. This is the myth of science! It deals only with objects, giving us access to and dominion over objects by transforming us into objects ourselves. As Paul Ricoeur has remarked, "Since the Renaissance only the non-living is held as being knowable. The living must then be reduced to it. In this way all our thinking is today under the domination of death."[5] This situation creates a "real" that is inaccessible to the "self," or to what we are, truly and totally.

According to Lacan, who expresses himself in difficult jargon, the scientific project "thinks where it is impossible for the subject to articulate" itself, where the subject cannot gain access to self-consciousness: "I think where I cannot say that I am." To say "I," "where it was (where the truth of the subject was), there as a subject must I occur."[6] Thus the subject as a complete or true man cannot develop in the real offered up by science; his reality exists in another dimension. To occur he must find or create the "there"

that is precisely the center of the labyrinth.

Rather than describe the object of science, the myth paints the other face of truth, the universe of the "subject"—in other words, the universe of the entity at the origin of a scientific project that was eclipsed by the development of a science that deviated. Thus it appears that the knots described by science and those evoked by myths are linked by another knot, described by Lacan, that represents the structure of both language and the unconscious.

Alongside the decoding of the world by science, the way we perceive the world directly with our senses also depends on topology. The pathway of the gaze, in exploring a painting or a landscape, also constitutes a sort of knot that brings together, synthesizes, and discovers meaning. The labyrinth of the ear absorbs and reconstructs sounds in a similar way. As Piaget remarked, young children intuitively use the language of topology in their drawings and scribbles that resemble prehistoric or primitive graffiti. A child's hand follows the arc of its vision. The interlacing designs of primitive peoples or those that can be found in Islamic, Celtic, or Chinese art can be considered as a consciously reconstructed version of what children draw unconsciously. Mysteriously, we decode the hidden knots of nature by drawing new ones.

Today we are faced with a knot that takes on many forms, serving as a model for all sorts of phenomena.

The modern knot replaces a knot that was the symbol of everything, and it reveals an unexpected dimension of the ancient symbol. Brought together, all of these knots form an "internet" that we could learn to "surf" with the greatest expectations. Today, instead of a Gordian knot to be untied, a path to be discovered, or a grail to be won, the quest that scientists present us with consists in discovering a unified theory and understanding the role of mind and consciousness in the scientific experiment. Does not this problem also consist in finding a common cord on which to tie both the ancient and the new knots?

Language is discovering that its own roots run as deep as those of nature, and that there is an enigmatic correspondence between the knots of language and those that science has discovered in nature. As Walter Benjamin said: "Inasmuch as it communicates itself, the whole of nature communicates in language and finally in man. Man is the orator. Through the word, man is linked to the language of things."

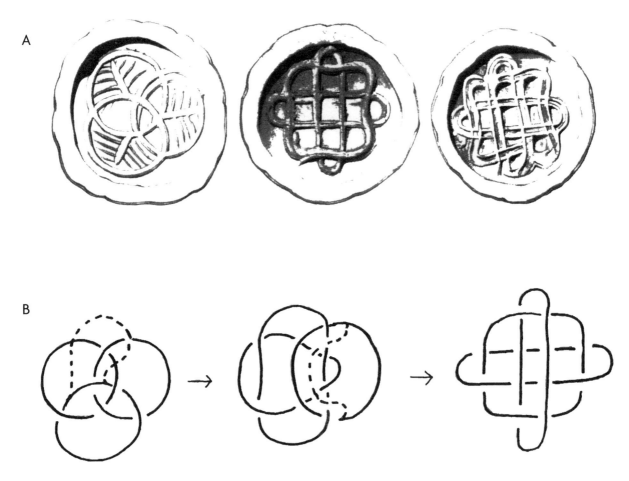

Fig. 15.5. Cretan seals
(A) Borromean knots or a projection of them, as the superimposition of the cords is not clear.
(B) The modification of the Borromean knot corresponding to the designs on the seals.

3
The Geometry
of the Labyrinth

16

The Ball of Thread
and Ariadne's Technique

The straight and crooked path is one and the same.
—Heraclitus

We have now reached the geometry or the topology of the labyrinth itself—a subject that might put off many readers. The topology discussed in the following chapters, however, has little to do with topology and algebra as it is taught in college—even if it can lead to similar conclusions. Here it is only a matter of observing and manipulating the knots and their projections, or shadows, and the reader is asked to play the part of a botanist observing the growth and motion of some strange heliotrope or sunflower. The nature of this topology can be found in the paraphrase of an Egyptian inscription: "Between the Fingers and Below the Shadow of the Forehead," in which everything must occur, as in a cat's cradle, between the fingers, and to which no additional concepts may be added. If we observe diligently, we can discover that the object of our study becomes a structure. There is a transformation brought about by the act of observing. It is such that our vigilance and observation are also gradually transformed.

The myth never explicitly reveals how Theseus used the ball of thread. As we mentioned previously, the unwinding of the thread must indirectly allude to a geometric method or to a strategy to discover the structure of the knot or how to chart it. The Malekulan myth furnishes complementary information that mustn't be neglected about a central axis that divides the knot into two symmetrical parts.

As in the case of dream interpretation, to reach a solution we must consider each mytheme as being a condensation of disparate elements and as displacing or reversing the different steps of a process that we would find rationally expressed in a geometrical demonstration. Things being jumbled, it is only afterward, once we have discovered a geometric process of transformation to which the myth alludes, that we can verify how the myth and the logic of geometry correspond. At the beginning, we can only progress intuitively, trying to reunite and associate data that appear to be crucial.

One of the implicit meanings of the Greek myth is that the labyrinth represents a matrix or a womb within which a process of gestation and emergence is accomplished. Thus Ariadne's thread is a symbol of the umbilical cord. But instead of emerging from the womb twisted and bent, it is wound into a ball and reintroduced into the womb/maze to show Theseus his way.

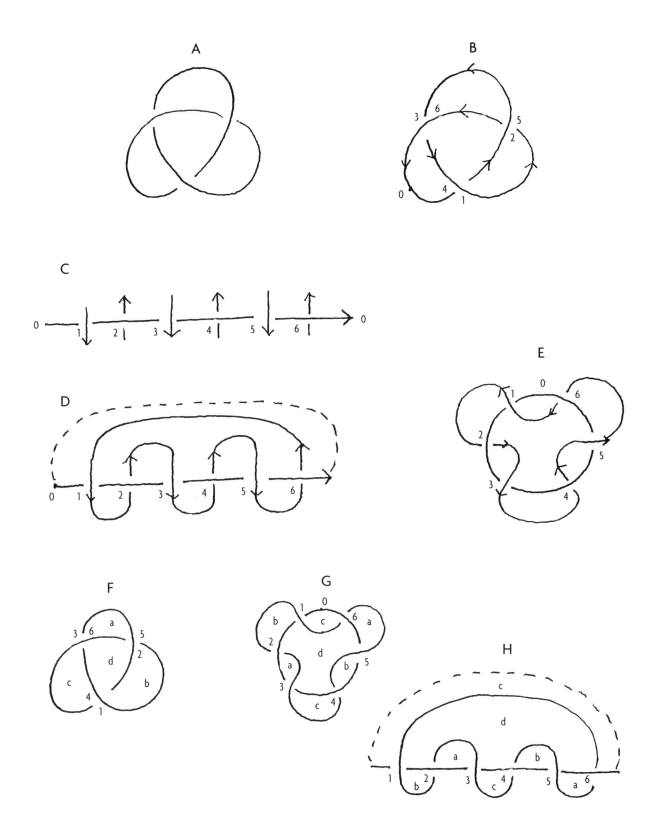

Fig. 16.1. The mapping of the knot

(A) The simple knot. (B) The knot is oriented and each crossing is numbered in order starting from point 0.
(C) The string is stretched and becomes an axis upon which the crossings are marked. (D) The arrows representing the crossings are joined as they were on the knot. (E) If the axis is circular, one obtains a torus knot. (F, G, H) Each space in the knot (labeled with lower case letters) is found twice in the torus knot, except for the central space, "d."

According to the rules of structuralism, we must find a second version of our theme against which to place the first. We can take up this "leading thread" first in connection with the Gordian knot, which is presented in the myths as being a complement to the labyrinth. Not only will we follow the path presented by the knotted string, but as the Malekulan myth has informed us that the path to be followed is the axis of the knot, instead of preserving the pattern of the thread as it presents itself in the knot, we will set the string straight and use it as an axis to chart the sequence of crossings in the knot. This tortuous reasoning gives rise to a very simple method to chart the structure of the knot. Moreover, this method also corresponds to the definition given in chapter 11 where we reversed the message of Malekula and suggested that the solution will be reached by taking the thread that constitutes a knot as an axis, which will allow the knot to be doubled and unknotted by a projection.

To demonstrate this method, which must be carefully followed at every step, we shall first use the simplest example and apply it to a clover knot lying flat.

In figure 16.1B, the ends of the cord constituting the knot join at point 0. If we follow the direction thus indicated, we can number the points where the cord crosses itself as we meet them. Thus each crossing is represented by two numbers.

In C and D, if the cord is then held taut so that it forms a straight line that can be used as an axis, the numbered crossings can still be marked on this line. The crossings are then joined in accord with the way they fall in the knot. The part of the cord that crosses the path of the axis above and to the right of point 1 will cross the axis again from beneath and toward the left at point 2. By continuing in this way, we obtain a drawing depicting two interlaced cords.

In E, we can also bend the axis into a circle. This pattern presents meaningful symmetries that we shall find useful for what is to follow. The pattern appears more clearly as that of a torus knot—in other words, a knot composed of two interlacing rings, reminiscent of a Hindu *kolam*. When the clover knot has a triangular form, as in figure 16.2A and B), the torus knot resembles Solomon's seal.

Our knot is thereby divided into two lines or two cords. One of the lines is an axis that we will call the *self axis*; the other takes on the form of a *meander*. Thus mapped, our knot has been deconstructed. The knotted thread or line representing it is now divided into two threads or lines, neither of which is knotted anymore. If we consider that the meander is the final result of the mapping while the self axis was only a means, each line takes a different meaning and we can conclude that we have undone the knot. We can say that with the meander we have mapped the situation of the string in relation to itself or in relation to

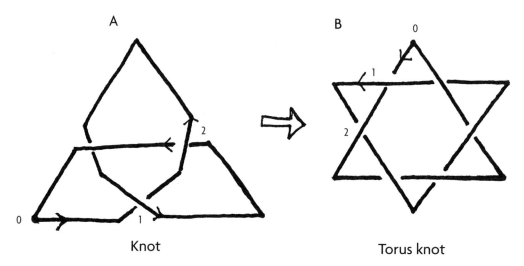

Fig. 16.2. If the knot is angular, the torus knot becomes a Solomon's seal.

the axis that it constitutes. (In fact, in a knot each section of the string is an axis around which a loop is coiled. The knot is made of axes joined end to end but also of loops joined end to end. With the mapping or analysis in situ, as topology was first called by Leibniz, we have divided these two aspects of the string.) Since the two lines in the torus knot are knotted or ligatured together, however, the unknotting is somehow relative or virtual.

We have thus found what we have been looking for, a method of finding a meander or path through the knot that doesn't cross itself and a method to untie a closed knot. To assimilate this technique, the reader can try to apply this mapping to a knot crossing itself several times. A solution can be found in figure 16.4.

The meander doesn't represent exactly the unknotted thread, but rather the thread's path in another dimension. "Dimension" is not taken here in a strict mathematical sense, but since everything is doubled by the mapping, there are now two dimensions where there was one before. This notion will be developed gradually. This new dimension is not simply added arbitrarily as when we add a new axis of coordinates; rather it is discovered by following the path of the knotted cord, and it becomes visible in a doubling of the cord and of the knot. It is at first difficult to ascertain whether this dimension is mental or whether it corresponds to or describes a divided consciousness, a "double inscription," as Freud called it, or whether it describes a concrete phenomenon. The geometric solution corresponds to, and clarifies, the Hindu philosophical notion that compares freedom to an independent or liberated thread that only "resembled a knot," and that would appear differently in a space with more dimensions rather than simply being cut or untied. The Hindu metaphor is grounded in a concrete geometric formula.

Simple yet at the same time mystifying, the geometric procedure leading to this doubling of the cord is difficult to understand. We could object that the process that consists in transforming the pathway of the cord into a rectilinear or circular axis is an ille-gitimate subterfuge and that the transformation obtained by the mapping corresponds to a geometrical sleight of hand. But if we consider that the knot is in motion, and that as we map the knot, it turns in on itself while circling like a planet around the sun (see fig. 16.3), then the circular path of the self axis coincides with that of the orbit and that followed by the thread, and one obtains yet again the pattern of the torus knot. The map of the knot thus describes simultaneously a structure and a movement of the knot, and therefore includes a cycle of time. The place of this structure and that of the maze becomes difficult to define; it exists only in space-time and thus in another dimension. As the Greek philosopher Laërce expressed it, "What moves does not move where it is nor where it is not." The ambiguous situation of what exists in another dimension is brought to our attention. The image corresponds to the implicit message of the Hindu myth, where the sun is followed and captured by Varuna's lasso, which represents the apparent path of the sun, a path reaching the sun in order to catch it, and the structure of a maze imprisoning it. The mapping of the knot while it turns around the sun or a center presents the sun enclosed as in a castle or maze. The knot that represents the whole and thus somehow contains us also becomes like a vehicle that transports us. Through the transformation and mediation of a map we are carried away, on the way toward the center of the labyrinth, which resembles the sun in the labyrinth.

This transformation or projection of the knot is original in that it makes no reference to Cartesian or any other coordinate system arbitrarily applied from outside. Space, like time, no longer exists as a system of reference established a priori, but rather as a relative notion. The only axis of reference is the self axis, which represents both a dimension of space and time. The self axis also represents the entire cord—that is, the entire substance of the object. The object is thus transformed from within, hence the name "self axis" that we have chosen. Thus in some odd way, a geometrical image corresponding to the Self or to

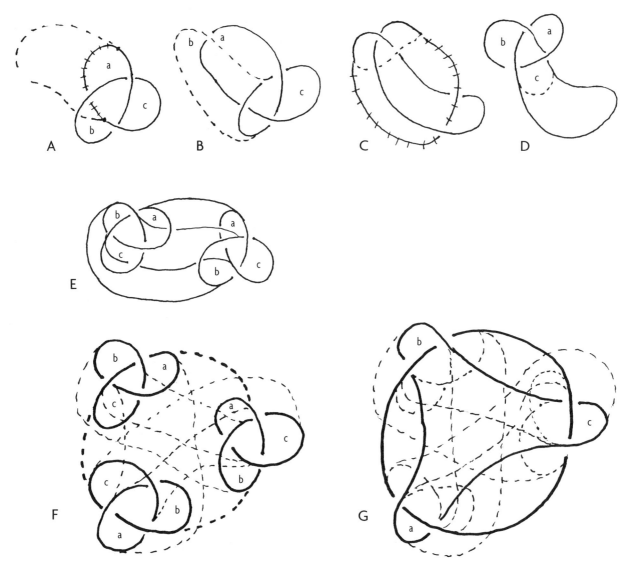

Fig. 16.3. The circulating knot

As we follow the string (charting the crossings and their connections), we can imagine the knot turning in on itself and following an orbit, moving as in illustrations A, B, C, and D. If this movement is repeated three times, the knot accomplishes a full circuit. Illustration E represents a third of the entire motion, or the sum of A, B, C, and D. Illustration F shows the knot in orbit with its entire circuit traced. Illustration G shows the map recorded by the observer as he follows the string while the knot moves. The dotted line represents the full circuit of the knot. The diagram is the same as in figure 16.1.

self-knowledge is produced. The map of the knot produces a representation that is as "real," or even more real, than that of a drawing or a photograph of the knot, as the transformation actually refers to an experience, both visual and tactile, of living through and with the knot without having any preconceived notion of what it is as an object. Geometry illustrates in a new way how difficult it is to define the real and proposes a way to reach it in another dimension. One can note

here that while primitive men like the Aborigines of Australia can identify all the details of complex paintings or patterns that we are completely unable to recognize, it was very disconcerting for them to identify the subject of a photograph. An ethnologist describes the difficulties an African man had in recognizing a portrait when confronted with a photo for the first time; with some help, he finally distinguished one eye, then the other, and it was only after much hesitation that he managed to assemble the features of a face.

An examination of figure 16.1 F, G, and H shows that not only is the rope divided in two and each crossing of the knot represented twice, but likewise each space delimited by the cord is doubled, except the central region D. In this way the labyrinth offers a dual representation of the knot, and thus of everything. This suggests a less obvious interpretation of why Janus, the god of doors and secret passageways, who is associated with the labyrinth, is represented with two opposing faces, simultaneously gazing into two different worlds. This doubling can represent the foundation upon which rest all the other doublings we have mentioned up until now (two lives, two deaths, and two kinds of consciousness). Once this geometry has been assimilated and accompanied or replaced by a symbolic system, we can imagine how a primitive mentality could conceive of totemism, giving to man both a spiritual and an animal nature and to the soul a double role: at the same time gestating within the human body and manifesting a particular power in a totemic animal. The Minotaur, inextricably linking these two opposing natures as if with a taut knot, can be seen as presenting a principle directly opposed to totemism. The Minotaur's existence eliminates the betwixt-and-between space occupied or traveled by the soul, and it assimilates the superman or the overman to a monster.

From a psychological point of view, it is interesting to speculate about the fact that our diagram is what an ant would come up with if it lived in a knot and, like a primitive astronomer, tried to understand the structure of its world (this ant should remind the reader of the one used by Daedalus to pass a thread through a shell, thereby accomplishing a task similar to that of Theseus). Imagine a huge but invisible three-dimensional knot and lines of other ants moving along the thread. Like primitive man, the ant is badly equipped to understand the movement and the form of its world. It cannot guess directly the form of the invisible knot whose pattern it follows. It can only notice that after a long journey, it comes back to the same spot that it had previously marked. It cannot fathom that the other ants that it crosses on its path through space are following the same thread. Even if it meets or passes another ant on the same thread, it cannot know if it happens to be one of the ants whose path it noticed moving through space. Thus, for it, the path of the other ants is similar to that of the stars, the angels, or the gods described by the myths. Mentally, this ant lives in the dual world of our diagram, projecting each region of its world into separate domains. In its universe, ants, their gods, and heavenly bodies mysteriously meet and communicate. Its mentality is the one described by myth.*

Quipu Knots and Knots with Four Intersections

We must now make sure that this mapping or transformation of the knot into a torus knot can also be applied to more complex knots, and that it always produces a meander that doesn't cross itself. This method can easily be applied to the knots in the traditional quipu. As the knot becomes more complex, the meander folds in a more complicated manner, as shown in figure 16.4. Certain difficulties arise, however, when we try to map a knot with four intersections, or any other even number of intersections, as shown in figure 16.5. This difficulty can be avoided by twisting the knot in such a way that it forms an additional cross. Since all knots can be obtained from a combination of simpler knots, we can assume that if we turn or twist the knot correctly, this method can be applied to all knots. As the knot becomes more complicated, however, the solution becomes more difficult, but we shall not need to analyze such a complicated knot to find the path of the labyrinth.

---

*A doubling that brings to mind our geometry can be found in the non-commutative geometry or geometry of incertitude recently developed by Alain Connes. Space is constructed from a fictive universe of functions, and each point in space has an indispensable twin alter ego. There even exists a technical operation that consists of fusing objects together, which gave rise to the name "Connes-fusion" humorously given to this operation by other mathematicians.

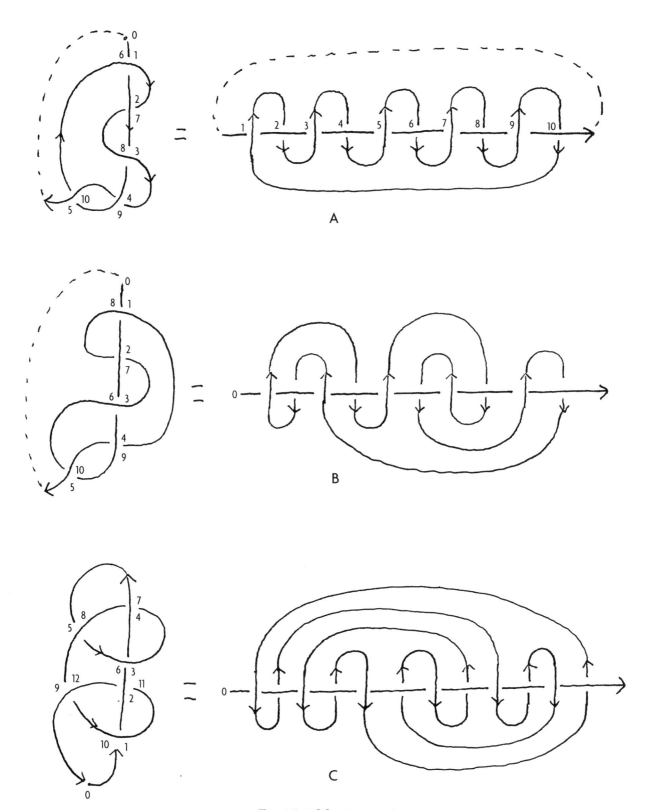

Fig. 16.4. Mapping a quipu

(A) Mapping of a quipu knot crossed five times. We apply the same procedure as in figure 16.1. The wave pattern is similar to the one obtained with the threefold knot. (B) When in the knot the string changes direction, the pattern of the meander in the torus knot becomes more complex. For example, the arrow crossing at 1 jumps farther away on the self axis at 4. (C) Mapping of quipu knot crossed six times. In this case we have a knot with an even number of crosses that is easy to map. But in general, as in the case of the knot crossed four times (fig. 16.5), that kind of knot can create a problem.

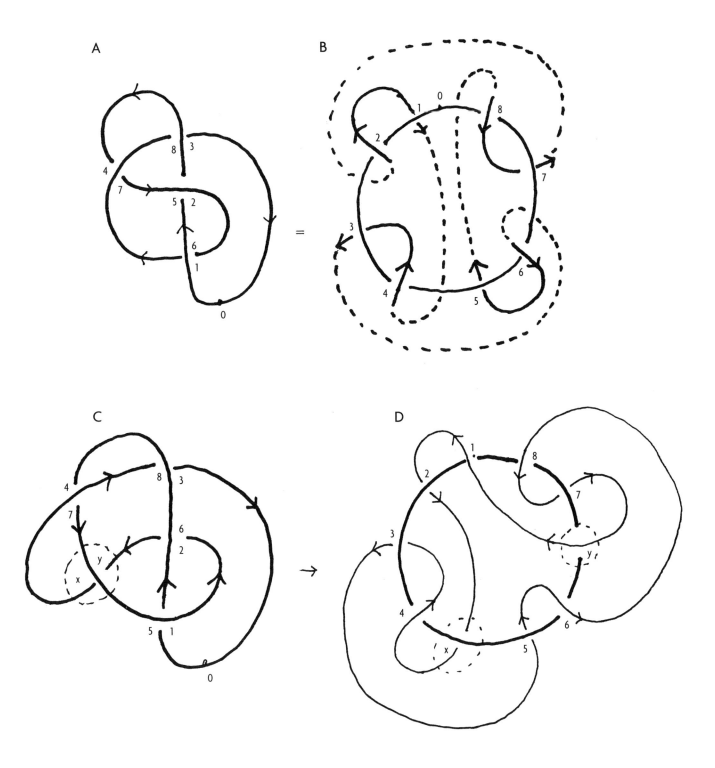

Fig. 16.5. A knot with four intersections

On these figures we have used the pattern of the torus knot and the self axis in a circle instead of using a straight self axis.
(A) The knot crossed four times. (B) Because the direction of the arrows poses a problem, the meander cannot be drawn without
having the axis intersect four more times. (C) By swinging one loop, the knot in (A) is transformed into a knot with five intersections. The new intersection is represented by x and y. (D) The map obtained from the knot in (C). Thus, in order to map a knot
with an even number of crossings, we first transform it into a knot with an odd number of crossings. The difference between the
knot with three intersections and the one with four can be explained in terms of the twists of the rope that occur when the
knot is made. There is a different ratio in the equation n links = n twists + n writhings.

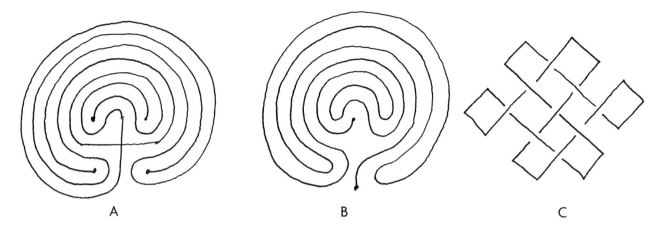

Fig. 16.6

(A) The Cretan labyrinth. (B) The path in the labyrinth. (C) Pal-be-ü, *the Buddhist knot of eternity*

The Path of the Cretan Labyrinth Is Obtained from the Knot of a Man's Tie

Does a knot exist that, once transformed into a torus knot according to our mapping technique, would produce the same meander as the path of the labyrinth shown in figure 16.6B? Then the origin of the labyrinth construction might be identified. Furthermore, this knot would be significant and be somewhat equivalent to the maze or to the Gordian knot that must be undone. At least it could represent the basis from which a confused or inadequate mapping would produce a more complex maze or Gordian knot.

As the path in the labyrinth forms seven rings around a center (fig. 16.6B), we must apply the transformation to a knot that intersects seven times. The classic men's tie knot perfectly satisfies this condition. It may originally come from the ritual knot found tied behind the neck of the priestess at Knossos, or else from the Isis knot tied around the *djed* pillar. In this way, when we wear a tie, our neck or spine replaces the pillar of Osiris. Another knot that has seven intersections but is presented with two supplementary twists is the Tibetan *pal-be-ü,* or knot of eternity, or *srivatsa* in Sanskrit. This knot represents the interdependence of all things, and thus the true nature of reality. Since it has no beginning and no end, it also symbolizes the knowledge of the Buddha and can represent the union of skillful means

and knowledge, or the inseparability of emptiness and clarity.

Actually, the classic tie knot is a false or composite knot; it is composed of a clover knot (which represents the principle of the trinity), with two of its loops crossed. This kind of knot must have had a particular symbolic meaning, but to keep things simple and the geometry rigorous we shall change the order of superimposition of the cord in order to work with a real knot crossed seven times (see fig. 16.7).

In figure 16.9 (A, B, C, D), by following the same procedure as in figure 16.1, we obtain a more complex meander with a labyrinthine character, but it is still different from the drawing we hope to obtain. If we examine the new torus knot, we can notice that it presents a symmetrical axis and that each delimited space is represented twice, except the one labeled "e." Here one must follow one's intuition; since we often encounter the notion of symmetry, somehow it is tempting to—by a twist of the axis—make the symmetry complete. One can sense that this modification can change the pattern of the meander in the right direction. It is only later, in retrospect, that we shall find the logical necessity of this new twist and the validity of the intuition.

If, however, as in figure 16.10, we twist the circle of the self axis around this symmetrical axis so as to form a figure eight, all the spaces become doubled; as

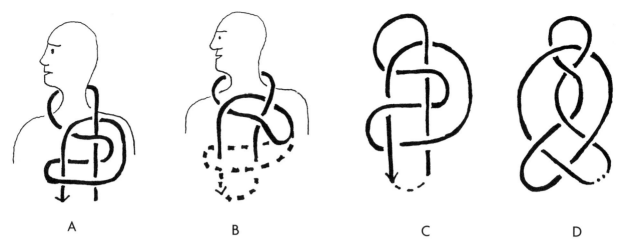

Fig. 16.7. The tie knot

(A) The knot as it is made is B, a simple knot with two intersecting loops. (B) shows how illustration A is partly a false knot with one loop inside the next one. (C) and (D) represent two different aspects of the real knot we shall use.

the pattern of the self axis is modified, the pattern of the meander also becomes modified, precisely like that of the path of the labyrinth.

We can thus conclude that the path of the labyrinth is obtained by mapping the tie knot in a particular way. We have discovered a complementary position to that expressed by the myths. The thread, which is a solid part of the knot, becomes empty space or the path between the walls of the labyrinth.

In figure 16.9C we see a symmetrical axis that is reminiscent of the one mentioned in the Malekulan ritual, but this time, instead of directly showing the way, it does it indirectly and only modifies the path. Since the self axis and the meander can exchange their relative positions, however, the self axis also corresponds to the path in the Malekulan maze leading to another dimension. The better we understand the geometry, the clearer the language of myth and ritual will become.

The self axis is also a labyrinth because it represents and commands an "eternal return." This straight labyrinth path was recognized by Borges in his short story "Death and the Compass": "I know of one Greek labyrinth which is a single straight line. Along that line so many philosophers have lost themselves that a mere detective might well do so, too."[1]

Fig. 16.8. Cretan seals depicting diverse torus knots
The presence of these knots suggests that the Cretan scribes knew the geometry of the labyrinth.

The Meaning of the Crossing

We shall consider the mathematical and logical meaning of the crossing and twisting of the self axis in geometrical terms later on. We must first become archaeologists or detectives, tracking down and assembling the pieces of a puzzle, reassembling and examining the symbols associated with the geometric figures. As we gradually explore the geometry of the labyrinth, each phase of transformation and each element of each figure must be considered as the source of a symbol that infuses geometry with a new meaning, displaced though it may be in different contexts. In exchange, the geometry will more precisely indicate how the symbols are interlinked, leading us to discover the profound structure of signs and signification.

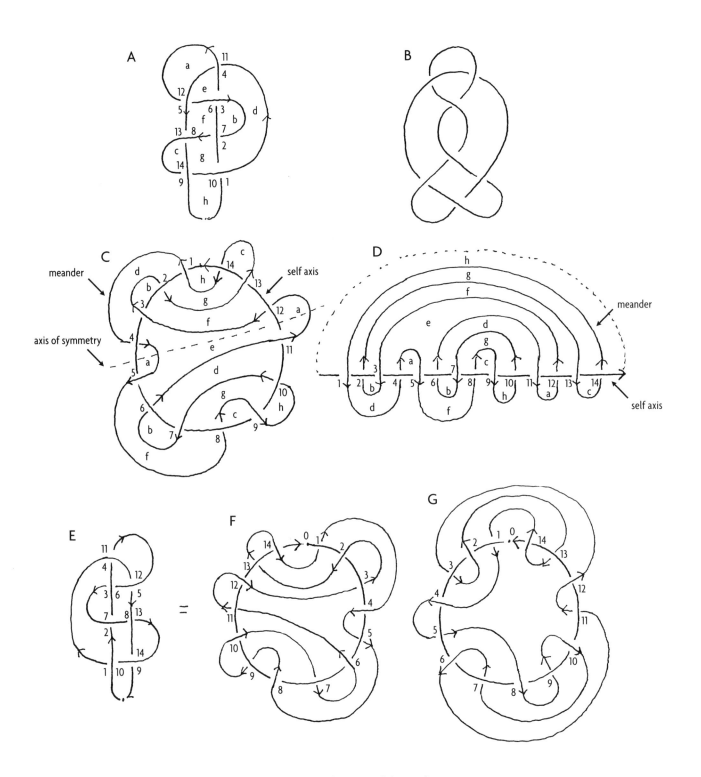

Fig. 16.9. The map of the tie knot

(A) The crossings are represented by numbers, the spaces by letters. Those used in A correspond to those used in the following illustrations. (B) The modified tie knot. (C) The torus knot and its axis of symmetry. (D) The meander when the axis is straight. (E), (F), and (G) The knot seen from the other side or mapped in reverse. We apply the same geometrical mapping to a knot, as in A and B, crossed seven times. The mapping produces a torus knot that can be presented in two different ways: In C an axis of symmetry becomes apparent; in D the near similarity between the pattern of the meander and the pattern of the path in the labyrinth is more apparent. The mapped knots in E, F, and G are not useful right now but they will be later. In F we have mapped the same knot seen from the other side, and in G we have mapped the same knot, but on the torus knot we have oriented the self axis in the opposite direction. Thus we can see that there are apparently two possible patterns for the meander, but when the axis is straight they become the same. (They are only oriented differently or symmetrically.)

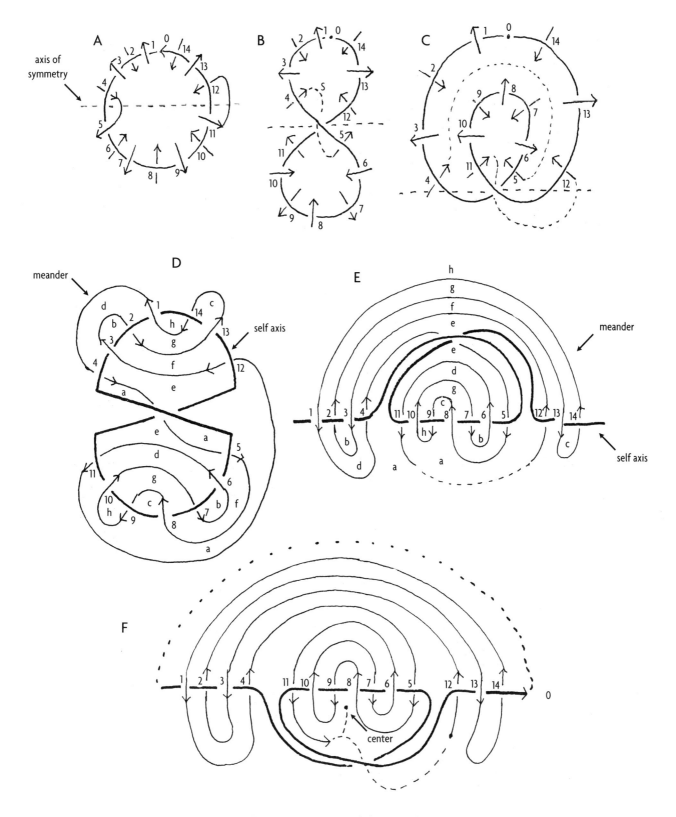

Fig. 16.10. Twist of the torus knot

(A) The self axis. (B) The self axis can be twisted along the axis of symmetry. (C) The self axis can also be overturned.
In this case, the new crossing meets the meander where it gets broken; it is thus the best model for the path in the labyrinth.
(D) The meander pattern when the self axis is twisted, as in the figure eight in B. (E) Same figure as D with a straight self
axis. When the self axis is a straight axis, we can recognize the pattern of the path in the labyrinth taken by the meander.
(F) Same pattern of the labyrinth when the self axis is first twisted, then flopped, as in C.
Then the meander seems broken by the cross of the self axis.

Thus, to the geometry we must join a cryptography, a term selected by Deleuze to describe "the art of inventing the key of a thing which is wrapped" or shrouded.

It is as if "the infinite had two stories: the recesses of matter and the folds in the soul. . . . A labyrinth corresponds exactly to each story: the labyrinth of the continuous in matter and its parts, the labyrinth of freedom in the soul and its predicates. A cryptography is needed which at the same time enumerates nature and deciphers the souls, sees in the recesses of matter and reads in the folds of the soul."

Ancient iconography often directly suggests the existence of a link among myths, rites, and geometry. The images representing the symbols are transformed, slipping from figurative images to abstract or geometrical signs. Such is the case with a series of Cretan seals (fig. 16.11A) that are directly linked to the labyrinth and that illustrate "the gate of horn"—that is, the entrance to the labyrinth, above which can be found a representation of a double ax, or labrys. The seal shows how the double ax becomes a diagonal cross, suggesting an intersection. This cross is itself replaced by the intersection of the diagonals of the embedded rectangles that seem to suggest the enclosure of the labyrinth. Elsewhere, in figure 16.11C, the double ax becomes a knot or even, in (B), a winged goblin that brings to mind Daedalus escaping from the labyrinth with his wings made of wax and feathers. Thus the elements of geometry are attached to other symbols through the series of mutations illustrated in the figures. But this kind of transformation merely indicates associations without ever explaining them.

We shall attempt to find the symbolic meaning connected to different parts of a geometric drawing and reveal how a crossing, reversal, or twisting of the self axis is suggested by the myths and symbols. First, there is no doubt that, just like the meander, and even though it isn't represented in the symbol of the labyrinth, the self axis has a symbolic meaning. Represented as a straight line, it can again be associated with symbols like the world axis, the pillar of Osiris, the path folowed by the ghost of the dead, Gilgamesh's stick, the golden bough, and Hermes' caduceus—in other words, with the instruments necessary to gain entrance to the Underworld. As is indicated by the pillar of Osiris, which is first a tree, then a trunk floating in the current, and finally the

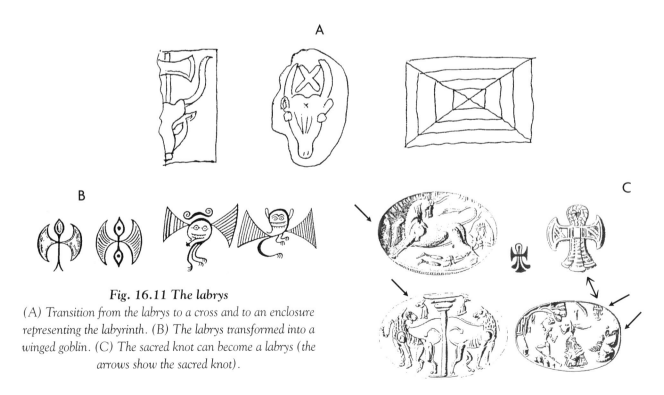

Fig. 16.11 The labrys

(A) *Transition from the labrys to a cross and to an enclosure representing the labyrinth. (B) The labrys transformed into a winged goblin. (C) The sacred knot can become a labrys (the arrows show the sacred knot).*

pillar of a temple, this axis is neither still nor unchanging nor completely determined by the object it represents. It can appear in many forms when it is put into relation with other symbols; it travels, in a certain sense, toward diverse horizons, which change depending on one's point of view. Bent into a circle, it can be associated with the rim of a wheel, which also represents the border of the world, the horizon, the sky, or the Ourobouros serpent that eats its tail and that represents time and the eternal return. To the circle representing both the sky and the border of the world corresponds the twisted circle forming a figure eight, which represents infinity, but also the universe. It is significant that the infinite isn't represented by an infinitely extending circle but rather by a twisted and crossed circle that can suggest the two halves of an hourglass or the two vases of the Aquarius sign exchanging a transformed content. The Ourobouros drawing that is associated with it is also sometimes twisted like a Möbius strip (in other words, crossed), indicating that the cycle cannot be completed without a reversal through which the exterior and the interior become one (fig. 16.12B).

For primitive man, the concept of a crossing, a torsion, or a reversal associated with the activity of brewing or churning was seen as inseparable from the concept of the whole or of completeness. The look of the ankh, the Egyptian cross of life suggesting a circling and a knot, can correspond to Saint Andrew's diagonal cross inscribed in a circle, which also ex-

isted in ancient Egypt. It is as if the second cross were necessary to find the path symbolized by the first cross. The combination of the directions indicated by the two would suggest the existence of a dynamic intermediary cross expressing a rotation or a reversal similar to that of a swastika, a variety of which is found in the center of the labyrinth.

In the Chinese sign of the Tao, the axis and the border of the whole are both represented by a single continuous line. The central point of the inflected axis is where the bend changes orientation and where yin becomes yang. At this central point the axis undergoes a torsion, called *san-su-chin,* that is not explicitly represented on the diagram but which is essential in the practice of tai chi, which uses the diagram of the Tao as its foundation. This twisting, which signifies a reversal or a crossing, indicates a reversal of the polarity of the sign, which spins in on itself as it were. The line of the Tao becomes like a thin Möbius strip. Moreover, the sign of the Tao can be traced with the right hand, or backward with the left hand, and it is interesting to note that these two superposed signs produce once more the projected image of a simple knot. Thus the sign of the Tao represents, in a different way from that of the Malekulan ritual, a knot divided in two (see fig. 16.13). On a funerary banner—dating from 166 B.C.—one can actually find a knot replacing the sign of the Tao (see plate 5).

To signify the unity of the whole, the ancient

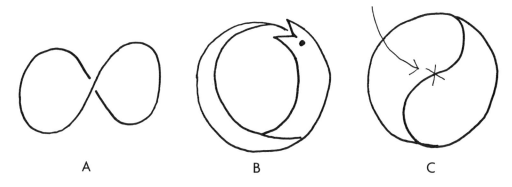

Fig. 16.12
(A) Infinity. (B) Ourobouros, comparable to a Möbius strip. (C) Tao, showing san-su-chin, *the twist of the axis.*

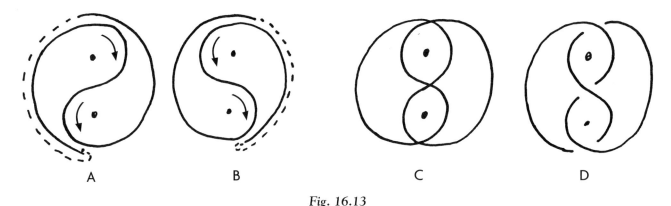

Fig. 16.13
(A) Movement of the right hand following the Tao. (B) Movement of the left hand following the Tao.
(C) Combination of the two motions. (D) The resulting knot.

symbols cannot be built and connected in an arbitrary or random way from objects perceived in an essential or obvious way. The variety of symbols linked to a rudimentary dance of signs would have no meaning and could not serve as a model for the tropological games in the myth if it didn't correspond to the subtle links established by the geometrical transformation. When linked to this geometry, however, the relationships among the symbols resemble an algebra that probes the deep meaning of the geometric process of transformation.

The symbols always suggest an exchange and a third term or a connection that reunites things. As the relationship between Horus and Osiris indicates, we are first and foremost dealing with an emanating and nourishing absolute sun, which, as it rises and sets, is born and dies in order to be reborn. It is thus a question of the conservation of energy, as in the formula $E = mc^2$. But we are also dealing with the relationship between light and darkness, with a light in the darkness, or with the unconscious that can become true consciousness. In the earth, as in an athanor, energy or light is absorbed and transformed. The earth, once it has absorbed the energy of the sun buried in its depths, is like the ball of manure that the sacred Egyptian scarab pushes before it, containing the eggs from which it will be reborn.

The symbols describe neither the apparent movement of the sun nor the real movement of the earth encircling it, but rather the interaction between these two movements. Thus in *Hamlet's Mill*, Giorgio de Santillana and Hertha von Dechend suggest that we not confuse the mythical earth with the earth as we normally consider it:

> In the most general sense, the "earth" was the ideal plane laid through the ecliptic. The "dry earth," in a more specific sense, was the ideal plane going through the celestial equator . . . the words "flat earth" do not correspond in any way to the fancies of the flat-earth fanatics . . . who in the guise of a few preacher-friars made life miserable for Columbus. . . . [Moreover] the name of "true earth" (or of "the inhabited world") did not in any way denote our physical geoid for the archaics. It applies to the band of the zodiac, two dozen degrees right and left of the ecliptic, to the tracks of the "true inhabitants" of this world, namely, the planets.[2]

If, instead of considering each symbol as representing a specific object, we consider its meaning by the place it holds in the entire system of symbols, then it suggests a reversal that unites contraries, a crossing that is a chiasmus, a passage leading to the hidden side of things and finally to the whole. But since the chiasmus, or the crossing, represents the meeting of complementary worlds or domains without which unity is impossible, it is also the symbol of a center where the different regions meet or fuse.

The possible fulfillment or awakening of a person is also considered as a crossing, or a passage, or a reversal. In terms of his potential evolution, man's internal structure is as if upside down, and his awakening corresponds to a somersault that reconfigures this structure, transforming an egocentric man into a man centered on his Self or true "I." This passage is equivalent to that leading from geocentrism to heliocentrism. If the transformation or awakening of the hero in the labyrinth is like the somersault of unconscious man, it must correspond or be caused by another torsion that transforms the maze and the path within the labyrinth.

This somersault can be represented in a perfectly figurative and literal manner. The fresco depicting the bull vaulting in the palace at Knossos suggests this same reversal accompanied by a torsion (see fig. 16.14A). The three positions of the acrobat, who ends her vault facing the tail of the bull, not only describes a somersault but also a half turn that corresponds to the way we reversed and twisted the torus knot. If this fresco suggests a bullfighting game or a ritual sacrifice, its border, representing the phases of the moon (see fig. 2.1), has been interpreted by Herbinger as constituting a calendar that must be read in a labyrinthine manner by following the diagonals of the diagram.[3] The acrobat's vault in the central part of the fresco must then also have an astronomical and cosmic meaning. It represents the sun passing through the gate of horn—in other words, descending into the Underworld or the labyrinth before being reborn (this explains the acrobat's change of color). But it can also suggest man's "flip" in relation to his own psyche, the reversal that enables him to attain true consciousness and a rebirth, a metanoia, or a "vita nuova."

From an astronomical point of view, this torsion can also correspond to a reversal of the earth's poles, which, according to Bellamy and Allan, is described on the ancient portico calendar of Tihuanaco, Peru, which also possesses labyrinthine characteristics.[4] According to Velikovsky, such a cataclysmic reversal actually happened, caused by the colliding of the earth with a second moon, which disappeared in the collision.

There is also an Egyptian fresco that presents a situation inverse to that presented in the Cretan one (fig. 16.14B). In it, the body of Geb, the earth, sometimes called the bull of the sky, seems to somersault while turning around beneath the celestial vault, Nut, represented here as a woman, but elsewhere often as a cow. The papyrus tells us that like Geb, "man conceives himself in his soul (sky)."[5] Geb's erect phallus suggests an axis or a pillar linking the earth and the sky and can in fact be replaced by Shu (space, but also the intellect) holding up the sky (fig. 16.14C). We can thus suppose that Geb's somersault can be applied to this axis, like in geometry. The similarity between the Cretan and Egyptian images illustrates yet again how the composition of figures can be reversed while retaining an equivalent meaning and suggesting relative points of view that correspond to a comprehensive, holistic concept.

It is interesting to note that this crossing finds its equivalent not only in the cosmic catastrophe in which the earth's poles would have shifted, but also in the chiasmus of the optic nerves, as well as in certain fundamental processes of morphogenesis (fig. 16.15). Thus man is truly crossed, a "crusader." He carries within him the trace of an organic crossing that, according to tradition, he must repeat at another level to gain access to the absolute center of his universe.

The Snake and the Topology of Manifolds

If there is a somersault representing the daily apparent motion of the sun, there must be for one year or for eternity many such loops. With eternity, the meaning of the loop must change; it can now represent the movement of creation linked to a final coming back to the original naught or vacuity, or again the turning from involution to evolution.

In Egypt, this cycle is represented first by a serpent surging from darkness with the outflow of primeval waters and representing the first phase of creation or the emergent form of the creator spirit or Godhead, Atum. The rearing serpent represents life as spontaneous movement; he is the "provider of

A

B

C

Fig. 16.14. The somersault and the reversal
(A) The vault over the bull (from Knossos). The somersault is accompanied by an about-face.
(B) "Like Geb (earth), man conceives himself in his soul (sky)." (C) "Intellect—the KA, or soul,
as 'SHU' (space) separating earth (GEB) from sky (NUT)."
(From Bika Reed, Rebel in the Soul)

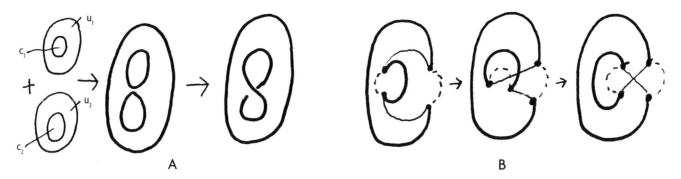

Fig. 16.15
(A) Reunion of two chromosomes with the fusion of two energies. Chromosome C_2 captures chromosome C_1 by crossing.
(B) The successive steps of gastrulation in vertebrates interpreted by the rotation of the endodermic sphere.[6]

attributes," the "serpent with many coils." (Here the coil can be that of the *ren* surrounding the sacred name, but it can also have the connotation of expanse of space and totality.) Thus, since it contains within himself Atum both as a written name and as the indwelling soul, the serpent is also a symbol of creation by the word. He says: "I am scribe of the divine book, which says what has been and effects what is yet to be." Like Atum, the serpent can represent creation, the beginning, but also the end, "the great surviving serpent when all mankind has reverted to the slime," and the menace of a return "to darkness, to nowhere, nothingness in the infinity."

The division of sky and earth by Shu (space) corresponds to the preceding division or slaughtering of the serpent (see fig. 16.17A), which occurred before the birth of Shu and is somehow its cause. As the serpent is cut, what was only potential becomes actual. After its dismemberment and dispersion, the reunion of the body of Osiris corresponds to the erection of a pillar; similarly, from the cutting of the serpent the tree of life emerges. From one thing or one seed, all things appear. The reciprocal loopings of sun and earth correspond to the reciprocal loopings of Osiris and the serpent (fig. 16.16B and C). Osiris is also a representation of Atum at a later stage when the serpent has been cut. He stands for the "coming into being," but before the snake is cut and after his death, when he is in the Dwat, like the sun during the night, he appears as the mummy of the potential but inert form. It is difficult to decide if the circling

of the inverted world of the Dwat by Osiris (fig. 16.16D) results from the circling of the potential world by the serpent or if it represents its reversal. The bringing together of both suggests a Möbius strip in which, after a cutting, a crossing, and a gluing, the opposite sides become one and seem to result from each other. We are back where we started. As in India, where we find a yoga, a dance, and a gestural language of *mudras* that must be integrated in order to free ourselves from our tethers, in Egyptian iconography we find a complex *gymnastique* that corresponds to a topology linked to a symbolic language.

There is never a single meaning in this topology; before manifesting as Ra or Osiris, Atum is also the primordial mound or horizon, or, for example, an egg whose shape is like that of the looping serpent. Atum says ambiguously: "I was also he who came of existence as a circle." In our geometry as well there cannot be a single meaning for the self axis, the meander, or the cross. In a similar way, finally, the serpent, dividing, attributing, and making whole with his coils, freeing time and form (see fig. 16.17A, B), represents the labyrinth path or perhaps rather an acentric circuitous path in a maze that potentially can become the path in the labyrinth (fig. 16.16A). In a hymn from the coffin texts, the serpent exclaims:

> I extended everywhere, in accordance with what was
> to come into existence,
>
> I knew as the One, alone majestic, the indwelling
> soul . . .

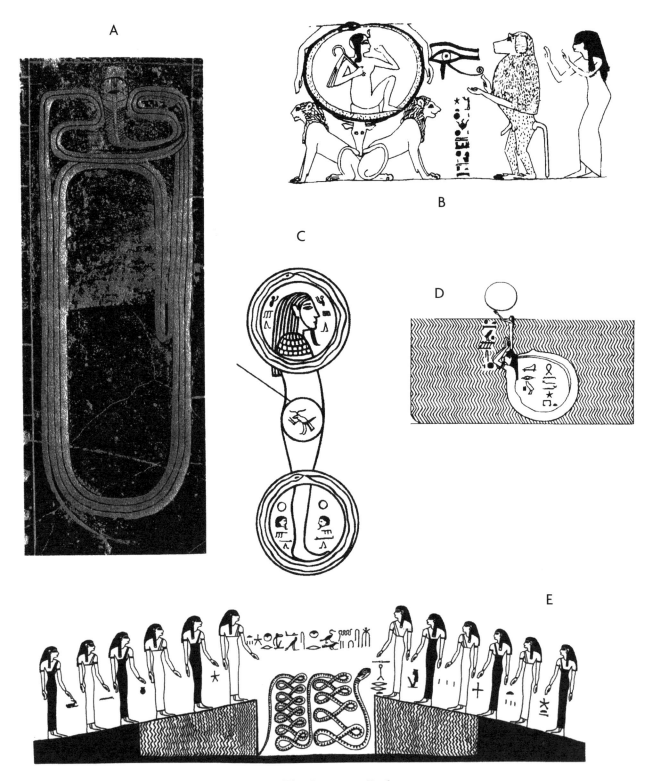

Fig. 16.16. The Circuitous Path

(A) The circuitous path or an acentric labyrinth. (B) Presence is a symbol. The present moment is eternity. Horus the child sits between the two Aker lions (yesterday and tomorrow) wearing the braid of the crown prince. He is seated on the sign of the horizon, inside the solar disk, which in turn is encircled by the serpent biting his tail, the symbol of eternity. (From R. A. Schwaller de Lubicz, Symbol and the Symbolic.*)(C) Two serpents enclose the cosmic form (the potential inert form occupying the whole universe bounded by the serpents of earth and sky). (D) Osiris enclosing the Duvat or inverted world, carrying on his head Nut, the sky. (E) The hours of the night. Between them the serpent representing the dark force of chaos and non-being, threatens the sun's journey through the Underworld. (From Lucy Lamy,* Egyptian Mysteries*)*

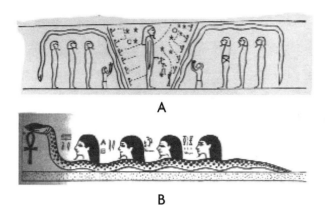

Fig. 16.17
*(A) Time and Form emerge from the Cosmic Serpent
(tombs of Ramses VI and IX). (B) Serpent
containing the Cardinal Points.*

I bent right around myself, I was encircled in my coils,

One who made a place for himself in the midst of his
coils.

So we see that in the center of the labyrinth, in addition to the serpent, is Atum, the absolute, the beginning and the end. There is thus an evident relationship between the Egyptian cosmic serpent and the Indian *kundalini* serpent, which represents the same force individualized. The inner is the same as the outer; the outer is a projection of the inner; but the outer is also the reflection in the mirror by which the inner is recognized.

Let us now find a way back to the meaning of the crossing, which is the subject of this chapter. In Egyptian iconography, the serpent is depicted not only as a line, but also as a ribbon or a tube. A serpent biting its own tail can be represented as a torus (the surface presented by the inner surface of a tire or a doughnut), or a Möbius strip as well as a circle. When the two edges of the Möbius strip are joined, the result is a torus with two opposite holes joined by a twisted piece of ribbon—a very accurate or expressive picture of a serpent biting not only his tail, but his entire rear end.

Behind the myth, we discover a reference to a topology of manifolds or membranes that precedes and complements the topology of knots. As we shall see, when in the myth the serpent is slain and cut so as to liberate its potential content (see fig. 16.18A and plate 26), this topology can produce knots. In effect, a Möbius strip crossed three times will produce, when cut along its median, a simple knot. When it is crossed seven times, it produces a knot with seven crossings (see fig. 16.18). The knot is then simply a representation of the configuration of the two sides of the strip that have united. The operation consisting of forming the torus and then cutting it appears as an action opposite that of the geometry of the labyrinth, which divides a string or ribbon and undoes a knot. We also discover an interesting cycle suggested by myths.

As if by magic, cutting makes apparent a structure that is almost impossible to visualize or comprehend when the strip is not cut. For Lacan, who constantly uses topological figures to illustrate the functioning of

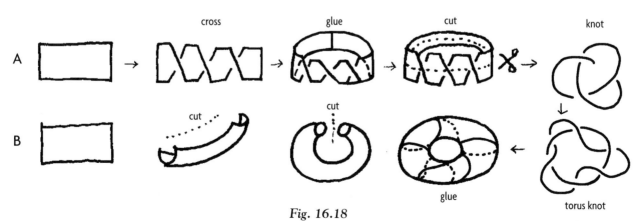

Fig. 16.18
(A) We can obtain a knot by forming a Möbius strip and cutting it. (B) From the torus knot, we can come back to the original strip.

the psyche, the cutting is an interpretation of the surface: "The interpretation is the cut."* In his statement the word *interpretation* refers to the psychoanalyst, who is able to lead the subject to the identification of a symptom. The symptom itself can be represented by another topological figure—for example, a fourth ring connecting the three rings of the Borromean knot—assuring the subject the "consistency of their relation." With Lacan, the topology of surfaces represents the place of the body, something that language is incapable of presenting. The knot is then related to another dimension, the "dit-mention," in Lacan's French jargon, a word than can be translated into English as "said-mansion" or "the place of what is said"—that is, the unconscious revealed by the way a tongue twists when we talk about ourselves.

Interestingly enough, the symbolic dimension of this topology is brought to our attention by the very effort to define its figures with words or to say what we see. The saying makes us see more. As we describe it with words, the figures of topology are replaced by a tangle of paradoxes and antinomies that can also describe other strange phenomenon. Thus when observing a Möbius strip, we have found that its twist is also a crossing and that this crossing is what brings a "unity" of two opposites sides and edges. We could say that it brings a coincidence of opposites. The twist of the band can also present itself as a hiding or a plunging of the plane of projection illustrating what would otherwise be difficult to represent, like a passage from the conscious to the unconscious. The Möbius strip is rich because it represents abstraction bound to the real.

The torus (which can be cut into two Möbius strips or into a torus knot), being a closed surface without a hole, is, says Lacan, "without a mouth to scream," without any means of the inside communicating with

the outside. In the torus, the center and the exterior are one and the same space, figuratively answering the question, "How can the exterior become central?" For Lacan, the conscious and the unconscious are supported and communicate by a toric world. Performing surgery on the torus using scissors and glue, he demonstrates the function of what Freud called "the double inscription"—the fact that the same memory is inscribed in both a conscious and an unconscious chain. He also interprets the meander of the torus knot as "desire" and the longitudinal axis (that which we have called the self axis) as "demand." Desire then circulates around Demand without ever reaching it. As he concludes: "The unconscious is the desire of the other."

The questions relevant to us here are these: Can the interpretation of Lacan and his symbolism join and fit with the symbolism of the labyrinth or does it belong to a different domain? What are the relationships among all the possible interpretations of topology belonging to physics, mathematics, biology, psychology? If the topology shows an articulation between the elements of a structure and their interpretation, what is the complete structure? At any rate, we must recognize that the labyrinth, which includes the twist of the self axis, is likened to a succession of crossings even more fundamental than the knot itself. Hence, the liberation that the labyrinth offers is not only a liberation from fetters or from a knot that we impose upon ourselves, but also from a more profound bondage linked to the presentation of the unfolding of the universe. Such bondage corresponds to the Fall, a twist or crossing involving a serpent that transforms Paradise into Earth (see fig. 16.19).

◎◎

What appears finally to be most meaningful is that originally, the cross that is associated with a torsion, a reversal, a crossing, and a conversion is not a static structure, but rather corresponds to a dynamic process. The cross with folded and tangled arms that forms the wall of the labyrinth perfectly suggests (like the swastika) a subtle synthesis of two apparently contradictory meanings, the first being an absolute

---

*Along with Jacques Lacan's own writings and seminars, many books distill or develop his topology. I recommend, for its completion and clarity, Jeanne Granon-Lafont, *La topologie ordinaire de Jacques Lacan*, 1985. It has been a source of quotations and the main inspiration for the following pages.

center and the second a reversal that is equivalent to a crossing. The exploration and the contact with different regions that this cross represents as it suggests a whirling movement, or by containing the path of the labyrinth, implies a variety of experiences and points of view that explain the variety of images symbolizing the vertical axis. The vertical axis, the *axis mundi*, has been represented by a multitude of different objects: a cosmic mountain, a tree, a fort, an altar, a stake or a plug, a cork that can contain the flood, a pillar or a pivot, and soma obtained by churning the ocean, which rises like a column. Curiously enough, this axis can also be replaced by a vessel, a ship, or a vase (a chalice), which would seem to have the opposite meaning, but which is precisely a symbol for the communication between different realms.

The English word *[vessel]* denotes both a container of liquid and a vehicle through which liquid is carried. . . . Functioning as an Axis Mundi, the central vessel offers controlled contact with the formless chaos symbolized by liquid. The movable central vehicle carries culture through the fluid, undemarcated outer space.

The establishment of spatial order achieved by the journeys of heroes (and the knowledge of the universe gained thereby) is not limited to ascent and descent along a fixed passageway. Heroic and creative movement, which established the bounds of order, was imitated by human ancestors and continues to be reenacted by pilgrims, travelers, and adventurers during their wanderings.

The image of the Axis Mundi as a vessel intensifies the intrinsic semantic connection between, on the one hand, travel to all realms of the universe and, on the other, the convergence of diverse forms of being from distinct world planes. . . . Drinking and control over travel are both symbolic strategies for containing potential chaos, which threatens to drown articulate experience, while gaining knowledge of forms of existence in other realms.[7]

Fig. 16.19
A *detail of the tapestry of the Triumph of the Cross, Coptic, 6th or 7th century* B.C. *In this image Jonah comes out of the mouth of the sea monster which is replacing the snake. One can also see the modified Pillar of Osiris and the Tree of Life.*

This equivalency is made even more complete and more complex by symbols related to particular mythical events. During the Flood, when the vessel is Noah's ark, it signifies a condensed version of the entire world being transformed. Inversely, this symbol can be replaced by the receding water that allowed the Hebrews to cross the Red Sea and gain the Promised Land.

The two rings of Minos and Nestor (fig. 16.20A and C) illustrate perfectly the two complementary aspects of the crossing accomplished on a vessel and on the world axis, represented in C by the trunk of a tree whose branches form a cross. Since, according to Evans, the drawing of the tree suggests the river of paradise described in Mesopotamian myths and thus a liquid current crossing and irrigating another world, the two images perfectly counterbalance each other. This transformation of a river into a tree echoes the myth of Osiris, who is identified with the Nile before he becomes a tree.

The ring of Minos is also mentioned in the myth of Theseus. When Theseus arrives in Crete, Minos doubts that he is really the son of Poseidon and thus under the protection of the god. To test him, Minos throws his ring into the sea. Theseus dives without

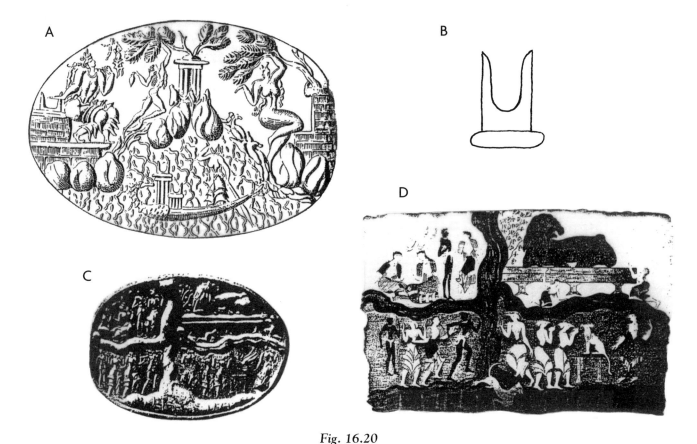

Fig. 16.20

(A) Intaglio design on the "ring of Minos" showing the passage or crossing of the goddess across the sea from one sanctuary to another. One can recognize the gate of horn representing the entrance of the labyrinth twice on the boat and once on the left altar. The message can be interpreted thus: The crossing provides the entrance to the labyrinth. (B) The gate of horn. (C) "Ring of Nestor." The cross is represented by a tree. (D) Fresco reproducing the intaglio on Nestor's ring. According to A. Evans, the ring describes the Minoan afterworld: "The effect evokes first the four rivers of paradise, or the water course with three branches of the field of Ialu on the island of the blessed."

hesitation and brings back the ring from the depths of the sea.* In this way the myth completes Theseus's horizontal journey of arrival at Crete (and another, similar, sea journey portrayed on the ring) with a vertical descent to the unfathomable depths of chaos represented by the liquid element, a descent and successful return that prefigures that in the maze or in Hades. The two journeys together thus form a cross.

This anecdote permits us to observe a curious and accidental new relationship between the pictography and the story of the myth. If, according to the symbolic code, this dive or this other journey, this time

---

*The dive to the bottom of the sea as an allegory for the recovery of ancestral memory buried as if in the silt of the deep, is taken back by Platon with *Glaucon* and by Schiler in his poem "The Diver."

into the liquid element, is equivalent to a crossing and a reversal, this incident could mean that the symbol on the ring thrown into the sea by Minos is reversed, and that it thus takes on the meaning of Nestor's ring, its counterpart. It thus could signify that Theseus will discover the center of the universe. If we push this analogy even further, the incident can also show that in geometry, the ring of the torus knot must be crossed. Of course, this sort of message cannot be consciously calculated, but it can arise by way of a perfectly coherent crossing of codes.

The symbol (ship + vessel) and the crossing of the sea would correspond only to the horizontal axis of a cross, while the axis of the world would correspond to the vertical axis. But it is rather as if the cross were continually turning, sometimes diagonally and sometimes vertically as the axes change roles. It is as if this exploration led to a communication with beings from other worlds, allowing us to discover a spiritual dimension and permitting us to travel vertically on a version of Jacob's ladder. Reciprocally, this access to a vertical dimension can be seen as granting powers in this world. Thus, during the journey, the stem becomes the mast, the pillar becomes the whirling sword that cuts the knotted sphere representing the whole or that serves to reveal the chalice of the Grail, the tree becomes the pipe of the Sioux, as well as the flute and its enchanting melody, the serpent becomes the Nile that nourishes the earth and the sea, and so on. The cross of the crucifixion does not become the symbol of Christianity before the conversion of Constantine. Constantine has a vision that this sign will lead him to victory and he makes Christianity the official religion of the Roman Empire. Later his mother, Helena, makes an expedition to Jerusalem where she is supposed to discover the true cross. At the beginning of Christianity one can find the cross mixed with the I and X of the Greek initials of Jesus Christ, as in the Basilica St. Vitale (5th century) (see fig. 16.21). This image can also represent the sun and its rays. Sometimes the cross presents itself, as in Buddhism, like a wheel with a hollow hub as can be seen in the window of the oldest church of Assisi. This wheel will become divided into a rosace and a cross, to be reunited much later in a different manner by the Rosicrucians. "The interchangeability . . . [and] the enrichment of significant imagery at the center contributes directly to the edification of a symbolic universe. The elaboration of symbolic forms extends the sacrality, power, and meaning of reality that is found at the center . . . it enables the construction of the world-system."[8]

It becomes clear that the mythic center that is also represented by the center of the cross of the labyrinth cannot be conceived of as a precise place situated in Euclidean space. For the truth is that we do

Fig. 16.21. A detail of the mosaics of the choir. Ravenna, Basilica St. Vitale (5th century).
At the center of the cross is the sign Alpha.

not live so much in the outside as in an internal world that determines our perception of the first. The world is like a dream. The center is a symbolic image of what appears as real, essential, and knowable in a multidimensional space.

> The ambivalence . . . of the *axis mundi* conjoins planes of being, but, at the same time, its images are visible signs measuring the gulf that separates the different realms. . . . [T]he journey to the center, the achievement of other states of existence, is a dangerous task, requiring a complete transformation of one's spiritual being. . . . On every plane of space, the meaning of the symbolism of the center of the world emphasizes that the heart of existence consists in an experience and a quality of being different from the ordinary world around it. Paradoxically, it is from this central conjunction of different qualities of being that the unity of the universe derives.[9]

The ambivalence doesn't end here, however, for to define a center we must also define the limits of the world that surrounds it. In the myths there is also in a kind of identity between the periphery and the center corresponding to that between outside and inside. The marginal expresses, in an alternative way, the values that we find at the center, and all the mediating elements are also associated with the center. Thus we shall gradually discover an intrinsic relationship among the path of the labyrinth, its exit, and its center.

> The relation between the circumference of the circle and its center is intrinsic: the circular shape is produced as a ripple by an object plunged into the water. Only time marks the difference between the center and its outward-bound expression. They are distinguishable moments in a dialectic. The image of the periphery becomes reflexive in language . . . the images of the limits of space define the power and intent of language.

> In the Warao universe, journeys between cosmic zones and the cardinal and intercardinal points are effected by means of bridges and slippery paths that lead out from the center of the earth or from the central zenith-point of heaven.[10]

This interchangeability of images is perfectly expressed in the sign of the Tao. The axis continues to the periphery. The yang (suggesting the vertical, the penetrating, and the full) has its source in the yin (the horizontal, the containing, and the empty), and vice versa. We are therefore dealing with a reversal and a chiasmus. But this sign also illustrates how all kinds of symbols can be linked to a concept of the whole and of space-time or being-time that takes this reversal as its foundation. It is well known that as one traces the sign of the Tao, trigrams can be found representing the elements but also the phases of the moon. Combined into hexagrams, the results are symbolic images and judgments about living. The symbols met on the path of life can thus be found projected onto the axis and the sphere of the whole. They are produced by a perpetual exchange between two adjoining and intersecting universes. To grasp how

Figure 16.22. The correspondences between the tai chi postures or gates and the trigrams
We can see the progression of the full bars with the yang and of the broken bars with the yin. The yin corresponds to the back of the hand and the yang to the palm of the hand.
Adapted from The Tao of Tai-chi Chuan *by Jou Tsung Hwa.*

the hexagrams appear, one must imagine lines that join the trigram and cross the circle (see fig. 16.22). But we have already seen (fig. 16.13) that the sign of the Tao also represents both a sphere that reverses itself and a knot that, in its turn, can be doubled and transformed into a torus knot that is crossed. It is also in this way that the trigrams can meet and the hexagrams can arise. We thus find a link among a system of calculation, an ancient writing system, and the geometry of the labyrinth.

We know that the hexagrams were used for a divinatory art. But the sign of the Tao is also the foundation upon which the discipline and the art of combat that was tai chi was based. (I am using the past tense because many masters such as master Jou consider the essential core of this ancient art to be almost entirely lost.) In the progression of movements, the orientation of the hands as if holding or juggling with an imaginary sphere also corresponds to the trigrams or to their positions along the axis. The combined positions of the two hands thus form hexagrams, but the hexagrams can also be formed by the succession of moves or gates, which also correspond to trigrams (see fig. 16.22). The transitions, the "changes," are as important as the fixed postures. But the rotation of the hands is the manifestation of a more fundamental movement; basically the tai chi practitioner must unite the movement of his hands and his body to his breathing and to a spiraling current of energy (*chi*). The energy accumulates or comes forth from a center (*tantien*) situated below the navel and is itself connected or rooted in the ground by the movement of the legs. In some way, the exercise aims at connecting all the movements of the practitioner and his opponent to an indestructible but elusive axis that allows one to use the force of one's opponent by reversing that force.

Just as there is in the geometry of the labyrinth a doubling of the knot and a perfect connection between the twin parts, the movements of tai chi opponents become intimately connected as if they were the double aspects of a whole. The exercise thus consists in a sort of alchemy. The ultimate goal is to "melt the essence and transform it into breath, melt the breath and transform it into spiritual energy, melt the spiritual energy and make it return to emptiness." The tai chi practitioner mimes the movement of the universe with his whole body while at the same time he unites his center to that of the universe and his energy to the cosmic energy. He guesses and "hears" how to unite his whole body with the Tao. Once achieved, this unity must have formed an awe-inspiring warrior, but also a wise man and healer, as the energy that the practitioner accumulates and develops can also be used to purify and vivify. Though dealt with too summarily here, this example is intended to show how ancient geometry not only was used to organize a world system, but also corresponded to diverse practices intended to produce a direct experience of union.

It finally appears that the entire system of symbols and myths rests on a crossing that constitutes a chiasmus and indicates a center. We can now examine how the geometric crossing can be used to organize this system in a coherent way—in other words, how geometry can organize and produce meaning.

The geometry we are rediscovering can create meaning first because it deals with objects, which become symbols and thus carry meaning. But for geometry or topology to create a real meaning and not just an imaginary one, it must correspond to a specific way of seeing, following, and understanding—that is, to a pathway leading to an experience. This is how we shall attempt to consider it.

Fig. 16.23. Cretan seals depicting bull vaulting

17

The Geometric Crossing

Against the Word the unstilled
world still whirled
About the center of the silent Word.
—T. S. ELIOT

We have examined how the concepts of crossing and reversal play out in myths and symbols. We shall now attempt to show geometrically how the crossing of the self axis is used to produce a complete of view of the knot and of its structure. Until now, we have studied only a particular projection of the knot—namely, its image projected on a flat plane. In a certain sense, we have acted like the troglodytes in Plato's myth who are only acquainted with the shadow of the world projected on the wall of their cave. We have ignored the existence of the three-dimensional knot, which can be manipulated and turned, which can transform itself by taking all sorts of configurations, and which presents itself differently depending on whether we turn around it or cross it. The crossing of the self axis will give us a complete vision of the knot, a synthesis of all its aspects and facets.

Let us clarify how we reached this conclusion. When the self axis is crossed, the meander presents two identifiable aspects, as shown in figure 16.10D. The top half remains unchanged, but the bottom half presents exactly the same form as the meander obtained by mapping the knot from the other side as in figure 16.9E, F. This means that at the point where

the self axis is crossed, we are looking at the knot from the other side, or, in what amounts to the same thing, as we mapped the knot it flipped over, presenting us with its other side. This equivalence is similar to the one presented by the myth of Pacahusta lasso and many Egyptian myths between an apparent movement of the sun and a real movement of the earth.

The labyrinth presents the structure of the knot in a complete way by presenting a synthesis of points of view, but because of this, it includes in its representation the movement or the trajectory by which the observer obtains different points of view. It simultaneously represents both the structure of the knot and a circular movement around the knot (or else a new rotating movement or spin of the knot).

But we have already seen that the self axis can also represent a rotation of the knot as in following an orbit. Thus, three inseparable movements are included in the representation. In a way that is difficult to conceptualize, the structure is represented by the synthesis of a trajectory through and around a knot and a complex combination of movements of the knot itself. Two important principles are demonstrated once again. First, there is no longer any distinction or separation between the structure of things and the movement that animates them and links them; and second, the way one observes alters the nature of what is observed and is included in what is perceived as reality. "This truth corresponds to the most important concept of quantum mechanics, i.e., that the status of an object is determined by the act of perception of the observer and the nature of the observer determines the condition of the object."[1] As in the myths, reality is found in complementary and contradictory aspects perceived simultaneously. The mythic center of the world can be attained only in this reality. The center is not discovered preexisting somewhere as such; it is reconstructed within an event.

When the three-dimensional knot pivots before the observer (or when the observer turns around the

Fig. 17.1. Manuscript page belonging to Caesar's Universal History of the Creation (Histoire Roger)
The text mentions that the picture refers to the enclosure that houses the monster. The spherical form of this labyrinth suggests a knot or a ball of yarn. It can also evoke the travel around a three-dimensional knot described by the geometry.

knot), multiple new intersections appear while others disappear. The relative position of the crosses, like that of the regions determined by the segments of the cord, ceaselessly change, and this in an indeterminate order (because the observer charting the path of the cord can observe only a segment of the cord at a time). If this upheaval of relations between the crosses corresponds, as we have suggested, to the changes and permutations of symbols and of their relationships in myths and rites, we can understand that here as well, they cannot be directly determined. The indeterminacy that doesn't allow one to calculate the position and the energy of a particle at the same time is a basic principle of physics. Thus, one finds that the fundamental paradoxes of quantum physics are already produced by the topology upon which it rests. This is why myths present the same paradoxes. The paradoxes seemingly produced by nature belong first to the mind, and the myths seem to explore this mental process.

In the following sections of this chapter we shall illustrate several ways to turn around and cross the knot or to turn it while recording its movement. They will permit us to explain how, in the end, only two supplementary crossings between the self axis and the meander will be recorded or added by the crossing of the self axis and how the other apparent crossings observed as the knot is turning will cancel each other out. We shall prove in this way that the crossing of the self axis is effectively equivalent to different rotations of the knot or to different journeys of the observer passing to the other side of the knot.

All the different ways of turning the knot, whether turning it around or crossing it while following the string, correspond to different trajectories through the knot and different ways of creating or reaching a center. These paths can all be suggested by the myths as well. They represent the diverse ways the psyche of a pilgrim or a hero can be transformed by traveling through the labyrinth. To the extent that they produce the same configuration of the labyrinth's meander and lead to the same center, all these trajectories are ultimately equivalent. Thus one cannot

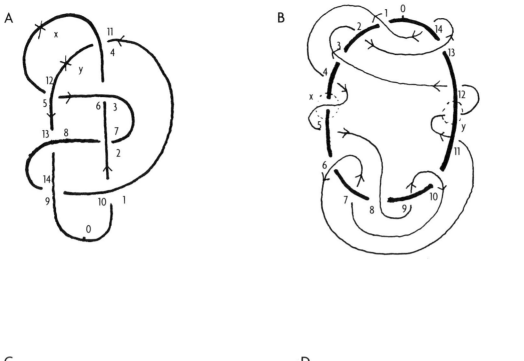

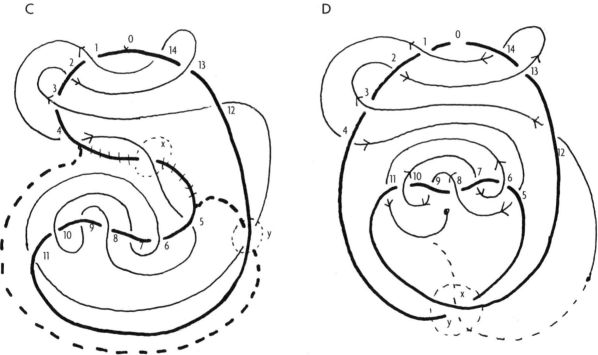

Fig. 17.2. The new intersection of the self axis corresponds to a motion of the observer around the knot or around the rope

(A) To observe and map the knot from both sides, the observer must cross to the other side at some point during his or her recording of the intersections and then cross a second time to find his or her original position. The crossing or rotation of the observer around the string (described in fig. 17.3) occurs at points x and y and in such a way as to record the whole string from both sides. (This is possible because he or she passes twice at each crossing.) Each time the observer changes sides, a new crossing is recorded. (B) The mapping obtained in this way before twisting the self axis. (C) and (D) When we twist and flip the self axis, we obtain again the same pattern of the labyrinth path, but this time the original meaning of the crossing between the meander and the self axis at x and y (which coincide) is more explicit.

determine exactly to which particular trajectory the labyrinth's pattern corresponds. The symbol of the labyrinth, rather than corresponding to a single perspective or to a single path through the knot, corresponds to an indeterminate whole, a sum of perspectives and pathways, and to many voices in the myths. The intersection of the self axis constitutes an invariant, a common denominator for all these elements. This allows us to understand how there can be several interpretations of a myth, or how a myth is polysemic.

The geometrical demonstrations presented in this chapter demand some effort to be followed, but they do not require any particular mathematical knowledge, and they offer the advantage of presenting an image of the structure of the myth that is difficult or even impossible to express verbally.

First Interpretation: Turning around the Knot or Turning around the Cord

As we have already noted, for an observer to see the other side of a knot, the knot must turn before him, but this observer can also turn around the unmoving knot, the two movements being equivalent. This turning and its result are illustrated in figure 17.2. To simplify things, let us imagine a flat knot and that the observer, instead of facing the knot, finds himself standing at a particular place on the thread staring at another segment of the thread whose trajectory he just crossed (fig. 17.3). The observer then decides to place himself on the other side of the knot by turning 180° on the cord, without letting his eyes wander from

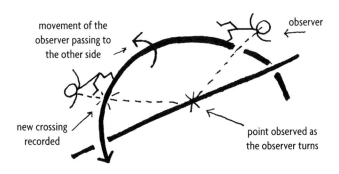

Fig. 17.3 The observer changing sides

the particular spot he has been staring at. As he turns, the trajectory of his vision staring at the same spot crosses the cord on which he is walking. He sees two segments of cord crossing each other. He records a new intersection between the cord he observes and the one he moves on. This will be the first supplementary intersection recorded beside those recorded by the mapping. The second supplementary intersection will be recorded in the same way when the observer returns to his first position, facing the front of the knot.

These two extra intersections are the same as those obtained between the self axis and the meander when twisting the self axis. The path of the labyrinth thus represents not only the structure of the knot but also, at the same time, a journey around the knot, or through the knot, or again a change of position of the observer on the knot.

Second Interpretation: A Gyroscopic Movement of the Knot

Let us come back to the case when the knot turns in front of the observer. It remains to be seen how all the new intersections that appear when the knot turns around in front of the observer cancel each other out. To achieve this end, we can imagine in the place of a rotation that happens in one movement a gradual change in the configuration of the knot. The knot's rotating movement becomes decomposed in a series of distinct movements for each loop or each part of the knot.

As the position of the loops or the segments of string are shifted, the number of intersections grows larger and then diminishes before becoming the same as at the beginning. The resulting figure presents the knot backward. If we imagine that the observer, placed at a particular place on the knot, suspends his observation during the dance of the knot to once again stare at the same spot once the knot's rotation is complete, we notice that its place, or the place that he observed marked in figure 17.4A by the symbol α, has been displaced backward in relation to the crosses

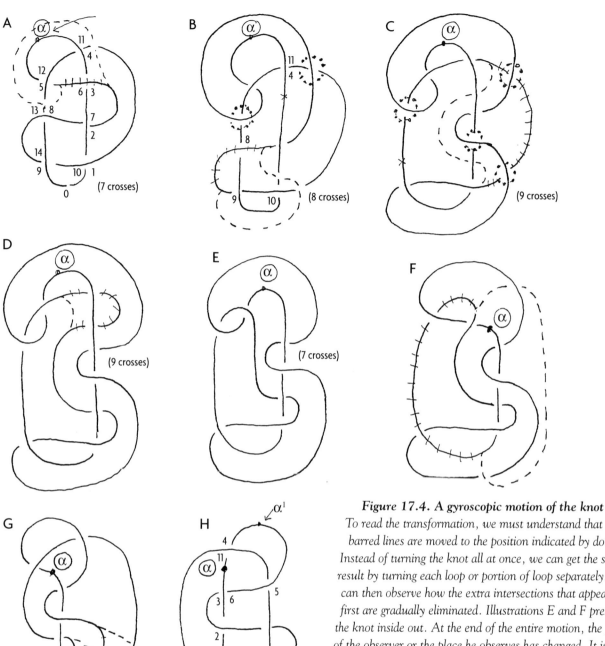

Figure 17.4. A gyroscopic motion of the knot

To read the transformation, we must understand that the
barred lines are moved to the position indicated by dots.
Instead of turning the knot all at once, we can get the same
result by turning each loop or portion of loop separately. We
can then observe how the extra intersections that appear at
first are gradually eliminated. Illustrations E and F present
the knot inside out. At the end of the entire motion, the place
of the observer or the place he observes has changed. It is now
in α¹ instead of in α, as it was at the beginning. The result is
that for the observer to retrieve his position, a new intersection must be recorded. When the knot returns to its original
position, an extra intersection will be recorded.

(A) First change. Instead of one crossing at (6, 3) we now
have two crossings and a total of eight crosses.

(B) Second change and one more crossing.

(C) Third change. The number of crossings remains the
same. (D) Fourth change. We come back to seven crosses.

(E) This position corresponds to the knot turned inside out.

(F) With this change there are still seven crossings. Gradually
with G and H we return to the first knot pattern, but seen
from the other side. However, the observer is now in alpha
and, in order to return to his original position in alpha¹, a
new crossing must be mapped. Then, to return to situation
A, the same process leads to another new crossing.

(see fig. 17.4H). Thus, each time that the knot turns around showing its opposite face, we shall record an extra intersection so that the observer returns to his original place once more. A total of two intersections are needed so that the knot comes back to its initial position and we once again obtain the same diagram of the labyrinth.

During this transformation, we also obtain an image of the rotated knot as if turned inside out (fig. 17.4E). The inside of the knot becomes the exterior and the undefined space around the knot becomes the protected place at the center. We can thus conclude that the labyrinth can also represent a sort of gyroscopic dance of the knot as it turns itself inside out. Such a transformation, which again coincides with a circumambulation in which everything is reversed, can be expressed in a different way in the myth by using figurative language or tropes. The reversal of metaphors corresponds to the reversal of the loops that can cancel each other out. The meaning of a rotation can also be transposed and applied yet again to the state of the pilgrim in the labyrinth. At some point in his progress, the latter discovers that the exterior as he perceives it is nothing but a projection of his interior world.

The various rotating and twisting movements or spins of the knot-maze can be suggested by Greco-Roman frescoes that present a sort of maze produced by a knot whose intersections are rotated or twisted so as to represent swastikas (see fig. 17.5). In these images, the vertical rotation of the loops is replaced by a horizontal rotation of crosses.

Since this dance of the knot finally leads to a new position of the knot, or to another state of the knot that reveals its hidden face, we can deduce that the path of the meander can also correspond to a leap from one knot to another, similar yet reversed knot (fig. 17.6). This leap suggests again another interpretation of what the labyrinth can include in its representation. The undulating movement of the loops and of the knot as it turns inside out is equivalent to a sort of quantum leap accomplished by the knot or

between two similar knots. Once again, we are curiously confronted with a paradox similar to that of quantum physics, where light has a double nature and presents itself both as a wave and as a particle propagating itself by quantum leaps.

Third Interpretation: The Path of the Labyrinth Represents the Knot as It Tightens

Let us observe the tight knot. Although structurally it remains the same as when it was loose, symbolically, and from the point of view of our geometry, its nature has changed. When drawn tight, it is as if frozen, presenting itself as an opaque ball that is difficult to map. Instead of having spaces between the loops to define the regions, the cord is now in constant contact with itself. It is as if all its crossings had fused. In this form the knot could symbolize unity, or, more accurately and from the opposite point of view, the ego.

If the loose knot is gradually tightened, we can observe, as if the knot were alive and made taut by a series of convulsions, a new movement of the knot and the appearance of two new intersections (see fig. 17.7).

We can also include this movement of the knot as it tightens in the successive movement of the loops that reverse the knot—in other words, in a movement similar to that illustrated in figure 17.4 and presented in figure 17.9. As it tightens and loosens, the labyrinth can thus represent the knot as breathing, symbolizing a contracting and dilating universe. This interpretation explains the difficulty and the danger that would arise were one to travel through a maze that continually expanded and contracted, requiring an itinerary in accordance with its particular rhythm to avoid getting crushed by its transformations. The lasso of Varuna, or the whale swallowing Jonah only to regurgitate him on a foreign shore, could suggest such a labyrinth.

The labyrinth therefore captures not only the structure of the knot but also the movement by which it is drawn taut and loosened, the movement by which it accomplishes a function. The function of linking and uniting thus suggested could also be called a

A

D

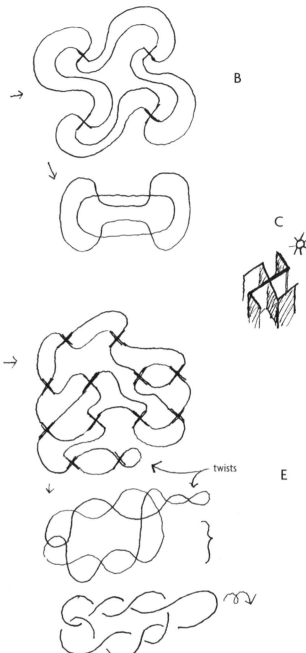

B

C

E

twists

Figure 17.5. Mosaic of labyrinths in gestation

(A) This mosaic suggests a maze, but it presents the projection of a
torus knot (B)which, when transformed, can become a labyrinth
path. At the center is the head of the Medusa. Either the chicane is
her emanation or her picture is caught, as in a mirror that returns
her own paralyzing spell against her. As in (C), the dark triangles
can represent the shadows projected by the walls. Their placement
suggests that the knot turns or even twists itself as it is observed. It
can also suggest that the light turns around the knot. The twists at
the end of the knot can indicate that the knot itself is twisted or
crossed, much like the cord of a phone will get tangled if we twist it.
The drawing E represents a simplified version of the design D.
We also find two twists on the Tibetan pal-be-ü.

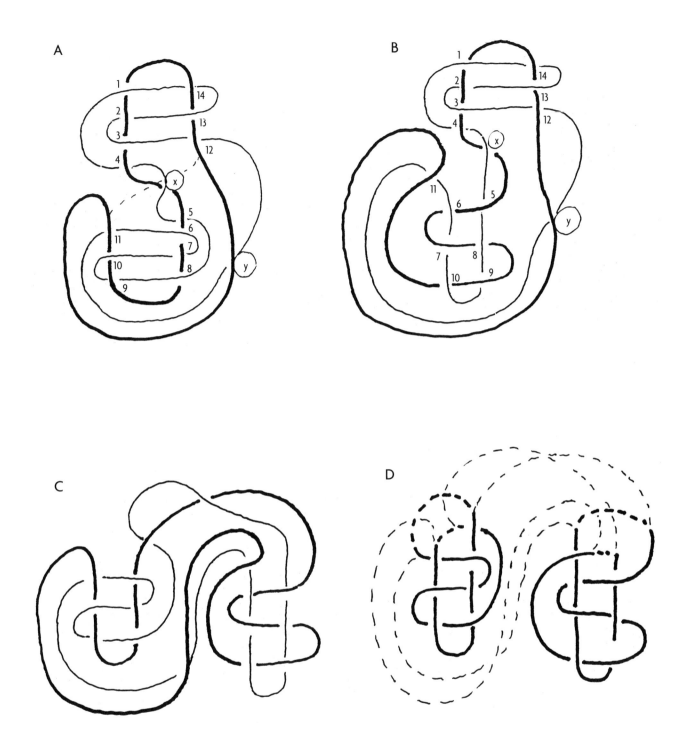

Fig. 17.6. The torus knot can represent a leap between two reversed knots.

The torus knot A is exactly the same as the one we use for the labyrinth and figure 17.4C. We can slightly modify the shape of A into B, C, and D in order to recognize the two sides of a single knot. Figure D is the same as figure C, but shows more explicitly how two knots marked by fat lines are broken and then linked by the self axis and the meander. The path of the labyrinth can then be seen as representing a leap between two reversed knots or a leap of the knot changing position.

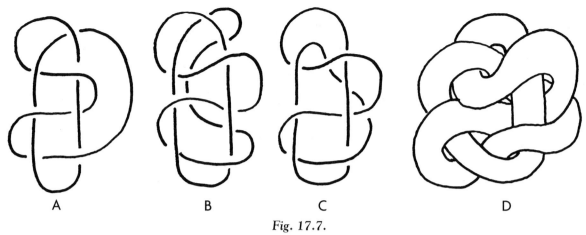

Fig. 17.7.

(A) The tightening knot. (B) Two new intersections appear. (C) The pattern of the tight knot. (D) The tight knot as it appears.

centripetal force, or even Eros. Structure and form are linked to a gestalt and a function in a precise manner. In the labyrinth, the geometric symbol captures the inherent principle of the knot and finds a "signature" in its structure. This signature distinguishes itself from the form by expressing a latent movement, a behavior, or even a destiny incorporated within form. In the form of a boomerang, for example, we can discern a signature that anticipates the arc of its trajectory and a particular way of being thrown.

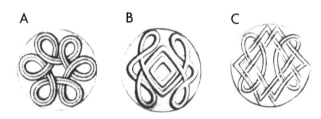

Fig. 17.8. Cretan seals depicting false knots and interlaced true knots.
Illustration C shows the geometry of two reversed knots linked by a path.

Fourth Interpretation: A Leap within the Knot

Several other interpretations of the knot could be advanced that would all lead to the same diagram of the meander and enrich our interpretation of the path through the maze. But for the sake of brevity, we shall consider only one more particularly meaningful pathway.

In the classical drawing of the labyrinth the self axis is absent, and the path of the meander is delineated only by the walls of the labyrinth. The question then arises as to whether the same meander pattern could be obtained without intersecting the self axis—in other words, by passing directly on the self axis from intersection four to eleven and from intersection five to twelve, as is shown in figure 17.10.

To obtain this pattern, we can imagine that each cross that appears on the knot's projection represents a point of contact between two segments of the cord. This actually happens when the knot is completely flattened or taut, and we have seen in the last section that this factor cannot be neglected. An observer following the thread could then jump from one part of the knot to another or from one cord to another at the points where they cross. If we follow the path marked by arrows in figure 17.10C, we obtain precisely the pattern we are seeking. We can thus conclude that the final drawing of the labyrinth can also represent a change of trajectory obtained by jumping from one segment of the knot to another.

Each intersection represented on the projection of the knot thus becomes a door or a potential drawbridge that opens or closes depending upon the movement of the knot. This gives rise to an abstract system of crosses interlinked in a complex manner—in other words, a sort of grid or matrix for diverse combinations of itineraries, a network of temporarily usable pathways.

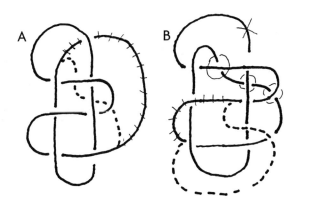

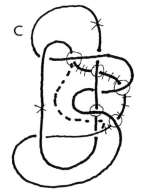

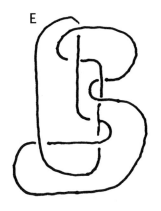

Fig. 17.9. The motion of the knot as it is reversed includes that of the knot as it is made taut.

The circles in illustrations B, C, and D represent new intersections; the crosses mark the places of the former intersections. The dotted line in illustration A shows the configuration of the taut knot. Illustration E is the same as E in figure 17.4. The drawing of the labyrinth can thus include the motion of the knot as it is successively tightened and relaxed.

We can now see the nature of the link suggested in the myths and the rites between an inextricable maze and a dance that includes the knotting and unknotting of complex figures in a new light. As the knot configuration changes and evolves in space, different segments of the cord are connected or separated, creating doors or bridges that suddenly disappear. As a result, shortcuts, detours, and vicious circles, as well as new knots, are formed. The path followed on the knot changes constantly, constituting an acentric maze wherein to find one's way, one needs a calendar of events, like the one explaining the Egyptian labyrinth of Lake Moeris. We are confronted with another concept of space-time, or rather of path-time (this without trying to make a pun).

The possibility of an ever renewable choice between diverse trajectories can thus create a new maze. In the same way, in life, infinite choice can lead to a

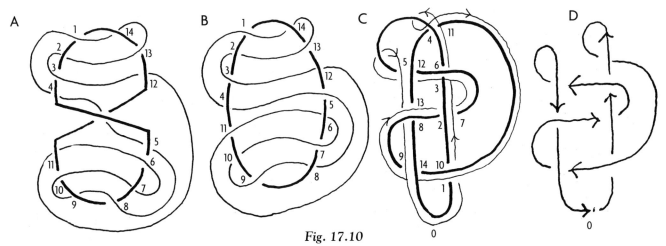

Fig. 17.10

(A) The crossed torus. (B) Torus obtained with a leap from one segment of the cord to another.
(C) A new path on the knot. (D) The new path of the self axis.

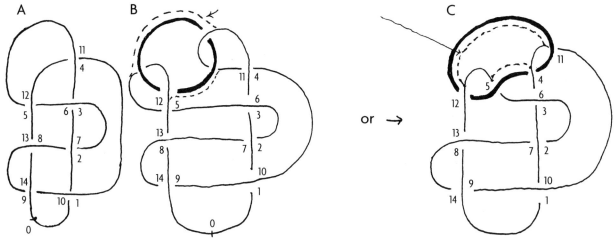

Fig. 17.11

(A) The knot. (B) A new structure built with a ring showing different possible paths along the knot. (C) In this picture the crossings are now between the strings of the old knot and the new ring. Thus we eliminate two loops that made the knot in B a false knot. The dotted lines in illustrations B and C demonstrate an outline of the old knot and the old path.

blind existentialism or a profound enslavement, if it is not correctly understood, or if it completely replaces the idea of an inner balance that must be established.

In mathematics and physics as well, it is not beyond the range of possibility that the continuous discovery of new connections and new arrangements could end up creating or complicating a maze and, paradoxically, preventing the discovery of a unified theory.

Fig. 17.12. Cretan seals depicting torus knots and knots
We shall discover similar figures later in which the self axis and meander are joined.

Fifth Interpretation: The Structure of the Knot Replaced by a System of Rings

Having established the existence of a network of pathways obtained by jumping from one part of the knot to another, or from one part of the string to another, we must now determine whether the knot can be replaced by this network of pathways. A complementary structure to that of the knot can in fact be built by

using a ring to hold the new path in such a way that the outline of the first path is preserved (see fig. 17.11).

In order to make the transformation more systematic, we can also simply replace each cross in the knot with a ring (see fig. 17.11). This ring will represent all the possible pathways offered for each cross. These rings can also be broken and joined two by two so as to reproduce the same number of crosses as appear on the knot. The result shown in fig. 17.11C is the same as in figure 17.13B. Figure 17.14C and D show some of the pattern obtained when all the crosses are replaced by rings.

In terms of the paths linking a system of crosses, the structure of the network of rings is equivalent to that of the knots. Once the rules of transformation from crosses to rings are established, we can slide the rings one on top of the other, and then seek again in this modified system of rings the original knot whose configuration has changed. The equivalence between the ring and the cross is reminiscent of the equivalence between the symbol of the vase and that of a crossing or a journey on a boat. The Egyptian diagonal cross inserted inside a ring (see fig. 17.14 B) can also suggest the complementarity between cross and ring. In fact, the image includes all the different paths that the intersection of two cords in the knot can offer.

Fig. 17.13
(A) The knot. (B) The crossings are replaced by rings. (C) The rings are joined two by two.

By judiciously choosing the rings that replace the crosses, we can recreate the pathway of the self axis. Finally, by joining all the rings in the correct manner, we can also recreate the pathway of the meander that corresponds to the path of the labyrinth (see fig. 17.15). There thus exists at least one more method to construct the pattern of the path in the labyrinth.

The path of the labyrinth can thereby represent the structure of a network of rings (a concatenation or maze like those presented by the Hindu *kolams*), as well as the structure of the knot. It reveals a common denominator for apparently different structures. The path of the labyrinth corresponds just as easily to an undulating movement of the string in the knot as to a series of jumps joining and uniting virtual and real rings.

The path can represent the fabric of the universe as well as "such stuff as dreams are made of." We meet again the same perplexing paradox presented in physics by the nature of light.

Apparently we feel a similar perplexity when faced with myth. Were we to study the Egyptian pantheon, for example, and as we discovered new connections, we would be confronted with a disturbing proliferation of antinomies and apparent contradictions. For the student lost in this maze, the myth seems to follow the formula: "Once upon a time there were two times at once." Yet this complexity becomes clear if understood as being produced by the juxtaposition of several points of view so as to reveal something invariable.

In myths, a ring is often a talisman obtained as a reward for a good action, and, like the golden bough, it can help to accomplish a difficult task. The transmission of a magic ring can be seen as equivalent to a passage or a transformation that enables a cycle to be closed. This transmission that we find, for example, in the Niebelungen is a major theme in Celtic and Germanic mythology. Let it be remembered that the word *symbol* derives from *symbolon*, which signifies the action of uniting, but also and more specifically a broken ring. In our geometry, it is also a broken ring, broken in order to be linked anew, that, after uniting with other rings, can finally lead to the center of the labyrinth.

As in physics, we have come face-to-face with a principle of indeterminacy: It is impossible to decide exactly what the path of the labyrinth represents. A well-defined path of Logos exists, but its own relation to the parts of the whole remains indeterminate. This path represents the process by which we seize and reach knowledge of things as well as the one by which they are linked and by which they mutually transform each other. As in quantum physics, it is the observation that colors and determines the aspect of the parts, their relations, and their evolution.

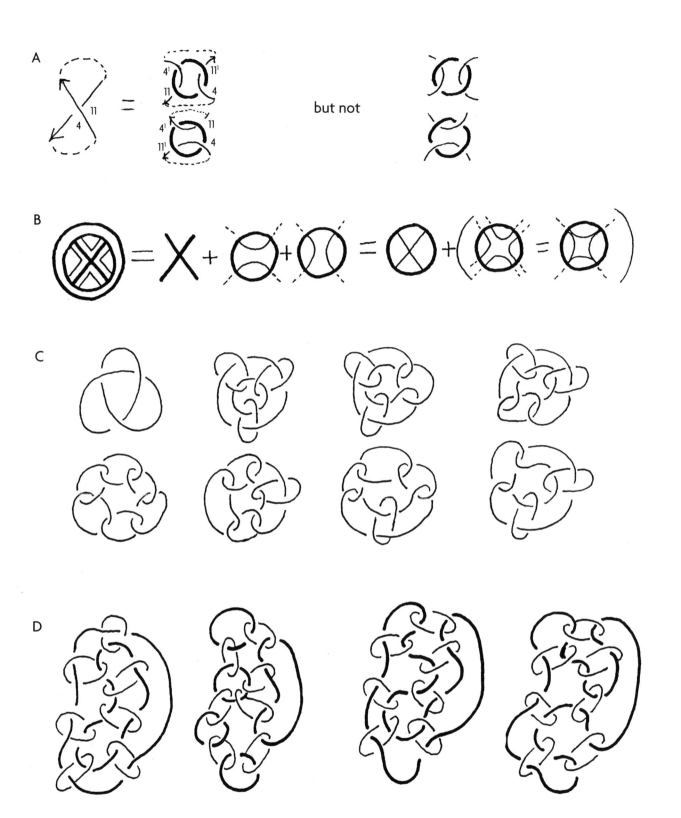

Figure 17.14. Some ring networks

(A) A rule is necessary in order to be able to come back from the system of rings to a knot. Each time we change a cross into a ring, we have a choice between two possible transformations. But in each case we will keep the superposition of the crossings. The other solutions are eliminated as the superposition of the crossings changes. (B) The Egyptian cross contains all the different elements of the change between a cross and a ring. The doubling of the central cross could evoke an equivalence between different paths and the totality of paths presented by a cross. (C) The different ways of replacing a simple knot by a network of rings according to the method detailed in A. (D) The knot with seven crossings replaced by a network of rings.

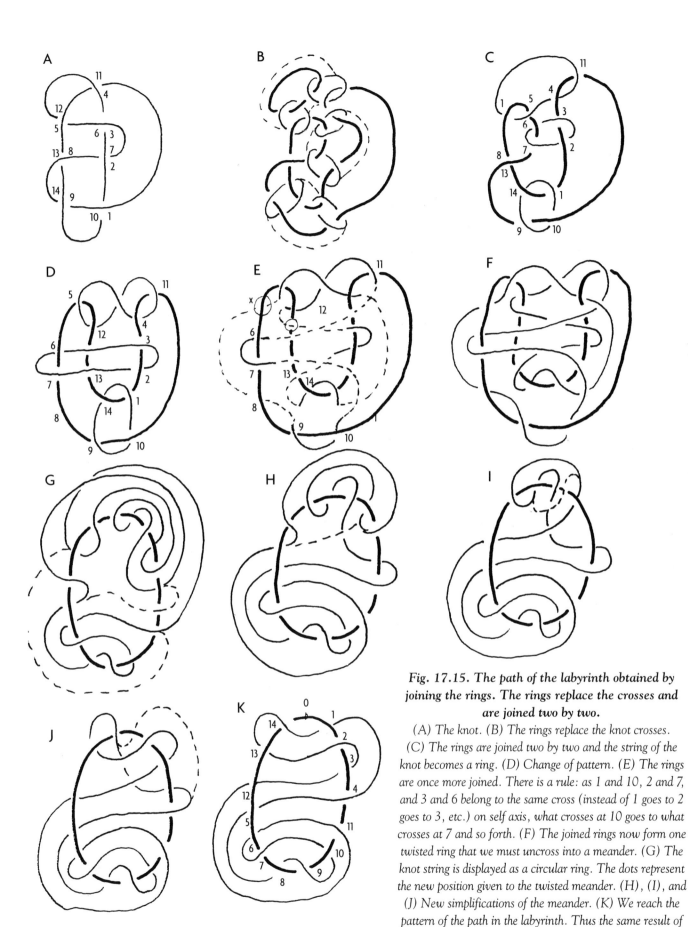

Fig. 17.15. The path of the labyrinth obtained by joining the rings. The rings replace the crosses and are joined two by two.

(A) The knot. (B) The rings replace the knot crosses. (C) The rings are joined two by two and the string of the knot becomes a ring. (D) Change of pattern. (E) The rings are once more joined. There is a rule: as 1 and 10, 2 and 7, and 3 and 6 belong to the same cross (instead of 1 goes to 2 goes to 3, etc.) on self axis, what crosses at 10 goes to what crosses at 7 and so forth. (F) The joined rings now form one twisted ring that we must uncross into a meander. (G) The knot string is displayed as a circular ring. The dots represent the new position given to the twisted meander. (H), (I), and (J) New simplifications of the meander. (K) We reach the pattern of the path in the labyrinth. Thus the same result of a doubling of the cord and of a mapping of the knot can be obtained with the system of rings.

The path of the labyrinth represents a flux of consciousness that brings into being a latent project of the world by contemplating it. It does not represent a structure of matter or space or spirit, but that of spirit-space-time-matter. It allows meaning to be created, but this meaning is incomprehensible for an incomplete man. This path corresponds precisely to the path of wisdom as defined by Heraclitus:

> Wisdom is whole . . . the knowledge of how things are plotted in their course by all other things." (fragment 41)

> Wisdom alone is whole and is both willing and unwilling to be named Zeus. (fragment 32)

What prevents us from being able to understand the ultimate meaning of myths is the same as what prevents us from being able to define concretely the geometric symbol. When we are confronted with new figures of language or the reversals of metaphor, we understand only how a new image affects us; we cannot understand simultaneously the complexity and the meaning of the transformation, under way. Each instance of figurative language, each metaphorical transformation, also corresponds to a geometry and a symbolic algebra, which themselves correspond to events in cosmic, biological, and psychological games. But just as we cannot simultaneously understand what we perceive and the phenomenon of perception, or how perception corresponds to a scale of stimuli and to an inner process, in the same way we cannot understand how the path of language in myth so totally affects us; the connection happens without us being aware of it. We can perceive only one dimension of myth at a time, but through myth we penetrate unconsciously and profoundly into the nature of the whole and into our own nature. Myth is exemplary in that it maintains a link and a balance between all possible meanings. It contains the meaning of the whole by concealing it.

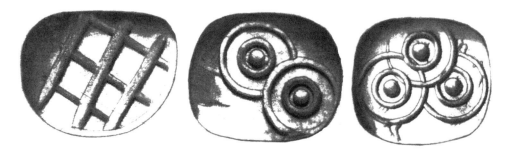

Fig. 17.16. Engravings on a three-sided Cretan seal
Is there a relationship between crossings and interlocked rings?

18
Time

The beginning signifies an instant in time.
—THE BOOK OF MOTZU

Up until now we have accentuated the spatial aspect of geometry, but the self axis and the meander also represent time, since, as we have already noted, their appearance corresponds to different motions of the knot in the string and the observer. Moreover, self axis and meander can also represent the gesture or movement that produces the knot. For the simple reason that tying the knot takes time, both can also represent the time it takes for one end of the cord to form the knot. Time and space were also equivalent for the ancients. There was thus a concept that corresponded to our space-time. We will attempt to show how the geometry of the labyrinth elucidates this ancient concept to such an extent that the concept, or at least its formulation, seems to rest on the model of the labyrinth or even constitute its exegesis.

Hindu philosophy distinguishes the past and future from the present moment. The latter, placed between past and future, is defined as being situated outside of time, or as representing time standing still. Paradoxically, it contains eternity, where the past and future are both united. The present moment thus represents absolute Time, containing the relative past and future time within it. So there are two different kinds of time, and eternity is not time indefinitely prolonged, but rather reveals itself in the blossoming of a present moment that escapes from time while containing it.

> Lord of what hath been and shall be, He (Time) is both today and tomorrow."
> —KATHA UPANISHAD

> Wherein what hath been and shall be, and all worlds are instant, tell me thou of that pillar (axis mundi), what it may be.
> —ATHARVAVEDA SAMHITA[1]

According to this passage from the Atharvaveda Samhita, absolute Time, or the present moment, is also represented by the world axis that structures space. Moreover, like space or emptiness, Time is in an absolute way the source of all things and of all relative times. Another Sanskrit text, the Maitri Upanishad, seems to replicate, and, in a certain sense, explain the Buddhist Heart Sutra: "Form is emptiness and emptiness is form." "For one who worships, thinking 'time is Brahma' (*kalam brahmeti*) time (*kala*, also 'death') reflows afar. As it has been said: From Time flows forth all beings, from Time they advance to their full growth and in time, again, win home. 'Time' is the formed and formless, both."[2]

To comprehend fully how the present moment is linked to eternity and how eternal Time is equivalent to emptiness, we must look at the Hindu theory of the atom. The moment that suspends or interrupts relative time is similar to a single point (perceived in the blink of an eye) on a line. Just as the moment, outside of time, contains or opens to eternity, so this point is situated outside of space and contains or opens to infinite space, or the void. In the same way as eternity unites past and present and contains all worlds, the void represented by this point, being the source of all lines and all forms, completely contains the segments on either side of it, uniting them in a totally different way than would classical geometry.

> The word *anu*, often synonymous with *suksma*, subtle, or "acute" (*suci*, "needle"), is not literally "atom," but does mean "indivisible particle or principle," so that *anu* or *paramasu* and *anutva* are the real equivalents of "atom" and "atomicity," and may be translated accordingly; the related *ani* is the sharp point of anything, such as an axle or needle. . . . Furthermore, just as *atomos* can be used for either spatial or temporal minimum, so the reference of *anu* may be either to a "point" in space, or to a "point" in time, without duration.
>
> In the Rigveda *anu* occurs only as the adjective "fine," qualifying "fingers" that prepare and qualify the Soma. But *ani* as "axle point" is significant in 1.35.6, where "as upon the axle-point of the [cosmic] chariot stand the immortals" . . . the "axle" here must be identified with the pneumatic Axis Mundi.
>
> Atomicity and immensity are attributed simultaneously to the ultimate reality in which these two, and all extremes, meet; and this implies at the same time a total omnipresence, and the coincidence in eternity of that which is everlasting with that which is present. [As the Mundaka Upanishad says,] "Less than the atoms in which the worlds and their inhabitants are, THAT IS the imperishable Brahma, immortal truth. . . . Both immense and very subtle, that is the atomic 'self.'"[3]

Which of the two theories, that of the point or that of the moment, is the original model? It is impossible to decide. But just as the point corresponds more to a way of perceiving than to a material object, and cannot be identified with even a tiny segment of the line, in the same way the "moment" here mentioned must be distinguished from a psychological moment where time seems to stand still. When it becomes absolute Time, the moment corresponds to an extinction of ordinary consciousness and to the vivid experience of a presence or even an omnipresence. Omnipresence, like omnipotence and omniscience, can certainly never become a personal quality; they are experienced as such only in a process of participation. According to Henry Corbin, scholar of comparative philosophy and esoteric Islam, they correspond to a complete annihilation and an exile where the awakened yogi or pilgrim "disappears from himself and is concealed from both *universes*." He becomes the instrument through which God or the gods still watch over the world. "As it is said in a *hadith* famous among the mystics of Islam, it is of this exile and stranger that God says: 'I am the eye through which he sees, the hand with which he feels, the foot with which he walks.'"

This moment is not fortuitous, for, as the geometry has shown, the break of the meander results from a complex process of division and a twisting of the thread. The experience of the present moment requires a complex process to bloom fully. With the moment expressed in this way we have an indication of what links the experience of emptiness to that of the infinite for the yogi. Zero and infinity are related like emptiness to spaciousness and the void to a vortex of infinite potential creativity. The theory of Time thus serves yet again to describe the process of alchemical transformation or of a spiritual evolution leading to liberation in a new way.

> The whole world passes through a mutation at every moment; thus all the external qualities of the world are relative to this present moment" (*Yoga Sutra Bhasya*). The control of moments and their sequence

leads to a discriminative gnosis, whose final development, "the deliverer," has all things for its object, and all time without regard for their course or its object." It will be seen that this is the same procedure as that described in the Buddhist Kalachakratantra; it also reminds us of Meister Eckhart's saying: "Not till the soul knows all there is to know can she pass over to the unknown good."[4]

In the labyrinth, this point or particular moment corresponding to infinity and eternity is represented by the center, the goal and end of the path. This center is often considered as the nucleus of concentric hierarchical worlds; it is sometimes represented in iconography by a tower or mirador from which one has a view over all things past, present, and future.

This central point that marks the end of the meander is where the meander was interrupted or broken; it is thus also represented by the other end of the cord—in other words, by the entrance to the labyrinth. The entrance and the center are the same point that has opened itself to eternity and the void. The infinitesimal point has become indefinitely immense, containing simultaneously the entire pattern and its transformation in time and all things (in that the knot represents the whole). Although it is difficult to admit from the start that in accordance to the ancient science a point on a line contains the entire line, the geometry and construction of the labyrinth render this proposition more acceptable. In a reversal, the entire knot is also contained in a point that is at the same time interior and exterior, the beginning and the end, alpha and omega. It is then actually the whole seen from this point of view that the knot symbol represents. This information helps us to clarify how symbolically the whole can be contained in a knot. "Nonspatial and non-temporal intuition is the condition of the interpretation of the space-time world itself."[5]

The labyrinth can then represent what Stephen Hawking calls the "form of time" and its center the "origin of time" in a more complete and intelligible way than physics.[6] We find also the notion of directions of time in example in some Mayan codices.

But if modern physics speaks of a time form, it is because the theory of relativity is applied to the notion of a uniform time represented by a straight line, a notion that does not make any metaphysical sense. The form of time becomes then nonsensical for the metaphysician.

This formulation rests on the position that Hawking assumes, that of the positivists, and for them the real is undeterminable and real time unconceivable; there are only clocks. But for the gnostic, the "form of time," which can be taken as a humorous way to present some important facts, ultimately describes a universe in a nutshell.

The geometry of the labyrinth reveals a subtle difference that remains ambiguous in the myths and tradition. It is not really the knotted cord that is directly interrupted or broken, but a time-space dimension represented by the meander (the self axis itself is not necessarily broken). And so if the center of the world is described by tradition as being everywhere and its circumference nowhere, it must be because it is situated outside of conventional space and time, in another dimension. It can therefore be projected anywhere in our familiar space and time. Moreover, as Time, or the infinite and infinitely subtle point, contains relative time and all things, the break in the meander can also represent the rupture of anything—the umbilical cord, the vital breath (sometimes represented by a line), a strand of DNA, or even the path taken by a photon as it is transformed into an electron and positron or a muon and antimuon. Only ancient geometry allows a symbolic meaning to be elaborated that is connected to the essential nature of an interruption or a rupture found at all levels. In Egyptian iconography time is represented, like DNA, by an intertwined double cord, but also by a broken line suggesting a sort of quantum jump (see fig. 18.1).

The geometry seems to indicate that it is the achievement represented by the final crossing of the meander and the self axis that decides where the

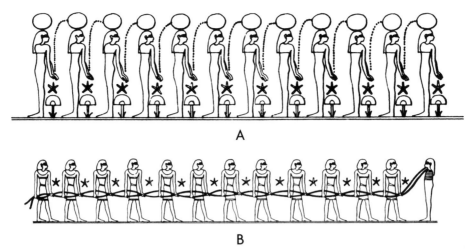

Fig. 18.1

(A) "The Hours of RE are thus. Their forms are between their fingers, their shadows are lower than their foreheads."
(B) 'Those who carry the intertwined double cord out of which come the stars.' Thus are designated the twelve persons who extract the double cord from the mouth of Aken. Knowing that at each hour a star is born, we can understand the rest of the text, which says that at each new twist, an hour is born, then, after the passage of the Great Neter, Aken reswallows the cord (thus making time go backwards). (Book of Gates, 5th division).

meander will break. This crossing itself corresponds to a passage to the other side of the knot and to a twist or reversal of time. The self axis cuts in a much more subtle and efficient way than the sword of Alexander. There thus exists a correspondence between the cross that cuts, which represents a time reversal, and the moment represented by the expanded point where the meander is cut. This relationship helps us better understand the apparently contradictory descriptions that we find in diverse traditions describing the way to reach salvation. They sometimes describe the self as a bridge as thin as a razor blade, and elsewhere, speaking of time, they mention a cut caused by a sharp blade.

> If now ultimate reality, that Brahma, and truth, which is the target we are aiming at, is so minute, if the Janua Coeli [the door in the sky] is so tiny as to be imperceptible to deluded man and visible only to those who have overcome anger and mastered the powers of the soul" so also must be, and so is, the Way that leads to and through it, "the ancient narrow path whereby the contemplatives, those that know Brahma, enter on high to the world of heavenly light" [Brhadaranyaka Upanishad]. The self, in

other words, is the razor edged Bridge that holds these worlds apart and must be crossed by all who would reach the Farther Shore, Trans-ethereal, Hyperuranian.

The most precious human thing is the state where a being is caught up between the past and the future . . . and the sheykhs have said that "Time is a cutting sword" because it is characteristic of a sword to cut, and "Time" cuts the roots of the future and the past, and obliterates care of yesterday and tomorrow from the heart. (Kasfh al-mahjub 67)

Feed me, for I am hungry, and make haste, for the Moment is a cutting sword, and the Sufi is a "son of the moment"; it is not the rule of the way to say tomorrow. (Rumi, *Mathnawi*, vol. 1, pp. 132–33)

Having crossed and reached the Farther Shore standing, means to be an "Arahant." Samyutta Nikaya[7]

In the Mahabharata, the "Active Door" is an ever revolving razor-edged wheel (as in the "flaming sword which turned every way" of Genesis), between the spokes of which "the skyfarer, diminishing his body, darted in an instant."[8]

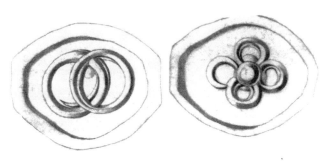

Figure 18.2. Cretan seals
Do these engravings found on a two-sided Cretan seal represent absolute time between the past and the future? Are there many directions for time, as there are for space?

Time in Ancient Greece, the One and the Many

> *In this world of sense it is indeed necessary to examine carefully*
> *What time and place are, so that what delights in a part,*
> *Whether of place or time, may be undersood to be far less beautiful*
> *Than the whole of which it is a portion.*
> —St. Augustine, *De ordine*

With the double notion of time in ancient Greece, we also find an emphasis on the "Logos," and an attempt to define a principle corresponding to the concept of eternity within the "instant." The moment that contains infinity, where all things are united, is the realm of the "One," a self-sufficient and unchanging plenitude. The whole that exists in relative time, on the other hand, is composed of the "Many" or the "Others," which are always changing, always different with respect to each other, always seeking what is other than themselves. The Many that composes the cosmos, and the whole, is obtained from a division of the One.

The One and the "Others" are united by the Logos. We can effectively observe that the dual functions of the "present moment," or dimensionless point, that divides and unites extensions of time or space are in fact logical functions or, more precisely, the functions of the Logos, which is at the same time the separator and the link uniting all things. This is pre-cisely the vision Philo had of the Logos: "He divided them in the middle, and laid the pieces opposite each other" describes the created world "as consisting of an almost infinite series of opposites held together in harmony by the very creative impulse or agent that had originally separated them out from primitive and unformed matter by a series of bisections" . . . and so "the Logos as being God in relation to the world . . . is at once the cutter of the universe and the glue binding it together."[9] The ambiguity of this double function of the Logos that cuts and glues back together is the same as what is expressed by Zeus's golden cord that unites things by keeping them separate, or by the Sufi who cuts himself off from time in order to fully merge with it. But the terms used also belong to the language of topology, where surgery is the term employed to cut a cord that is then glued back to-gether rather than spliced. The terms are thus suit-able for a God who is also geometer or topologist.

The idea that all creation implies a distinction and a separation of contrary concepts continued to exist in the Middle Ages, notably with Nicholas of Cusa: "It is of these contraries that the wall of Para-dise, wherein God dwells, is built, and no one who has not overcome 'the highest spirit of reason' [i.e., the Logos] that guards the undimensioned point that divides the contraries from one another and unites them can attain to the coincidence of opposites that subsists in the divine intellect."[10] The mention of op-posites or contraries as material to build the world—that is, to build the mythic world and thus the myth itself—is instructive, as it reveals how to interrogate the myth. This is the fundamental principle of struc-turalism, expressed well before this movement ap-peared. Structuralism effectively explored the struc-ture and meaning of myth through investigating the interplay of opposites (others) such as the raw and the cooked, honey and ashes, downstream and up-stream, and so on. But at the same time, the limit of this method's efficacy when it aims to find an ulti-mate or unified meaning is indicated by the relation-ship between the "One" and the "Others."

The "others" participate in the One, but are not parts of it, for it has no parts; so that their participation is both in the whole (of which they are parts) and in the One, and it results for these others than the One "because of what they have in common with the One and with themselves, both that there are differences among themselves by which they are limited in their relation to one another and to the whole," and that "their own authentic nature is unlimited." So that the things that are other than the One, whether as whole or parts, are both unlimited and participant in limitation."[11]

We must thus distinguish two different meanings for participation. In an article on the primitive mentality, Coomaraswamy mentions how this is possible: "The lineage of [or participation with] a totem animal is not what it appears to the anthropologist: a literal absurdity, but a lineage from the sun, the progenitor and Prajapati of everything, in the form by which it is revealed to the founder of the clan in a vision or a dream."[12] Rather than alluding to a simple hyphen linking a man to his totem, totemism corresponds to a triangle whose apexes are man, the totem, and the absolute sun or progenitor.

It seems that by differentiating the participation with the one and the whole, Parmenides defines at the same time the difference between the language of myth and that of symbols. Symbols express participation with the One, and the myth expresses participation with the whole as composed of the "others." Structuralism, which addresses itself only to mythic language, can recognize only relations among "others," or the relative aspect of the whole, but cannot lead to the One. It can explore only the limited dimensions of the symbol and thus lead in the end to a relative "truth." Only the unlimited nature of the symbol gives access to what we shall call with Philebus a "truer" meaning. "There are [in our existence] two things, one authentic Self and the other ever pursuing something other than itself. . . . The truest knowledge is of that which is, and really is, and that is ever

natured in accordance with itself."[13] This truer knowledge merits a bit of thought. By finding in the One a title for what is truly true, have we obtained a truer knowledge or simply added a new "name" to the labyrinth? Where does this knowledge hide? It seems as impossible to locate and understand as the smile of the Cheshire cat that Alice meets in Wonderland. So far we have recognized a representation of the mythical world produced by the unconscious or by the mind-spirit, but now we are dealing no longer with a description of the world of spirits or the world of the spirit, but with the spirit in and of itself.

In his *Cratylus,* Plato describes the One in the following way: "It is all things and nothing at all."[14] This formula reappears in Jacob Boehme's work: "Nothing and All, or that nothing visible out of which all things proceed . . . whosoever finds it, finds nothing and all things."[15] This last definition is appropriate for the labyrinth as well, which can be identified with no precise object, but which, at the same time, takes on a multitude of forms and corresponds to myths offering apparently contradictory interpretations. The definition also suits the symbolic significance of the labyrinth, since it corresponds to a knot representing the whole and potentially containing all and everything, while at the same time leading to an empty point or to a void left by a broken line. The title "One," given to the labyrinth's center, is similar to the painted title of Magritte's painting of a pipe, *Ceci n'est pas une pipe* (This is not a pipe), which refutes the reality of the image and at the same time undermines the validity of the signifier. The word "One" that is announced is itself defined only as a negation or a privation of what remains "Other." We can ask ourselves if this double negation produces an archetype of the absurd or if it actually hides an authentic way of affirming. To escape from this strange circuit, we must examine what appears to be paradoxical or even absurd in the existence of the One. In his *Physics,* Aristotle wrote: "If simultaneity as to time, and not being before or after, implies *coincidence* and is in the now, if the before and after are both in one and the same Now, then what happened ten thousand years ago would be simultaneous with what is happening today, and nothing would be before or after anything else. . . . Then everything would be in anything, and the universe in a grain of millet, only because the grain of millet and the universe are both existent at the same time."[16]

The error in Aristotle's reasoning consists in placing the One and the whole in the same category, whereas they are united rather by a concept or a specific experience of space-time-spirit. The true "coincidence," revealed to us by geometry, exists between the limited, concrete object perceived by the senses and the limitless symbol (in other words, between the knot as an object and the knot as a symbol).

Fundamentally, the symbol is born from an experience or, we could say, from a spiritual view of the object. This latter produces in return an awareness of the nature of this view or vision and of its source, as well as an awareness of the essential nature of geometry, which maps the process leading to the vision. Geometry furnishes a model to capture the essence of the otherwise ineffable immediate experience of the object. As it operates on objects transformed into symbols, each intuition and each of the geometer's operations takes on a profound meaning that is incorporated into new symbols. The geometer who thought he was skillfully manipulating a knotted cord suddenly finds himself unconsciously guided as if by a thread, or else manipulated like a marionette, tied to the system of strings he thought he was controlling and transforming.

By capturing in this way the spirit's gaze directed at the object, the trace of the path of his vision and the sign leading to it, the geometer produces an image that is neither an idol nor a copy but is nonetheless more than the object represented. The image becomes similar to a reflection in a mirror, which, like all mirrors, can send back the gaze and the image of the person gazing at the same time as it produces the image of what is seen. The object and the seer fuse and are connected by the path traced by the gaze.

The object can be seen as the hatching of the gaze fused with its pathway and its source. Everything is both distinct and united in the moment. The symbol teaches us to read an aura with a piercing gaze. The seer is encouraged to discover in himself the image of the creator, about whom it is said: "He created man in his image"—that is to say, according to his vision. The image of this gaze, which, for example, can be symbolized by the Oudja, the Egyptian cosmic eye, remains invisible but is present everywhere.

> The complex meshes of eye symbolism are woven all around the mother goddess—The Eye is the key to the religion—Egyptian literature of all periods abounds in allusion to "the bringing back of it," meaning the Eye.—When it is wounded and exiled the Ouddja is called Wedjat. Thoth is the one who brings him back, who claims: "I am he who returns the Wedjat eye, I am he who abolishes its dimness, when its brightness was damaged." This return took the form of a hunter that comes back to his people and whose name is Onuris, "He who brought back the distant one."[17]

The Egyptian mind nearly always envisages a notion with its inverse that is indissociable from it.[18] It points to a reciprocity; thus, if the myth speaks of an exiled eye, which can represent the eye of Horus wounded by Seth (the right eye of the supreme being is the sun, the left eye the moon that mirrors it), there is also the implicit meaning of a distant vision that becomes available or nearer (we shall say through the geometry or in the labyrinth), thanks to Thoth, the scribe (we shall say the divinity of the *gramme*). In fact, the wounded eye must be healed or "filled," which means that its wounded parts must be gathered together, and this filling is explicitly a mathematical operation represented by the parts of the Oudja. "Egyptian arithmetic was based on dimidiation—halving—rather than on addition, and the eye plays a part in the notation. The *hekat,* the unit of volume used in the measurement of grain, is represented graphically by the Oudja Eye, and its fractions by the

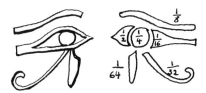

Figure 18.3. The Oudja

individual strokes of the glyph"[19] (see fig. 18.3). This process of halving that we find also in the geometry of the labyrinth is at the base of all pharaonic mathematics and represents the processes of creation.

One can add that the Oudja is sometimes represented with a uraeus, a serpent surging out of it; thus it is related to the circuitous path. It is also related to the dilation and contraction of space, since Shu (space), with his companion Tefnut, is pursued and brought back three times by the enraged Wedjat. The relation between the two eyes, or the crossing of the optic nerves, is represented by Sia, the goddess of weaving and knowledge.

In the symbol of the labyrinth there is thus a coincidence between a gaze and the image of an object that throws back this gaze like a mirror. This gaze, adopting and creating a pattern, presides over creation and also represents an instantaneous vision containing eternal time. It follows a wave motion and at the same time is contained within a nondimensional point.

Like the cord used by Seth to tie up Osiris and the slipknot of the lasso used to capture the sun, the mirror is used in myths as a symbol of the spirit and as a weapon. In Greek myth it takes the form of a shield used by Perseus to vanquish Medusa, whose powerful gaze petrifies all those who look her way. We can interpret her gaze as that which transforms living symbols into inert objects. Medusa's accomplishment is inverse to that of Daedalus, who gave life to statues by "opening their eyes" and thus, in a certain sense, converting objects into symbols. The shield/mirror throws Medusa's gaze back at her. Confirming the hypothesis of a mirror labyrinth, the Greco-Roman mosaic in figure 17.5 represents the image of a maze formed by a torus knot at the center of which is reflected Medusa's head. There must therefore have

been a recognized identification between the maze and the mirror/shield. Thus depicted, the maze suggests an equivalence between imprisoning or losing a bad spirit in a knot and neutralizing it in a deflection or a reflection that turns the evil gaze back on itself. But this mirror can also be seen as containing a more powerful gaze than that of Medusa: that of the One hidden in the maze with the path of the labyrinth.

There are sacred Celtic and Chinese mirrors whose surfaces don't really reflect but rather take the form of a disk upon which are engraved a kind of labyrinthine drawing (for example, see the Desborough mirror, fig. 18.4). It appears more than likely that these objects attempted to substitute our limited gaze with an infinite gaze connecting all things and linking them to a single source.

The symbol of the mirror representing the spirit can also be found in the Persian tradition in Attar's *The Conference of the Birds*. At the end of a dangerous journey that the birds accomplish to seek out their lord, the latter presents himself as a mirror in which the seekers must recognize their own faces and those of the others. It is also present in Orthodox iconography (see plate 15) and in Dzogchen, the direct path

Figure 18.4. The Desborough Mirror

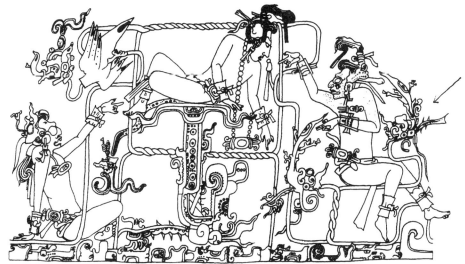

Fig. 18.5. Kauil
At the extreme right, the smoking mirror, Kauil, is represented on the knees of one of the twin heroes. The resurrected god gazes at it from the center. One cord emanates from the mirror. Another comes from the waters of the Underworld. The intertwining of the two cords symbolizes the union of opposites. The knot formed by the cords is also used to illustrate the ancient concept of the binding of space-time.

of Buddhism, where it represents the natural, primordial or perfect state of the mind. Among the Maya the mirror is called Kauil, "the smoking mirror." Kauil is considered to be an emanation of the sun and is most often represented by a real mirror or by a mask. In figure 18.5 we can again observe a relationship between this mirror and a cord that forms a knot. Kauil has an equivalent among the Aztecs in the person of Tezcatlipoca, who represents God the creator but also the mirror (which sees the whole world in its reflection). In Egyptian iconography we can also sometimes find a mirror at the top of the pillar of Osiris or in the ankh loop. According to Lévi-Strauss, the structure of myth is itself like a play of mirrors. This brings to mind Indra's net, where each knot in the net reflects the whole (another example of a myth describing its own structure), a structure then also similar to that of a hologram or to that of fractals.

Today, we can find another interesting coincidence in the fact that the problems posed by knot topology can be resolved by a play of mirrors: "Knot complements (in other words the space that surrounds them) have a natural geometrical structure that can be used to specify the difference between knots that are not equivalent. Non-Euclidean geometry appears. . . . In fact, we can also create non-Euclidean geometries with mirrors assembled into a sort of kaleidoscope."[20]

Thus the geometry leading to the symbol of an absolute mirror itself corresponds to a play of mirrors.

Time and Experience Betwixt and Between

The name that can be named is not the limitless name.
—LAO-TZU

The center of the labyrinth represents the One. But using the word *represents* is no longer appropriate, as the One cannot be represented. The truth is image but there is no image of truth. The verb *to signify* is more fitting, as the labyrinth is first a sign that signals the presence of the One, and where it is situated and how to participate in it. It shows us the way to an interior process and can thus also be seen as a grail or an empty vase that must be filled.

The sign points out three things: a view, a path, and a fruit, and it is only with the latter that the three fuse and that the sign becomes a complete symbol. The symbol is completed and fulfilled by addressing itself to a pilgrim progressing along the path.

The transition from sign to complete symbol acting as a mirror corresponds to a *metanoia*, or a leap from a given experience of the senses to a knowledge that springs from a new mind, or what the Greeks called *nous*. This is what the apocryphal Gospel according to Mary Magdalene points to:

I had a vision of the Lord the teacher and I told him,

"Lord I see you today in this form." He answered:

"Blissful one, who does not trouble my view,

where the nous is found, there is the treasure."

Then I told him:

"Lord in the moment, does she who contemplates your form see thanks to the psyche (the soul) or to the pneuma (spirit, breath) ?"

Lord the teacher answered: "Neither thanks to the psyche nor the pneuma, but thanks to the nous (the natural mind), being *between the two*. It is nous that sees. . . ."[21] [italics mine]

The "where" or the "moment" that Mary Magdalene mentions is thus truly an "in-between," an emptiness that is between things as well as between us and things and between parts of things and which is like space, but which unites and transforms what it seems to separate.

This notion of in-between is also prevalent in the labyrinth and suggested by its design.

> Here we will simply note that mazes are in relation to directions what betwixts-and-betweens are in relation to opposites. In passing through a maze one is not going in any particular direction, and by so doing one reaches a destination that cannot be located by reference to the points of the compass. According to Irish folk-belief, fairies and other supernatural beings can cause a man to lose his bearings (just as they can upset his sense of time). . . . Conversely, in some of the "Voyages" it is when the voyagers have lost their course and shipped their oars—when they are not going anywhere—that they arrive in the wondrous isles.[22]

Thus, the symbol of the labyrinth corresponds first to a particular experience, a pure experience that is free from all reference points, and one that puts our being in contact with an emptiness that is a vastness and a matrix in a moment situated outside of time. The labyrinth corresponds to the essential nature of experience.

The nature of experience is not a thing present at hand, to which we return and upon which we then simply stand. Experience is in itself a circular happening through which what lies within the circle becomes exposed. This opening however, is nothing other than the between—between us and the thing . . .

. . . the question "what is a thing" is the question "who is man?" . . . A dimension is opened up in Kant's question about *the thing which lies between the thing and man*, which reaches out beyond things and back behind man.[23] [emphasis added]

This new definition, "the thing between the thing and man," is perfectly suitable for the symbol of the labyrinth. Moreover, it can be applied to symbols in general, as the symbol is that which reaches through an object to what is both "beyond it" and "behind man" or, rather, replaces the mysterious back and beyond by a new existential structure of time-space where the usual definitions of directions become meaningless.

The experience of the moment can be fundamental, but it needs an exact language like that of myth or of geometry to be communicated and to avoid an equally fundamental misunderstanding. The visible and the thing are needed in order to understand the invisible, and vice versa. As the *I Ching* explains, "All that is visible must grow beyond itself and extend into the realm of the invisible," and Heraclitus also: "Invisible harmony [that connects and orders] is stronger than visible" (fragment 54).

What is more, we have already met this in-between. The space or void in between is also the realm that the breath of the first Dogon genie occupies; it is the place of the path of the Logos and the realm where the medium of language becomes structured. In return, it is the mediation that will design, represent, signify, structure, or fill—one could say re-place—the space and the void in between with a medium.

The mediation and the medium are the message. As Bruno Latour cogently remarks, even modern science, as it progresses, reveals itself as a mode of representation. There is no longer a representing mind and a represented world but only a mediation: "The notion of mediation is much too weak and hazy to define the whole middle range between the bygone representing mind and the represented world. This is true even if one is careful not to define mediation as what is 'in between' (for this I reserve the word intermediary), but rather as that which produces, in part, the elements that come in and out of mediation. If the medium is the message, slightly different types of media (and mediation) will produce enormous differences in types of messages."[24] It is as if the space in between expands and merges with the containing space, the energy of the void, and invests itself in the things and between the parts of things, at the same time separated and united.

There is not on one side an intelligence and on the other a language that expresses it, but rather a logos and a language that represent two different or polar aspects of the same mediation. The Logos becomes the intelligence of the universe (the void) or of the Creator (silence), but it needs language to be communicated, and it is communicated *through* language rather than *by* language. It is as if the Logos was dispersed everywhere, creating and making us understand things and the void and conveying this understanding by enrobing itself with language so that this Logos could be rediscovered whole and pristine, with an eternal memory at the center of the labyrinth, contained in a point including all things.

We cannot decide when the breath becomes Logos, when the name that cannot be pronounced becomes a word, or when the Logos becomes language. Nor can we decide with certainty when an embryo becomes a fetus. The Logos exists even before conception. This is what is symbolized by the Annunciation to Mary by the angel Gabriel. As the void becomes structured and a source of energy, it is as if the Logos and the void become the same thing. This is what is expressed by "In the beginning was the Word" in the Gospel of John and by the Vedas in "At the summit of the distant sky is the word, enveloping everything."

We can find a comparable expression in a puzzling question in modern cosmology. The best explanation of the cosmological constant, the expansion of the universe, and the appearance of solid matter is given by a fifth element, or "quintessence," represented by the void. In addition to the energy of visible matter, which is 0.5 percent of the total, and that of two kinds of black matter, which constitute 29.5 percent, 70 percent of the total cosmic energy would be produced by the void. In thus producing a fluctuating energy, the void becomes structured. "It is a coincidence that the expansion of the universe accelerates at the very moment when thinking creatures appear, that is, us. Why is the evolution of (living) matter bound to that of the void energy?"[25] As Ostriker and Steinhardt conclude, "It is the void structure as it is presented by the quantic fields theory that must be revised."

The nature of the Logos, and of the Word, is the fundamental mystery and the essential message that myths and sacred texts transmit. All the definitions of the in-between we just mentioned are ways to circumambulate a notion of mediation and of Logos that in itself we cannot fathom. They indicate a way to circulate in a multidimensional space where the concept of direction changes constantly. The Logos is also what explains the origin and the hidden meaning of the ancient theory of the moment and the "One." The Logos that is unlimited and unites must come and return to the "One." In the One, the Logos, the void outside and the void inside (the nous in between spirit and soul) become one and the same. For us who do not understand, who see the Logos as absent or empty, the information seems meaningless and like pouring the empty into the void, but the message is also the form in in-formation, about an embodiment (as in "I am the word)," and about a messenger, a mediator, or a messiah who can show us the way out of the world mess, a messenger who uses the same language we do but in a different way, who by harmoniously joining words and actions indicates a path and a way to participate with the intelligence of the Logos.

At the absolute center the in-between appears, then, as a relative term belonging to a dualistic mentality. With the "One" and the completed symbol, there is no more duality, no more this and that, and thus no more in-between. The in-between subsists only as an appearance and the experience as a step away from the center or from the moment, as a return to duality. The symbol and the sign of the labyrinth, however, address themselves first to dual beings; thus we shall find again the concept of the in-between represented in a new way. In a Zoroastrian myth about the nature of time and related in the next section, the in-between is represented by angels.

Figure 18.6
Do these Cretan seals represent the expansion of the in-between?

Cyclical Time and the System of Rings

From the epoch of being comes the unfolding in epochs of its destination, which constitutes the veritable history of the world. Each time being contains itself in its destiny a world is suddenly and unpredictably created. All epochs of world history are epochs of wandering in a maze. The unfolding of being in epochs belongs to the secretly temporal character of being and thus characterizes the essence of "time," thought within being. What we ordinarily present beneath time is but the emptiness of a pure appearance of time gathered within a being understood as an object.
—Heidegger, *The Speech of Anaximander*

The symbol holds meaning in a way similar to how a grail or a cornucopia or even a seal holds its contents.

The symbol sends us off on a quest for an innate knowledge that, for the most part, remains latent or sealed in man. Alongside the symbols there also exist rituals, practices, and forms of gnosis that lead to this quest by bringing the symbolic world to life in the world we live in. If, in an ascendant movement of evolution, geometry linked to myth transforms objects into symbols, with the gnosis and the rituals the meanings telescoped within the symbol descend according to the force of involution once more to inhabit objects and beings.

For example, the symbolic meaning of the knot transformed into a system of rings (in the manner described in chapter 17 and figs. 17.14 and 17.15) can be revealed by such a gnosis, as, for example, by the Mazdean cycles of time described by Henry Corbin. Since there are few references on the symbolic significance of rings and their connection to knots, Corbin's research can be revealing. When presenting this gnosis we shall respect the point of view of Corbin, who saw in it an exegesis preexisting the Christian and Islamic religions and fully deserving the name it was given of *Weltreligion* (world religion). This gnosis, based on very ancient myths, expresses in a new way the implicit or nonconceptual content of an ancient mentality having the labyrinth as its foundation.[26]

In Mazdean cosmology we discover

the conception of a cyclical time that is not the Time of an eternal return, but rather the time of a return to an eternal origin. . . . Mazdean cosmology thus makes us recognize that time has two essential aspects: the shoreless Time without origin, eternal Time; and limited or "long domination time.". . . Eternal Time is the paradigm, the model for limited time, which was made in its image. And this is why our time itself, as a dimension of earthly existence, allows a dimension to be seen that differs from its own chronological dimension: a dimension of light that imposes its form and its meaning. Inversely, the absence or destruction of this dimension measures the depths of the darkness of a being in this time.[27]

This cosmology is built upon a myth that describes the struggle between two opposing principles, Ahura Mazda, who is pure presence, eternity, and light, and Ahriman, who is negativity, void, and darkness. From these two colliding principles are born the cycles of relative time, which are nothing more than delayed eternity used to stall Ahriman's force and ultimately vanquish it. "'Ahriman rose up out of his depths,' said Bundahishe, 'and he reached the frontier where the star of light shines.' . . . Seeing 'a splendor and an ascendancy superior to his own, he fell back into his darkness to produce his counter-creation.'"[28] Ahura Mazda gets even with Ahriman by establishing cycles of time capable of catching up with eternal time. As eternal time represents the glory and light that emanates from Ahura Mazda, these cycles are personified by angels of light, or *fravartis*, who descend to earth and who, when they incarnate, are confused with human souls. Each *fravarti* also has its own *fravarti*, establishing in this way a hierarchy that reaches all the way to Ahura Mazda. It is by recognizing or uniting with their souls or with their tutelary angels that men can retrieve eternity, uniting with Ahura Mazda instead of being subjected to Ahriman.

> Ahura Mazda revealed to his prophet that without the help of the *fravartis* he wouldn't have been able to protect his creation against Ahriman's assault. . . . Ahura Mazda put the humans' *fravartis* before the free choice that gave rise to their destiny (in other words, their time): they could either remain in Ahura Mazda's world or else descend and incarnate into material bodies to fight Ahriman on earth. The *fravartis* answered yes to the proposition to descend and fight on the earth. A doubling was thus produced. The incarnate *fravarti* ended up being identified with the soul, though this soul kept its archetypal dimension, since its celestial condition was to be an archetype. It is, in fact, but the person and the earthly part of a whole, a *syzygy*, completed by a celestial person, another self that is its destiny, its angel-soul, the celestial I (called Daena) who comes to meet it

> after death, on the Chinvat Bridge path called for this reason in the texts "the soul on the path". . . Losing this archetypal dimension is literally to stop having an angel, to die as a soul can die, to stop answering one's celestial partner, who can thus no longer answer from one's earthly soul. . . .
>
> This vision of an incessant ascent from hell shows us how an alchemy of resurrection operates from cycle to cycle. What it proposes is a series of ruptures, of laying bare and adorning to which one must consent, to avoid falling backward, beneath oneself.[29]

The syzygy or doubling of the person into a disciple and a guiding angel can remind us of the doubling of the cord of the knot, or of the creation of a ring replacing a cross in the geometry. It has nothing to do with schizophrenia, and it is obtained through a certain way of observing or perceiving. Thus, as with the mirror-labyrinth, time is confused with the trajectory of a gaze. The symbolic is considered observable. Time, which necessitated a specific way of looking at objects in order to be represented, now finds itself incarnate or even personified by a gaze and integrated into an intimate relationship.

It is immediately recognizable that the chain of angels representing the cycles of time perfectly corresponds to the system of rings that can replace the knot. This chain can represent Ahura Mazda's counteroffensive against Ahriman's incoherent world, symbolized by an inextricable knot. The conjunction of angels making it possible to reach the dimension of eternal time also corresponds to the junction of rings that makes it possible to reach the center of the labyrinth or the One.

What is particularly striking in this form of gnosis is the way its liturgy and practices can lead to a recognition of hypostases and the creation of visions in which all kinds of things appear embedded or fused together. The angel that can be recognized within oneself or in someone else is not only Time and the soul but also destiny, glory, light, the robe of Ahura Mazda, or even the liturgy (the cycles of time are established by a song sung by Ahura Mazda that prefigures the liturgy). Time is also represented by a new kind of knot, the *kosti*.

Thus we meet again, linked in a new way, symbols that remained latent in the symbol of the labyrinth.

[T]o attain the *paredros* angel is to attain immortality. . . . In the same way, the meeting with Daena "on the path" of the Chinvat Bridge signifies the reversal of limited time into eternal time, the attainment of one's destiny, and the plenitude of the light of glory, or *xvarnah*.

It is thus only in anticipation that the vision of his eternal time in the form of his archetypal angel can be presently given to the soul; and this prediction, by manifesting what is not yet and what is meant to be, reveals its true being as "belated eternity." In consequence, anticipation is the vital law of an existence, which, by understanding itself in this way, reaches toward its superexistence, or else eternally delays itself. This anticipation is manifested by rites, injunctions, an enchanting mental iconography, or visions of ecstasy.

We have been able to rightfully interpret the symbolism of the *kosti* along these lines. The *kosti* is the sacred braid, woven with the wool of a lamb that Zoroastrians wear as a belt and which is revered as their distinctive religious sign. Four knots are tied when putting on the braid, which must encircle the waist three times. The symbolic meaning traditionally given to these four knots helped to identify them as a Zervanite tetrad (Zervan is time) to which is added, as in the myth of the "Magi's chariot," a fifth member that renders the tetrad coherent and sums it."[30]

It is as if the rites that use these symbols had the goal of rediscovering, in order to use it in life, the gaze that produced the symbol and that is as if hidden within it. To understand the symbols, to see the angel is to see with Ahura Mazda's eyes; it is to climb on the ray that joins him to what he sees.

Finally, the preceding discussion of symbols can lead us to another realization. The homology among all these overlapping meanings can influence the interpretation of iconography by revealing a multitude of meanings that can apply to a ring. If the Ismaelian gnosis really corresponds to a *Weltreligion*, it allows for both a more complete and more ambiguous interpretation of all the images related to myths containing rings or circles.

It is as destiny and personal fate that Zervan (time) also presents himself as *xvarnah*, in other words, as the celestial light of glory, "victorious fire," which is first the property of the celestial Yazatas; this glory manifested itself visibly as a nimbus and halo of flame surrounding the princes of the sacred dynasties before our chronologies; it retained this visibility in the stylized nimbus, which was transferred from the figure of the Mazdean Saoshyant to the Western representations of Christ and the oriental Buddhas and Bodhisattvas. But it is not only the royal and sacerdotal charisma; it is the power that constitutes and makes coherent the being of a being of light. In this sense, this "glory" signifies the soul itself as it preexisted the body. Accordingly, if this "glory," figure of eternal time, is bestowed to each being of light as its very soul, it is true to say it is its destiny and eternity.[31]

In part 4 of this work we shall examine a variety of images linked to myths and containing full or broken circles. These circles or rings can represent the sky, the sun, or the horizon, or, as in the Knossos calendar, they can represent time in the form of moon cycles or, by association, the tides linked to these cycles. But they can also implicitly carry a meaning as *symbolon* (the broken rings offered as tokens that are at the origin of the word *symbol*). Finally, depending on the context, they can become symbols, bearing a significance that has apparently very little connection with the thing represented. They can carry all the other meanings attached by the myth to the cycles of time, whether epochs, destiny, souls, light, victorious fire, the nimbus, wisdom, or "the power that constitutes and makes coherent the being of a being of light." In the words of Basarab Nicolescu:

"They never have an ultimate or exclusive meaning . . . they are capable of embracing an unlimited number of aspects of reality. We are thus obliged to accept the relativity of our way of looking at it: this relativity can be present only if the symbol is conceived of as in movement and if we ourselves experience it. Symbolism entails a decreasing entropy of language, a growing order, an augmentation of information and comprehension, as it crosses different levels of reality."[32]

If myths are polysemic, so are primitive images; it is this quality that ultimately renders them a representation of a unifying vision.* Thus, the sign linked to the symbol impregnated thought.

This way of applying an interpretation given by the exegesis of one myth to seemingly unrelated designs can appear completely illegitimate, but as Griaule has learned from the Dogon: "The painting does not get its efficacy entirely from its form but also from the words pronounced at the time when the Awa[†] operates. The man succeeds in the painting operation by incorporating the force of his word in the stroke. It is obvious here that the name is pronounced before the symbol precisely at the moment where it is painted and that this symbol has only a tenuous relation with the represented object."[33]

We must then distinguish between the meaning as content and the form of the symbol as an adequate container. In addition to a meaning assigned to the content there is also an essential meaning in the container that corresponds to the geometry and the algebra of symbols and which makes possible or enhances the specific content. As a deep exegesis, the myth of the cycles of time informs us about the essential original meaning of a circle or ring both as container and content, belonging then to all symbols of the circle. Although this meaning is often ignored or forgotten and replaced by that of a new content, it is an integral part of the full symbol.

---

* We shall be reminded of this aspect when we examine drawings composed of circles in chapters 27 and 29.

[†] *Awa* means mask, or the fibers of the dance costume, or, in common language, the group of dancers.

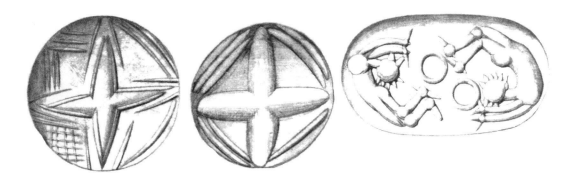

Fig. 18.7. Cretan seals depicting stars representing the light of eternal time and personified stars that evoke the cycle of time

19

Axis and Center

Only the backward path will lead us forward.
—Heidegger

The Enclosure of the Labyrinth Corresponds to the Knot's Axis

So far, we have examined only the origin of the path in the labyrinth. We must also ask ourselves what the meaning and origin are of the enclosure or surrounding wall of the labyrinth, in other words, of the labyrinth itself, perceived no longer as an imprisoning maze, but rather as an enclosure containing a unique path leading to a center. Is the enclosure of the labyrinth just a line added arbitrarily to separate and close off the convolutions of the meander, or does it correspond to a specific element of the knot? We can answer this question by following the progression of the geometrical transformation backward and finding the place occupied by the walls of the labyrinth, first in the torus knot and then in the original knot (see fig. 19.1).

This process reveals that the walls of the labyrinth originate in a path doubly joining the spaces marked by the rope in the knot. This double path, through the space of the loose knot, reveals itself as a double axis of the knot. The discovery of this double axis is surprising because there are a large number of different ways to join the spaces defined by the projection of the knot, and because we cannot define a single axis for a three-dimensional knot whose configuration can change. When we switch from the geometry of solids to knot topology, the notion of the axis becomes more complex. It is only when we face

a fixed geometrical projection of a knot, as with the *nahals*, that a single straight axis can be found.

There is thus a polarity and a perfect balance between knot and labyrinth, path and enclosure:

The cord of the knot	becomes	the path in the labyrinth (or the enclosure of the knot)
The double path through the knot	becomes	the walls of the labyrinth (or the double axis of the knot)

In a reversal, the contents become the container and the effect becomes the cause. As in a circumambulation of the knot, everything is inverted.

We can find here an explanation for the fact that the labyrinth is sometimes called "the corridor of the double ax." The labrys, or double ax, that can cut or split in opposite directions was an important emblem for the Cretans and the Celts. It is associated with the double face of Janus, the god of doors and passageways, and through this association with the labyrinth. The word *labrys* was even considered to be the root of the word *labyrinth*. We can accept that the ax that splits in two different directions was a symbol for an axis that accomplishes a similar task in geometry. With this analogy, the

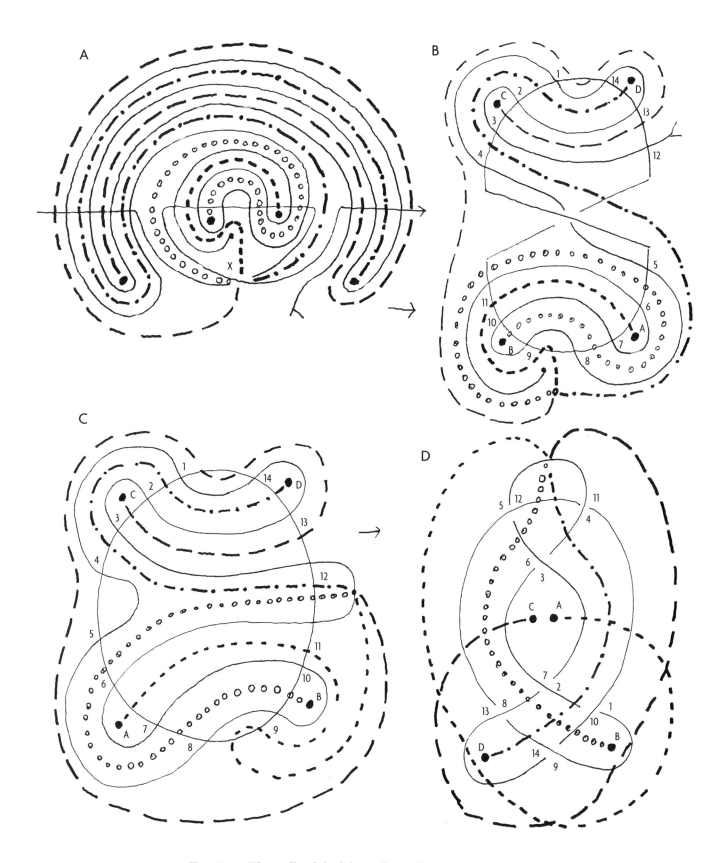

Fig. 19.1. The walls of the labyrinth are the double axis of the knot

One can trace back the place that the walls of the labyrinth take in the knot by following in reverse the transformation of the knot into the path of the labyrinth. (A) In dots, the four branches of the wall of the labyrinth. (B) The Torus knot crossed. (C) The Torus knot. (D) The knot and its double axis.

labyrinth, geometrically the corridor of the double axis, could also be called "corridor of the double ax."

Even if the objection is raised that this name only applies to the one room in the palace of Knossos that is decorated with double axes and with double entasis shields, we could answer that this room could have been used precisely to commemorate the labyrinth. The name is particularly appropriate, as it echoes the ancient Egyptian "corridor of double truth" that is mentioned in the papyri known as Book of the Corridor of Double Justice, Book of the Two Ways, Book of the Double House of Life, and the Book of Caves. These papyri deal with the weighing, judgment, and transformation of souls in the Underworld—which is to say, in the labyrinth.

If, as we have assumed, the geometry unveils the structure of myths as well as that of the labyrinth, we find here another indication of the complexity of the deep structure of myths. Not only does this structure involve an assemblage of tropes corresponding to the reversal of loops and a correspondence between different structures, (knots and concatenations of rings), but the metaphors must also serve to achieve inversions and correspondences that make the notion of symmetry, which is fundamental in myths, more complex.

Axes—Causes or Effects?

We have seen how the walls of the labyrinth correspond to the double axis of the knot. But what exactly is an axis? What is its essence?

Schwaller de Lubicz drew our attention to the meaning and the importance of the concept of the axis for the ancient Egyptian mentality. These "imaginary lines" are not an abstraction from a concrete phenomenon, and it is impossible to decide if they are causes or effects. Which came first, the circle or the center? Or as the Taoists say, "What causes the chariot's movement, the hub of the wheel or its spokes?" Schwaller de Lubicz doesn't hesitate to call the axis the *will* of a figure.

In modern physics, the notion of a continuous whole that contradicts the classical idea of a world that can be analyzed into separate independently existing parts and which refutes the theory of local causes appears to revive this same question. Where is the center of things and of the universe? Where is the origin of all things? What turns around what? The ancient theme that Samson was induced to ponder when he was attached to the wheel of a mill has become once again the crucial question.

Without becoming too involved in a philosophical discussion, we can first understand that the principle of the axis is the foundation for the making of a knot. To make a knot is to use one end of a cord as an axis around which the other end of the cord is coiled (fig. 19.2). To complete the knot, the same end of the cord must be introduced like an axis in a loop formed by the first operation. Each knot obtains its characteristics by a specific alternation of these two maneuvers.

The double axis concludes and reveals the order of this process; it follows the path of the cord when it is placed as an axis and at the same time binds together all the real and potential axes. It represents a potential development of the knot and a structuring capacity of space that made the making of the knot possible. Can we call this principle a "will"? Will is itself a difficult concept to define. It cannot be confused with the desired object or with the goal toward which it is driven; it is rather a capacity to accomplish and materialize that which is only potential or nonpolarized energy, to explore the void left by a longing or a latent

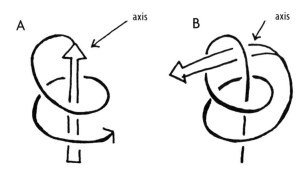

Fig. 19.2
(A) *First phase: The cord is rolled around an axis formed by the cord.* (B) *Second phase: The cord pierces a loop following its axis. What was axis in A becomes loop in B.*

hope and to discover the nature of a wish that transforms and defines itself with its accomplishment. A riddle from the Arthurian legends clearly expresses the link between desire and will: "What does a woman desire most in a man?" The answer: "His will." It is perhaps Theseus's almost blind will that seduces Ariadne when she already holds the secret of the labyrinth. This aspect of will is manifest is the pattern of the labyrinth where the double axis, once it becomes the enclosure, is what guides the hero or pilgrim toward his desire or his source, or rather toward the source of his desire. "The character of this will is that which will always compel spirit—nonpolarized energy—to define itself in time and space, hence in the form of the symbol."[1]

But how does this unveiling of the meaning of the double axis occur? In the geometry of the labyrinth, the existence of the double axis doesn't appear immediately; first we encounter the self axis. The entire cord becomes the self axis, and then an axis of symmetry that appears is used to twist the torus knot. It is only once the pathway of the meander is established that the concrete self axis is erased and replaced by the double axis that was represented by space or structured void beforehand. In the construction of the labyrinth, each phase unveils a meaning that remained hidden in the previous phases. There is a dialectic that progresses as it reveals the essence of the knot and the relation among three different kinds of axes. This dialectic can be implicitly suggested in the myth by the transformations of the Osiris pillar, presented first as a tree or stream, then as a temple column, and finally as the world axis. Ancient geometry does not construct complex notions from simple assumptions. Rather, it unfolds layers of meaning that overlap and interpenetrate each other. It reveals what is latent, grasping and making apparent what is unconscious. Geometry unfolds like the Egyptian "hours" (see fig. 18.1A) in a way that can be paraphrased as follows: "between the fingers and below the shadow of the forehead."[2]

In imitation of the way the ancient Egyptians ex-

pressed themselves, we could say that the self axis reveals the nature and the will of the double axis. The self axis is the offspring of the double axis, just as Horus is the son of Osiris and reveals his potential. As the Egyptian text puts it, "The son reveals the face of his father." In the knot the double axis is like Osiris and in the labyrinth it becomes like Ra. In the myth, the father-son relationship suggests the seminal power of the axis.

The parallel between the structure revealed by geometry and the one that appears to underlie in the myth can lead us further. The relationship between the knot and the axis seems also to correspond to the relationship between the physical body and the more subtle bodies as these were conceived by the Egyptians. As figure 19.3 illustrates, this relationship is itself reflected in the way the protagonists of the Greek myth interact and in the structure of language.

It follows that the geometric transformation and the work of the geometer Daedalus could present an analogous model for the work of self-knowledge, a work that leads at the same time to a development of the subtle bodies of our being. The geometric model certainly doesn't offer a simple technique or a user's manual for work on the self, but the geometry does allow one to grasp a hidden relation between invisible and ineffable processes. Many mandalas, which help one to develop a specific visualization for contemplation or meditation, are made according to a sort of symbolic algebra combined with geometry.

The architecture of the Egyptian temple also reproduces this relation between the axes in another manner. In *The Temple in Man*, Schwaller de Lubicz shows how the key to the meaning of the temple of Luxor is found in the study of its different axes. The entire temple is built according to three axes, and its alignment is displaced from one axis to another by a pivoting motion. This explains why the angles of its walls are not orthogonal and why the plan of the entire temple is slightly bent. The interpretation of the frescoes and the hieroglyphs painted or engraved on each wall depends upon the axis toward which it is oriented. The temple itself thus suggests a transformation and a process of spiritual evolution for man. Schwaller concludes: "Once and for all we must see the pharaonic temple like the process of a seed bearing fruit."[3]

Polarity and Reality

Always beyond concepts
That we may intuit its backroundness
Always in the realm of conceptual desire
That we may discern its manifestations
These two are the same, yet they receive different names
That they are the same is the mystery of mystery
The door of all subtleties.

—LAO-TZU

But why this polarity and balance between knot and labyrinth and between path and wall, a polarity that echoes that of life and death established by the myth? It is much more than a game, and it bears witness once more to a will to embrace the knot completely. The knot defines itself by the two aspects of the openness of the spaces and the closed nature of the cord, and by their correlation. Like a piece of Swiss cheese, it can also be seen as a structure of holes. If we watch children playing on a jungle gym, it is impossible to decide whether they are climbing upon it or crawling across it. The balance offered by the pattern of the labyrinth resolves the dilemma at a more fundamental level by describing a whole that is more than the sum of its parts and which leads to a particular conception of reality. Reality is expressed as the simultaneity and the reconciliation of opposing principles. The balance allows the dualism that prevents us from grasping the whole completely to be overcome. This whole seems self-evident, but it is precisely its apparently obvious character that hides its true nature and the reversal it implies.

This reversal of polar relations allows us to see more clearly how the parts of the whole and the symbols that are attached to them change meaning and are transformed according to the relationship in which they are presented. To geometry corresponds a kind of algebra of symbols, and the value or the meaning of these symbols changes according to the composition of the equations. This is probably also true of

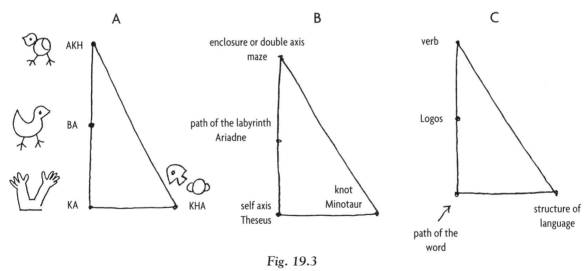

Fig. 19.3

(A) The akh is the universal mind or light. It is the aspect of the spirit that preconceives the object of creation, and is represented by an ibis. As its spelling indicates, it is seen as being the inverse of kha, perhaps in the same way as the labyrinth built with the double axis is the inverse of the knot. The ba is represented by either a crane or a bird with a human head. The ka is vital energy or the double. The kha is the physical body or corpse; the ba is the soul or etheric body or vital breath. (Picture borrowed from Lucy Lamy, Egyptian Mysteries.) (B) The same triangle with the elements of the Greek myth. (C) The same triangle starting with the structure of language.

the symbols of modern algebraic equations, but those who use these equations are not preoccupied with this aspect, as only the final quantitative answer matters to them. The meaning of the combined equations remains unknown until they are solved and replaced by quantities. As Nietzsche saw it: "Since Copernicus, man is rolling out of the center into an *x*."[4]

Here, for example, the double axis of the knot first represents (according to the Dogon myth) the path of the word that finds its way into this knot. The path of the word invests itself in a structure, thereby creating language. Yet in the pattern of the labyrinth, the double axis, transposed into another dimension, becomes that which guides and contains the path of the Logos. It becomes the symbol of the unfolding Word-Creator, signifying the thing in it-

self, the original unity, or the essential element represented by the central cross.

The unity of this whole can then be represented as the pyramid that surmounted the Egyptian labyrinth (fig. 19.4), a pyramid whose golden top could represent the word and corresponded then to the center of the labyrinth. But the pyramid is complete only with the transformation of the knot. The erection of this symbolic pyramid then corresponds to the geometry of the labyrinth.

The materialization of the double axis that becomes the wall of the labyrinth and a containing structure instead of a content illustrates how, by way of symbols created by geometry, that which is intangible becomes concrete and that which is concrete takes on an absolute meaning. Emptiness becomes a pillar,

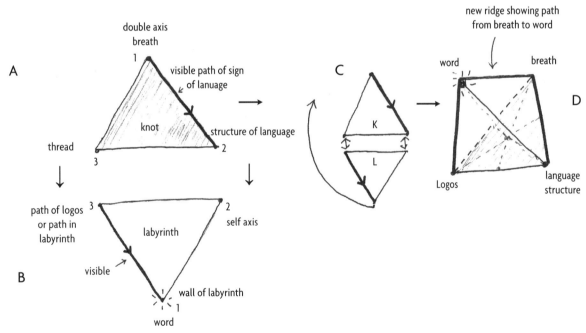

Fig. 19.4

(A) In the knot we have three things that can be represented by the apex of a triangle: (1) a double axis, which represents the breath of the path of the breath of the genie that becomes articulated as an audible sign of language as it penetrates the structure of knots, which become the structure of language. (2) The knot as a container representing the structure of language. (3) The thread as a link, which will later become the path of the logos. It is the ambiguity between the knot as structure of spaces and as pattern of string that will allow the creation of the labyrinth. (B) In the labyrinth we have: (1) The walls of the labyrinth with the central cross representing the "word" unfolding. (2) the self axis that was used to discover a structure but then becomes absent. (3) The meander or void in the labyrinth as logos or path of the logos. (C) As the transformation occurs, the two triangles join and belong to different planes, thus creating a pyramid (illustration D) showing new relations, and a new ridge, representing the path from breath (pneuma) to Word (verbum), which is a mystery.

energy becomes the sound "OM," and spirit becomes a flame or a bird. Yet the message of the myth isn't that space is a pillar or that the spirit is a pigeon, but that everything is a sign, everything signals.

The Center

As we come to a better understanding of the role played by the central cross of the labyrinth and its symbolic meaning suggesting the "One," the Creator-Word, or Brahman wishing to become the many, we can better grasp the complexity and ambivalence in the ancient notion of the center, a center that is everywhere and whose circumference is nowhere.

It is impossible to define a center in a loose knot, as the configuration of the knot can change. In the labyrinth on the other hand, the center is well defined by the central cross, though in an ambiguous way. The labyrinth's center can be defined both by the cross whose branches form the wall of the labyrinth and by the end of the path located between two branches of the cross; it is thus defined by a conjunction. But in another sense, as we have seen before, since the point at the end of the path in the labyrinth corresponds to a break of the meander, it is the same as the point marking the entrance to the labyrinth. Somehow the center (or the point that breaks the line of the meander) is no longer a dimensionless point; it becomes as a wave progressing in all dimensions and enveloping the whole pattern. The center is then also suggested by the entrance to the labyrinth, which represents the point of emergence into this world or else a door leading out of this world. This entrance therefore represents the center here on earth connected to a center located elsewhere. There would thus be two double centers since both of them establish contact with the central cross, which is also a center. (The fact that the pathway touches the central cross two more times is puzzling, but can indicate that the process of transformation must be completed in order for the goal of the mythic quest to be reached, or for the central cross to take on its full symbolic meaning.)

So we are dealing with a dialectic of centers which corresponds to the dialectic of the axes and which includes the entire network of relations among all the centers presented by the crosses that appear on the projection of the knot (each cross being the symbol of a center). A similar dialectic governs the relationship among the centers represented in the human body by the *chakras*. Each *chakra* is both an entrance and a stage on a pathway that unites all the other centers and leads to unity. Together, the *chakras* suggest a progression and a sort of ladder that finally leads to a center situated outside of the body, above the head or everywhere.

The double center of the labyrinth is not really the same as the center of the knot. Before the transformation of the knot, the center existed only in potential. The center in the labyrinth is located in another dimension and can be projected anywhere in the three-dimensional world, depending on the point of view or the perspective taken. *Thus the mythic center is re-created or actualized in a geometric or spiritual process rather than rediscovered; it is man's task to re-create his gods and reconstruct his source in an evolving world.* It is perhaps this power that constitutes his freedom. Since the center is anywhere in ordinary life, it is as much at the center of the labyrinth as between each step of the pilgrim, who must not expect anything different to be given to him on a silver platter at the end of his journey. Neither here nor there can the center be found. The labyrinth simply indicates that the re-creation of the center requires a complex process. This can explain why skeptical philosophers are so vehemently opposed to the idea of "logocentrism," since for them there is effectively no absolute meaning, no single truth, but rather an infinite potential inherent in a world that allows an indefinite number of meanings to be discovered or elaborated. This elaboration may seem to correspond to our pursuit, but, in fact, since it does not lead to unity, it corresponds to the maze and not to the labyrinth.

This apparent inconsistency between a dual or fourfold conception of the center is also apparent in

India, in Rome, and particularly in ancient Ireland. The center of Ireland is located at Tara but also in Uisnech. In Tara the center is represented by a fort where the kings of Ireland came together, but also by a stone called Fál or the Stone of Knowledge, which cried out when touched by the man destined to be the next king; later on it was also called the "Penis of Fergus." "One story speaks of a more elaborate ritual in which the cry of Fál is preceded by a symbolical rebirth. There were two flagstones at Tara, called Blocc and Bluigne, which stood so close together that one's hand could only pass sideways between them. When they accepted a man, they would open before him until his chariot went through. 'And Fál was there, the "stone penis" at the head of the chariot-course; when a man should have the kingship, it screeched against his chariot axle, so that all might hear.'"[4]

The center is also represented at Uisnech by a blaze originally lit by Mide, the chief of the druids. There is a seat associated with this hearth under which the cut tongues of the druids were buried. But at Uisnech a double of this center is also presented by the "stone of division," which is like the navel of the earth and near which there is a well from which, legend holds, the great flood would surge forth. This duality, which is itself doubled, is recalled in yet a different way by the numerous minor centers spread across Ireland.

Fig. 19.5. Cretan seals showing three images of an axis on the same three-sided seal

20

The Hopi Labyrinths

The word does not come alone.
—Dogon saying

The Hopi Indians of Arizona also use the symbol of the Cretan labyrinth, especially during the Wuwuchim ceremony, but they combine it with a second labyrinth that has a double entrance and a square shape (see fig. 20.1).

In *The Book of the Hopi*, Frank Waters describes how the meaning of these two symbols is connected to the emergence myth:

> In the circular type [which corresponds to the Cretan labyrinth] . . . the center of the cross . . . symbolizes the Sun Father, the giver of life. . . . All the lines and passages within the maze form the universal plan of the creator which man must follow on his Road of life; and the four points [where the branches of the labyrinth wall end] represent the cardinal or directional points embraced within this universal plan of life. "Double security" or rebirth to one who follows the plan is guaranteed, as shown by the same enfoldment of the child by the mother. The additional meaning this circular type offers is that it also symbolizes the concentric boundaries of the land traditionally claimed by the Hopis, who have secret shrines planted along them.

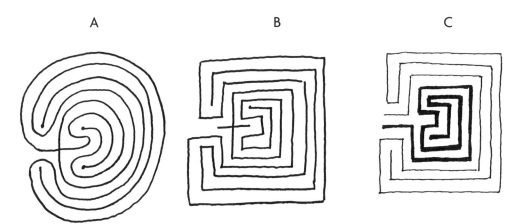

A   B   C

Fig. 20.1
(A) The first Hopi labyrinth; four branches of a central cross. (B) The second Hopi labyrinth; two branches of the central cross are eliminated or indicated only by a short bar. Note: The doubling of the path corresponds, then, to a dividing of the wall.
(C) The two paths in the second labyrinth.

Plate 1. *Shoowa textile from the Congo.*

Plate 2. *Shoowa textile from the Congo.*

Plate 3. Mola made by the Cuna Indians of Panama.

Plate 4. Mola made by the Cuna Indians of Panama.

Plate 5.
Funerary banner painted on silk—found in the grave of Dame Dai at Mawangdui. It shows the lady in old age (in the middle), dead (at the bottom), and resuscitated as a young woman (above and within the knot, replacing the sign of the Tao).

Plate 5 detail.
The knot replacing the sign of the Tao above. This knot can correspond to three cycles of the Tao sign linked together.

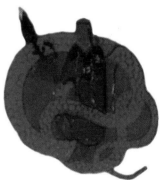

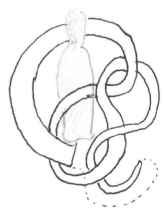

Plate 6.
Suzhou, *by Brice Marden, 1995–96.*

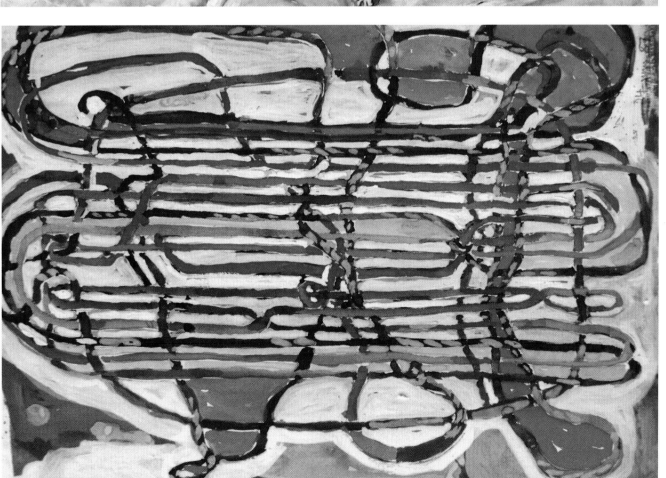

Plate 8. Emanation and Absorption (*in the Tibetan Mode*), 1999.

Plate 7. Ariadnae, 1980.

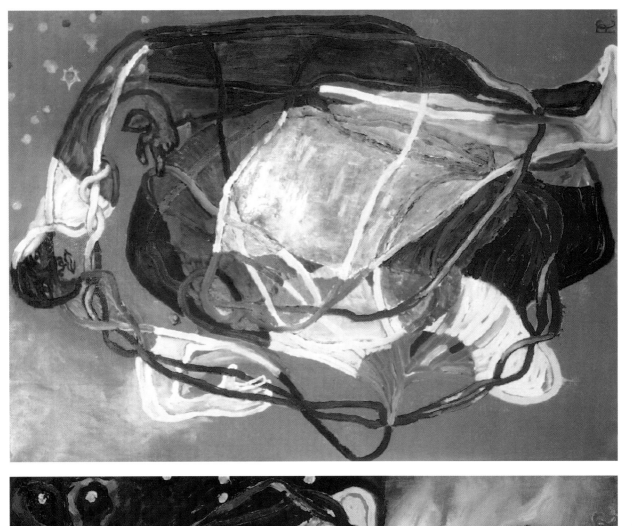

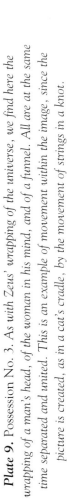

Plate 10. Possession No. 1.
Here the woman plays cat's cradle with the man's mind.

Plate 9. Possession No. 3. *As with Zeus' wrapping of the universe, we find here the wrapping of a man's head, of the woman in his mind, and of a funnel. All are at the same time separated and united. This is an example of movement within the image, since the picture is created, as in a cat's cradle, by the movement of strings in a knot.*

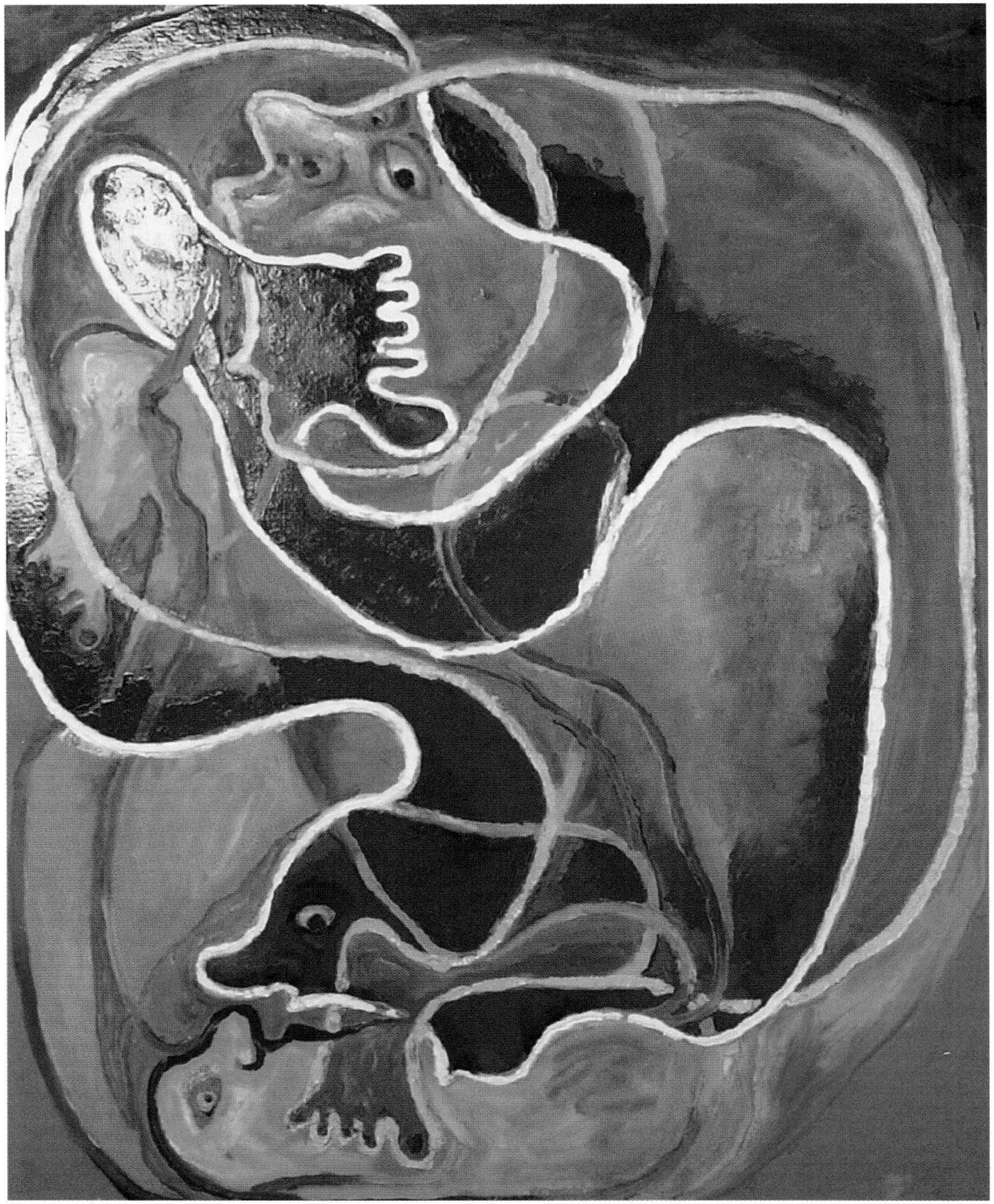

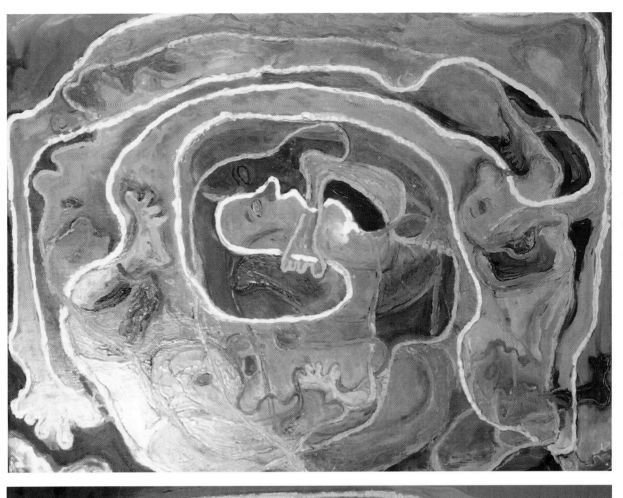

Plate 11. In the Labyrinth No. 3, 2001. This is an example of the formation of the simplest labyrinth, starting with a moving figurative knot, as in fig. 26.1C.

Plate 12. In the Labyrinth No. 2. Here the labyrinth corresponds to a knot crossed five times.

Plate 13. The Perilous Seat, 1998.
Application of the topologic transformation to a chair.

Plate 14. The Seat of Oblivion, *1997. Geometry applied to several chairs.*

Plate 15.
*Volotovo Fresco.
The archangel
Gabriel is holding a
mirror reflecting the
Divine Word.*

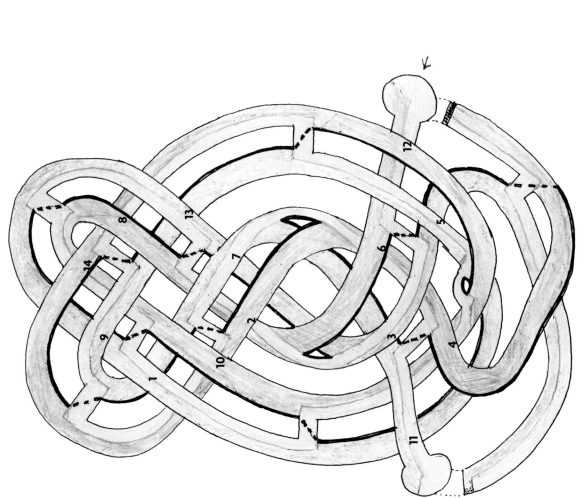

Plate 16. *The maze containing the path of the labyrinth. Two knots crossed seven times and intertwined can also constitute the new path of the maze (one in red, the other in blue). The path of the labyrinth (in yellow) and that of the self axis (in black) that joins these two knots and borrows the path of the image, also become like knots with seven crossings. This image contains many other paths that use a combination of the path of the labyrinth and that of the maze, and since all of them will become knots that have seven crossings, this image can become like the one in Plate 17.*

Plate 17. *This maze contains only six knots. To reach the center of the maze one must follow each knot and find a connection between them. The connections are marked a, b, c, d, and e. The colors of the different knots and the few connections make the travel to the center easier. This maze corresponds to the computations of a pilgrim trying to find the structure of the knot, not the center of the labyrinth. The pilgrim proceeding this way can never find this center and he will wander incessantly in a maze that becomes ever more intricate, invisible, and proliferating.*

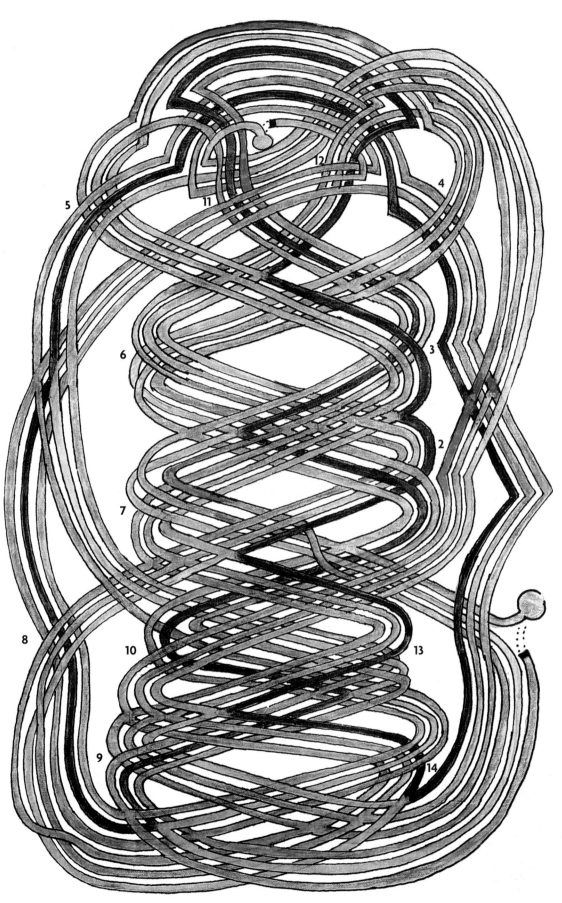

Plate 18.
A maze evoking a vortex based on two separate knots.

Plate 19. *The maze of the Book of Durrow, 680 A.D.*

Plate 20. John the Forerunner, *Sr. Sophia Novgorod School, late 15th century, now at the Moscow Museum. One can note the resemblance between the writing on the parchment and the letter-like lines for the folds of the cloth.*

Plate 21. *Detail of* The Transfiguration *mosaic of the 6th century. Refectory of St. Catherine, Sinai. The rays of light continue the lines of the folds.*

Plate 23. *Detail of* The Last Judgement, *St. Catherine in Chora, Istanbul. The scene showing the sky rolled into a book is inspired by Revelation 6:14: "and the skies will withdraw like a book that is rolled." This shell can also be the one that Dedalus symbolically crossed with a thread and the help of an ant.*

Plate 22. The Giving of the Law to Moses, *early 13th century, St. Catherine of Sinai. The cloth is like a continuation of the book or of the pages of the book, which now become folded in such a way that the text can present a new meaning.*

Plate 24. In Assisi, a man extends a cape at the feet of St. Francis. Fresco by Giotto, c. 1300.

Plate 25.

St. Francis gives his coat to a beggar.
Detail of a dyptic by Sasseta. Sasseta
Sienese School, c. 1430, National
Gallery, London.

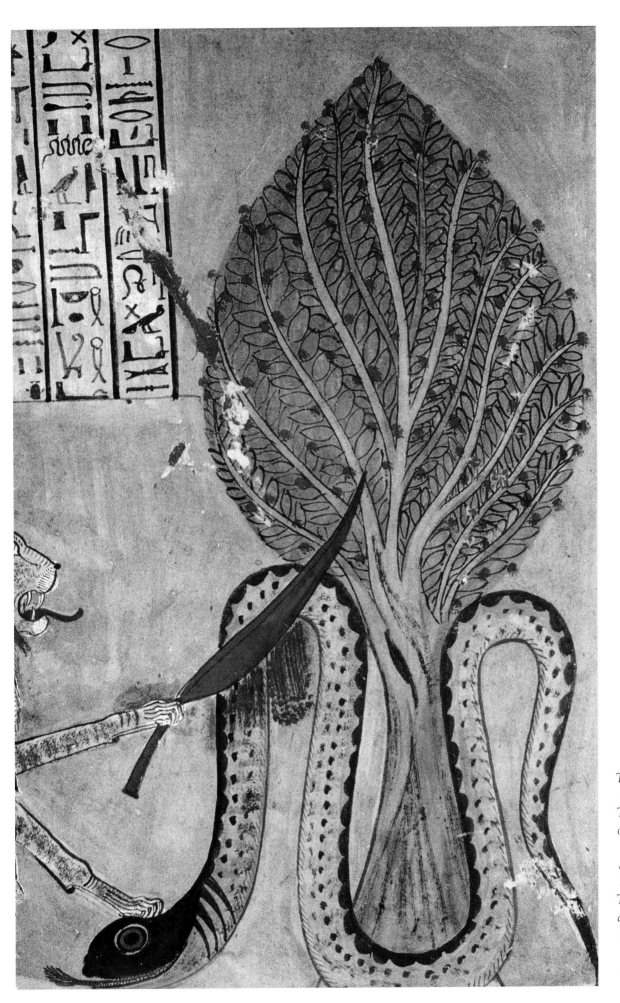

Plate 26.
*The cat of Re cutting
the serpent Apopis.
This is also an image
of the Creation or of
the Tree of Life
appearing out of the
body of the serpent.
The feather replacing
a knife indicates that
the whole scene has
many possible
symbolic meanings.*

Plate 27. Interlaced initials. From the Book of Kells.

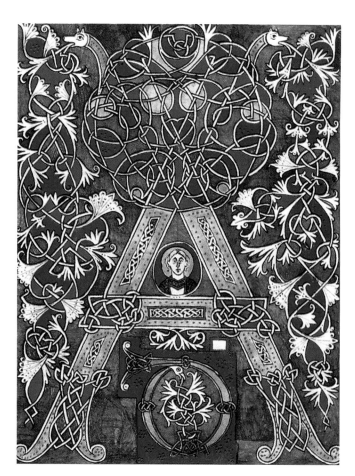

Plate 28. Letter A from the Gradual of Albi, 11th century.

Plate 29. Writing called "mason kufic," 1659–60, mosque Tilla Kari, Samarkand. It represents a blend of the code of the Arabic alphabet and the technique of the laying of bricks. The writing forms a sort of maze and spells the name of the first four caliphs.

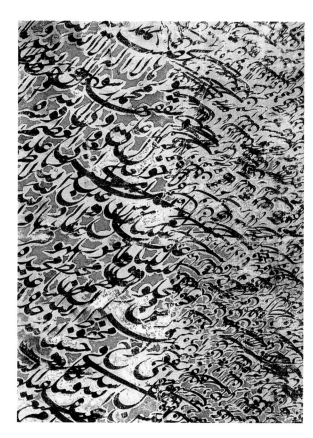

Plate 30. A combination of shikasta and nastaliq calligraphy from Persia.

The square type commonly known as Tapu'at [mother and child] represents spiritual rebirth from one world to the succeeding one, as symbolized by the emergence itself. In this drawing the straight line emerging from the entrance is not connected with the maze. Its two ends symbolize the two stages of life—the unborn child within the womb of the mother and the child after it is born, the line symbolizing the umbilical cord and the path of emergence. . . . The inside lines represent the fetal membranes which enfold the child within the womb, and the outside lines the mother's arms which hold it later.

A structural parallel to this mother and child symbol is the kiva, itself the mother earth. The *sipapuni*, the small hole in the floor, represents the womb, place of emergence from the preceding world; and the ladder leading out through the roof for another Emergence to the succeeding world is the umbilical cord. Enactment of the Emergence is given during Wuwuchim, when initiates undergo spiritual rebirth."[1]

The complementarity of meaning (father-mother) given to the two symbols is in accord with their shape. The circular labyrinth presents a single path limited by a double enclosure, whereas the second one presents a double path limited by a single enclosure (if we don't take into account the short bar of the central cross, which doesn't play a structural role). The fact that both symbols are engraved on opposite sides of a single stone can be interpreted as showing that the new labyrinth is like the reverse of the first.

If the geometry of the labyrinth is truly the origin of the pattern, the second Hopi labyrinth should be obtainable from the same knot by way of a new transformation corresponding to this new reversal. Based on the previous analysis, we can intuitively predict that the opposing side of the Cretan labyrinth will be obtained by pivoting its entire path around its axis of symmetry. To this effect, if we examine the torus knot (see fig. 20.2), we can observe that the new labyrinth can be obtained by pivoting half the loops of the meander around their partial axes of symmetry (which corresponds to pivoting the entire meander around half of the double axis).

A pivoting movement around the axes of symmetry is then translated by a reversal of meaning of the symbol that changes from a beyond or a hereafter in which the "map of the creator" of father sun is drawn to a life on earth describing a birth or emergence on mother earth. The processes of evolution and involution, of creation and procreation, are thus described as linked by a reversal that is more complex than a simple reversal of direction on the same path. As the center of the Cretan labyrinth represents an eternal moment containing all things past and future, it includes in a latent form all kinds of breaks and passages (including, for example, the expulsion of Adam and Eve from paradise). But in order to ensure that the birth and the severing of the umbilical cord are specifically represented, a new geometric overthrow is necessary. Thus the series of transformations and the symbols associated with them seem unending. The meanings of these symbols, which can be represented in so many different ways (and mentioned in myths in so many different contexts), are as if linked by a sort of algebra that itself corresponds to geometry.

The transformation of the Hopi labyrinth undoubtedly presents problems that we are unable to solve. For example, it is difficult to define rationally the principle according to which the meander is broken at the point where it crosses on itself (as is fig. 20.3E).

As I have already mentioned, in order to obtain the new pattern of the meander, we cannot simply change the order of crossings on the torus knot (as in fig. 20.2). Since we are dealing with a knot, even if it is a torus knot, in order to pivot the loops of the meander without having them twisted or crossed, the self axis must be crossed or twisted several times (see fig. 20.3).

The combinations of crossings of the self-axis that provoke the permutations can be obtained in several

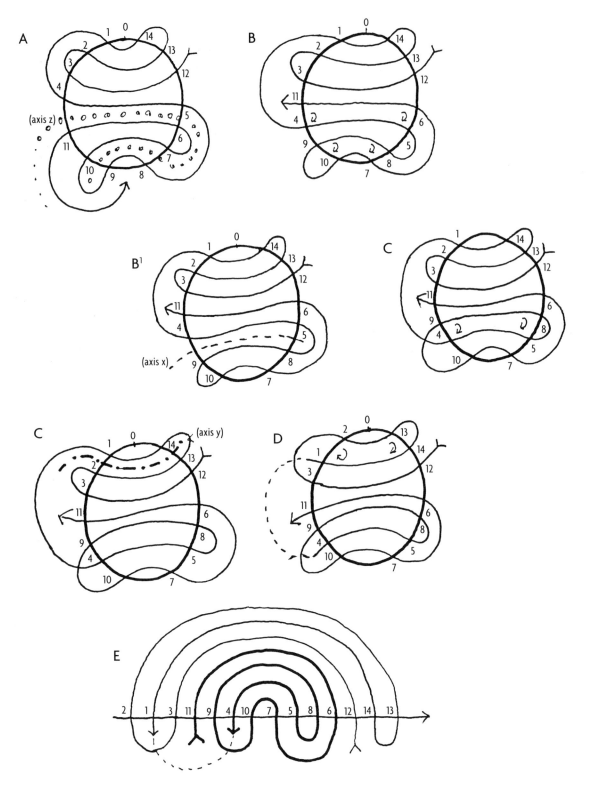

Fig. 20.2. The path of the second Hopi labyrinth is obtained by turning the entire meander around its axis or around half the double axis.

(A) We begin by marking one arm of the double axis. (B)When pivoting the arms of the meander around this axis the crossings 4, 5 and 9, 8 are changed. (B¹) Then we mark half of the second arm of the double axis. (C) One pivots the corresponding arms of the meander. The places of 9 and 5 are changed. In illustrations C and D, we mark half of the third arm of the double axis and then pivot the corresponding arms of the meander. The places of 1 and 14 are changed. We have thus turned around half the four arms of the double axis—and if we cut the meander where it crosses itself, we obtain the meander of the second Hopi labyrinth at 9 in (E).

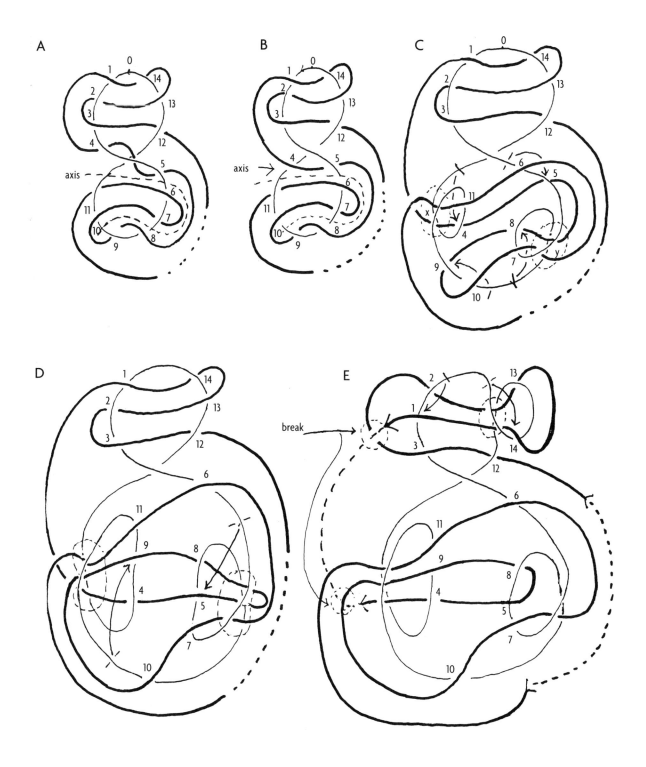

Fig. 20.3. The crossing of the self axis that produces the path of the second Hopi labyrinth

In order to obtain a complete shift of the meander, one must twist the self axis several times. With this operation new loops are formed on the self axis. (A and B) Path of first Hopi labyrinth with the first axis of symmetry in dots. (C) To pivot the meander around this axis of symmetry, one must twist the self axis at (x and y). One obtains the same order of crossings as in fig. 20.2B. (D) To pivot the meander around the second axis of symmetry, no new twist is necessary; one can slide the meander. One obtains the same order as in fig. 20.2C. (E) To pivot the meander around the last axis of symmetry, one more twist of the self axis is necessary on top. We obtain then the same display as in the second Hopi labyrinth.

different ways, and the relation between crossings and permutations poses an interesting mathematical problem. An ingenious mathematician should be able to solve this problem algebraically, perhaps with the help of a system like the matrix.

If we were dealing with the tie knot as it is actually tied, the superimposition of the crossings on the torus knot would be different (see fig. 16.7). The permutation of the loops would then be simpler and would not require new crossings of the self axis. It is then important to consider the symbolism of the actual tie knot.

It seems possible to find traces of algebraic operations in certain Cretan seals or on images like those on the ring of Minos. We can sometimes observe what appears to be a system of parentheses or brackets that are themselves represented by symbols that act as operators on other symbols contained within them. In the myth, the meaning of images produced by figures of language is also affected by other elements of figurative language acting as operators. Each symbol can be considered simultaneously as operator and as datum, as a sign for a process and as a product of it.

Moreover, since the geometry explains the relationship between myths and rituals, it can also reveal the relationship between, on one side, the symbolic figures corresponding to the images evoked by myths and, on the other side, the more abstract patterns describing the woven structure of myths—one could say between the symbols that are the data and the operators or between the algebra and the geometry. Sometimes they can replace each other, and sometimes they are combined. One discovers a fundamental unity behind the diversity of ancient arts.

Fig. 20.4. These Cretan seals seem to evoke a Kiva with its ladder leading out to a new emergence

4
The Maze

21

The Concept of the Maze

We are all immersed in language.
—NIELS BOHR

Up to this point, we have considered that the maze evoked by the myths was a knot that could be wandered through or crossed in many different ways. The number of choices could correspond to a branching of the paths suggested by the Greek myth. But does an image exist that represents a maze of branching paths more directly? We shall see that an analysis of the pattern produced by geometry results in just such an image.

Up to this point the fundamental method used to build the labyrinth consisted in following the thread and in observing the way in which the branches of crossed thread joined each other. For example, as illustrated in figure 21.1, we concluded that

the segment of cord that crosses the self axis at point *1* will cross it again at point *2*. But the segment that crosses at *1* could just as easily be thought of as meeting the self axis at point *5*, since on the knot these two segments are the same, or fused. There are thus two different ways to chart the knot, and by juxtaposing them we obtain a branching path of the meander.

In figure 21.2, if we replace certain parts of the ancient version of the torus knot by this new path, we can obtain, depending on the number of segments replaced, either two distinct knots, as in C, or a new knot similar to the Malekulan tracings, as in D, or a torus knot (equivalent to the torus obtained when a cross on the knot is replaced by a ring), as in E.

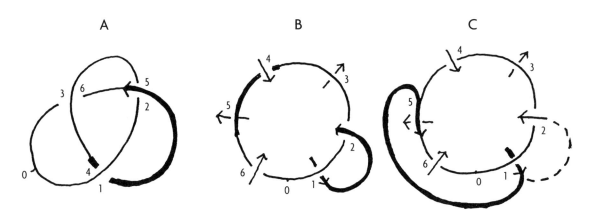

Fig. 21.1
(A) The knot. (B) The path of the labyrinth. (C) The other path of the maze.

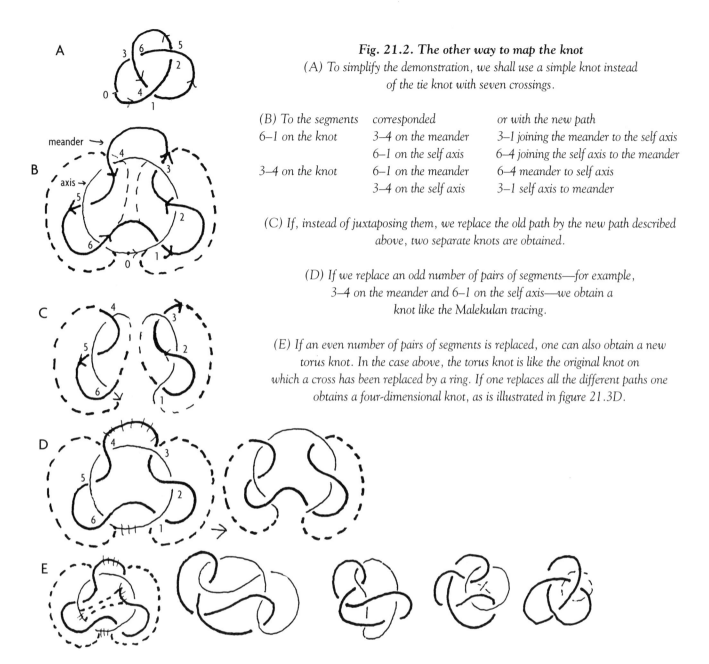

Fig. 21.2. The other way to map the knot

(A) To simplify the demonstration, we shall use a simple knot instead of the tie knot with seven crossings.

(B) To the segments   corresponded   or with the new path

6–1 on the knot	3–4 on the meander	3–1 joining the meander to the self axis
	6–1 on the self axis	6–4 joining the self axis to the meander
3–4 on the knot	6–1 on the meander	6–4 meander to self axis
	3–4 on the self axis	3–1 self axis to meander

(C) If, instead of juxtaposing them, we replace the old path by the new path described above, two separate knots are obtained.

(D) If we replace an odd number of pairs of segments—for example, 3–4 on the meander and 6–1 on the self axis—we obtain a knot like the Malekulan tracing.

(E) If an even number of pairs of segments is replaced, one can also obtain a new torus knot. In the case above, the torus knot is like the original knot on which a cross has been replaced by a ring. If one replaces all the different paths one obtains a four-dimensional knot, as is illustrated in figure 21.3D.

In figure 21.3, if we replace all the segments that constitute the path of the labyrinth, we obtain, according to the way the new segments are disposed and superimposed, either two more complex knots, or two knots similar to the original one. Depending on the way the segments are disposed, the knots can be interlaced, superimposed, or juxtaposed. Thus the geometry can produce not only a doubling of the cord but also a doubling of the knot.

In figure 21.3 C, if we represent the old path and the new path of the labyrinth at the same time, we obtain an image of the maze. The new figure presents

a path that continually branches and the image of a four-dimensional knot. The original knot constitutes a part or a section of this new four-dimensional knot, and the path of the labyrinth becomes an interdimensional path that is difficult to distinguish.

In figure 21.4, the same pattern of the new path of the maze can also be obtained by modifyng the original torus configuration (we then arrive at two interlaced false knots). Thus the new path can also correspond to a movement of the torus knot.

In figure 21.5 we discover that reciprocally (in the special case when the new path is presented as

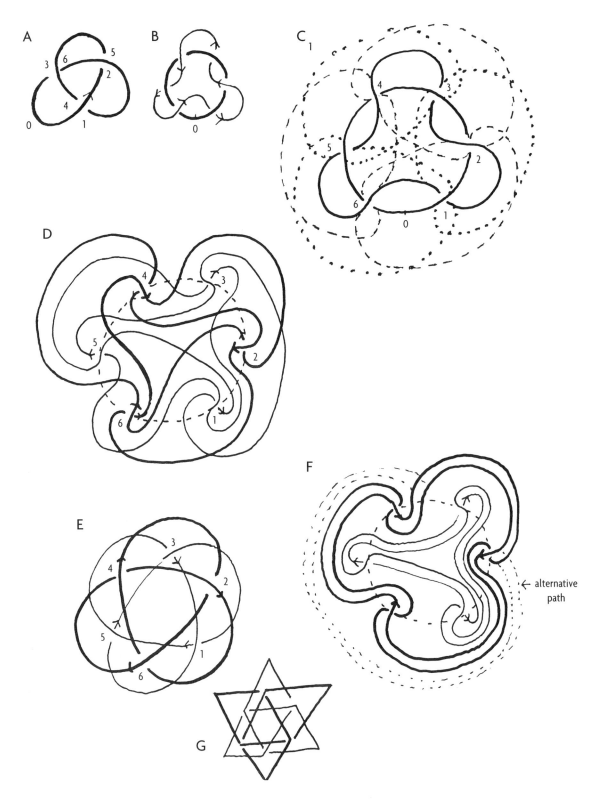

Fig. 21.3. The four-dimensional knot of the maze

Here again for the sake of simplicity we shall use a threefold knot, but the reasoning applies to the knot crossed seven times, which produces the labyrinth. (A) The simple knot. (B) Path of labyrinth. (C) By mapping together all the possible paths, we obtain a four-dimensional knot. The overlapping of the string is undetermined and thus so is the exact nature of the knot. (D) Here, only the new path is presented. By following another way, the path shows two simple knots interwoven as in illustration E. The twist in the knot is similar to that on the mosaic in figure 17.5. (E) Shows illustration D simplified. (F) The pattern depends on the placing of the new path. It can also be modified to represent two knots contained within each other, or two knots separated. (G) Shows illustration E, transformed into a Solomon's seal.

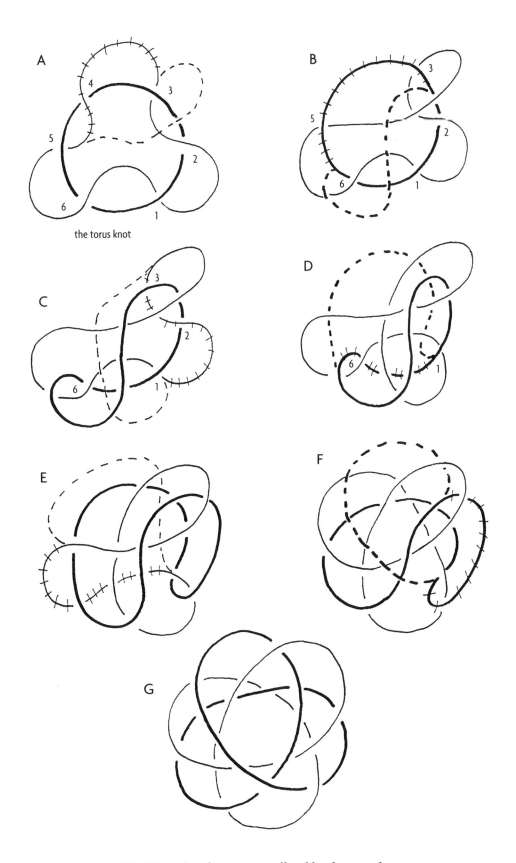

A

the torus knot

B

C

D

E

F

G

Fig. 21.4. Another pattern offered by the torus knot

Each path described as a barred line is moved to the position marked by dots. Starting from a simple torus knot, we can obtain in illustration G the same pattern as in figure 21.3E. (G) The torus knot modified. Two interwoven false knots present the same pattern as the two interwoven real knots in figure 21.3E. This drawing could also be obtained with a particular overlapping of the string of the new path, as in figure 21.5. Thus, reciprocally, the new path of the maze can coincide with that of the labyrinth.

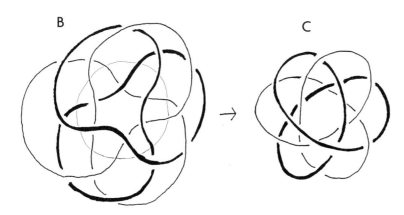

A — Former position of the self axis

4
3
5
2
6
1

↓

B **C**

→

Fig. 21.5. One particular example of the maze's new path

The pattern of the new path in the maze depends on the superimposition of the branches of this new path. For example, in illustration A one possible new path in the maze finally produces two entwined false knots, the same pattern as in figure 21.4G. (The dots represent the change of position of the path). Thus it is shown how the path of the maze can coincide with that of the labyrinth. (B) The two entwined knots in a simplified pattern. (C) The pattern as in figure 21.4G. Because, as in figure 21.4G, this pattern can be modified and transformed into the original torus knot, the maze can finally coincide with the labyrinth.

two interlaced false knots), the maze knot can take on the form of the labyrinth or coincide with it.

By joining all the possible trajectories, we have obtained a new image that coincides perfectly with that of the maze suggested by the myth. The new combination of pathways corresponds to logic and is a rational way of considering the original knot, though this new way, which adds a second degree of reasoning, is no longer coherent with the process or the vision that produced the path of Ariadne's thread. Thus the maze of the myth corresponds to a hybrid way of perceiving the knot or the whole. The confusion produced by this maze comes from another confusion, or a mixing of heterogeneous conceptions at the origin of its construction. The maze, like the Minotaur, is a hybrid and a bastard.

We can retain the following principle from this observation: The diagrams cannot be considered separately from the method or the vision that originally gave them form. According to Kant, mathematics essentially consists of a method for building diagrams. It is perhaps because the principle we have just formulated is not always respected that the math and physics that rely on it proliferate without offering a unified system that corresponds to a coherent vision.

The new image of the maze does not only represent the world or the whole as we confusedly perceive it, or language as we use it. It can also represent how consciousness produces an image of the world. According to recent scientific theory, this consciousness would be produced from a flux of information transmitted through a complex network of neurons. This network can itself be represented schematically by the new knot-maze. A strange new coincidence results between the image of the multidimensional knot as a symbol produced by consciousness and the same image representing the process producing this consciousness. Ordinary consciousness produces its own image, and the unconscious, when it becomes true consciousness, would correspond not to an added complexity, but to a more simple itinerary through the labyrinth and to a coherence that would, progressively and paradoxically, lead to both an extinction and a plenitude.

This maze could be compared to a diagram like the one in figure 21.6. This acentric diagram, called by its author the "Geometry of the Spirit," constitutes a maze, for if each station is the destination to which all the others lead, we can also say that each station indefinitely sends us toward the others and thus cannot be considered an end in itself. The dia-

gram therefore represents a closed world. As Kafka has shown, a maze is not necessarily a chaos and can be organized in a superlative way, created precisely by an abuse of codification and considerations that reveal themselves contradictory, or rather disparate, like the geometry of the maze.

When the world becomes a maze, so does language. Thus in the ancient world, when alphabets were secret, we find codes like that of the Ogam Tract (fig. 21.7), which corresponded to laws of harmony and which could be used for both poetry and chanting as well as for magic and divination.

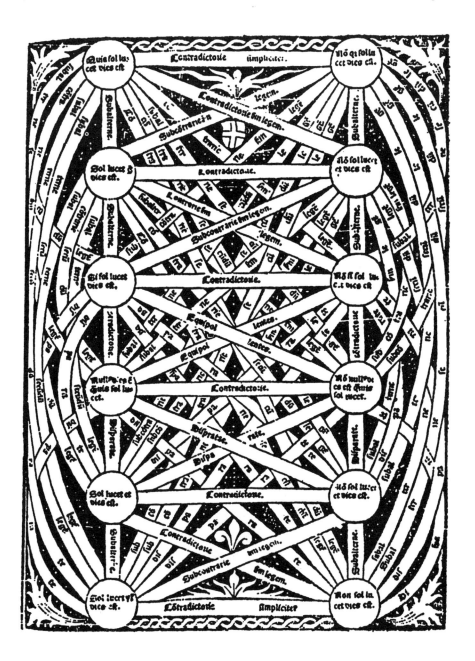

*Fig. 21.6. The Geometry
of the Spirit*

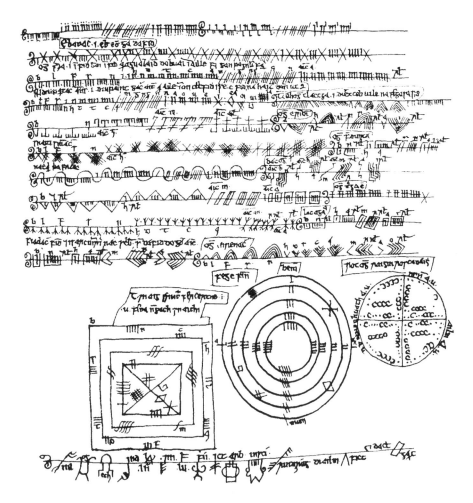

Fig. 21.7. Ogam Tract of ancient Irish script

It was supposedly used in poetry to show the relationships between different symbolic meanings of the letters of the ogam alphabet.
Illustration by Sean O' Boyle from *Ogam: the Poet's Secret*, 1980.

But we have seen that the construction or apparition of the maze depends upon that of the labyrinth. It follows that the Ogam Tract and the diagram of the Geometry of the Spirit can also correspond to a labyrinth, either a labyrinth in gestation or (in the eyes of the uninitiated) a labyrinth in disguise. As in the Tree of Life of the Kabbalists, each station of the diagram of the Geometry of the Spirit would thus correspond to a local or transitory center giving access to an ultimate center representing unity. In the same way, the letters of the Ogam Tract could be organized into mantras, which were considered to be the residence or dwelling place (one might say the phone number) of gods or spirits, or else they could constitute the heraldry of the organic erotic body, itself considered a gestalt uniting the subtle and gross bodies. In tantrism, there are mantras that correspond to the chakras on the human body. Their effective recitation by the practitioner represents a path leading to freedom.

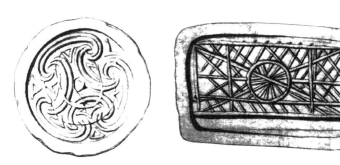

Fig. 21.8. Cretan seals
On the left is a design similar to figure 21.3.

22

Why a Four-Dimensional Knot?

square can be thought of as a two-dimensional section of a cube. The cube is represented on a plane by joining the corners of two squares two by two. Similarly, to represent a four-dimensional cube, the angles of two cubes must be joined, as shown in figure 22.1B and C.

We have spoken of the maze as a four-dimensional knot, and this leads us to the question, How might a knot be represented in four dimensions? The answer is simple: by drawing two identical knots and joining the corresponding crossings. This is precisely (and unexpectedly) how the new figure of the maze is produced. We are thus dealing with the image of a four-dimensional knot.

But as was previously indicated, the labyrinth already included a fourth dimension of time and space, and we should recognize in the new pattern at least five space-time dimensions, even if we have difficulty defining or conceptualizing them. The new knot-maze thus abounds with different interpenetrating and transforming worlds. It contains the original knot, tracings similar to those of the Malekula, ring systems, and finally the path of the labyrinth.

The image offered by the maze of the multidimensional knot constitutes a kind of hyphen between an ancient concept of space that remains psychological and blurry for us and the more obscure concepts of modern science. The topologist René Thom, who created catastrophe theory, follows another line of reasoning to conclude that "there is no major discontinuity between primitive magical thought and modern scientific thought."

In his description of the magical world, G. Simondon presented space-time as a given, a universal substratum of the reticulation defined by the "key points."

A

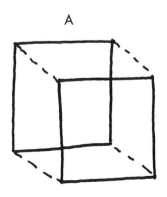

B

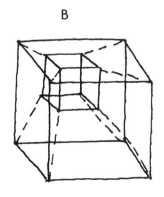

C

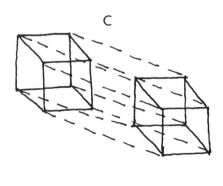

Fig. 22.1
(A) A three-dimensional cube. (B) and (C) A four-dimensional cube.

But we can ask ourselves if reticulation is not the first datum, where the global construction of space-time only comes into play by a process of concatenation from spaces engendered by the bursting process associated with the central points. . . . It is striking to see, in any case, that this image appears in the model of the Big Bang that is currently accepted in cosmology, as well as in the basic pattern of quantum mechanics where a particle that is at first located spreads into a wave that . . . immediately occupies all of space. . . .

Perhaps there is the image of a biological behavior underlying this archetype: an embryo that develops and, once adult, explores its vicinity in order to deposit an egg that will perpetuate it.[1]

The image of the knot with n dimensions leaves us with some new questions. For example, does one who, like a shaman, travels psychically in another dimension find oneself in another world, or does one remain in the same world that is only perceived differently? The symbol representing the world also corresponds to an experience and a perception; is there consciousness of new dimensions as we have described them in this experience, or only a change in appearances? Does the experience give access to new knowledge that is incompatible with the ancient, or does it modify knowledge by relativizing it? Does a shaman change the world like Christopher Columbus discovering a new continent, or does he discover a new world like a child who leaves his mother's womb? Is this new world an absurd and aggravating topsy-turvy world like the one discovered by Alice in Wonderland? If this journey corresponds to a doubling of consciousness that accompanies the doubling of the knot, are there then two separate understandings of this doubling, or rather of a threshold that reveals a pre-existing division of the world in several domains? Are the sky, hell, and limbo elsewhere or within us? Does the inner world also exist beyond our familiar sphere?

The myth seems to offer several different answers, like that of the Minotaur, that of Theseus or Aeneas, and that of Daedalus, but it is the questions that correspond to these answers that remain naive and difficult to formulate. The answers send the one who decodes the myth back to himself, revealing how little he knows of the human condition and how limited his language and experience is. In myths:

> The multiplicity of world-planes and of qualities of space indicates the richness of manifest being. It demonstrates that known existence cannot be rendered by any single image. More important than that, this multiplicity proves that space itself is, in its essence, a manifestation of the meaning of existence in whatever form. Furthermore, the variety of perceptible spaces shows that human awareness, enriched by the imagination, can encounter multiple kinds of beings on its own terms.[2]

Other conclusions that are comparable to those the myths offer us are proposed in quantum mechanics by theories that attempt to explain the collapse of a wave function when a particle is localized.

> According to the Everett-Wheeler-Graham theory, at the moment the wave function "collapses," the universe splits into two worlds. . . . There are two distinct editions of me. Each one of them is doing something different, and each one of them is unaware of the other. Nor will their (our) paths ever cross since the two worlds into which the original one split are forever separate branches of reality.

> In other words, according to the Copenhagen Interpretation of Quantum Mechanics, the development of the Schrödinger wave equation generates an endlessly proliferating number of possibilities. According to the Everett-Wheeler-Graham theory, the development of the Schrödinger wave equation generates an endlessly proliferating number of *different branches of reality!* This theory is called, appropriately, the Many Worlds Interpretation of Quantum Mechanics.

> The theoretical advantage of the Many Worlds Interpretation is that it does not require an "external observer" to "collapse" one of the possibilities

contained in a wave function into physical reality. According to the Many Worlds theory, wave functions do not collapse, they just keep splitting as they develop according to the Schrödinger wave equation. When a consciousness happens to be present at such a split, it splits also, one part of it associating with one branch of reality and the other part(s) of it associating with the other branch(es) of reality. However, each branch of reality is experientially inaccessible to the other(s), and a consciousness in any one branch will consider that branch to be the entirety of reality.[3]

The dialogue between the ethnologist and the physicist is difficult to establish, as the consciousness that the quantum theory of plural worlds speaks about cannot be the same as the one suggested in the myth. An essential difference between the ancient and the new models is that the n-dimensional knot of the maze also represents a semantic volume in which the meaning attached to the concept of consciousness is transformed; this concept changes with each dimension of the knot and, at the center of the labyrinth, consciousness that was consciousness of something becomes reflexive, aware of its own creative process. It becomes a liberated consciousness that "immediately occupies all of space," insinuating itself at once into all things.

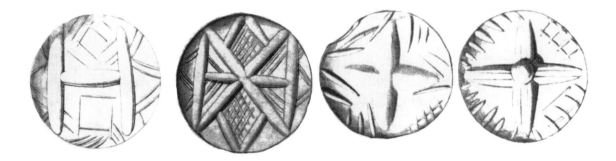

Fig. 22.2. Cretan seals: Inner vision or outer architecture?

23

The Equivalence of
Samsara and Nirvana

Until now we have examined only a new way of mapping that can produce a maze, but not the maze itself as it presents itself to us or as it is created by the mind, which amounts to the same. We can now consider the configuration of the maze that corresponds to the Cretan labyrinth (and therefore to a knot with seven crossings). This maze will lead us to some surprising interpretations. Figure 23.1 represents the new pathway of the maze superimposed on that of the labyrinth. But as we have seen, there are numerous ways to trace the new pathway of the maze. For example, according to the method illustrated in figure 21.3, we can also build it, as shown in plate 16, with two interlaced knots that are similar to the original. We must examine this drawing carefully:

◎ The two interlaced knots represent the new path of the maze.

◎ These two knots are joined by crossing paths or bridges (in yellow), which correspond to the pathway in the labyrinth.

◎ With the simplification of the shape of the maze, the path in the labyrinth in yellow and that of the self axis in black are deformed accordingly, and they also resemble a knot crossed seven times (but since they appear this way because of a folding of the torus knot, this time they are intertwined false knots and not real knots).

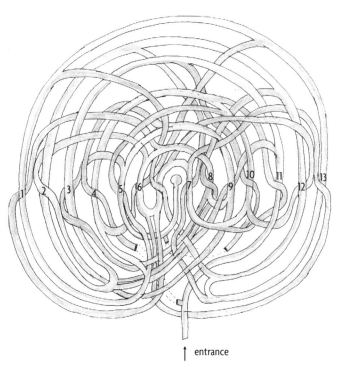

↑ entrance

**Fig. 23.1. The maze corresponding
to the Cretan labyrinth**
*To build this maze one must construct bridges or tunnels.
The new maze is comprised of two knots intertwined
and joined by the path of the labyrinth.*

◎ Somehow the labyrinth path is the same path as before, but it is now folded on itself and leads not to a center but to a place on the exterior surface of the maze knot; the center becomes the way out.

Thus in this maze, the path of the labyrinth leading to freedom becomes folded and acentric, taking on the appearance of the knot that holds us in bondage. From a relative point of view, it seems that the maze becomes completely inextricable. But at the same time, this path through the maze is not a real knot and it can unfold itself when we change the pattern of the maze knot. As we have demonstrated in figure 21.4, when the conditions are favorable, the new path of the maze can coincide with that of the labyrinth.*

Fundamentally and from an absolute point of view, the path through the maze symbolizing bondage and the path through the labyrinth symbolizing freedom are one and the same. With the path of the labyrinth folded like a knot, we obtain an image that can become the symbol of the equivalence or the harmony of samsara and nirvana, the latter being the supreme goal of Mahayana Buddhism. (Line 16 of the Ocean Seal text in figure 2.3 also declares that "samsara and nirvana are always harmonized together.")

The maze in plate 16 presents a great number of possible courses. Now, as we look at it, we must imagine that it corresponds to a situation in life where there is no knot with seven crosses that matches our experience. Nor is there a visual knot that can serve as a symbol of the whole, but only the random discovery of relations between things, between experiences, and between experiences and things. With no overview of the map, the apprentice pilgrim has only vague connections from which he or she attempts to create order in the mind. Without apparent connections among the different courses presented by this single image, all possible paths should be represented separately, just as they appear in the real-life maze. The maze can then be subdivided so as to contain and represent all the pathways combining a part of the path of the maze with a part of the path of the labyrinth. (All of these pathways can become somewhat distinct because while they are followed, the basic knot moves and can change its configuration.) One then obtains a very large number of similar knots. All of these knots can be joined in diverse ways, thereby creating an extremely complex network. The maze in plate 17, which, for reasons of clarity, contains only six such knots, can give some idea of the complexity of the complete maze, which would contain at least thirty connected knots.

But the complexity of this maze that keeps growing as its contours are explored doesn't end here, as the two knots that constitute the path of the maze can be displayed in different ways, either contained one in the other, or separated, or even interlaced in different ways, as in figure 21.3F. The complete maze thus includes a combination of all of these, depending on the whim of its explorer. Constantly changing, proliferating, and becoming infinitely complex, the maze is—for a being bound by the mind—absolutely inescapable (see fig. 23.2).

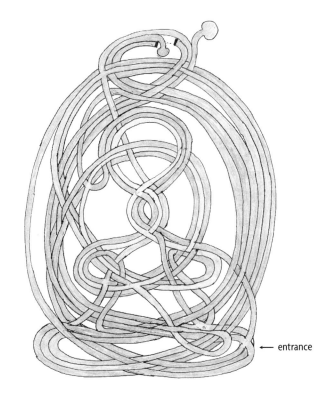

←— entrance

Fig. 23.2. A maze made of two knots contained within each other

---

* We must bear in mind that the order of superimposition of the crossing is aleatory, or dependent on our whim. Thus the change of shape is always theoretically possible.

We have thus discovered the image corresponding to the maze described in the myths, but in order to understand the symbol and the maze in which we live, we must consider it from opposing points of view. To be elucidated fully, the meaning drawn from the context of myths must be projected onto the matrix of the symbol. For Daedalus, who like us built the maze on the base of the labyrinth, it represents the way the universe can organize itself freely and still be connected to the Logos; it represents the perfect integration of knowledge and understanding. On the other hand, when the path of the labyrinth is no longer recognized, the maze represents our knowledge of the universe, whose every part can be infinitely divided and organized in an indefinite number of ways. This is a knowledge that depends on the arrangement of points of view, choices, or the throw of the dice, but that can never be definitive or complete. The maze can then represent the relativity and vanity of our knowledge when it claims to reach a real understanding.

By representing a system of pathways, the geometrical symbol always represents a process rather than a determined object. Hence the difficulty in grasping a precise or unchanging meaning. The process represented by the symbol when the path of the labyrinth is recovered is essentially the one produced by contemplation, a contemplation that, in revealing the basic nature of our illusions, destroys or dissipates these illusions. In contemplation there is no geometry per se, but rather a direct communion and understanding of relationship and the interpenetration of all things. What happens is an immaterial *solve et coagula,* or emanation and absorption, that can be translated into topology only with the use of material cuts, fusions, and amalgamations.

When the lines in the maze become concrete, they represent not only a path for thought processes and experiences but also a path of creation, the lines of force potentially able to produce forms. We encounter once more the principle illustrated by the cat's cradle. As they change configuration, the knots can blend with the contours or the fragments of the volumes or structures representing beings, organic systems, or things. Like those studied in embryology, these structures can be complex, having borders constituted by several different knots fused together. As in quantum physics, the knots of the maze represent both the dance and the dancer, the ray confused with the trace of its moving source. They can represent the diverse aspects of the dance of Shiva.

I have tried to render this maze or this dance in

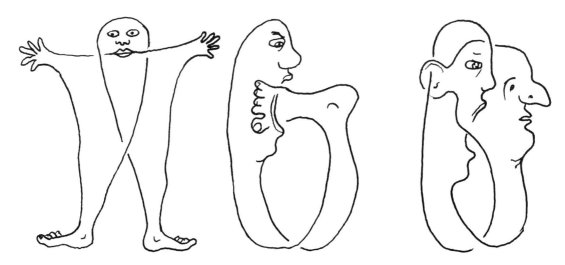

Fig. 23.3. Figurative knots
Starting with a torus knot and two strings superimposed onto the shape of a head interwoven with that of a woman (see plates 9 and 10), and then removing the loops of the torus knot produces curious psychological effects—in this case, the interesting image of a yin-yang interplay, as if the woman surges out of the man's skull and plays cat's cradle with his thoughts.

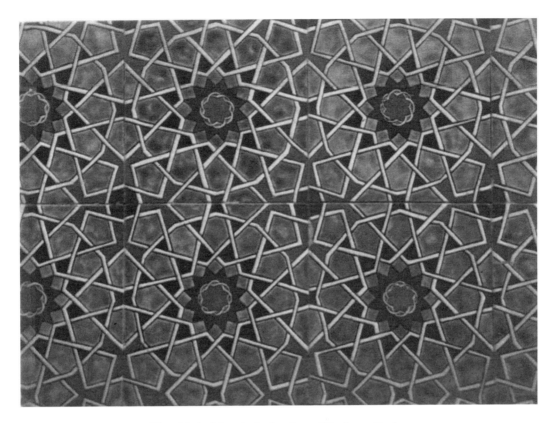

Fig. 23.4. Islamic design from Kütahya, Turkey

other terms by replacing the basic changing and moving knot with a human shape that can express openness or bondage (see fig. 23.3). As in a comic strip, the different positions or shapes taken by the knot can then suggest a story and the resulting figures can provoke new questions about the meaning of the labyrinth geometry and about the different ways to present it in primitive and modern art (see plates 11 and 12).

Besides conforming to all kinds of potential organic structures, the patterns can also surround and delimit shapes or ideal forms that are not topological. This is illustrated by the maze in plate 17 whose shape includes starred polygons. This design was not invented for purely aesthetic reasons, but produced directly by the geometry of the labyrinth. It is interesting that it is reminiscent of Islamic art (see fig. 23.4). It seems to reveal a principle that could have influenced the birth of this art, a principle that would have been partially obscured since, most of the time, Islamic interlacings show examples only of closed mazes, with neither entrance nor exit.

In Islamic art, the forms that appear between the paths of the maze suggest a constellated sky. But these forms can also evoke inner constellations contained within the organic structures just described. The stars of these inner constellations linked by the maze are like the immaterial points of energy known as *bindus* or *tigles*, which are perceived by the yogi through contemplation as being either in space or in the body, like the chakras that are connected by *nadis* or channels. There is no longer a distinction between what is exterior and what is within. When the maze is projected or flattened, the star figures that seemed undefined, broken, or dispersed in a multidimensional space appear distinctly, as if crystallized. One could say that such shapes correspond to those taken by the void when it becomes structured. This can suggest that what the yogi perceives in contemplation is the void taking shape, or the energy of the void becoming structured.

Islamic art thus entails a passage and conversion from topological symbolism to a symbolism of ideal forms, such as circles, triangles, squares, and polygons. As Seyyed Hossein Nasr writes, "Through revelations of this Word or Logos come into being the sacred traditions which, although outwardly different, are inwardly united into a Centre which transcends all forms." Speaking of this mystery at the center, Keith Critchlow adds: "This supreme mystery, manifesting itself as paradox in the human mind to remind it of its inherent limitations, can be expressed variously as: no God but God; no part without whole; no reflection without source. It is no less applicable in the field of geometry: no dimension without all dimensions."[1]

It is this conversion or coincidence among topological, biomorphic, and ideal forms, such as those found in crystals, that becomes crucial in order to understand symbolism as a whole. The topological geometry corresponds to kaleidoscopic optical games, (reflection, refraction, diffraction) that can be evoked by the crystals. It explains the passage from the natural to the conceptual, a passage that corresponds to the one between labyrinth and maze, since the first stands for the Logos, while the second represents the world of discursive thought.

Different mazes based on the same principle, but with some knots separated, could again help us interpret and understand other ancient arts, most notably the Tibetan *tankas*. In the *tankas*, emanation and absorption between guru or master and disciples can be suggested by the outline of flames or clouds of smoke linking the diverse figures represented in different realms. In plate 8, I have replaced figures and joined lines with knots. But I will not pursue this interpretation here, since my concern is not with material questions and historical influences, but rather with other kinds of influences that cannot be demonstrated. I am concerned with developing a way of interrogating an ancient art that always transmitted information and a teaching, or as Gurdjieff called them in his book *All and Everything*, "legominisms." It is a question of discovering a common source at the root of its expansion, a unity, and a continuity behind its diversity. This sort of investigation could open up new possibilities for a contemporary art that would be based on analogous principles, on principles that can transmute and reverse themselves, depending on the circumstances.

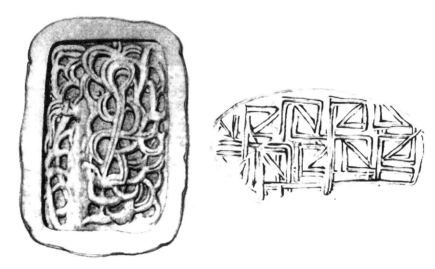

Fig. 23.3. These cretan seals could suggest mazes in formation

24

Different Aspects of Reality

When we contemplate an actual knot made with a cord, it is difficult to accept that it is part of a more complex knot with n dimensions. It seems undeniable that the actual knot constitutes a separate and autonomous entity and that only it is real. But by thinking this way, we confuse the real with a sort of consensus. In a perception we don't really understand, we are satisfied to receive passively a form of the cord as manifesting the presence of the object. We perceive the form as if it included, in an obvious way, the structure of its different pathways and a knot of relations, but without necessarily understanding that the search and the discovery of this structure modify the perception of it.

Even when we examine the substantial, actual knot, however, we can note that the cord is composed of strands or finer threads twisted together. If we imagine a cord made of two strands, for example, then by separating and untangling these two strands, a new, more complex knot appears that includes the first knot as one of its parts. This new knot was already there as a hidden and ignored possibility behind the simpler knot. If we were only to untangle a part of the cord, we would obtain a path of the cord that branches.

In the same way, we can imagine a cord made of three braided strands, themselves composed of fibers twisted together. If we untwist all these fibers, the form of the knot disappears completely. All that remains is a chaotic mass of fibers and the memory of a knot made of twisted space holding all the fibers together.

There is thus a coincidence between the reality

described by geometry and the reality that manifests itself before our eyes and between our fingers when we deconstruct the substantial object or analyze its composition. The truth objectified by the symbol corresponds to a concrete aspect that is directly observable in the object that becomes the symbol.

In figure 24.2, the pattern of a labyrinth is carved on a Chinese incense burner and the incense placed in the groove. As the incense burns, following the path of the labyrinth, the swirls of smoke that rise and drift away produce an ever-changing, ever-new cloud or four-dimensional volume that cannot be memorialized or represented by a single drawing. The smoke is like a composite ribbon or braid, made of incense, that becomes tangled as it unfolds, like a continually changing maze. In this chaotic and blurry image we can recognize continually transforming knots, rings, and meanders, but in the evanescent and

Fig. 24.1. Egyptian designs representing what were probably tombs

Fig. 24.2. This very elaborate incense seal was featured in the Hiang Ch'eng, *a work on aromatics and incense popular in medieval China.*

changing volume of smoke spread out over time, we can no longer distinguish the original labyrinth. Yet this latter constitutes the origin and a section of this volume of smoke that develops in space-time until all of the incense has been burned. The form fades away and melts into space, suggesting the fugitive character of time, while the perfume can perhaps bring back the memory of a garden, perhaps even the labyrinthine Chinese garden with forking paths described by Borges. This suggests how ordinary consciousness is incapable of distinguishing an original form behind those that manifest in a veiled or dissolved fashion, or those that are the goal of an organic process of morphogenesis.

Henri Allan reminds us that this smoke structure can suggest the organization of life itself, which is always between a repetitive order in the crystals and an infinitely complex and unforeseeable variety like that of the evanescent forms of smoke.

> The living organizations are fluid and moving. All attempt to set or fix them—in the laboratory or in our representation—makes them fall in one or the other form of death. Oscillating between the ghost and the corpse . . .

All cell organization is thus made of fluids and dynamic structures. The liquid eddy—overthrowing the crystal order—has become, or become again, its model as well as the candle's flame, somewhere between the rigidity of the mineral and the decomposition of smoke.[1]

The same principle at work in the incense burner is used inversely in the labyrinth game practiced in South Africa by the Zulu (see fig. 3.2E). Two opponents smoke hashish and spit puffs of smoke mixed with saliva toward the ground, where they take turns tracing a labyrinthine drawing similar to the one projected by the swirls of smoke in such a way as to maneuver each other toward a destination "like two bands of warriors advancing toward their chief." The saliva-wetted smoke is like speech, reminiscent of the humid breath of the Dogon genie coming between the strands of a rope. The swirl of smoke is like inspired discourse, which itself is similar to the flowering mouths of certain Mayan sculptures. The players let the smoke speak and write for them. By capturing and joining the shape of the swirls of smoke to draw a labyrinth or a maze, it is as if they recognize and distinguish the path of the Logos in their mute conversation, or, captured in their own voices, that of the genie or spirit who first breathed forth the Word.

In comparison, the patterns of the four-dimensional knot and of the maze that we have obtained somehow seem to be the product of a modern mentality. In addition, the knot-maze cannot be completely represented because it is constantly changing. It will therefore be impossible to find a drawing of the ancient maze that exactly corresponds to it. In the archaic world, there are no purely geometrical drawings produced solely by analytical logic. What we find are symbols, syntheses of art and geometry whose meaning is suggested by myths and whose anonymous creator is the unconscious. We can thus assume that the "fourfold sphere of wholeness," which is another name for the philosophers' stone or the Hebrew Bethel (the house of God), also corresponds to a four-dimensional knot. Sculptures like the Glas

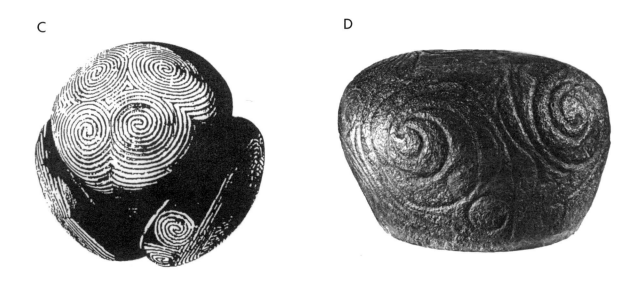

Fig. 24.3. The "fourfold sphere"
(A) *The omphalos at Delphi.* (B) *Stone of Turoe, Ireland, end of the Iron Age.* (C) *Stone ball from Glas Towie,*
Scotland, ca. 3000 B.C. *(D) Stone from Castlegrange, Ireland.*

Towie balls, the Turoe and Castlegrange stones, and even the Delphi omphalos (see fig. 24.3) and the Desborough mirror (see fig. 18.4) present a synthesis or a sort of compromise between knot and labyrinth that suggests at the same time an *n*th dimension.

There is no doubt that ancient peoples perfected a symbolic topology that included the study of surfaces, volumes, and manifolds just like modern topology. We must understand ancient geometry more completely in order to grasp precisely the meaning of each symbol, the link between all the symbols, and the complete structure of myths. The meaning of each symbol depends precisely on its relation to the others and to the whole.

Fig. 24.4. Cretan seal depicting a braid or a rope and its unfolding

25

The Cord

Our concepts are like a thread made of fibers. The solidity of the thread is not due to the presence of a single fiber running its full length, but to the intertwining of a large number of fibers.

—Wittgenstein, *Philosophical Investigations*

The examples that we have just studied show that next to the relation between knot and labyrinth there exists another important relation, mentioned by the Dogon, between the maze and the cord made of interlaced threads or fibers. The interlaced strands already form a kind of knot, and the division of the knot leading to a maze or a labyrinth also corresponds to a separation of these strands. The archetypal knot representing the whole can be seen as representing a quintessence of the whole, or a virtual whole, but in any case, its symbolic elaboration is the result of a complex process. For there to be a knot, there first must be something like a thread.

As they are tangled, twisted, braided, or woven together, the joining of the fibers can be seen as representing a first phase in the creation of the concept and symbol of the whole. Or these fibers can symbolize the way the mind manifests itself by building entities from raw data that become somehow tangled and stuck together. Strangely enough, this idea, which seems to belong to the mythic world, was recycled in the modern world by Bernhard Riemann, the inspired mathematician who, by elaborating a new model of space, helped Einstein formulate the equations of his theory of relativity.

Riemann considered that beyond the habitual space of lengths and masses governed by a mechanics of objects, the description of the universe demands that a "space of thought" be taken into consideration, a space just as real but non-physical, inciting matter to be seen as just a part of reality. This was the first tentative attempt to explain consciousness scientifically, and Riemann's reasoning must be taken seriously.

We would not have had the idea that masses could attract, he says, if we had only been able to observe small objects: only the observation of large masses led to the discovery of gravitation. In the same way, Riemann links consciousness to relations within a system, one aspect of which is the way of connecting a network. This latter is usually rudimentary. At most it manifests itself in man's brain with effects that are tangible enough to be an attractor in the space of thought. In this latter, Riemann admits, there would be non-physical objects, which he calls "thought-masses," that are capable of getting larger by accretion, or we could say by agglutination of other thoughts, as in the solar system, where the germ of a planet appropriates the materials it meets; its gravitation insures the cohesion of the object to itself and makes it capable of attracting others.

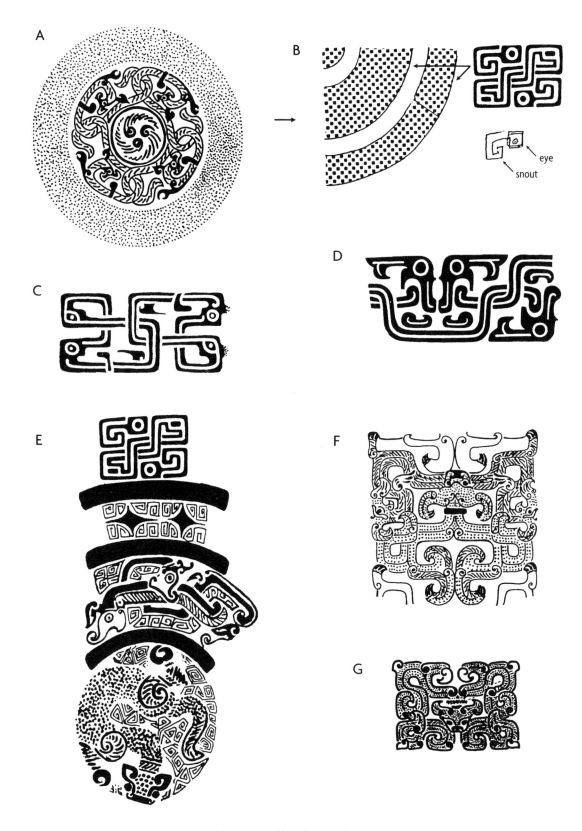

Fig. 25.1. Chou bronze designs

(A) From the cover of a cauldron. (B) A section of the rope and projection of its lateral view. (C) and (D) are transitions toward the more abstract illustration B and can explain its composition and what it represents. In illustration C, the snout of one animal is the beginning of the next. (E) A section of the rope replaced by the front view of a tiger. The whole composition is similar to A. (F) and (G) A front view of the face with a split lateral view of the body that can replace A.

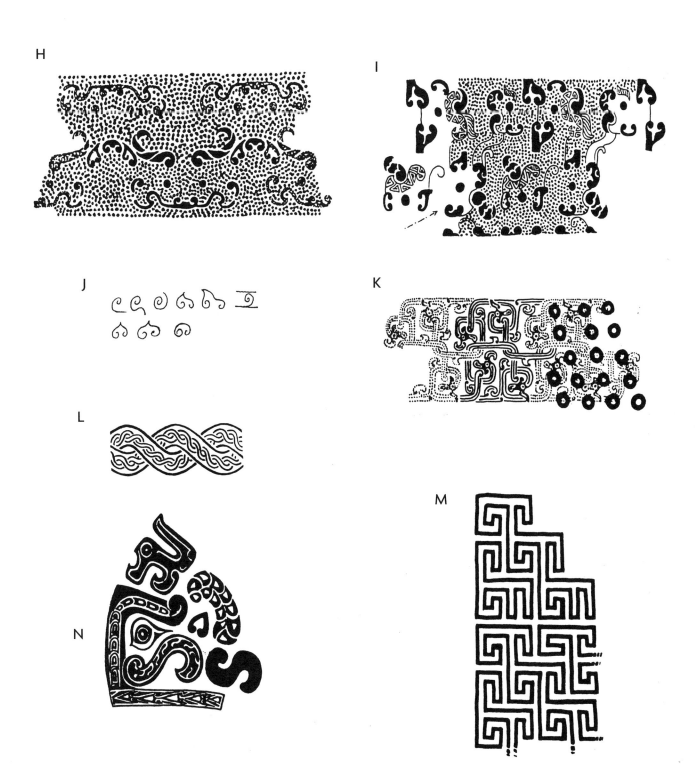

(H) and (I) Here we see silhouettes of intertwined animals appearing in a mist of particles. (J) Different comma shapes used to build the designs, including hook volute, feather, fur, and silkworm patterns. (K) Transition toward illustrations H and I. The design is covered with warts, which can represent eyes or articulations. (L) A braid with a circling motif within it. (M) A maze on a weapon. (N) Dispersal of body parts equivalent to the undoing of the rope.

Von Neumann uses this scenario to explain an assimilation of data originating in the physical world: when integrated with our self they become information. . . .[1]

The symbolic representation of the cord that can represent thought-matter, or for the Dogon contains primal speech, can also be found suggested by motifs decorating certain Chinese ritual vases (see fig. 25.1) from the Chou period (1050–221 B.C.). The grouping together of these drawings will offer another complementary image of a maze.

In figure 25.1A, the central medallion engraved on the cover of the cauldron can be seen as representing a cross section of the cord around which different lateral views of interwoven fibers or strands unfold in successive layers. This center could also represent the center or the entrance of the labyrinth, since it is there that the cord is cut. As we move away from the central section, the repeated design figured in B can represent strands or fibers twisted together, or again these strands as they appear later when they are included in the map of the knotted cord—in other words, in the maze. We have here yet another representation of the map of the knot in successive layers, but this time, instead of a relationship among the segments of the cord, it is the relationship among its strands or fibers that is mapped. The repetition of the

motifs as in figure 25.1 is puzzling and can suggest new comparisons. If these motifs really correspond to the strands or fibers twisted so as to form a cord, then they become similar to the geometric figure representing space in superstring theory, or to the representation of extra dimensions in Kaluza-Klein space, which are also curled up around the three usual dimensions of space (see fig. 25.2). They also present increasingly complex shapes (such as those called Kalabi-Yau shapes) when the number of dimensions increases. These extra dimensions are the key to the final success of superstring theory, and one must visualize the superstrings also knotted within those dimensions. A difference between the Kaluza-Klein and the Chinese designs is that the latter represent at the same time the extra dimensions and a map of the strings or threads, tied together within a knotted cord.

On the Chinese vessels, the mythic animals replacing abstract or concrete strings suggest that their dimensions are like those of the subconscious, appearing on a different level but modifying the logic of common experience. There is again a connection between inner and outer worlds.

In figure 25.1A, the strands are first illustrated in the second circle by long, thin tigers or dragons with hanging tongues and striped bodies that suggest twisted fibers. Biting, tearing, interlacing, and grip-

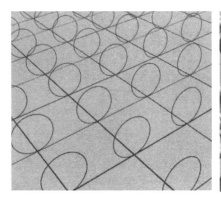  

Fig. 25.2. Disposition of the added curled-up dimensions on a frame representing the usual coordinates according to Kaluza-Klein geometry
(A) One more curled-up dimension. (B)Three more dimensions. (C) Kalabi-Yau spaces, or shape taken by six or seven new curled-up dimensions. The shapes are disposed in the same way as the repeated Chinese motifs on the cauldrons.

ping each other in different ways, the animals seem to attest to the fact that the strands remain attached or braided even though they are not directly knotted; they suggest a cohesive force that manifests itself in many different ways. We simultaneously obtain a representation of the knots and the images or things they can contain knotted together. Instead of a maze seen as a container and representing the structure of a knot or a textile, we find a representation of beings and forces that haunt the maze and have informed it.

In figure 25.1E, another, similar motif seems to indicate that the central image of the cross section of the cord can be replaced by a dragon or a winged tiger, or even by the head of an animal seen from the front, while the strands representing the body of the split animal are projected laterally (fig. 25.1F, G). This is a classic motif of Chinese pictography, and it is also prevalent among the Indians of North America. The dragon would then represent a force or a power dispersed in the knot that becomes accessible in the center of the labyrinth.

In fact, archaeologists agree that the dragon represents the materialization of a spiral movement without which he is nothing:

> "The climbing serpent wanders amidst the fog, the flying dragon rides the clouds. May the clouds disappear and the fog go away, they are similar to the earthworm, for they have lost their mount."[2]

The movement could be the combination of two spirals and the dragon a symbol like the labyrinth, for there is a pearl hidden under his chin that can stand for a sacred center or the price of a quest, and supposedly there is on his back a map made of complex meanders. If reaching the center brings all sorts of virtues, the dragon is also the symbol of supreme virtue:

> After his interview with Lao Dan, Confucius came back and did not utter a word for three days.
>
> His disciples asked him, "Master, you have seen Lao Dan. What instructions did you give him?"
>
> Confucius replied: "I finally had the occasion to see a dragon, this dragon which, when the elements agregate, takes shape, and when they scatter, becomes scenery; which rides clouds and vapors and feeds on yin and yang. Mouth gaping, I stood flabbergasted. What instructions could I have given him?"

In those Chou designs, there is indirectly the suggestion of a labyrinth or of its latent power appearing within the structure of a complex knot similar to a maze.

A complete interpretation of these designs would necessitate a long study, as the code that corresponds to the drawings is certainly very complex. First, the bestiary includes not only existing animals but also composite imaginary animals like dragons, chimeras, and griffins, and not only animals mating or devouring and gripping each other but also giving birth to each other, both out of the womb and from the mouth or head. The ways of uniting the animals are varied. What is more, the code communicates at several levels, as most often the animals are built from a scale of juxtaposed comma shapes that could also represent the fibers that make up the strands, as in figure 25.1J.

Alternately, in some designs, the grains that punctuate the bodies of the animals seem to come from or merge with a vibration of space. Sometimes the body of the animal represented in a pointillist style seems to dissolve into space, and sometimes the silhouettes of the animals appear as if they were solidifying out of a cloud or suggested by the eddies of an atmospheric bubbling or a haze (see fig. 25.1H, I, K). Those images can represent in a more explicit way what was suggested by the Chinese incense burner and by the labyrinth drawn with the help of the swirls of smoke spit out by the Zulu. They can suggest how all things and the whole are formed and dissolved, and how "[i]t belongs to perception to pulverize the world, but also to spiritualize dust."*

All of Chou art seems, then, to have as its theme

---

* Quoted by Gilles Deleuze in *Le pli Leibnitz et le baroque* (it is in those terms that Gabriel Tarde defines *monadology* in *Monadology and Sociology*).

the representation of cords and knots being tied and untied. This is corroborated by the fact that we find next to these animals the representation of braids as well as typically labyrinthine motifs (fig. 25.1K, L). Like in the Dogon myth, which simultaneously describes different layers of the structure of language and the succession of genies leading to the first ancestors and to different activities, the map of the knot is fused with a representation of life and the impulses and forces that occupy and perpetuate it. We no longer find the representation of an empty path, but a more subtle one of a way of living as it is experienced by those who find themselves wandering through a maze or by those who, like the Dogon genies, use it to cohabitate with and help men.

This is all rather gripping, as this vase ornamentation constitutes the prototype of an art that can be found in Crete as well as among the Celts, the North American Indians, and even in Islamic art, where animals are often replaced by plants. We could easily conclude that all this ancient art that is qualified as decorative corresponds or comes from a complex science of cords and knots linked to a science of language. Based on this origin, all the stylized intertwined animal figures will continue later on latently to represent the forces presiding over creation and the unfolding of the universe according to a topology. The complex rapport among animals classified according to different directions of space, which is narrated in many myths, and in particular in Native American mythology, could also be related to this aspect. In the art of the Chou, we find the key for one of the codes that translates abstract designs related to knots and weaving into figurative images of mythic animals, whose relations, as they are described in myths, take on symbolic meaning.

Fig. 25.3. Cretan seals
Pictured at the bottom of the center seal is a sacred knot, which can suggest that the representation
of the animals is still linked to the symbolism of the maze and cords.

26
Labyrinths within Labyrinths

As we progress in our exploration of the labyrinth, we discover a number of geometric approaches that all open the way to different interpretations of the nature of the labyrinth and of its relation to the maze. All these interpretations correspond to specific myths or different formulations of the truth or to ancient patterns, and if they appear contradictory, they are more exactly complementary. It seems that all these geometrical approaches form a "group," in the mathematical sense of the word, that must be complete in order to give a complete understanding of the labyrinth. To support this idea, we shall offer here an example of another geometrical approach.

As shown in figure 16.2, the geometrical transformation of a knot into a labyrinth makes complete sense only if the torus knot is obtained by a mapping of the knot synchronized with its rotation on an orbit (see fig. 26.1). This circulation of the knot is included in the final structure of the knot and cannot be ignored.

The circulation of the knot, however, as it is represented in figure 26.1A, cannot be used for the transformation of the knot with seven crossings. But a satisfactory result can be obtained by a flip of the knot, which is then shown as spinning back and forth. As shown in figure 26.1B and C, we must also visualize the knot expanding and contracting during this oscillation. This new motion of the knot is symbolically more complete, since it can represent, as in the Durrow carpet (see plate 19), a creation and dissolution of the world, and thus both the history and the fate of the world.

When we now consider these trajectories of the knot, we must accept that there are a multitude of pos-

sible mappings, all equally valuable. The different readings of the knot's trajectory are obtained by using a variety of positions of the knot while it makes several cycles of rotation (or expansion and contraction) instead of a single one, as is illustrated in figure 26.2. Thus it is different synchronizations between the reading of the knot and its motion that creates different mappings.

With each new mapping, the torus knot and the path of the labyrinth become distorted; folded or knotted in different ways, they become like the new path of the maze, and in fact the path of the labyrinth and that of the maze have become one and the same. Yet ultimately all these patterns can unfold and fuse with the labyrinth, as they correspond to an imagined trajectory and to a process rather than to something concrete. Like the trail left by a bee's dance, the pattern does not correspond to a tangible string. It is as if there were a concerted dance of all the different paths of the maze that unite and fuse when the center of the labyrinth is reached.

All this leads to a new, equivocal interpretation and deepens the paradox of the maze. Just as we could consider the labyrinth included and hidden within a complex maze, we can now conclude that, like a cornucopia or a Pandora's box, the labyrinth contains a multitude of other labyrinths and mazes that ultimately all fuse when the center is reached. It follows that if we can recognize the dance of all things as that which is evoked by the dance of Shiva, we are never lost in a maze, but are always in a labyrinth on our way toward the center. All is always perfect and complete as it is, and all that is required of us is to be aware of what is. It is as if all laws coincided and reflected each other in a final unity.

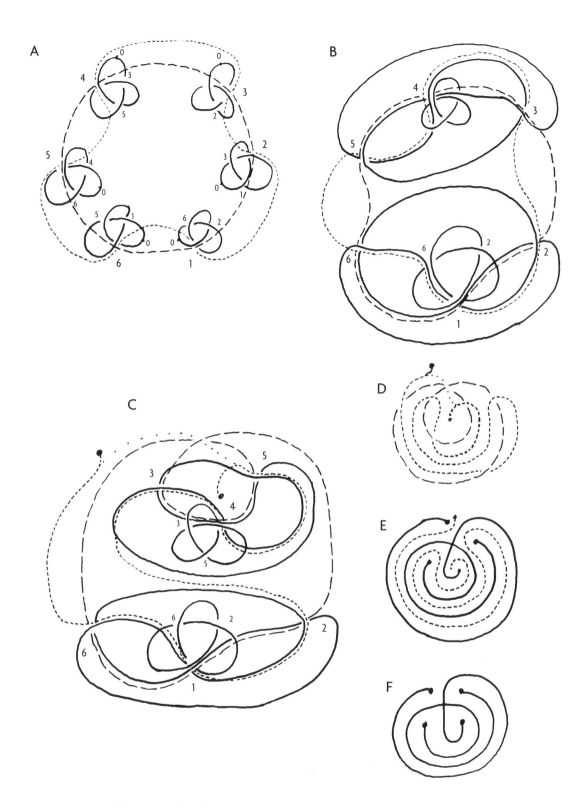

Fig. 26.1. Circulation of the knot and production of a torus knot

(A) This pattern is equivalent to the one in figure 16.2. The torus knot is produced by a mapping of the knot synchronized with the circulation of the knot on an orbit. (B) A simple rotation of the knot on an orbit cannot be used satisfactorily to create a knot crossed seven times. Instead, we must imagine the knot expanding and contracting. Here, to simplify the picture, we still use a threefold knot, but a similar process using eight knots instead of four will produce the torus knot corresponding to the Cretan labyrinth. (C) If we want to represent the self axis crossed so that the meander becomes like the path of a small labyrinth, we must flip the knot so that it is reversed on its top position. (D) Path of meander as in (C).
(E) Path of meander with wall of labyrinth. (F) Small labyrinth.

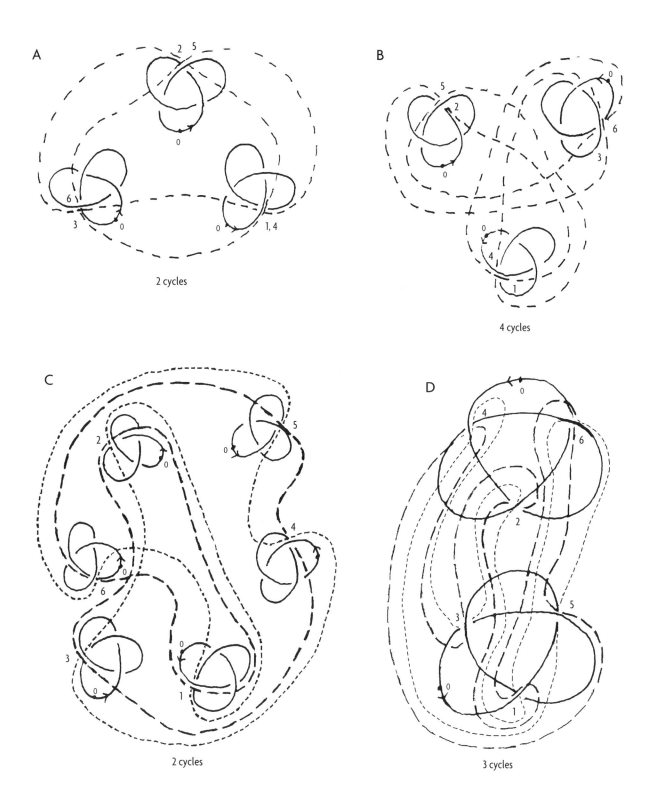

Fig. 26.2. Some other mappings of the circulating knot

Instead of using six positions of the knot while it circulates once on its orbit, as in figure 26.1, the torus knot can be created using six or three or two positions of the knot while it completes several cycles on its orbit. We obtain then a torus knot folded on itself and a path of the labyrinth that becomes confused with the mapping of a maze. (A) This reading corresponds to two cycles of the knot in its orbit. It produces a torus knot folded like a knot; the meander and the self axis are superimposed and become confused. (B) This reading corresponds to four cycles of the knot in its orbit. It produces a double threefold knot folded on itself. (C) This reading corresponds to two cycles of the knot on its orbit. It produces a twisted torus knot. (D) This mapping corresponds to three cycles of the knot in its orbit. It produces a convoluted torus knot.

5
Images of the Labyrinth

27

The Image, the Whole,
and the Changing Aspect

Going from leaves to birds is easier than from roses to letters.
—Borges

The geometrical explanation may change our attitude toward the symbol, but it does not completely replace the rather vague but penetrating image produced by the myth that allowed us to imagine the world as a maze and life as the experience of wandering through it. If we can see life as a maze and be touched by the images suggested by the myth, it is partly because the spectacle of the world also presents imprecise or incomplete images of mazes that suggest life. The symbols and the geometric drawings can also contribute, like a ferment, to the emergence of these images from their resting place in the unconscious and to the revival of indistinctly received impressions, which are like the negatives of pictures that must be developed.

My interest in the labyrinth was first crystallized by playing cat's cradle. The changing pattern of a knot connecting disparate images that emerge like mirages in a rebuslike succession brings to mind the play of maya and the image of a maze where we wander as if hypnotized. This fascination is partly due to the fact that the eye is busy completing the images suggested by the pattern, while at the same time following the starlike movement of the interlacing. The invisible path connecting the images becomes confused with the path of the thread. The eye and the fingers seem to cooperate to suggest a reality normally inaccessible to the senses and the mind. But at the same time, because the enigmatic relationship linking the continuous pathway of the thread to the successive aims of the fingers and the discontinuous succession of images is difficult to grasp, this perception provokes perplexity and a sense of being lost that can instigate a fruitful questioning.

There are many different ways to be lost, all of which complete and reflect each other. I can, for example, contemplate the plywood board that I use as a table. The grain of the wood, grouped in narrow or wide strips, follows a labyrinthine meander that has an irregular patina and reflects light unevenly, so that, intrigued and fascinated by the moiré pattern it produces, my gaze jumps from a luminous tracing to a more obscure one, following a path suggested by accents, highlights, and contrasts rather than the less evident texture. But it is partly due to my inclination to seek out light and dark patterns and the trajectory of my gaze captured by their arrangement that leads me to identify the blurred pattern of a continuous labyrinthine meander presented by the tighter grains of wood. My eye follows two different trajectories that complete each other and seem knotted together.

We might be surprised that a tree trunk made up of concentric rings can produce a labyrinthine meander. But this can be explained once we realize that the layers of plywood are obtained by cutting the tree lengthwise in circular layers that follow its average circumference instead of following the rings, since the trunk is not perfectly straight. The sawmill thus puts into practice another geometry that produces a labyrinthine drawing from concentric rings. As for the movement of the gaze following the accents of light by jumping from one line to another, it is due to the physiology of the eye, which is guided by an inherent rhythm produced by the cones of the retina. But by rediscovering a path that connects luminous or dark, incomplete, or broken rings, the movement of the gaze seems also to rediscover the way the tree grew. It recombines the pattern of stringy fibers with a movement of the light that stimulated their growth, and follows a maze or knot that surrounds and contains the path of the meander. The path of the gaze sketches the outline of an imaginary, indescribable form similar to the one produced by the cloud of incense rising from the Chinese incense burner shaped like a labyrinth. The meaning of this fugitive form seems to question us in an unknown script. Subconsciously, we vaguely perceive a complex knot, which, latently, contains a labyrinth, but this labyrinth doesn't need to be reconstructed, as it is already drawn by the grain of the wood.

The same hypnotic effect is created by the play of ripples and eddies produced by the current of a stream. Here, the time dimension is introduced by the current; the lines constantly change while perception isolates a still image and sees the repetition of a single motif and a transformation it cannot identify, or an incomprehensible maze, constantly modifying itself before the immobile observer and spreading out over the entire stream. Each form leads to another without allowing us to determine a cycle or to perceive the complete whole. Saussure also used this image of a stream or a river to represent the structure of language. As wind currents and atmospheric pressure influence the movement of water, the association of ideas influences language. We could add that the bed of the stream, which also contributes to the formation of eddies, could represent the subconscious activity.

In these examples, the elements constituting the parts of a whole are combined in different ways and distributed between visible and invisible, conscious and unconscious domains. There is a pathway shared by the process of vision and the movement of objects. The gaze explores an external structure by extending the body it emerges out of. According to Merleau-Ponty's description, the body becomes "the body in its preconscious, dialectic, non-causal relationship with its environment or given world, like a knot of living meaning."[1] The external structure is produced by a gaze that weds it to the body and the life that animates it. Life is reflected in an enigmatic vision that seems to contain its meaning.

The pathway of the gaze creates or rediscovers a palimpsest of images and structures. It connects patterns belonging to different dimensions but without understanding the space it explores. It forms Gordian knots, a maze in which one wanders between an interior and an exterior world, but without being able to distinguish them and without knowing how to reach the center, where the exterior and interior merge. The labyrinth that leads to the center thus presents, in a certain sense, the reverse side of a perception that forms a maze surrounding and penetrating the object whose meaning it sought.

We could mention many other phenomena that similarly interrogate our gaze, as, for example, the flight of migrating geese. One after the other, the geese take their place at the head of the formation, drawing a moving braid, a wave carried onward by the ever-changing V. This wave breaks on a shore that the geese recognize as the place where the egg that contained them hatched, as their place of origin. Why is this flight so fascinating? Is it because the changing pattern seems to braid the void, or rather is it because it constitutes a sort of language illustrating how a common effort and a common will and instinct permit the geese to better orient themselves? According to a Greek myth, it was from observing the patterns of flying geese that Hermes invented the alphabet. Thus, originally, writing would correspond to articulations of changing formations, the tracing of braids or network patterns. In the Hermes myth there is the indirect suggestion of a link between the alphabet and a script made of knots, like that of the quipu or ancient Chinese writing. The situation is similar for cranes, and it is well known that their flight as well as their mating dances are intimately linked to the labyrinth. Dances imitating cranes are part of the rituals associated with the labyrinth. It is as if the ritual recognized a hidden connection between the geometry that produced the labyrinth and that which governs the dance and the migration of birds, those masters of space and symbols of the soul.

In the dance of the Maypole, which is also obscurely associated with the labyrinth, the dancers each hold a colored ribbon that is attached to the top of the pole. As the dancers weave in and out, a colorful braid is gradually formed. As the braid becomes tight, it draws the dancers closer together and closer to the pole, until they are assembled like a bunch of grapes attached to a vine. This suggests how the movement of dancers can serve to draw them closer to a common center that could also be found within each one of them.

One of the marvelous sights that nature offers is the gathering of hawks prior to their individual migration. As they circle, they create the image of an aerial well composed of a double spiral that seems to magnetize the atmosphere by a sort of magic. The effect is produced not by the group of hawks that rises while the other group descends, but by the combination of spirals and loops that each bird follows, creating a whole that suggests a strand of DNA in which each molecule is free to play musical chairs. The force that maintains the cohesion of the whole pattern is stronger than the force of entropy and the force that leaves each bird its freedom of direction. It is as if

without understanding or even perceiving the whole picture, each bird was instinctively connected to the movement of the others, as if by a sort of ritual each bird exteriorized an innate common pattern that helped it to orient itself. Unlike the message in the form of a knot delivered from one bee to another concerning the place of and distance to a food source, there is what resembles a ballet or a concert intended to help the hawks remember their respective destinations in a vast territory. As with the Malekulan ritual, the hawks seem continually to recompose the missing part of a knot that is erased as soon as it is sketched, with the goal of designating an axis that will direct them and around which they will be distributed. The axis becomes defined and concrete when they start to emigrate while the memory of the knot appears intangible and perhaps exists only in the spectator's vision.

This more or less direct connection between movements or dances and a labyrinth is also expressed by the most ancient petroglyphs (see fig. 27.1). These drawings prefigure or accompany the purely geometrical drawings of the classic labyrinth. Labyrinthine meanders can be discovered among a jumble of symbols and sinuous lines that seem to form a map. The meander can be constituted by an animal's prolonged tail, thus suggesting a pathway it has wandered (fig. 27.1A). It can also be suggested by a dancing body whose elongated limbs curve in and embrace themselves in the form of a labyrinth (fig. 27.1D). Sometimes the meander leads to a central face, suggested by two eyes, thereby suggesting a field explored by the gaze (fig. 27.1B and C). Sometimes, on the other hand, the path becomes a straight line like a flattened axis and it leads from a center defined by concentric circles to a point located in a mapped territory (fig. 27.1E). The latter seems to describe both a ritual and an initiatic journey, and it presents a middle term between the straight path taken by the Malekulan ghost and the circling in the labyrinth.

The drawings illustrating a labyrinth are answered by other drawings corresponding indirectly to

Fig. 27.1. Ancient labyrinths

(A) The path is suggested by the tail of an animal; petroglyph from the Camonica valley ca. 2500 B.C. A similar motif can be found on the Bogomil grave in Bosnia. (B and C) The labyrinth can become like the field of a gaze. (D) The labyrinth built with the arms of a man, Camonica valley ca. 2500 B.C. (E) From Auchnabreach, Scotland, a style called "ring and cup." Similar motifs are found in Scotland and in Sweden.

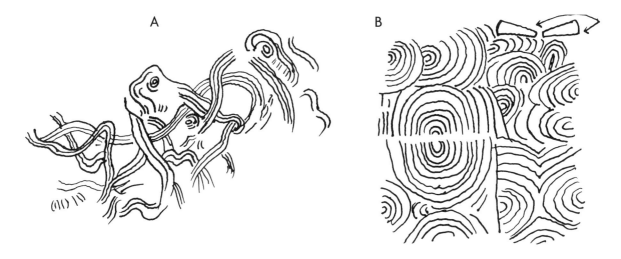

Fig. 27.2

(A) A bull in the macaroni style, Altamira. (B) From Gavr'innis, Morbihan. At the top, two opposed ax heads that suggest a labrys.

mazes in which the figure of an animal is entangled with that of a knot or a ripped or unfinished interlacing. Drawings with jumbled lines called "macaroni," typical of the Altamira frescoes, represent, in an equivocal way, both the movement of an animal and the trajectory of a gaze trailing the animal (fig. 27.2A). Instead of a game of cat's cradle schematically suggesting an animal, we have the outline of an animal that could suggest the movement of a game of cat's cradle.

Each line seems to represent either a trace left by the animal or else the trajectory of an eye or a blow that is inflicted on it, or again that of a wave that envelops and penetrates it. Perhaps according to the code established by the Chou vases, the animal is also the materialization of a link in an energetic network. The trace no longer belongs to an exterior world, but rather seems to have been transposed from the powerful vision of a hunter or shaman who recognizes a double nature within himself and thus identifies with the animal and becomes one with it. The drawing suggests a doubled vision that answers and announces the doubling of the cord in the geometry of the labyrinth. The woof of the sinuous lines and the spaces between the lines capture the gaze and suggest a magnetic field in which the shaman rediscovers a path joining him to the animal.

The decoration of archaic pottery, and in particular the pottery of Crete, also shows an intriguing mix-

ture of grooves and ridges preceding the more accomplished spiral drawings, meanders, and geometric waves. These latter are the result of impressions left by the grain of a knotty piece of wood or by a cord that is knotted, braided, or rolled and that leaves a trace resembling a pathway. The pot thus becomes similar to a piece of basket or wickerwork, but the movement of the cord can also remind us of the technique of a potter who makes a pot from a strand of clay rolled in a spiral (this spiral could be replaced by a labyrinthine meander). The vase enveloped in a wave can appear to float on a net or on the liquid element, just as it is capable of containing it, and it is a fitting reminder of the symbol of a vase-vessel connected to the labyrinth that we have already shown to be equivalent to a crossing or a reversal. The container and the contents of the vase are no longer opposed, and the outline of the cord thus suggests, like Zeus's tying method, a path that is both penetrating and enveloping. Although it is not obvious, in primitive art there is constant allusion to the transition from a labyrinth to a knot and to a maze, or to part of a maze that links phenomena, as well as a transition from nature to techniques and geometry.

The concentric grooves carved on the hallways of the Gavr'innis tomb resemble the eddies of a stream (fig. 27.2B), and they can represent, as in the Knossos calendar, the phases of the moon as well as the succession of tides or the movement of swelling waves before they break. These are not the only interpretations, as in other petroglyphs they can also represent a field of perception and different ways of questioning memory and space-time. As we have already seen in the chapter on the cycles of time, the rings can represent latently and simultaneously relative time, a glory, a nimbus, a mandorla, a womb, a soul, and a destiny. In a primitive person's interior vision, all these meanings can be associated, joining and completing each other. Finally, it appears that at Gavr'innis a particular theme cannot be dissociated from other themes and that the drawing can represent something common to a multitude of rhythms occurring at different levels. The similarity of the arrangement of circles with those used in a tantric drawing representing the creation of the universe (fig. 27.3) suggests that the Gavr'innis circles can also represent a cosmic and biological rhythm that would affect the growth and decline of all things. In their turn, the perfectly drawn geometric circles included in the tantric drawing can suggest both a perception of creation that emerges with the awakening of the chakras and the chakras themselves. "The reactivation of the chakras, the 'wheels' or circles that are seen as the points of intersection of cosmic and mental life, is homologous to the initiation that constitutes the penetration of a Mandala. This awakening of the Kundalini is equivalent to a break on an ontological level; in other words, to the plenary realization of the symbolism of the center."[2]

It is often only the title given to a drawing that, by indicating a relationship between ritual and myth, can inform us of its intended meaning, the meaning conveyed by the word of the artist-priest but a meaning that must find its way and transform itself in the mind of the observer. As seen in figure 8.3B and its subsequent caption, the Malekulan tracing showing a typical labyrinthine meander represents a hero called Hambut who is pushed back in successive stages by the incoming tide as he is sharpening an adze on the beach. The title of the drawing is surprising, since without a context, the pattern suggests neither the movement of the tide nor that of Hambut. The connection among the action of slicing that is suggested by the adze, that of sharpening, and the movement of the tide that, linked to the cycles of the moon, erodes or fills in the coast is intriguing, and leads one to seek out the link and the metaphor that is alluded to. What do we sharpen and what do we peel away to find an essential core or center during our lives?

The relationship between the adze and the labyrinthine pattern can be compared with that between the double ax and the Cretan labyrinth. The function of the adze, which slices layers, complements that

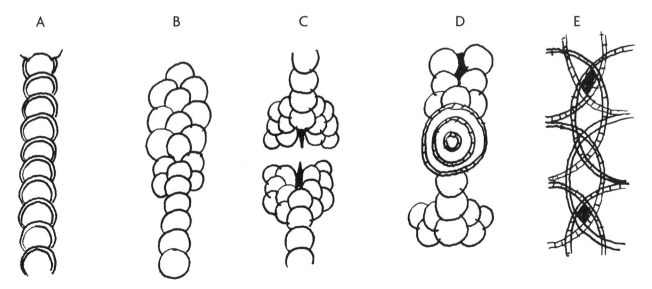

Fig. 27.3. Schemas of tantric drawing representing the creation of the universe

of the double ax, which splits along an axis. It suggests another aspect of the axis and implicitly connects the symbol to a geometry. The adze thus suggests a geometry that is similar to the one that produces the plywood meanders from the concentric rings of a tree trunk. The process of decortication and cutting into finer and finer layers suggested by the adze as it is progressively sharpened can also suggest a pathway modifying itself according to a finer and finer scale of dimensions; it is a question no longer of directions in space, but rather of a scale or of a passage from the macro- to the microscopic. As is indicated by fractal geometry, there is a correspondence between the two aspects, for as the line or the limit follows details more meticulously, it becomes more and more sinuous, branching out into a bush until it finally fills and describes a surface or a volume. There is thus an allusion to a geometric approach complementary to the one we have studied that makes it possible to explain the labyrinth in a more complete manner. In fact, the labyrinth, which itself seems built of strata, represents superimposed or embedded worlds. It can also correspond to a telescopic view of the universe and of the whole, a whole that brings together macroscopic and microscopic worlds whose images reflect each other. The backward and forward motion of Hambut according to the tides corresponds as well to the centripetal and centrifugal movement of the path in the labyrinth, leading back and forth from the macroscopic to the microscopic and thus from the furthest exterior to the most interior world and joining them together. This sort of interpretation will always seem contrived when rationally explained, but it reveals the existence of overtones pertaining to symbolic language.

It follows that ancient patterns, like myths, have an indeterminate meaning. Besides being polysemic, they connect diverse meanings. It is the comprehensive view of all the drawings and all the myths that will lead us to understand their ultimate meaning more completely. For example, the Malekulan tracing we just discussed could also illustrate the legend describing the wizard Merlin, who, as a child, fought with the dragon that was shaking the foundations of the Pendragon castle by provoking earthquakes. Once ousted from its home and chased by Merlin, the dragon circles the walls of the city and retires into the sea at low tide to attack with renewed vigor at high tide until Merlin finally slays it. In this legend, the labyrinth that housed the wandering Minotaur is replaced by the path and the strategy of the dragon. The legend reunites a spacial pattern to a rhythm and a cycle to the surging and the control of an energy. The wizard Merlin's budding power corresponds to the activation of the chakras or the *kundalini* that awakens a force equal and finally superior to that of the dragon. To the patterns representing the surging of a creative force correspond those adopted by an opposite, destructive force. All is accomplished according to a cycle, and Merlin's first adventure announces his final misadventure. At the end of the Arthurian cycle, it is Merlin as an old man who takes a place similar to that first occupied by the dragon. Vivian magically locks him into a cave beneath a mazelike forest (representing the unconscious) that the hero to come must once again explore.

Fig. 27.4. Three images on a three-sided Cretan seal
On the left: geese or a dance of cranes? In the middle: dance of a bee or dragonfly or lion mask? On the right: flying griffin.
Is a dance conveying a message but also transforming the dancer?

28
Gestalt

I have seen a horse, a horse with horns,
I have seen a cow, a cow with a beard.
What is this? It's another world.
—Dogon song

opology is the study not of form but of relation. The geometry of the labyrinth presents a logical method for transforming a knot into a labyrinth, and for relating many different patterns and concepts, but it does not completely explain the final form given to the labyrinth. Yet this form, which suggests a vase or a womb, is a determining factor in the creation of a balanced image and an eloquent symbol. How is this form determined? We can ask ourselves if the form is simply invented intuitively to make the symbol explicit or if the transformation of the form responds to a structural transformation. Are the reversal and invagination that give the labyrinth its final form the effects of the series of other movements that allowed the knot to be transformed?

The language of ancient symbols appears to be connected to a morphogenesis, but the form, like the appearance, does not seem to exist independently and is difficult to define. The compact pattern of the path through the labyrinth, which cannot be identified in one all-embracing gaze, somehow escapes from the realm of form while being more or less contained by a form. It reveals what the form veils. It is impossible to decide whether the form of the labyrinth is defined by a contour, by the fact that its enclosure is square or round, or by its path.

The form, however, is unique in that it is directly accessible to us and our understanding. It is itself the symbol of a presence. Things are born, appear, and become with a form. Though life itself has no form, it is nonetheless made manifest through the language of forms. Each form is the outcome of a genesis, a development, and an involution. It corresponds to an idea and a map, or a relationship, of forces. But at the same time, form veils the meaning of this becoming to express something else, a function, an existence, or a new way of corresponding and electing affinities. The Zen master Dogen captured this mystery in a poem:

Like grass in winter
invisible in the snow-covered field
the white heron in its own form
keeps its body hidden.[1]

The symbol also appears as such only when it invests itself in a form. It tears itself away from geometry and the support of an object to guarantee a meaning or an ineffable pact. Form becomes similar to the name by which one invokes and evokes. But we have seen that the form of the labyrinth is as much the form of a perception as it is a form perceived. It is this balance between form and perception—in other words, this gestalt, or configuration—that gives the symbol its authority.

If the concept of form linked to that of perception is imprecise, it is because the phenomenon of perception is itself difficult to define. Merleau-Ponty pointed out how a pure perception is impossible to isolate because it is always affected by a predetermined knowledge, whether conscious or unconscious, of what is perceived.

> Science presupposes perceptual faith and does not elucidate it. We commit what psychologists call the "experience error," which means that what we know to be in things themselves, we immediately take as being in our consciousness of them. We make perception out of things perceived and since perceived things are themselves accessible only through perception, we end up understanding neither. . . .
>
> We are caught in the world and we do not succeed in extricating ourselves from it in order to achieve consciousness of the world.[2]

Fig. 28.1. Sixteenth-century Italian engraving from Symbola Divina, Prague
The motto his artibus (*with these arts*) *refers to the tools and weapons in the image: a thread to lead, a club to kill the minotaur, and three balls of wax to wedge tetween his jaws and prevent him from biting, or perhaps from talking.*

In other words, we are prisoners in an inescapable maze. This view is in accord with the Buddhist philosophy that recognizes form as devoid of inherent existence, as the product of what is called dependent origination. Alongside the realm of geometry and the study of ideal forms, we must thus discover form in its relation to gestalt, or how knowledge and perception affect each other.

The perceptual theory based on the gestalt rests on the recognition that perception includes more than something perceived that is suddenly embodied in a form, or more than a form signifying something perceived. Rather, "A perceptual something is always part of a field . . . each part arouses the expectation of more than it contains and elementary perception is therefore charged with meaning."[3] In this notion we once more encounter the principle of a whole that is more than the sum of its parts. Each part, like each color or sound or note of the scale, suggests beyond or within an indeterminate structure beyond or within that includes its harmonic or complementary form. In the same way we have seen that a knot can suggest a structure of space that in topology will be used to define the knot and differentiate it from other similar knots. Reciprocally, form is perceived and takes on a meaning from a field where it is discovered or from a whole that includes a group of potential relations. A gestalt can thus be understood as a dynamic balance. The unconscious knowledge obtained is that of an immanent meaning surging out of a conglomerate of information and out of a dialectic that is experienced through a complex process.

But where is this gestalt field? Just as we cannot define the field or the structure of language, we discover that we cannot overdetermine or limit the field in which perception is charged with meaning. The perceptive field comprises the whole world, including the subjective world of the perceiver and the realms of his or her subconscious and unconscious. The outer vision includes the seer and the aggregate of the seer's mind-heart-body. The gaze invests the perceived object just as the object solicits a specific trajectory of the gaze.

> The gaze is itself the incorporation of the seer into the visible, in quest of itself, in the visible and part of it. . . .
>
> What we call visible is . . . the surface of a depth, the cross section of a massive being, a grain and a corpuscle engendered by a wave of being. . . .
>
> Each of these two beings (the object and the seer) is an archetype for the other, because the body belongs to the order of things just as the world is universal flesh. . . . The flesh we are speaking of is not matter but the coiling of the visible on the perceiving body.
>
> There is a reversal of the seeing and the visible, and at the point where the two metamorphoses cross what we call perception is born . . . the reversal that is ultimate truth.[4]

The transformation of the knot into a labyrinth is also a vision "in quest of itself." It is simultaneously the study of an object, the pathway of consciousness, and the discovery of an "ultimate truth" in a reversal. It is a reunion of art, geometry, and science. The center of the labyrinth designates an absolute center where the visible and the invisible, the interior and the exterior, the object and the seer, are joined.

The labyrinth has replaced the form of an object (a knot), tacitly accepted, by another form that defines an archetypal pathway of perception, allowing one to grasp the thing in itself. It is with this pathway that a gestalt appears and is created.

The path of the Logos, which allows things to be understood without being separated from the whole, also corresponds to a path of perception discovering an exit from the maze of the gestalt field. The Logos would correspond to "thoughts by form," whose importance is emphasized by Gurdjieff. There are thus two kinds of perception; one corresponds to the ego or an imaginary "I," imposed, as a result of fundamental ignorance, judgment, and attachment; the other corresponds to an awakening. The transformation of

a consciousness of something out there into a consciousness aware of its own process would be accompanied by a transformation of perception that frees itself and sees itself. Perception would then coincide not with an acquired knowledge but with the emergence of a natural, innate, latent, or hidden knowledge. Like the world and the word, the indeterminate gestalt field changes with the archetypal pathway and becomes defined with it.

Modern gestalt theory, which attributes the genesis of a perceived object to a multitude of gazes scrutinizing an undefined field, can lead neither to a definition of this gestalt field nor to a definition of the archetype that the object and the seer reciprocally represent for each other. It consists in assimilating the field of the gestalt to the total horizon of a gaze wandering indefinitely from one thing to another. This theory does not explain how these gazes are knotted together and organized. The multitude of gazes corresponds to a divided person or a shattered vase, and the gestalt field

Fig. 28.2. Ducit idem deducitque (the same leads and misleads). Early seventeenth-century engraving.
The motto is an allusion to the thread of Ariadne, which almost looks like a serpent. In the center of a labyrinth is a Tree of Life.

remains a multidimensional, indeterminate maze where objects and hybrid seers like the Minotaur remain prisoner. A duality exists between what is perceived and the gestalt field, which is similar to that between the Word or Logos and the structure of language. To resolve it is like trying to square the circle.

On the other hand, the notion of an archetypal path of perception leading to the thing in itself by reuniting it to the whole or to a gestalt that suddenly becomes clearly defined can seem absurd. But it is in accord with the concept of creative imagination, or with creation from the "One," or a Brahma desiring to be multiple. The trace of this path would still remain potentially or latently in man and in space; it corresponds to the union of clarity and emptiness that the Buddhists seek to achieve and whose existence is confirmed in ancient texts.

If view operates on contact, we consider that light produces a disposition both in the object and in the organ . . . if view operates on contact, the visual rays are helped by the light which is of the same species. . . .

For those who have the plenitude of light whose spirit is not obstructed, knowledge of past and present does not differ from a perception. . . .

The clerks whose faults have been completely consumed, whose thought is unveiled, see in a direct perception that is like a reflection of their own thought, the totality of things including all reunited forms and this without any possible error.[5]

Like the field of language, the new gestalt field is indeterminate and cannot be represented as a whole. Yet a gestalt field is also directly represented in primitive art. By studying this art we can discover ambiguous patterns that invite a multitude of different readings and offer the image of a moving and decomposing object that suggests relations among all of its possible aspects. There thus appears a knot uniting all things, a knot from which the path of the labyrinth representing an archetypal path of perception can be rediscovered. Such an art is visible, for example, in certain Malekulan tracings that we shall analyze in the next chapter. We shall attempt to show that this gestalt field is not only given but is also constructed with a pathway.

Fig. 28.3. Images from a three-sided Cretan seal
Two seals represent a boat. In the center, two crosses; are they symbols for a voyage, a crossing, a symbolic voyage?

29

The Tennis Ball and the Path of the Grandmother

Expression reaches beyond language.
—MERLEAU-PONTY

We have just seen how, according to gestalt theory, the visible is the surface or the cross section of a nonexhaustive depth. This depth should therefore be impossible to represent, yet certain geometric Malekulan tracings manage to suggest this inexhaustible gestalt field. In an ambiguous fashion, they suggest both multiple aspects of several objects and a path of the gaze that links these aspects together. Engulfed in the woof of the drawing, the schematically represented objects are imbued with an ambivalent meaning that can be transferred to their corresponding symbols. In addition, it is the reciprocal ambiguity of the silhouette being decoded that gives the field its depth.

We shall not attempt to analyze the authentic or original intended meaning of such a tracing, which appears to be impossible, but shall simply look at the meaning we can discover today. To analyze such a pattern we shall reverse the habitual method by first seeking an intention capable of motivating it, or a rule of construction capable of building it. In order to do this, we shall choose an object and consider how all of space (or the surface on which this space is represented) can be occupied by both the displacement and the unfolding of the object at the same time.

The object we have chosen for this experiment is a tennis ball. It can be drawn in several different ways: In figure 29.1, A reproduces the sign of the Tao; B depicts the iron of a double-bladed ax or labrys;

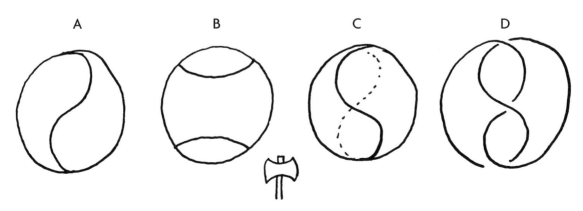

Fig. 29.1. Different representations of the tennis ball
(A) The sign of the Tao. (B) The labrys. (C) A transparent ball. (D) A simple knot.

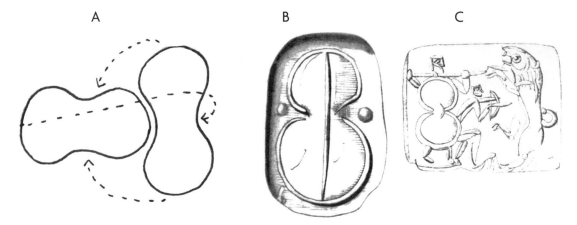

Fig. 29.2

(A) The envelope of the tennis ball. (B) and (C) Shields on Cretan seals. We can ask why there are two balls at either side of the shield and if the figure on the right represents two warriors or a warrior and his double fighting the alchemical symbol of a lion.

C can represent the ball transparently, which leads to the image of the projected simple knot in D. With just these aspects of the ball, we already obtain the embedded images of four objects: a ball, an ax, the sign of the Tao, and a knot.

The specific form of the stitched seam of the tennis ball makes it possible for the ball to turn and rebound evenly from all angles. Thus this seam is also a kind of axis used to balance the sphere, and this fact seems especially significant when one notes the embedded Tao symbol. The form of the seam also allows the sphere to be built with two equal elastic surfaces (see fig. 29.2).

We can notice that these surfaces have the form of the double entasis Cretan shields that are painted in the "double ax gallery" at Knossos, and that could have been used to ward off the blows of the double ax. The two symbols are thus intimately linked both geometrically and functionally.

To tile a surface, we can imagine several trajectories of the ball turning on itself, and represent the path of the ball by using the embedded ax heads as the basic design element (see fig. 29.3).

In these patterns we also find the elongated image of the ball's envelope. When it is big enough,

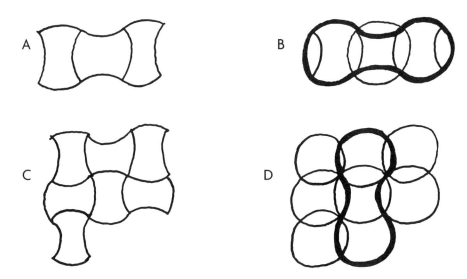

Figure 29.3. The movement of the ball covering a surface

(A) The horizontal movement of the ball. (B) The thick line can also represent the elongated image of one of the envelopes of the ball. (C) The horizontal and vertical movement of the ball combined. It now includes a diagonal direction. (D) The ball moving and one envelope elongated.

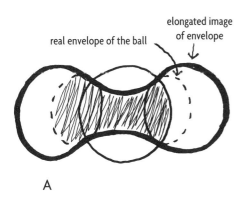

real envelope of the ball

elongated image of envelope

A

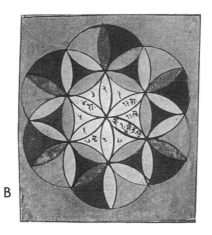

B

Fig. 29.4
(A) The envelope of the tennis ball. The central zone of the double ax can represent the intersection of the sphere of the ball with that of its flattened envelope. (B) Indian tanka. *Here we have the representation of a circular movement of the ball.*

the pattern uniting all the different trajectories of the ball can thus also represent a movement along which the two halves of the ball's envelope separate to become flattened before uniting once more. We can explain the fact that the ends of the envelopes are proportionally enlarged by the use of a reversed perspective or by a design suggesting a back-and-forth, wavelike motion of the ball as it is stripped and reconstituted (see fig. 29.4).

The form of the ax head becomes ambiguous in that it represents both the intersection of the ball and of its flattened envelope, and thus the intersection of one image suggests a volume while the other represents a surface. If we recognize the intention to represent a ball, the perception will oscillate between seeking an image with depth and seeing a puzzle composed of flat elements. In a drawing like that of the Hindu *tanka* (fig. 29.4B), we can again recognize the pattern of the Tao, but the double ax that becomes very thin is more difficult to identify. In figure 29.3D it is the contour of the Tao sign that is deformed. We

can visualize these same objects and symbols more easily when they are included in Malekulan tracings that are much more astonishing and ambiguous.

In the Malekulan drawing called "Path of the Grandmother," (fig. 29.5A) the eye does not at first follow the path of the thread; instead, it recognizes an entangled system of rings. It is only when the line is looser, as in the "octopus" drawing (fig. 29.5B), or when one tries to follow it in the pattern, that the projection of a complex knot and the continuous pathway of a thread can be recognized. In this way, we can identify the movement of the line as that of a meander or a wave diagonally crossing the page but compressed in on itself in such a way as to cross itself and suggest a knot (see fig. 29.6B and C). Finally, by accepting the intention that we have suggested behind the construction of the design, we can recognize the tennis ball zigzagging, or as if floating on a wave that carries it (fig. 29.6A). Different ways of interpreting the drawing merge, and the entire image appears to be a palimpsest on which superimposed images coincide.

A   B

Fig. 29.5. Malekulan tracings
(A) The path of the grandmother.
(B) The octopus, food of the phantom. Its modern title could be, according to Einstein's words, "The mollusk of reference."

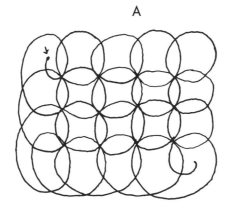

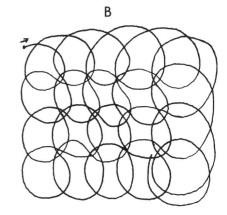

A
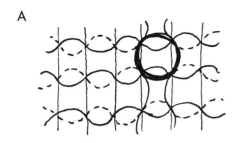

B

C
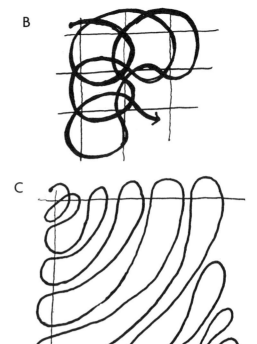

Fig. 29.6
(A) The "floating" tennis ball, or the ball caught in the net.
*(B) The beginning of the meander. (C) Illustration B pulled
taut in such a way as to cancel the crossings.*

In these Malekulan tracings we can recognize:

1. A false knot or the projection of a complex knot.

2. Many trajectories of the spinning and rolling tennis ball.

3. A movement by which the envelope of the ball comes undone and is flattened, as if the ball were opening as it rolled, continually dividing and recomposing itself. We could also say that the ball is replaced by a vibrating ring representing a superstring.

4. A net in which the ball is captured.

5. The pattern can also be seen as constituted of regular waves reticulating the page (as in fig. 29.6A). The sphere of the ball or of the Tao line included latently in the pattern can suggest the virtual sphere of an atom. Each ball or localized sphere is like an elementary corpuscle carried by waves, or else created by their intersections. The whole knot simultaneously represents a particle and its movement, like a dance and dancer. We find the same paradoxes

as in physics and an image that can illustrate the double nature of light.

6. The tennis ball can also be seen as schematically describing Ariadne's ball of thread unrolling to indicate the path of the labyrinth. The image that the myth describes of a ball of thread that can unravel and then roll itself back up at the exit of the maze seems a response to the image in quantum physics of a corpuscle transforming itself into a wave and suddenly invading and diffusing itself through space.

7. Finally, the pattern can be seen as a complex puzzle composed of diverse symbols: labrys, Cretan shields, swastikas, knots, rings or circles that can evoke moons, glory, destiny, the creation, and so on—all the different interpretations of a circle we have noted. Certain symbols seem to emerge from the tumultuous sea of the gestalt field, others are partially obscured, and yet others appear partially deformed by their motion.

The entire image suggests the mysterious semiological path where we discover metamorphoses, analogies, and affinities (the meaning is induced by an oscillation between sign, image, object, and symbol that can be represented by a knot in which the symbol takes the position of the central space, as in fig. 29.7). The Malekulan tracing produces the image of a knot that suggests an ambiguous concatenation of meanings. By presenting a path joining fugitive images, the Malekulan tracing is the counterpart to Mayan hieroglyphic figures that combine several figurative images with abstract symbols, connecting them with the help of knots. This tracing is also complementary to the ever-changing drawing of the cat's cradle that transforms schematic images. It represents space "pierced with ambiguity" by an active contemplation that grasps a latent object, but also, and paradoxically, a "complete object" as it is defined by Merleau-Ponty: "The completed object is a translucent being shot through from all sides by an infinite number of present scrutinies that intersect in its depth leaving nothing hidden."[1]

According to geometry, for there to be a labyrinth there first must be an archetypal knot, and we could conclude that it is precisely the gestalt field that offers the primary rough draft of this knot. It seems at the start that the knot corresponds to a pathway of the gaze exploring the gestalt field, but if we consider the construction of the drawing, we must conclude that instead, it is the pathway that creates the gestalt field. The gestalt field is not given by the exterior

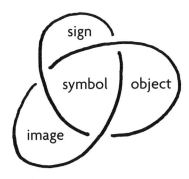

Fig. 29.7. Meaning is deduced by an oscillation between sign, image, object, and symbol.

world. Instead it is built by the gaze from simple elements, and the knot seems to preexist in us. The pathway of the Malekulan tracing is like that of a labyrinthine meander or a wave that folds in and gets tangled, thereby constituting a mold wherein the completed object is formed.

Recent research on the process of vision can help to understand this phenomenon. It leads to the conclusion that vision is not due uniquely to a sensorial flux and that it is not passive but fundamentally active. Albert Ducrocq notes that one researcher "considers perception as a directed hallucination."[2]

All of this leads us to a parallel consideration. We have already established that the labyrinth can represents both the path of the Logos and a path of the gaze leading to a perception. The gestalt field as a source of perception corresponds, then, to a gestalt field of language, or to a definite net of language enveloping or enwrapping the Logos. This field must also be structured and built in the same way by an innate knowledge, and must be different from the undefined structure produced when the net is tangled by language at large. This field is not exactly undefined, as the structuralists assumed, but it appears infinitely ambiguous. It is this ambiguity that is exploited by the modern deconstructionists, but they seem to explore only a maze. This field or net of language is also evoked by the Malekulan drawing that traditionally represents not only a perceived path of life but also the writing of a secret name.

One could object that this improvised interpretation of the Malekulan tracing using a tennis ball does not allow us to pierce the vision of primitive man. It is evident that we have not described the way the Malekula native actually sees in these patterns what their titles suggest—that is, an "octopus, food of the phantom" or a "path of the grandmother." Yet the equivocal character that we have attributed to the drawings is typical of primitive representation. We find, for example, a Malekulan pattern (fig. 8.4E) explicitly representing both the phantom guardian and flying foxes (a kind of bat). The reading is reversed when the interpretation of details changes, and at the same time the two meanings are connected. It is also clear that the images of the octopus and the path of the grandmother (grandmother nature) can be induced during ritual dances when the same patterns are traced and as if woven by the dancers representing heroes, gods, or totemic animals whose actions and behavior are described by the myths. But it is not only in rituals that the patterns come to life. The entire activity and life of primitive man lends itself to a communion with symbols.

When primitive man traces these patterns like generations of ancestors have before him, he does not act to express a personal vision like modern artists. He traces the pattern so that it can be inhabited by a spirit vision, or simply by the spirit or the genie that first inspired the vision. He does not see the pattern only as a representation of the world of the spirit, but also as the path by which the force or spirit invoked can inhabit him. He recognizes a method by which to invite and capture. The pattern reflects a way of being and of entering into relation, a way of communicating, and a mode by which the spirit visits or inhabits.

Each form in the pattern can bring back the memory of an ancient incident, glittering alternately as a familiar object, a window or a breach in the veil of the world, or an obstacle barring the path leading to another dimension. As he becomes familiar with the gestalt, primitive man learns to recognize the forces that invest and appropriate things and the forms that can invoke and invite these forces. He learns to live fully in the world by becoming a receptacle or a channel for these forces, and he begins to understand them when they act through him. At this stage, the vision he reproduces is more that a gift received so that he can fully perceive; it also leads to the exercise and control of a will: "to command and obey within a social structure composed of many souls."[3] In this way the Malekulan pattern also becomes a "divine graffito" and represents "a furrow that magically traces itself under our eyes without a tracer, a certain hollowness, a certain interior, a certain absence, a negativity which is not nothing."[4]

Fig. 29.8. Cretan seals comparable to the designs considered in this chapter
The design on the right could suggest an unfolded Tao symbol showing its two sides.

30

The Book of Durrow: The Reversal

Like in an Eleatic paradox, a dream disintegrates into another
And this one into yet another and again into others
Weaving pointlessly a pointless labyrinth.

—BORGES

As we have already mentioned, alongside the topology of knots made with a cord and drawn with a single line is another topology of folding and unfolding surfaces and volumes. Through studying different patterns specific to ancient Celtic, Chinese, Islamic, or Australian cultures, we can discover other branches of ancient geometry corresponding to those of modern manifold topology. We have explored only the surface of a buried realm.

We can recognize, for example, in one of the ornamental pages of the Book of Durrow (see plate 19) a complex labyrinth that is supposed to represent the continual creation and dissolution of the world. The motif of the central labyrinth is certainly obtained, like the Cretan labyrinth, by a transformation of the knotted braid illustrated in the border. The composition of the center is similar to that of the border: The two larger circles in the center are composed of four principle spirals, in the same way the circles in the braid are composed of four knots. We can also count twenty-four circles in the border and twenty-four figures linking the spirals in the two central circles.

By presenting one of the rare examples where knots are juxtaposed with the corresponding labyrinth, the whole design can be seen as constituting, like the Rosetta Stone, a key to decode a geometry. Thus Durrow's gospel, which was compiled and illuminated in the sixth century, when Christianity penetrated Ireland, is the hidden legacy of a more ancient knowledge destined for the Christian era, or perhaps even for our own. But here the geometrical transformation, applied to an interlacing apparently composed of two distinct cords, is more complex and is probably founded on different principles. It seems that the geometry follows a pathway of loops rather than that of the thread, and I have not been able to figure it out yet.

In the page from the Book of Durrow, a third dimension is suggested in a subtle way. This is due to the fact that we can follow the path of the labyrinth just as easily by following the surface of the spirals, or as if penetrating inside them as in tubes, cornucopias, or trumpets whose openings are perfectly drawn. In addition, instead of following the path of the luminous copper tubes, we can follow the obscure path of the funnels, blending with the background that opens into vulvas. There is therefore a "tunnel effect," as in quantum cosmology, and the trumpets are like the time cones represented in a similar way in modern cosmological diagrams.

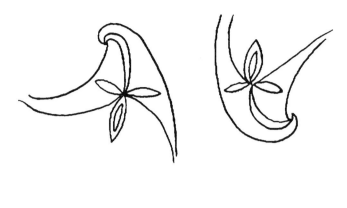

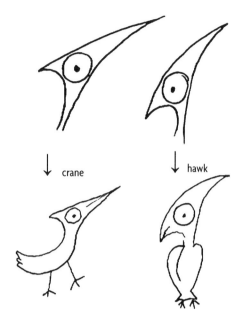

crane   hawk

Fig. 30.1
(A) Hood, mask, or Phrygian cap. (B) Fox head.
(C) Crane and hawk.

The geometric drawing also presents ambiguous figures that can be interpreted differently according to the angle from which they are seen. This reversal of the figures seems to accompany the reversal from one sphere to another. When they are turned, hooded beings wearing Phrygian caps can appear as malicious foxes with long ears and twisted noses. Embedded between these forms, as in an Escher drawing, we can also imagine dark hawks with solar eyes and pointed skulls, which, when pivoted, suddenly resemble cranes (see fig. 30.1). By following the paths of the labyrinth, we end up somehow in the eye or the head of an entity or a disguised god who shares his vision with us to guide us further through a sort of cyclotron that transforms us or transports us through time from one world to another.

The Durrow labyrinth presents a compromise between a maze and a labyrinth and between a purely geometric yantra and a mandala. Each way out of a labyrinth is the entrance to another one. We no longer find a single center, but rather a multitude of centers, or else a center that seems to move as it is discovered in different spaces and in an evolving and involving universe that dies and is reborn.

The braid surrounding it is traditionally a symbol of eternity or of perpetuity, but it can also represent the movement of a knot turning in on itself as it circles in an orbit (as in fig. 16.2), and thus a cycle. Hence, the corresponding labyrinth represents a universe that is constantly renewing itself, a world absorbed by black holes that reappears in another dimension as the mirror image of itself, perhaps in such a way as to reverse the matter-antimatter relation. The dissolution that this labyrinth is supposed to represent constitutes nothing other than a reversal permitting a perpetual creation. When reversed to become that of a menacing and helmeted guardian, the image of a fox, who in myths is a cunning rascal caught in his own stratagems, can suggest how all principles contain their opposite and can be reversed. It suggests the necessity for a middle path, an absolute center that must be continually rediscovered and which, when fixed once and for all in a rigid space, leads to a duality that excludes instead of reuniting.

Each kind of knot, whatever its cultural context, corresponds to a different way of envisioning a center. The entire group of these knots belonging to different cultures and civilizations forms a new knot that itself suggests a moving center. It is in this way that the symbol of an absolute center is maintained and comes to life. The center of the Cretan labyrinth is linked to a center presented by the totality of sym-

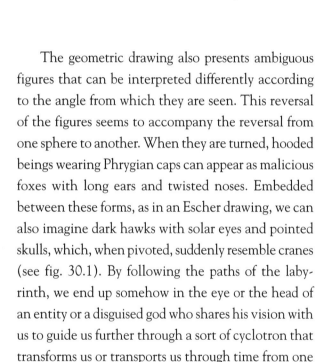

bolic language, or by what would be its complete understanding. The meanings of these two centers (the absolute center and the center of the Cretan labyrinth) are codependent and are in fact the same center reached by different means in an ever-changing world.

Each ancient cultural system is thus also comparable to a knot that presents itself as the cross section of a more complex multidimensional knot uniting them all. Ideally, each culture maintains its cohesion and universality only by maintaining its respective place in a whole that it reflects. An emptiness must be maintained to leave room for an infinite potential and so that other, complementary cultures can take the place of those that disintegrate. Each ancient cultural system reveals a path leading to the center and at the same time locates this center outside of the system, in an outside that is potentially everywhere and within each individual. Each system contributes to defining a dynamic and perfectly balanced whole that cannot be directly described and which reveals a path leading to the truth, while refusing to appropriate all possible aspects of an absolute truth that cannot be encapsulated in a formula. Uniting all systems, the knot can offer a model for a profound ecological science or for an ecumenism that would avoid the trap of syncretism. With new dimensions, the notion of direction changes. There are no more absolute opposite directions, right and left, rightist and leftist, above and below, but a search for harmony and for what links opposites. This model is also suggested by the reversal of the Tower of Babel and the division of languages or "confusion of tongues" that followed. As Humbolt remarked, it is by a separation of tongues that language starts.

It is perhaps for this reason that we do not find a treatise on the geometry of the labyrinth in ancient cultures. Ancient geometry is never dissociated from a continually renewed activity that occurs, like weaving, "between the fingers and under the shadow of the forehead"—in other words, in the unconscious. If it were separated, the mental realm, whose nature

is dual, would appropriate it as it has modern geometry, which has become a separate science.

If an absolute center and an undivided whole do exist, however, this implies that misunderstood ancient science and our actual, fragmented modern science, which is incapable of offering a meaning for life, must be complementary and part of a whole. Modern science is a reversal of ancient science, and the mode of this reversal should be reflected in the way the ancient and modern topologies correspond and are differentiated. A comparison of these two topologies could be fruitful and lead to a more complete or total science. We can imagine that with the support of modern topology, the geometry linking ancient symbols would be thoroughly investigated, and we could end up with a perfectly rational logical system. But if this hypothesis were realized, the symbol would lose its ancient meaning as a *symbolon*, which is literally a broken ring testifying to a pact or alliance and ensuring a possible participation with the Logos. In and of itself, isolated from any context—in other words, from myth and ritual—the symbol cannot procure the experience it suggests or the psychic transformation it offers. The rational system thus would correspond to an impossible and arrogant Tower of Babel. The knowledge of ancient geometry could also lead to an evolution of modern science, but without its symbolic dimension; it would not lead to a unified theory that could unveil the meaning of existence.

Hesitation about the method of engaging the symbolic turns on the fact that over the centuries, our relation to the symbol has been reversed, and thus at the same time the symbol's nature itself has undergone an upheaval. Ancient ritual consisted in sacrificing the antiquated to offer the promise of a renewal, and the symbols associated with the ritual contributed toward this renewal. But with time, the ancient symbols seem to have become the guardians of fossilized concepts. The mode of relation changes everything, and we cannot grasp what the symbol unites independently from the experience of the relation, nor can we understand the relation when the symbol separated from its context becomes mute. The reversal, "which is the ultimate truth," also escapes our understanding.

The mode of a reversal illustrated by the geometry of the labyrinth can nonetheless lead us to question our relationship to the images of a reality that remains imaginary or conventional, or to the images produced by modern science. We are continually living this reversal, but without being able to realize it or reach full awareness of it. It is through experiencing it fully and consciously that we can rediscover its meaning.

In Martin Heidegger's words: "We draw much closer to what IS by thinking about all this in an inverse way, on the condition of course, that we can see, first and foremost, how otherwise everything turns toward us. If effectuated for itself, the simple reversal gives nothing."[1] We still have to come to some sort of agreement as to what this "everything," this "we," this "inversion" or reversal, this turn, and this "otherwise" mentioned by Heidegger mean. With the geometry of the labyrinth, these words and their rela-

tionship to each other take on a very precise meaning, but it appears to be the task of art to express this "otherwise" by which "everything turns toward us."

Even this study, which presents itself as an attempt to investigate myth methodically and in such a way as to lead gradually to the discovery of a geometry, reverses the path that I have followed to uncover the structure of the symbol, a reversal that cannot stop reproducing itself at different levels and along different axes. In fact, I am first a painter and it is while I was questioning the role of the gaze in painting and the meaning of this "otherwise" that gives meaning to art that the geometry of the labyrinth unexpectedly presented itself to me. Once discovered, the labyrinth can lead to all kinds of connections and logical and analogical demonstrations, but what led to the labyrinth itself are the age-old questions "Who am I?" "Where am I?" "Where do I go?"—questions that are always being asked in serious art. It is only afterward, and in order to understand better into what kind of lock I should introduce what appeared to me to be a key, that I was led to investigate the myths.

Fig. 30.2. A two-sided Cretan seal
Do these images also evoke a labyrinth similar to that of the Book of Durrow?

31

The Labyrinth in Painting

To all appearances, the artist acts like a mediumistic being, who, from the labyrinth beyond time and space, seeks his way out to a clearing.

—Marcel Duchamp

As a boy, I remember being intrigued by a Giotto painting in the Louvre, the stigmatization of St. Francis, in which rays joining Christ's body to Francis praying beneath him became like beams revealing an invisible structure of the painting, or even like the stigmata themselves wounding the canvas or leaving scars on it. I had just started painting, and it seemed to me that Giotto had attempted to reproduce the play of visible and invisible rays. I recognized this play of rays in van Gogh as well as in the "X-ray paintings" of aboriginal Australia, and in my own work I adhered to the rayonism of Larionov. But I soon came to feel that the imbroglio of all these interfering rays would be better expressed by an arrangement of dots or spots that could represent a section in the maze of rays or rays seen from one end. In addition to radiation, they could also suggest emanation.

I became fascinated by Seurat's pointillism, which presented for me the goal the impressionists had been striving toward. I interpreted the post-impressionist movement not so much as a return to nature, but as a search for what is behind nature and as an attempt to rediscover, directly by the senses and in the most ephemeral perception, a vision of the world similar to the one science had led to. I recognized in it a return to the atomism of the ancient Greeks or the Hindus. Seurat, an admirer of Egyptian hieratism,

faced the problem of structure and composition in a new way by taking the simplest element as his building block: the point. His method of reuniting color and structure without having one dominate the other appeared to me as the most integral and radical endeavor.

In Seurat's last painting, *The Circus*, the points of color seem to be filings ordered by an invisible magnetic field. Is the field created by the crack or the arabesque of the ringmaster's whip, or does it emanate from the rider standing upon a galloping horse? Or is it rather the rider who executes a dance like that of the particles? Their sparkling seems to animate the spectators, inspiring in them different moods, expressions, and movements that anticipate futurist art. What magician could better harmonize this order, this freedom, and this virtuosity? Seurat's painting suggested that we could directly observe around forms in the atmosphere, as if through a prism, a spectral decomposition of light. In scrutinizing objects, the gaze could find a grain of light corresponding to a tactile sensation.

For some time, I worked in a mine, and emerging from the shaft into the daylight in the opening of the pit seemed to me like the eruption of flames at the entrance to a furnace. A similar effect can be obtained by focusing the eyes. It seemed to me that by focusing and following the effect of the law of simultaneous and successive contrasts in color and value, I could actually follow a rhythmic parade of light in nature that would obliterate forms, probing or enveloping them with an aura, itself having a form that suggested a center, a nucleus, or an axis. The light seemed to know and follow a course that unveiled the essential or archetypal structure of the object.

It was the intention to see and the intensity of the gaze that made this phenomenon manifest. A certain fixation of the gaze seemed to punctuate the light, suggesting a rain of photons or a whirlwind of projectiles enveloping the object. The internal physiological phenomena were knotted to the external optical phenomena. By sometimes superimposing spots and more minuscule points, Seurat had, in my eyes, rediscovered the phenomenon described by the Fresnel law, which establishes that within a very small light source the diffraction produces a darker central zone. Each punctuated luminous spot appeared then to be an atom with its nucleus, which was integrated in a conglomerate of other atoms or liberated itself from the rest of the image. By focusing my gaze to capture the fleeting moment when this nucleus would appear, the rest of my field of vision became blurry, occupied by the emptiness or fog that can be found in certain Chinese paintings, or else lured into a night where constellations once again shone, and swarms of sparks exploded as in van Gogh's landscapes, or imploded like in the paintings of Bonnard or Kandinsky. The role of these nuclei in the composition also reminded me of the role played by the "lice" in Cezanne's painting *Les Poux,* those voids or parcels of the canvas he left untouched and around which he is said to have organized his whole canvas as if he were rediscovering the emptiness that is the source of all creation. Thus I was rediscovering worlds that ran alongside, confronted, and interpenetrated each other, and the nude or the subject that I painted seemed free to become eclipsed or to escape from this world like the gods of antiquity, or to plunge and be embodied in diverse forms according to my will.

There is a Japanese tale of how a painter, wanting to describe the world to a bedridden child, brought him the leaf of a tree pierced with a hole that shone when the leaf was held up to the light. "Imagine," he told the child, "a myriad of these small windows. That is the forest." Each object could also become like a shady and labyrinthine forest feeding on light and offering the image of an abundance of stars, themselves sources of light.

I experienced, in fact, a certain inebriation in letting myself be drawn into a naive error of interpretation. Instead of recognizing in Seurat an analytical recomposition of color and a principle of composition founded on the harmony of verticals and horizontals that prefigured Mondrian, I persisted in seeing the representation of a direct vision that I saw as being more natural than mental. As van Gogh said, "La nature emboite le pas (nature follows suit)." As the will-o'-the-wisps and fireflies that I perceived and followed could not be the photons defined by science, being unable to identify them, I compared them to the *bindus* of Hindu philosophy and tantric art or to vital elementary particles.

As I struggled to follow and paint the bursting and eclipsing of minuscule suns that I believed I really perceived, and the phantasmagorical dance of successive images they provoked in reaction, I asked myself if the spots I placed on the canvas represented the traces of a dance that occurred only on my retina and which I could have followed just as easily by contemplating a blank wall, or if they corresponded to a more direct perception. How could I be transported or unified by this dance rather than frustrated by the impossibility of ordering and modeling such an elusive substance? As Balzac describes it in *The Unknown Masterpiece,* the organization of spots should be able to form a kind of cloud in which would appear, torn from the whole, a piece of reality, tougher and truer than that offered by concrete things; but this organization of spots depended on a path of the gaze that hesitated between its source and the object it wanted to invest. It seemed impossible to follow a precise pathway of vision that could indefinitely divide itself. I hoped that a *more* piercing gaze would finally force an entry into a vision that would impose itself and finally produce an image that would resolve the seducing chaos that I could not control. Was not such a transformation of vision produced by hallucinogenic drugs? Did there not exist an ancient promise stating that reality or truth could be attained in a direct vision? "The clerks whose faults have been completely consumed, whose thought is unveiled, see in a direct perception, that is like a reflection of their own thought, the totality of things, including all reunited forms and this without any possible error."[1] What was this plenitude of light? What fault veiled my thought and kept me prisoner of a centerless and exitless maze?

It is at this point that I became interested in the cat's cradle. In Lévi-Strauss's *The Raw and the Cooked* there is an Amazonian cat's cradle representing a tree (similar to fig. 7.6B). The drawing of the cat's cradle reminded me of the pattern of the juxtaposed spots scattered across my paintings. The way the drawing suggested the genesis of an image instead of reproducing an appearance corresponded to what I was vaguely seeking to portray in semi-abstract paintings. I saw the cat's cradle as a matrix in which I could order and transform the traces of the ephemeral impressions that I tried to capture on my canvases. The knot of the cat's cradle seemed to be a mold that could hold a fused matter that, instead of being dispersed, could rest, amalgamate, and weld itself together to find its source and its meaning.

The image of the tree suggested by the cat's cradle seemed to find its place between the trees painted by Mondrian and Klee and lead to an ideal synthesis between the vision of these two artists whom I admired. The path of the cat's cradle presented what appeared to be the negative of an image, or an emptiness left by its retreat; it somehow seemed more complete than that of the object, as it could indiscriminately include different possible relations with the tree. The more I thought about this image, the more it seemed to correspond to the tree I wanted to paint,

and to a tree that I carried in myself. I thought, for example, of the tree that had served as a refuge for a band of kids that included myself, and which we had transformed into a fort or a ship where we each had a lookout and an escape route; it was a pirate's lair where our dreams found shelter and secrets were shared. This tree could also be the shade-offering tree in the middle of immense cultivated fields around which crows circled, and that was a vestige of an ancient forest and the lone remaining witness of ancient stories such as the judgment under a tree by King Louis IX that I reinvented. Or yet again it could be the tree of paradise engraved on Nestor's ring. It could be the same tree under which the poet Michaux found himself, "The tree without end, the tree of life which is a source, dotted with pictures and words and proposing enigmas whose flowing without interruption, not even of one second, crosses man from the first instant of his life to the last brook or hourglass that stops only with it"[2] or the tree under which the Buddha awakened, thereby becoming the symbol of awakening. The tree was also a maze or a knot in which the ends of the branches were joined by the ephemeral traces of autumn leaves or spring pollen carried by the wind.

But if I tried to draw a particular tree, I could never manage to reconstitute the movement and pattern of the thread of the cat's cradle starting from simple impressions. In my frustration, the way the cat's cradle game could result in such an evocative image became incomprehensible to me. The initial ring suggested a center or an egg that hatched to liberate its potential contents. But I could not grasp of what this egg or the final image of the cat's cradle was constituted. The folding of the thread seemed to correspond to a ritual during which an invoked world suddenly surged forth in a strangely familiar form from an emptiness that perfectly enveloped it. The process seemed both opposed and complementary to that triggered by the symmetrical image of a Rorschach figure produced by folding the paper and transferring the still-wet stains, drawn without forethought, to the other half. In this case, the drawing leads us to discover a figure that seemed to haunt the subconscious and prevent or obliterate a purer vision instead of revealing it.

I was unable to grasp what could unite a perception produced by the senses to a concept that made it possible to gain access to a different order. In the cat's cradle, the concept that escaped my comprehension seemed to be like the word *cat* (*chat* in French), which could occupy the nest of the bird that it preyed on, or else transform itself into a screech owl (*un chat huant*, literally, "a cat that makes the sound *hoo*").

I had a dream in which, after climbing a mountain covered by a deep forest whose green color seemed very intense and vivid, I arrived at a castle where hung marvelous completely white paintings that seemed to contain all things (and thus were quite different from those of Malevich). Perhaps a white similar to the one described by H. Michaux, but more calm, since I was sleeping and had never tried mescaline. A white that was like a mirror of the world. "And white appears. Absolute white. White beyond all whiteness. White of the coming of the white. White without compromise, through exclusion, through total eradication of nonwhite. Insane, enraged white, screaming with whiteness. Fanatical, furious, riddling the retina. Horrible electric white implacable, murderous. White in bursts of white. God of 'white.' No not a God, a howler monkey (let's hope my cells don't blow apart). End of white. I have a feeling that for a long time white is going to have something excessive for me."[3] The lord of this castle appeared and showed me with his finger how to turn my eye inside in order to be able to see in this way. The dream left a strong impression, but when I woke up, I could not fathom either how to obtain this whiteness and this void by mixing all colors and all things, or how to represent the circumambulation or the transformation of all colored things in one white color.

I began to question the structure of the cat's cradle. If by discovering and analyzing a structure, Lévi-Strauss could make fragments of apparently incoherent Amazonian myths intelligible, there must also have been a way to pierce what, behind its apparent simplicity, made it possible for the cat's cradle to present itself as an imaginary theater giving a concrete form to myth. In this way, and to my surprise, going from the cat's cradle to simpler knots, I gradually discovered the geometry of the labyrinth and the path leading to a center, a white center that took the place of the cat's cradle ring.

This geometry revealed new and multiple relations between the forms woven into the cat's cradle, as well as a path connecting them. By projecting onto my canvas the geometry that transformed the knot of the cat's cradle, I found its forms doubled, decomposed, enlaced, and amalgamated according to multiple combinations. Images that were previously impossible to grasp because they were fused together were now separated, but only to invite each other to once again unite or become embedded. I discovered a sort of hieroglyphic writing whose signs were joined by a complex network (see fig. 31.1). At the time I was working in a studio by the sea at Key West, and I was surprised that the network could coincide with the impression the shimmering sea left on me. Gradually, new mappings could evoke other landscapes and movements other than those of the waves, and reciprocally they offered me a sort of master key for interpreting ancient primitive patterns. The more I elaborated new patterns, the more I discovered new views and new aspects of landscape and the more I was driven to deepen my geometric understanding. Arranged differently, this network corresponded to a system of perspectives applicable to a changing space-time dimension where all the escaping lines, instead of crossing at a single vanishing point, were extended and reconnected to form more or less deformed or interlaced rings or a tangled ball of thread. With the lines of this network, I felt I was rediscovering the subtle nature of the luminous rays painted by Giotto.

As I worked, the image before me seemed to suggest the "reflection" of "the totality of things, including all reunited forms," something I could neither un-

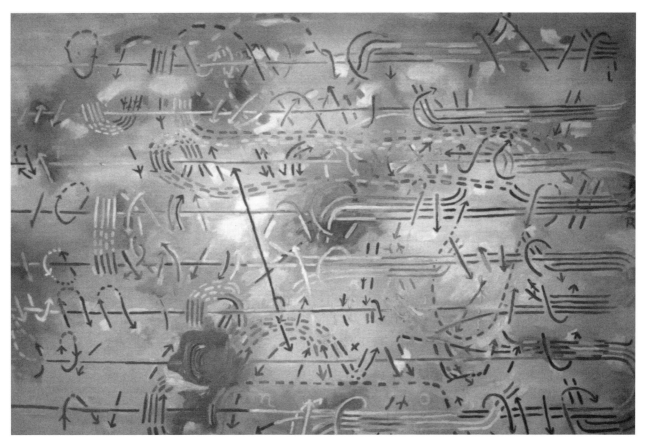

Fig. 31.1. The deconstruction of cat's cradle, Patrick Conty, 1987

derstand nor visualize without the help of geometry. At other times it suggested a spatiotemporal landscape, a field of transformation where forms gradually took on a new meaning. Deconstruction and structuration reconnected within a cycle, appearing as two inseparable but complementary forces.

The paintings I created with this method also suggested the figure of a latent myth as they became more detailed. The intentions of a painter like Poussin, who placed mythological scenes in a familiar light and a retreating perspective, were here reversed, as in the painting in figure 31.2 called *Destruction of Myth No. 1*. The map or landscape that I was painting described what could be seen as the other side or the hidden structure of myths, the dimension of spacetime where the transforming myths were united (also see fig. 31.3).

By exploring a network that connected the various puzzles of objects, signs, traces, movements taking form, and forms opening to emptiness, I felt I was

discovering the common language uniting all the currents of modern art. By opposing the tyranny of the perceived object, which had become suspect anyway, modern art seemed to trace the limits of the vague zone of a gestalt field that has lain fallow since a time when perception was more free. Thus the painter De Kooning, for example, compares painting to a ball of thread, leading to all desired things. But each modern school seemed to be stuck at a particular crossroad of a maze without being able to find the center. The proliferation and continual change of styles corresponded to the ever-renewed exploration of an inexhaustible and changing field. Each crossroad led irrevocably to another.

Recently, however, I felt a definite affinity with the work of some artists, like the American Brice Marden and the Australian Claude Heath. Their aim and ambition seemed quite different from mine, but through a perspicacious understanding of art evolution and dialectic, they also produced, and perhaps

Fig. 31.2. **Destruction of Myth No. 1,** *Patrick Conty, 1987*

more skillfully or elegantly than I, an interlacing of lines that suggested canons and fugues, a continual transformation that could reunite latent images (see Marden, fig. 31.4C and plate 6 and Heath, figs. 31.4A and B). Blindfolded, Heath draws with one hand while with the other hand he explores the volume of a head or a sculpture such as that of a tiger jumping on an antelope, thus suggesting that his technique also has a predatory quality. Other times his drawing accompanies the one-handed peeling of an orange, the lines following alternatively the baroque curve of the torn peel twisting itself and the more sober stripping of the flesh, the two motions enhancing and revealing each other. With a pencil or a ballpoint pen, he projects on a two-dimensional sheet the trace of a three dimensional exploration started from an original point to which he returns after every circuit. Thus he forms a sort of complex knot that differs from the

one accomplished by the natural course of the eye examining the motif.

Sometimes his drawing is projected on a wall, like a large-scale map, and the continuous line is replaced by a regular succession of dots, which, like *bindus*, can represent a moment of consciousness or a definite sensation. The accumulation of dots allows the spectator to discover new possible paths and make new choices, creating a gestalt field or a maze in which each spectator can rediscover the motif in an indeterminate number of ways. It is as if he were discovering hidden ways through a crowd. There is then an open invitation to an exchange between the artist and the spectator that reveals a dimension hidden in all great works of art.

When he draws a head, Heath explores its volume from all sides, and yet we get the impression of a facial expression lighted from within or of a presence

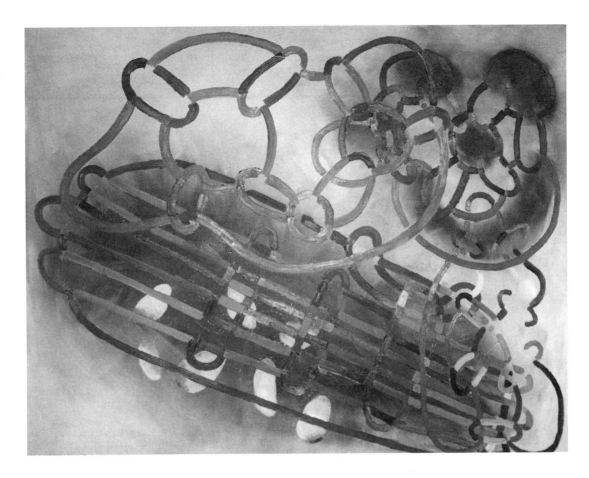

Fig. 31.3. The hidden structure of myths

(A) Eros and Thanatos, *Patrick Conty, 1988. This painting uses a system of rings to replace the structure of a knot.*
(B) Under the Volcano, *Patrick Conty, 1988. A deconstruction of cat's cradle transformed into a landscape.*

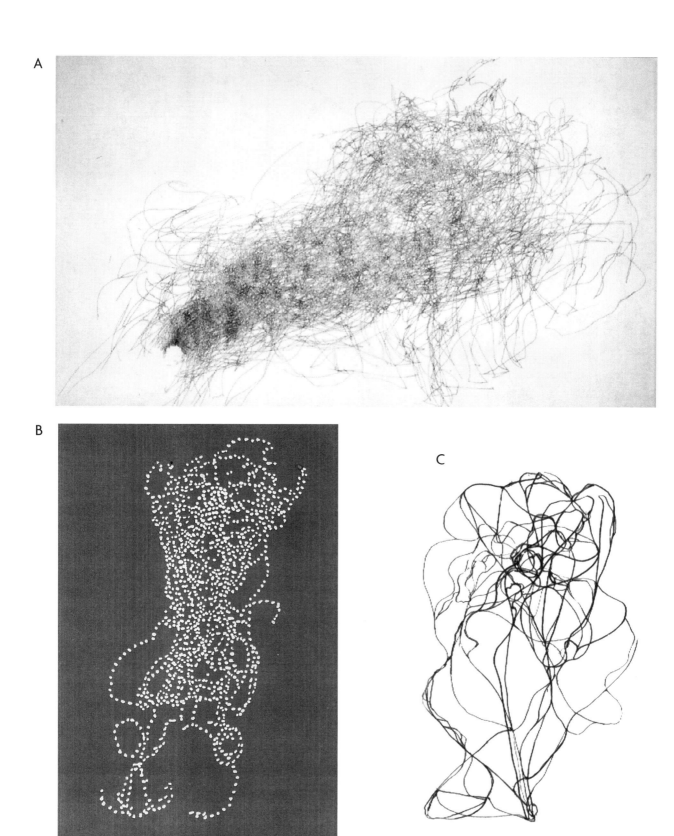

Fig. 31.4. Works by Claude Heath and Brice Marden
(A) Tiger and Prey, *Claude Heath, 1997.* (B) Study after Anthony Caro's Smiling Woman (1956), *Claude Heath, 1997.* (C) Solstice, *Brice Marden, 1993.*

that hides itself behind a mask. Remembering the labyrinth, one is led to ask: Toward what ultimate goal does the path of Heath's pen lead? Could it lead also to a center? What kind of consciousness or sub-consciousness guides his tactile exploration and its projection? What knot of relation links the sensation to an impulse and a mental image? At a deep level, could the process that provokes the folding of the drawn line become analogous to the one that folds the chains of amino acid proteins so that they function correctly? Is there a subconscious geometry like the one producing the maze that guides the pen? In my own work, I was trying to identify a hidden motif or the outline of some concrete thing within a cat's cradle or a complex maze representing an abstract knot of relationship. Heath's attempt is to produce an ambiguous image of an object with an uninterrupted path that itself corresponds to a knot of relations or to a maze. The two approaches correspond and can meet. This sort of convergence is for me a sign of this epoch in which we live.

Although the approach of Marden is quite different, there is a striking resemblance between some of his most recent drawings and those of Heath. With the fugal or musical aspect of his work, a time scale is more obviously introduced. It suggests that some forms exist that would be delineated by the shapes of new emerging paths combined with those of some more ancient ones or shapes subsisting only in memory. These forms exist then only within a time dimension, and could constitute the ones adopted by "spirits" or, what amounts to the same, by "states of mind" or even memories. In some way, even if we have grown out of our embryo, we are still connected to its life and to a nurturing womb. By creating designs that can suggest a path as well as a shape, with the means of color, Marden evaluates and accentuates the harmonious aspect of divers ancient magic tracings that represented the dwellings of spirits and could be used to invoke them. He thus acts somewhat as an exorcist. Besides, when Marden's lines are like traces joining different Chinese calligraphic ideograms, it is as

if he questions the structures of writing and language and their connection with the structure of things. Henry Michaux tried to paint the effluvium that circulates among people but Marden catches the effluvia that circulate among words. For a long time he painted scaffoldings, which, by the way, can be the symbol of the soul joining body to spirit. Marden should not be classified uniquely as an abstract artist.

With these two artists, I find a new approach to art and to art meaning that has nothing to do with the patching up of an old net. Both live an unknown adventure in an unknown space. Although many artists use the image of the labyrinth that they build with videos or mirrors or whatnot, without distinguishing it from a maze, I feel that Heath and Marden contribute perhaps involuntarily to the exploration of its deeper meaning. They show a path leading to it or to its transformation, instead of gobbling it up like a fish unaware of the hidden hook inside the wriggling worm.

But soon I noticed that by playing with images and forms that were disconnected from an ancient but defunct symbolic language, my painting as well was only exploring a maze, without finding the way out. The absence of a context produced by a coherent whole of modern myths and rituals rendered the symbolic content outdated, and there remained only remnants of forms having belonged to the symbols, forms that were eloquent only as ruins. Instead of finding a truer original nature, I saw myself puttering about like a genetic engineer, contributing, like Daedalus, to the conception and incarceration of monsters. Moreover, as I was limited by the composition of the geometry, I started to miss my ancient, more intuitive way of painting, when I simply pinned down the colors my eyes were catching, when it was a question of distinguishing what I really saw from what I thought I saw and of discovering how I saw. In opposition to this, when the construction and signification of the drawing predominates, the color is at the service of the meaning and the geometry. It has no life of its own, it becomes conventional or decorative like in the art of Escher or Magritte or even coded as in some scientific illustrations. To paint is not to depict. My strategy changed. Instead of trying to unveil the hidden structure and content of ancient or primitive patterns, I applied the geometry of the labyrinth to familiar objects that I could look at. I used, for example, chairs (see plate 13, *The Perilous Seat*) or step ladders that were in my studio. The first one reminded me of the perilous seat of the Arthurian legend or of Theseus's chair of oblivion. The second was kaleidoscopically deconstructed, multiplied, and recombined so as to suggest images of constellations, ships, or aliens, and could represent Jacob's ladder or the heavenly ladder of Climacus, which transformed itself into that to which it was supposed to lead. In some new way, then, I was recreating a symbolic image. The movement and the structure given to a banal object belonged to a vision that gave it a symbolic meaning.

After transforming knots into objects, the next step was to paint the geometric formation of the labyrinth starting with a moving and gradually transformed object instead of a knot. The result was that not only the labyrinth itself started to appear in my paintings, but also, somehow, what the labyrinth contained also began to appear (see plates 11 and 12). This came to me as a surprise and I soon realized that if the labyrinth could represent the process of perception, parts of it or phases of its formation also started to be perceivable. It presented itself as an answer to my most basic questioning in art. At a deep level, these parts could correspond to the encoded and embodied information that, in the constructive process of perception, is used as output to organize and interpret the flux of impressions and impulses corresponding to the input. The labyrinth, with all its phases, levels, and aspects, was the world hidden behind the motifs I was scanning and behind the changing apparitions I was trying to organize, but it was also the laboratory in which these alchemical transformations occurred.

There is, then, a continual correspondence not only between ancient art and the meaning of the labyrinth as it is expressed in myths and legends, but also between the new concepts of the labyrinth brought by modern topology and the new problems posed by the evolution of art. A correspondence between, on the one hand, all impressions, expressions, and visions of life continuously changing as we roam through a transforming maze and, on the other hand, an archetype of the labyrinth that we make descend only in determinate proportions according to our progress toward the center. The point is that as we can acknowledge the existence of different realms of realism, imagination, and symbolism, according to ancient tradition, the access to these different realms is opened by three different kinds of perception due to impression, embodiment, and union. It is the passage from the one into the other that is difficult to express.

In art or on the canvas, we cannot reproduce the phenomenon of perception or the changing of perception itself. It is always replaced by the elaboration of a structure, more or less obvious and achieved, which connects more or less consciously the brushstrokes, the marks, the spots, the washes and runs, or the basic elements; a structure that changes with the color system, the medium, and the messages delivered; a structure that art must constantly bring back into question. At a deep level there is a correspondence between the laws of perception, physics, and mathematics. When one law changes, all are shaken. Once again, the truth can be reached only by a coincidence.

In the blink of an eye, we can receive through the impact of color and light a vision of something. But we never know exactly what it is—perhaps the vision of a presence, or a unity, or a coincidence. The immediate always escapes us. When it is questioned, when the gaze interrogates the vision and tries to pierce through the conventional message that takes over, it discovers a sort of maze, a gestaltic cloud within which the first vision is hidden and must be searched methodically. We uncover a palimpsest (a superimposition of several images painted in different historical or cultural periods) containing a history of art, mediums, and mind structure—a storage of encoded embodied experiences that constitute the fabric of the constructive aspect of perception, the final product of which becomes either the result of inherited conformity, or chance and fate, or that of a creative freedom to interpret.

But how is it possible to follow with confidence and authority this process? How is it possible to bring to awareness and consciousness the hidden phases and mechanisms without modifying them, and to do so in such a way as to rediscover the true, original, pristine, spontaneous vision? We will never be able to discover the true image of the original vision. In art, as in myth, truth is reached only through a combination of learned lies. To evoke the original vision or "the truth of the lie," as Gauguin said, we must recreate, reverse, and transform the way leading away from it; invent a way leading back to the archetype. The process is similar to that leading from the maze to the labyrinth. The new aim of art then becomes the presentation of the succession or the movement, the more or less speedy unfolding of the transformation of images.

After the importance given by the impressionist painters to subjective colors and their simultaneous and successive contrasts, with "color as animated matter, as the body of an animated being,"[4] the conventional form was broken. With cubism Duchamp, the Italian futurists, Pollock, Bacon, and other artists started to represent movement itself, but even if the representation of movement further shattered that which was moving, it was still the movement of things. Now it is the movement or mutation and transmigration of the images that must be presented—a movement that can resemble the breaking and shattering of iconoclasm, but is really a return to the source, to an anonymous messenger, and to a center that is everywhere or to "a degree Zero of art," although not in the way it was announced. Bruno Latour called this new movement which imposes itself *iconophili*. But somehow, it presents itself once again as a return, a transformation rather than a restoration of a theory of the image already promoted long ago by St. Dionysios the aeropagyte:

> It is the trail through all discrepancies, puzzles, and breaches—in visual constructions, in the use of the themes, in the interpretations of programs—that provides meaning, or not, to religious icons. . . .What should be retrieved is their "shaking" and their "trepidation." What we have to retrieve is the carrying of a movement that uses the message to produce those who enunciate this message. Because it is nearly impossible, the only way it can be done is to render the message incapable of doing the job of information transfer in order to force the attention away. But this *away* is not the *beyond* of "beyond belief," and here again, the path falsely indicated by the message has to be broken, shattered, and interrupted . . .
>
> The meaning of the message is in a presence that becomes absent through the displacement of the mediation itself.[5]

This movement remains to be presented eloquently and successfully. The cats cradles, the Cretan seals, the paintings reproduced in the color plates section of this book all respond through different means and in a different context to the requested condition—but all with different results.

Now if the labyrinth can represent perception, one could ask: perception of what? The answer could equally be everything or the void. As always, it is a question of context; there is always the colorless "mollusk of context." There is the rub: When I observe the geometric patterns as a painter, I can always, as in a cat's cradle or a spot on the wall, see something, almost anything. When I manipulate it like a topologist, it is completely different. Even before realizing that the labyrinth was the symbol of all and everything, I had from the outset the conviction of discovering through its geometry a particular manner of exploring the structure of matter as physics describes it.

At first the knots and strings could represent the

trajectory of particles around a nucleus and the geometry explained in some way the double nature of light as particle (axis) and wave (meander). Already in 1860, William Thomson, who became Lord Kelvin, proposed a theory of "vortex atoms" composed of knots in order to reconcile the theory of corpuscles with that of waves. I felt I was following the same line of thought. Later details of mazes could become comparable to Feynman diagrams. Then, with knot topology becoming the mathematics of quantum physics, came a confirmation of what until then I only intuitively assumed. Actually the basic principle behind the Jones theorem (which revealed the coincidence between topology and quantum mathematics) corresponds to the transformation of knots into rings that I had already formulated in 1968. With the theory of superstrings and the fact that known particles correspond only to the few strings vibrating with low energy, it follows, as Brian Greene expresses it in *The Elegant Universe*, that "comparatively light fundamental particles should arise in a sense from the fine mist above the roaring ocean of energetic strings."[6] Then, I understood better what kind of "music of the spheres" the geometry of the labyrinth could represent. If only some among many patterns of vibration of the strings produce the ancient nondimensional pointlike particles, the strings are even more fundamental than particles. With the introduction of geometry and dimensional forms, it is as if an immaterial pattern like that of the Tao reappears on the stage, a form that is nothing in itself but the void and the relation between all things, a basic pattern that resonates and repeats itself with some variations at all levels, atomic, cosmic, molecular and genetic, embryological, psychological, and mental. This is something physics cannot recognize. Even if it can be acknowledged that there is a relation between mathematics and the mind structure, without metaphysics, physicists cannot even decide what are the objects corresponding to the models they propose, what really are the strings or the nondimensional corpuscles. Physics can predict

and give power over things, describe and control matter, but not our relation to reality.

With the geometry of the labyrinth and art, there is a different liberty with the forms and their interpretation. One can represent the movement of the knot and the crossing of the strings in an infinite number of ways. There is not only a connection with ancient symbols related to metaphysics but also all kinds of possible combinations of figures related to different aspects, physical, psychological, psychedelic, mental, and those related to language. All these aspects belong to the labyrinth. One can explore different worlds and hidden dimensions that are projections of what exist in the psyche or in the mind but become concrete out there. One can discover the in-between outside and inside and to which we are blind, the abyss that surrounds us and which is not only located in a black hole or represented by death. From the color point of view, the most interesting knot seems to be the one that, as in the paintings of Seurat and van Gogh, joins the motion of light and matter with the gestalt of things, the discovery with the lifting of the veil or the process of uncovering. The problem is again not to represent but to present; for this, the dynamic of color, texture, and geometry must correspond.

Science always seems to progress, but its theories get out of fashion. They always change; the idea of an ultimate theory seems illusory. By contrast, art seems to regress, but good art becomes eternal and its value increases with age. Art seems useless, but as Gurdjieff mentions, it is capable of containing information on universal laws that physics cannot reach. This is its task.

Before I start a new painting, I manipulate and draw combinations of knots sometimes for many days. One could wonder whether this exercise with knots that in a remote past were used as a script resembles more the work of the new physicists or rather the permutations of letters that according to Abulafia could bring new states of consciousness and prophecies. Could there be also a valid in-between? As Maurice Blanchot reminds us:

> The word *prophecy* does not only relate to the future. Much more important than the simple discovery of some events to come, it is a dimension of the spoken word engaged with time. . . . When the word becomes prophetic, it is not the future that is given, but the present that is withdrawn.[7]

Taken alone, geometry can lead neither to the symbol nor to a vision obtained in the center of the labyrinth or at its exit. There have always been diverse projective and perspective systems—in other words, "transversal visions"—that are fleeting, inverted, broken, or exploited in more or less methodical ways to confer a reality to images representing an inclusive vision. But these geometrical systems cannot replace the image produced by a "direct" vision or by a harmonious understanding. Geometry must give way to serve solely as a substratum for the image. Art consists precisely in linking an accentuated or punctuated alphabet that is either visible or underlies a wave of light that rolls and breaks, liberating a speaking image. We can discover such a dialectic between vision and the field of perception in ancient mosaics. The interstices among the stones form a network composed of concentric or broken circles that magnetize the image produced by the assemblage of colored stones, appearing as if suspended and carried by the magnetic field. The force of the image depends on the resolution of a conflict between the network of colored stones and that produced by the filigree of cement uniting the stones, a filigree that can remind us of Zeus's wrapping cord. These mosaics are often bordered with interlacing and waves forming small crests that could suggest the way the two networks interfere with each other. The geometry is thus transmuted between the image and the emptiness that crosses it.

A similar phenomenon exists in Eastern Orthodox icon painting, produced by partially superimposing successive layers of color. The border of colored zones also forms a network of hardly visible strata that have a subtle effect on the viewer. According to the ancient Russian tradition that consisted in painting with drops of tempera spread out or floated with the brush, three different layers of decreasing intensity representing a gradual concentration of light are superimposed on a dark background. The first covers a predetermined zone; the second, a part of this zone in a spiral movement; the third, a spot or a point marking the origin of the spiral. There is a light glazing of a darker hue forming a veil and making a transition between the three principle layers. The entire process of making the icon, which is transformed step-by-step with this alternative lightening and darkening, becomes a ritual. The network of folds and drapes in the clothing plays a fundamental role and constitutes a script; these folds are lit no longer simply from an exterior source as in Greek sculpture, but also from an interior source. They present a whirlwind of light surging through the clothing from the subject, who becomes like a veiled sun. In the icon, the reversal of light describes a movement that is both centrifugal and centripetal, and transforms the object into a symbol. As the people represented are always Christ, the Virgin Mary, or the saints, the draping clothes represent both what veils the Word (the Word made flesh) and the path of an interior energy or light that is visibly concentrated around the subject in the golden halo that illuminates the entire icon. "The picture that is the icon is not the feeble echo of a reality but what restores reality . . . the icons show a glorious reality, that is divine reality . . ."[8] as in John 12:45: "The one who sees me sees the one who sent me." The prototype of the icon is Christ himself or again his shroud. "The icon is the image of glory, as it is glory in image. With the consequence that it is the glory of the image."[9]

Responding to this fusion of centrifugal and centripetal, interior and exterior light, there is a conflict between a conventional perspective and an inverted perspective that places the spectator at the focal point. The combination of these two perspectives produces the effect of a curved or spiraled space where the object and the subject or spectator looking at the painting fuse. "One must be in the icon to see it."[10]

What is more, according to a sort of symbolic code, the buildings and temples placed in the background, themselves projected in an ambiguous manner, represent themselves as giving shelter to the person represented in the foreground, or else they suggest his or her spiritual status (the temple in man). Finally, the icon starts with the drawing of an armature based on the golden section, upon which are placed the harmonic proportions of the individuals. Apparently the building of this armature is not connected in any way to the combination of perspectives, but it is known that the golden section is used to create gnomonic spirals, which, oriented in opposite ways and combined, can reproduce the path of a labyrinth. There is a subtle connection, then, among the armature, the spreading of the color in spirals, and the movement of the folded cloth. At the end there is a sort of fusion between many geometric systems and methods of construction that is not apparent or obvious on the final icon. The geometry and the path of light hidden in the contruction of the icon are somehow comparable to those presented by the path of the grandmother in the Malekulan tracing; they also help define an object through penetrating, enveloping, and unfolding it. But by an effect of what is called *decoherence* in physics (defined as "a tangling with the environment"), the continuous abstract line of the Malekulan tracings, which loses its ambiguous meaning when colored or painted, is broken and doubled. It represents not the field of perception but rather its sudden occupation by the apparition of a meaningful image, or else of an appearance that allows the object represented to reveal its meaning. Geometry places the object in an ambiguous space to transform it into a symbol, and reciprocally the archetype takes possession of space by managing to signify it. As with the myths, in the "economy" of the icon the geometry is transposed, and we can even say that, in an alchemical circumambulation where everything is stirred together and individual distinctions are lost, it fuses with symbolic language. When perspective later becomes univocal, the symbols become conventional.

If it no longer appears possible today to produce a true image of reality that could correspond to an authoritative concept, it must nonetheless be possible to build an image corresponding to a vision obtained outside of the maze. Life continues to offer epiphanies and images that differ from a cultural medium or a proliferation of particles. The problem of art today is parallel to that of physics as it is expressed, for example, in *The Shadows of the Mind* by Roger Penrose, or *The Quark and the Jaguar* by Murray Gell-Mann. "How can we grasp in a single thought what is most elementary and most complex, the functioning with the completion . . . the transition that leads from quantum to classic, from foundations to appearance?"[11]

But it seems that thought alone can create only a new sort of dualism. In addition, there also exists a feeling and a sensing that correspond to a sixth sense and to the intuition reached by contemplation. This experience of sensing, which, when developed to its utmost possibility, could be defined as discovering an intelligence of the body acting as a mirror of the world, is the only experience that gives the certitude of the existence of a reality. It can be expressed and revealed otherwise by art.

As Mircea Eliade has affirmed, "All new valorizations have always been conditioned by the structure of the image," and "the image waits for the accomplishment of its meaning."[12] If the structure of multidimensional space-time constitutes the substratum of perception as well as of ancient and modern science, it affects the concept of reality and the image of it that we create. The role of art is, a priori, to reveal the nature of this relationship by reversing it and producing a concrete image of space-time-spirit or, in what amounts to the same thing, images corresponding to transmutation and metamorphosis. To rehabilitate the symbolic, art must indicate where, when, and how the invisible can be found. This appears to have been the goal of ancient art as well as Buddhist, Islamic, and Christian art. Primitive religions also strove, rather than to describe the nature of the divine, first to indicate where it could be encountered and how to position oneself in order to meet it. The question "Who are we?" is possible only after seeking to answer the questions "Where do we come from?" "Where are we?" and "Where are we going?"

In the Arthurian cycle the question "Where is the grail?" asked abruptly by Perceval, is the only question that can cure the Fisher King and help restore his kingdom.

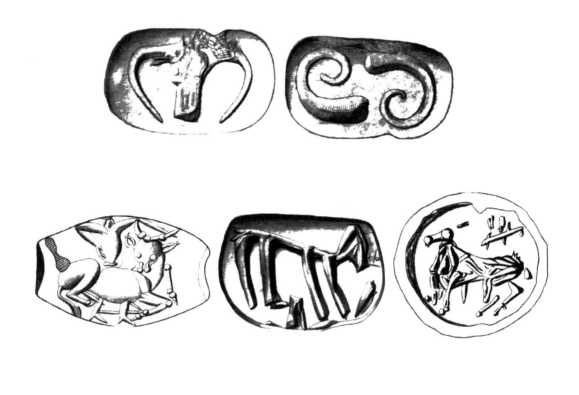

Fig. 31.5. Different styles of the art of Cretan seals

32

A Labyrinth Practice

Listen . . . your state is communicating with you
There is nothing else.
—The Primordial Buddha

The labyrinth is not only a symbol or a model to elucidate our condition and represent our universe; it is also a tool. Understanding the symbol is not enough to change us. The model must also be able to be used toward this goal by helping us to integrate our knowledge. The maze-labyrinth is also a tool for understanding.

If the labyrinth is older than tantrism, and if it constitutes a yantra before the word *yantra* existed, it also constitutes a recognized yantra later on—in other words, a mandala composed only of abstract lines. The yantra is a tool for spiritual and sacramental rites; it is a vase or receiver used to communicate with a god that is invoked in an internal vision. According to Hindu philosophy, the yantra is made of mantras and represents the energy of the mantra and the visual aspect corresponding to a sound. As such, it is also part of the deity. "What the body is for the spark of life, what oil is for the light of the lamp, this is what the yantra represents for all the gods. . . . If we worship the deity on a seat, separately, without a yantra, we tear apart what must remain united like the members of a body, and attract the malediction of the deity."[1] The yantra of the labyrinth thus suggests a very particular receiver, and its efficacy depends on how its content and nature is introduced or recognized or revealed by the officiating authority.

It is also interesting to note that the labyrinth presents a similarity, or at least a common origin, to the enneagram, a sacred symbol representing the potential growth of man and the combination of what Gurdjieff calls the law of three, the Trinity, and the law of seven that we find, for example, expressed by the musical scale. Its use is explained in numerous more or less authentic treatises. Introduced to the West by Gurdjieff, who may have brought it from a secret tradition on Mount Athos, or else from Sufism, the enneagram's affiliation with the labyrinth comes from the fact that the enneagram can be built in a similar way to the labyrinth from a tie knot as it is correctly knotted (see fig. 32.1).

The tie knot as it is usually tied can be represented with seven apparent crossings, but it is really crossed only six times. It then produces a torus knot with a different overlapping of the crossings.

In the case of the enneagram, it is no longer the self axis but the meander that is symmetrically crossed in such a way as to create twelve crossings with the self axis. These correspond to the six crossings of the tie knot. This construction is ingenious, for as we have seen, knots with an even number of crossings cannot be transformed directly into a torus knot.

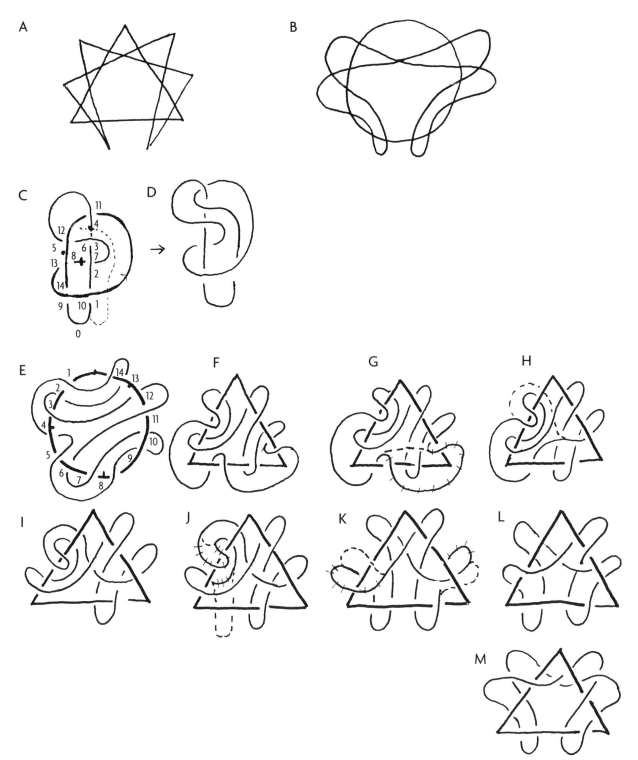

Fig. 32.1. The enneagram obtained from a tie knot

(A) *The enneagram.* (B) *The enneagram is equivalent to the projection of a torus knot, which (since the meander crosses the self axis twelve times) should correspond to a knot crossed six times.* (C) *The tie knot is really a knot crossed six times.*
(D) *A simplified version of C; but to map it, it has to be modified into a false knot crossed seven times, C.* (E) *The torus knot results, through a similar pattern as that of the labyrinth, but with a different overlapping of the string. Crossing the meander instead of the self axis, one obtains the same diagram as the enneagram.* (F) *Here we change the shape of the self axis into a triangle, as with the enneagram.* (G, H, I, J, K, and L) *The barred line is moved to the position indicated by the dotted lines.*
(M) *We finally find the pattern of the enneagram and a torus knot with twelve (six times two) crossings between the self axis and the meander.*

Instead of building a labyrinth, the construction of the enneagram uses the symbols represented by the crossings of the meander with the self axis.

To find a labyrinth practice, we must study in detail the role it has been given in tantrism, or among the Hopi, or even in Korea, where a labyrinth contains the Buddhist text called the "Ocean Seal" (see fig. 2.3). But it seems that in all these cases, the labyrinth is completely integrated into a complex system, which makes it impossible to distinguish a use that is proper to the symbol when it is isolated from its context. For example, in the Hopi Wuwuchim ritual, which lasts sixteen days and includes numerous ceremonies initiating neophytes in the passage from one world to another, it seems that the labyrinth is there only to contribute toward connecting the meaning of the different ceremonies.

Independent of all context, the virtue of the labyrinthine pathway is that it offers the possibility of coming into contact with a kind of sensing that alone can lead to the experience and certitude of the presence of the real. At the same time, it provokes a momentary dumbfounding of the pilgrim, because the labyrinth, even if it is like the body of a deity, first appears as a signifier without a precise signified (this body of the deity appears very differently from our own). As he circles within the labyrinth, the images and thoughts that the pilgrim projects are combined and dissolved instead of becoming fixated and associated. They undergo a circumambulation that transforms them and helps the pilgrim to communicate with his inner state. The practice of the labyrinth is thus similar to frequenting a master who teaches in silence.

Although I was skeptical at first, I was encouraged after a conference to lead groups of people into a labyrinth; I was quite surprised by the profound effect it seemed to have. There is no doubt—even if one does not realize it at the time—that the crossing of the labyrinth informs. Information brings into form what was formless and inarticulate. "To travel over distance, matters have to be changed into forms. If there is no transformation in the sense of encoding or inscribing into a form, then there is no travel or transportation and the only way to know something is 'to be there' and to point at features silently. . . ."[2] Thus a message that seemed incommunicable or not assimilable can be transposed and transmitted. Information can embody what was unfathomable and ineffable in us or in our body but which was not part of our body as we experience it. It presents a body under a new form and thus evokes new relations to the body, new modes of reception, expression, or action. It reminds us once again that as Nietzsche discovered and as I shall translate, "The amazing thing is the body." Hence, when walking the labyrinth, there is a resonance between an outer and an inner pattern and a process that is triggered within the would-be pilgrim. And so it is perhaps because of the effect my first run through the labyrinth had on me that I felt impelled to investigate it later.

Gurus or New Age promoters have attempted to elaborate methods to walk or cross the labyrinth in a fruitful way. Thus in his book *Labyrinths*, Sig Lonegren proposes placing key words corresponding to planets or chakras in each circuit. For example, he uses the words *mental, emotional, physical, spiritual, God, vision, manifestation*, and, in the center, *evaluation*. He suggests entering the labyrinth with a question and contemplating it at the level of the "capacity" of these words "to help those who seek a resolution to their problems." This sort of exercise appears to me inadequate in that it could present a consumer's attitude and offers only a psychological dimension. Without a familiarity with a precise technique of contemplation, or a complete openness, whatever activities one undertakes in the labyrinth will once again be translated into concepts and feelings coming from a dualistic mentality. The virtue of the labyrinth is precisely that it is empty; even if it presents itself like a vase or a dwelling waiting to be filled, this does not imply that it has to be furnished. A vase, even a cornucopia, is not the same as a pot.

According to Homer, the labyrinth was first a *choros*, or dancing floor, wrought by Daedalus for the fair-braided Ariadne; the dance performed was represented on Achilles' shield. Plutarch mentions that the *geranos*, or crane dance, in which the performers held a rope, was danced by Theseus and Ariadne on the island of Delos. And Virgil mentions the Trojan game that was performed on horses. Many ancient folk dances, such as Morris and sword dances and Basque snail and abduction dances, were related to the labyrinth. All these dances could evoke a process leading to unity, and their movement is a physical counterpart to the more abstract geometric transformation. Dancing may still remain the most appropriate way to run the labyrinth. Even when very simple (or reduced to steps with rhythm), a dance performed with awareness within the labyrinth can provoke a division of attention that prevents identification and helps to control the mind.*

Without attempting to elaborate a more precise labyrinth practice that would facilitate an awakening independently of all philosophical systems, whether they be esoteric or traditional, we can try to indicate how a familiarity with the symbol can help to understand the processes accompanying certain forms of meditation and contemplation that could have been associated with the labyrinth in the past.

First of all, the geometry of the labyrinth that consists in a particular way of observing can be compared to self-observation. To be efficient, this work of self-observation leading to self-knowledge must be simple and natural and performed without effort. "Without making efforts but remaining loose and natural one can break the yoke. . . . Whosoever strives to practice dharma will not find the truth beyond practice,"

writes Tilopa, Indian Buddhist teacher and master of mahamudra and tantra. But this work, using an impartial observer, who is at first virtual and must be imagined, is in the beginning necessarily artificial and constraining. Both simple and complex in its implications, the geometry of the labyrinth permits us to define precisely what "nature" and what "simplicity" we are dealing with. Given our condition, this loose and natural attitude can be the most difficult thing to achieve.

Other Eastern practices belonging to what is sometimes called the direct path consist in visualizing and locating in space a point or letter representing unity. This point is similar to the center of the labyrinth. The fixation of such a point has an organic and psychic effect that helps to control the mind. When accompanied by a profound relaxation, this practice can provoke an instantaneous presence and, ultimately, the state of union with clarity and emptiness that is the ultimate goal of contemplation. Tilopa wrote:

> If one sees naught when staring into space,
> if with the mind one then observes the mind
> one destroys distinction and reaches Buddhahood.

There is thus a correspondence between the method leading to the construction of the symbol and the inverse psychosomatic method that leads from a signifier to the signified—in other words, to the fundamental nature of the mind and to unity. The possible efficacy of this kind of contemplation constitutes the fundamental enigma that is inseparable from that of the origin of the labyrinth and of its construction.

Tilopa's statement could be converted in the following way: "If one no longer distinguishes the structure of the world from a knot of relations (or from a structure of space and void); if with the thread one then observes the thread, one reaches the center of the labyrinth."

---

*We have spoken of the division of the knot in the labyrinth. This division is what leads to a center, and it is provoked by a division of the attention and awareness in the observation necessary for the mapping. It is the same with consciousness. As Tilopa wrote: "With the mind one then observes the mind;" thus it is doubled.

Fig. 32.2. Cretan seals
Amphoras or vases, which, as on the left, can be similar to a bucrane. A vessel as a symbol of crossing? A cup for a transforming potion?

33

Structuralism and Contemplation

Meaning is like the other side of the sign: the explanation of what it implies.
—GILLES DELEUZE

After having investigated the symbol of the labyrinth, one may feel bewildered! It can appear that the ancient spiritual world rests entirely on symbolic language and geometry. One might then think, as many people do, that this spiritual world is not only a creation, but also a fiction. The paradoxes presented by spiritual doctrines are effectively even more difficult to accept than those of quantum physics, as they are built on experiences that can appear subjective. When "the kingdom is not of this world" and when, as Tilopa states, "the supreme accomplishment is to realize immanence without hope," it is difficult to understand to what or to whom words like *omnipresence, omniscience,* and *omnipotence* correspond.

When it rests only on concrete geometry, the symbol can suddenly seem similar to a skeleton, or to the lifeless corpse from the story "The King and the Corpse." Yet by interrogating us, this ghost guides us by the tip of the tongue or the tip of our thoughts and pushes us to finally throw these thoughts back into their element, into the void where they come from as we throw fish back in the water when fishing suddenly appears vain and hollow. Ultimately, it inspires us to throw ourselves into the deep. Contemplation promises to give life to this structure.

Rather than concluding that the spiritual universe is an invention elaborated from geometry, we can also think that the labyrinth that represents the whole, including our condition and our body, mind, and spirit, as well as the universe, also includes geometry as a product of the spirit, since, by definition the whole comprises all things, including that which renders its expression and representation possible.

Thus it is appropriate that it is by way of geometry and the structure of symbols, which are a creation of the mind, that the nature of mind manifests itself. In contemplation, the mind reveals itself to be like an empty mirror, but it manifests its nature by presenting the reflection of all things united and linked by a topology that corresponds to a sort of optics or hologram (a holistic *grammé*). According to Dzogchen, if its essence is emptiness, it is in its nature to reflect. The mind, when it becomes spirited or when it includes the unconscious becoming conscious, is likewise structured like a language or implied in this structure, a structure that becomes or reflects that of the world. It manifests itself in the image of a geometric structure in action.

Thus geometry is a language and the most appropriate only to signify the mind or the spirit and the world, but it only signifies it; it does not lead us to believe in Something. It does not present a substance opposed to the essence. The spirit exists beyond or becomes essential only when the world appears as substantial, when we imagine something standing hidden under the forms, some place below, which becomes a beyond. The language of geometry informs us only about a way that brings meaning into a form. With a form that can be moved and transformed, which becomes a vehicle and a "vessel," the meaning can be transported, transferred, communicated, but it is also transformed. This language informs us how a meaningful world is created or formed, how reality is communicated. Thus the source of this formation or revelation itself becomes very real; it becomes spirit. This language speaks about embodiment, informing us of a spirit that links a "father in heaven" to a son on earth and becomes one with them; it links that which is one, that which cannot be named or understood, to a messenger or a mediator and also a translator and transformer.*

Thus what is signified is simultaneously the same and different from the signifier or the sign. As it is said: "The Tao that can be named is not the Tao," but conversely, it is the images and the judgment accompanying the Tao that inform us about the way and the conduct that can keep us on the way, both here below and above. Geometry is a language of signs that can lead to the spirit or to an awakening, but an awakening that is itself a passage that calls for a new journey. Thus the geometry shows a path that in some way leads also to a new geometry and other structures of symbols, a new geometry that corresponds to the integration of contemplation in everyday life and to a participation of "all the distinct and independent parts that constitute our general presence."[1]

But aside from contemplation expertise, for those of us who are incomplete sentient beings, in order to understand how the mind can engender a structure like that of language, we first have to discover how language has a structure. This study of the structure of language and the meaning it conceals is precisely what structuralism devoted itself to revealing. We shall see that in return, the discovery of the geometry

of the labyrinth will modify structuralism. The fruit obtained through a process elucidates the process itself and transforms it.

If structuralism is no longer in fashion, it is owing to the fact that its methods often appear like fishing in troubled waters, or as pottering about, as Lévi-Strauss would say. Its theories were never formalized, and it never fulfilled the potential of its own criteria as Gilles Deleuze described them in *How to Recognize Structuralism*.[2] This state of affairs is discussed by J. Petitot-Concordat, who quotes Deleuze in *The Morphogenesis of Meaning*.[3]

"Structuralism's first criterion is the discovery and the recognition of a third order, a third reign, that of symbolism. . . . All our thoughts entertain a dialectical game between the two notions of real and imaginary." It is "the position of a symbolic order that is irreducible to the order of the real, to the order of the imaginary, and deeper than both" that will elucidate the relationship of the two first orders. But, as Deleuze admits, "[w]e do not yet know what this symbolic element consists in . . . if it remains difficult to recognize as such, this is because it is always covered by the properties of the substrata where the structures are actualized."[4] As we have seen, there is in fact a subtle difference between the symbol and its substrata (for example, between the symbolic knot and the knot as an object). As Lévi-Strauss perceives it, "The myth appears as a system of equations where the never clearly perceived symbols are approached by means of concrete values chosen to give the illusion that the underlying equations are solvable."[5] Structuralism is like fishing in troubled waters because it speaks of an order without truly understanding its authentic nature.

By connecting the symbol to a geometry that transforms the substrata, the study of the labyrinth resolves this fundamental problem of structuralism. It shows how, as the substratum is transformed, the symbol includes many connected images and becomes part of a new order. It helps to define not only the consistency of the symbol but also its place in relation to substrata within a multidimensional space.

---

* According to the Dzogchen and Mahayana traditions.

The second important criterion is one of locality and position. As Lévi-Strauss vigorously reminds us, the elements of a structure make sense or have a meaning "that is necessarily and uniquely one of position." Thus, "the scientific ambition of structuralism is not quantitative but topological and relational." According to Petitot-Concordat, if we consider only the relational, we are trapped in a logico-combinatorial structure that depends on subjective associations. If, on the other hand, we consider only the topos, we are left with the aporia of a pure spatium. It is only a mathematical science of topology that can create a strict objectivity and reunite the two aspects of place and relation. This topological science should be able to organize the descriptions of a morphogenesis correlatively with those of descriptive concepts such as tropes that transform and create meaning. The absence of this geometry, "its absolute lack . . . led to a major scission, a true transcendental Yalta opposing, right up to our time, reductionist and formalist points of view to romantic/dialectical/materialistic ones . . ."[6]

It seems that the geometry of the labyrinth also fulfills this request. The discovery of its structure and of its genesis changes the nature of structuralism. Its goal will no longer be to seek a structure, but rather to find the means of applying and filling it. Its new task will be to adjust the material to interpret to the structure. We can ask ourselves why this specific structure was not discovered sooner. Perhaps structuralists had some difficulties forming a single, all-inclusive structure out of the diverse deciphering grids that they elaborated. Instead of superimposing new mathematical models onto logico-combinatorial systems, confidence in the correctness of their endeavor should have led them to realize that a ready-made topology existed in the language of the unconscious and had to be expressed and signaled in myth and ritual.

With the geometry of the labyrinth, we obtain a coherent and inclusive structure that makes it possible to understand better the genesis of meaning. The structuralists first realized that "[t]he symbolic, the positional, and the structural is to semantic matter what morphogenesis is to matter."[7] They investigated this genesis of meaning but they did it in what now appears as an incomplete manner. They considered only an endless proliferation of meaning. According to Deleuze:

> It must be granted on principle that meaning always results from a combination of elements that are not themselves meaningful. As Lévi-Strauss said in his discussion with Paul Ricoeur, meaning is always a result, an effect: not only an effect as a product, but an optical effect, an effect of language, an effect of position. Profoundly, there is a nonsense to sense, which gives rise to the meaning; this is not a return to what has been called philosophy of the absurd, as in the philosophy of the absurd it is essentially the meaning that is missing. For structuralism on the other hand, there is always too much meaning, an overproduction, overdetermination of meaning, always produced in excess by the original and irreducible structure where it organizes itself."[8]

This overdetermination is the one the maze produces, and structuralists have not found a way out of it. Insofar as meaning is also obtained differently in the labyrinth, it becomes *immanent*, all-inclusive, and unifying, but incommunicable, except by way of a path or a language describing or signaling a path.

A final problematic aspect of structuralism is presented by its practice. As we have mentioned, until now structuralism has ignored and missed the fundamental consistency of the symbolic element. It becomes an unknown because its nature appears to be continually changing and because only the place of the symbol is recognized. But this place also appears as constantly moving. The symbol must be able to move, since it is constantly being transformed. For Deleuze, it becomes an object (*x*), a blind spot, what Lacan called (*a*), Lévi-Strauss a floating signifier, and Jakobson phenomenon Zero. This unknown remains nonidentifiable and floating, always displaced in relation to itself; it is a blank place that must remain vacant. "It must keep the perfection of its emptiness in order to displace itself in relation to itself and to flow through the elements and the different varieties of relations."[9] Watching over this blank space and protecting it becomes the work of the interpreter.

(This emptiness, however, is not a non-being . . . it is the positive being of the "problematic," the positive being of a problem and a question.) This is why Foucault can say: "It is nothing more, nothing less, than the unfolding of a space where it is finally once again possible to think." But if the empty space is not filled by a term, it is nonetheless accompanied by an eminently symbolic entreaty that follows all the displacements. . . . The *subject* [the identity of the structuralist interpreter] is precisely the entreating and pending authority that follows the empty place: as Lacan says, it is less a subject than subjected, subjected to the blank space. . . .

Structuralism is not at all a thought that suppresses the subject, but a thought that scatters and systematically distributes it, that contests the identity of the subject, that dissipates it and makes it pass from place to place, a subject that is always a nomad. . . .[10]

Thus the structuralism that leads us to chase a blank space or a center that is incessantly displacing itself leads to the dissipation and the dispersion of the *subject* or interpreter identified with it and displaced with it. It produces a subject who is bound to this moving emptiness, condemned to incessant wandering. Yet we have already recognized this "blank space" at the center of the labyrinth; this center is the place where the blank space stops transmigrating and becomes stabilized, the place where it can envelop all the symbolic, reunited elements. It is the place where the wandering interpreter finds space, but it is also the beginning and symbolic point in the imagination that the contemplator visualizes and from which he develops his contemplation. It is the vacant place where union and presence blend. It is amusing that with Dzogchen, as with Lacan, this point can also be replaced by the letter *a*, which becomes a mantra. We also find this letter representing the beginning (the instant) in medieval illuminated manuscripts (see plate 28).

Thus, by subtly guiding us toward this center while building an actual maze, the myth and the ritual lead to the reconstitution and the reuniting of the dispersed or scattered subject, a subject that finds a meaning for life or even gives meaning to life. It accomplishes the work of Isis in her care of Osiris. With the geometric structure of the labyrinth, structuralism could ultimately signal a threshold and an open structure. Besides exploring a maze, structuralism can become the study of a transforming chart, an ecological map of the house (*oikos*) of the Logos. Like Buddhist logic, structuralism's search can become, if not equal to, at least complementary and introductory to that of the nature of mind that occurs through the practice of contemplation. Even if it cannot lead us on the path toward the fruit, it can help us to formulate a view.

Fig. 33.1. Cretan seals
Lévi-Strauss compares myths and their structure to a musical language. Perhaps it is this music that is evoked by these seals?

34

Now What?

The accomplishment of dreaming depends on its interpretation.
—RABBI AKHIBA

Because of topology's central role in modern science, the contents of symbolic language and the yantra of the labyrinth have been modified. They include new information, and the knowledge that penetrated them has also changed. What was a harmonious whole is undergoing an upheaval. It appears then that the corresponding spiritual practice, or rather the way this practice is introduced and thought about, must also be modified to adapt to new paradigms of knowledge and to contemporary man. Since time immemorial, aspects of belief and religion have been modified as if in accordance with the movement of a pendulum in a continually changing world. "See how man also is machine, and that it is enough to activate a cog on the surface to make other cogs turn within."[1]

The elaboration of this modification is perilous, as it is not so much about creating a change as witnessing, interpreting, and integrating a change that has already begun and is developing without us even being aware of it. Ignoring this change means to live in the past or in a frozen world. But paradoxically, in order for the aspect in which a religion, gnosis, or spiritual practice is clothed to be changed, it must first be fully embraced and its essence and ultimate goal penetrated. We could think that the means of development of man and his psyche could be examined independently of all religion, but we must recognize that we are intimately connected to an already knotted network of understanding. It is the achievement of this penetration or assimilation that by itself naturally leads to the modification from the inside of an incompletely understood form that becomes rigid and fossilized. This is how Buddha, Christ, Muhammad, and other messengers renovated preexisting religions—that is, by presenting them differently in accordance with the needs of a new era, or, from within an established religion, by clarifying or revealing new approaches that lead to an awakening. To a lesser extent this process is ongoing. As Herbert Guenther noted in his book *From Reductionism to Creativity:*

> Any religion presents an interplay between a reductionist and a creative tendency. All religions need a structure, the elaboration of which requires a creative ability. But when this structure is imposed on the environment it becomes reductionist and leads to stagnation, rigidity and dogmatism.
>
> On the other hand, when the creative process is active and liberated it presents itself as a dissipative structure, and thus it produces a religion in movement whose form is in constant metamorphosis and somehow depends on the accomplishments of its adepts.[2]

The repercussions of the change presented by the merging of topology and symbolism reach mathematical and modern scientific knowledge as well. The new information that arises from studying the labyrinth does not only concern a New Age philosophy that compares aspects of ancient and new knowledge, but it also reveals the existence of a common foundation that the two traditions share. Mathematical knowledge, which is experiencing an upset, must also change and adapt in order to find or recover its essential nature. Mathematics could then once more become the support of a science of life, or a science that establishes a link between phenomena and noumena.

> The essence of mathematics is in its history, which is to say in the path it has followed. It is this pathway and not logic that reveals the essential links. The concatenation of mathematical notions or objects consists in effective gestures that themselves correspond to the effectiveness of a practice and a contemplation. Thus the origin of geometry is found in ritual. As the philosopher Jean Cavaillés has stated: "Mathematical thought is the result of the characteristic of thought to develop according to its essence." He also wrote, "Mathematics is more than logic in that it is effective thought, and all effective thought supposes applying abstract thought to an intuition. The difference from Kant is that there is no pure logical thought. Logic is nothing more than a constituent of all truly functioning thought that cannot be isolated."[3]

One principle stands out: To achieve unity or at least a unified science, the essential pathway must be distinguished from logical reasoning. As we have discovered, the relationship between pathway and logic is precisely the one that differentiates the labyrinth from the maze. When new dimensions are superfluously added, they produce nothing more than an inescapable maze. It becomes necessary to understand how diverse dimensions can appear, overlap, and proliferate in modern geometry, and how they can be explored existentially, or in an experience that corresponds to a state of consciousness. There cannot be an a priori privileged form or number of dimensions of space. The structure lent to space depends on a pathway, and it is this pathway that must be examined.

Western philosophy is founded on logic and leads to concepts that become unsteady as soon as their logical foundation is shaken. Eastern philosophy, on the other hand, is connected to a practice leading along a pathway to a transformation. The philosophy is like the view of the pathway. The translation from one tradition to the other is thus incoherent. Here as well, there is work to be done.

But for this work of bringing the traditions together to be accomplished and communicated, to grasp how its different dimensions and experiences correspond, it must coincide with the linking of signs in a multidimensional language. The model of language must coincide with the model of things.*

In fact, within language one must include several kinds of language that interfere. Besides conventional language, there is a silent symbolic language of signs and images that is used in myth, prayer, and evocations, and a seemingly incoherent language of sounds as found in mantras. There is a performative language that is a tool, used to accomplish a goal or to bring things together, or in other cases to seclude us. As the study of the labyrinth includes a particular way of interpreting myths, at the same time it outlines such a model of language.

Essentially the very concept of "signification" is questioned. The symbol and consequently the language sign more or less indirectly linked to it send us back to a protean interior image, and thus to a series of images. Ultimately, it can also send us back to the One or the Logos that was expelled from modern language theory. Rather than corresponding to a concrete and single thing, or sending us to an undetermined chain of signs, it functions like a yantra, as a recipient, a womb, and a tool for a process that has to

---

*Alberti in *De Trivia*, 1460. "The blitz, that lightning-flash within discourse, defines at once a 'way of speaking' and a way of conceptualizing the coincidence of contraries . . ." There is a correspondence between the blitz and the lightning of the Logos and the glance that represents the moment between speech and gaze.

be completed in order to reach the center of the labyrinth. This is where language draws its force.

There is a paradox here that is reminiscent of how light can be seen in physics as being either a wave or a particle. The language sign also has a double aspect. It can designate an object or a notion that is all the more difficult to localize in that it is (essentially or ontologically) more specified as being, and all the more difficult to specify (essentially and qualitatively) in that it is localized. But it also engenders a wave that floods the entire field of language or a function that can collapse to suggest again an object that moves and changes and is part of an uninterrupted whole. Actually, if light is described as both wave and particle, it is neither one nor the other, but something else and something unknown that will remain so. The same is true for the Logos or "light of mankind."

Does it mean that there is no identity possible for anything? If identity is defined as self sameness, it involves a duality—again a duality of an object and a witness who can observe and evaluate. It evokes something that is unknown in between the two. This in-between is what Rimbaud included when he said "I is an other."

To reach a complete understanding of communication and language, we cannot consider, as in psychoanalysis, the birth of language and the evolution of language as isolated processes. Inseparable from the genesis of the universe, the genesis and birth of language must also be considered as happening outside of time and space. This problem is the most difficult to overcome or to accept since, as has been indicated by the geometry of the labyrinth, the origin or center cannot be rediscovered as such, but only re-created or rebuilt from a whole itself issued forth from this same center.

Some questions remain: What practice of language will correspond to the theory of language? What strategy of elocution will offer a new dissemination of meaning or a multiplication of signs (semes) when the old and new science are juxtaposed or when the languages of East and West clash? If everything re-

peats itself, could a solution already exist in the past? In fact, a similar situation happened in Italy in the quattrocento. There occurred a split between the Byzantine and the Roman Germanic empires and a cultural revolution accompanied by the discovery of perspective. A different way of "seeing" produced a new way of constructing. In Icona, Nicholas of Cusa asks: "What does it mean to 'see?' How can a vision bring a new world into being?"[4] How do we share a vision?

A new mode of elocution was proposed: "The word will no longer be the immutable sign of an idea, but a provisional approximation, the support of an ever-renewed creation. The mass of thought . . . is not set aside, but caught up in a movement of thought that is entirely new."[5] In this study, coincidence is what links together objects and symbols, geometry's practice and gazes. It is the same for Nicholas Cusa:

"Coincidence of contraries is the infinite point around which is organized his [Cusa's] philosophy."[6] The movement which joins opposites, the old and new ways of seeing and conceiving, must not depend on one element. It is included in the potential of each element in play and by a mutual and reciprocal relationship. Only then will it lead to a flash within discourse that illuminates a reconciling profundity. The theory of this flash or "blitz" becomes the focal point of mystic science and announces "ways of thinking 'Oneness' within linguistic duality."[7]

What is required for this exercise, is a new sort of wisdom, which Cusa calls docta ignorantia (learned ignorance), a way of participating that cannot be categorized as discursive logic, but rather as extract gems, "seed of infinitudes" from the movement joining the opposites. It expresses itself by a continual transference leading from one element to another as from one perspective to another.

And so, just as we made sense of the meaning expressed by the labyrinth myths by turning to the labyrinth's image with perspective, Cusa uses the image as the "Other" of the text. The procedure he uses is of mutual reference between the movement of elocution and the movement of an image transformed by gazes and by geometry. There is an equilibrium between the sight of the eye and that of the mind. "Vigilance in looking for . . . oppositions in the undefined field of available knowledge stimulates the gaze, to which, in a "flash," the coincidence (of contradictions) is revealed."[8]

The image that Cusa uses in *Icona* is that of a portrait whose eyes, through the subterfuge of perspective, seem to look at you wherever you are situated. Several onlookers moving around exchange between themselves this astonishing or unbelievable fact: they are all followed by an eye, but they can verify it only vocally. Strangely, as in the geometry of the labyrinth, the gaze discovers an odd invisible eye, a mind's eye. Amazingly, the object looked upon becomes, as St. Paul wrote, like "a mirror presenting an enigma" (I Cor. 13:12) or, as it is sometimes translated, it makes us see "in a glass darkly," because, due to our imperfect state, we cannot see God directly. Cusa uses this portrait as a metaphor, but his text, which elaborates on a labyrinth of gazes, prefigures a topology; the metaphor fits the genesis of the labyrinth as we presented it. Thus the labyrinth becomes the model that coincides with that of Cusa, who ignored topology, the model that Cusa's learned ignorance evokes intuitively though unintentionally. The return to the image is also a return to a tying and a weaving made of gazes and exchanges between gazes, a return to a language that informs and directs the gaze and transforms it into geometry. But, by the same token, it is also a return to the birth of language as it is presented by the Dogon genie and to the relevant questions "Who speaks?" and "Who sees?" As the image is transformed by several eyes or witnesses and a reversal of the gaze, there are also many existences brought up by a new seeing. There is a spatialization of meaning, or a mandala of several I's. "The coincidence becomes the saying one (or One) in the place of the other, occurring at the center of the mandala. The elocution does not make us believe in "something" but leads us to recognize "the very act of believing, an act that posits the possibility of thinking,"[9]

an act of believing which is neither a belief in action nor in nonaction but rather in sharing, an act that brings a new world and a new age—an act that is perhaps the key to learned ignorance.

But, the "derangement" provoked by the questions "Who speaks? Who acts?" always repeated differently by different interlocutors is always accompanied by a hermeneutic of an image in movement which comes from the "night" of the ages. Somehow, it is this night that, with the "darkness of the glass that mirrors," becomes the black sun of learned ignorance, (Osiris becoming Horus). "The elocution becomes like the spontaneous manifestation of a primeval state of mind. It is a learned ignorance that makes it possible to think without being thinkable itself and which . . . remains a production of the mind, but a "generation" by means of which the mind produces outside itself the intimate surprise of its own infinite movement."[10]

Does this definition of the elocution of learned ignorance really belong now to Cusa or to the interpretation by the Jesuit Certeau, himself a student of Lacan? Does it offer today a potential for a new reality manifest, or only a utopia wrought with crafty words? After a long history of negativity, does a poststructuralism represented by believers such as Serres, Certeau, and Latour, turn to take a positive stand? To answer we can return to the beginning of the epistle of St. Paul mentioning "an enigma in a mirror" from which Cusa took his authority: "If I speak with the tongues of men and of angels, but have not love, I have become a resounding gong or a clanging cymbal." (I Cor. 13:1)

It seems that the elocution of learned ignorance means an art of listening as much as interpreting— and perhaps mostly listening to silence, the rich void between and beyond words. It means a sharing of silence. Could it be that this silence is the voice of enlightenment? If so, I cannot have a clear idea of what I am talking about, I am only guessing at something profiling itself on the horizon. It is then preferable to follow Cusa's advice and to try our luck in turning to an image in which to see as "in a glass darkly." For example, we may look at an image painted by Sasseta, a contemporary of Cusa, representing St. Francis giving his coat to a beggar (see plate 25). The folded cloth appears like a painting within a painting, and a strangely modern one, at that. It is the interrogation inspired by this image that makes this work a masterpiece.

It is said that beauty is a slow arrow, which can mean that in between the flash created by beauty and the revelation of beauty as truth lies an extended journey along a sinuous path. We shall now try to take that journey.

Let us first consider the symbolism of the coat. In the Byzantine icons, the convoluted or creased vestment is a symbol of the Logos. The design of the folds is painted as a script that is defined by the light coming through the cloth from a saint, or from Christ as the incarnated Logos (see plate 20). More specifically, it is defined by the interaction between two lights originating from different places, or from the coincidence of a light radiating and piercing through the cloth and the exterior light reflected on the folded cloth (see plate 21). Sometimes the symbolism is directly indicated, for example when the vestment of Moses seems to flow out of the scriptures (see plate 23). But the celestial vault or universe can also be shown as being folded and transformed into a scroll of scriptures (see plate 22). In this way, two signifiers are joined, and, as in the labyrinth, the cloth (either woven or knitted) reunites a meaning of the Logos, of the universe, and of the body-soul nexus. It is like a bridge between the body and the universe, a labyrinth which, because it is crumpled, becomes like a maze.

In Romanesque art the folds of the cloth become organized in whorls—vortex and concentric circles which at an early stage are sometimes very similar to those found in Celtic shrines such as the one at Gavrinis (see fig. 34.1 compared to fig. 27.2).

Not only are the old pagan shrines reused and transformed, but their decoration and their meaning is recycled and transposed. Now the scrolls more clearly represent the motion of the cosmos and the unfolding of the universe. With the transition from Orthodoxy to Catholicism, one passes from the mystic to the cosmic. In Catholicism, there is still the suggestion of an inner light, but it is a diffused remote stellar light, or a light that is observed in the darkness of the night.

In the Italian quattrocento, the influence of the Byzantine icon is still strong, but the symbolism changes with the evolution of the painting techniques. There is no longer a combination of two inverse perspectives and two sources of light but a unique one. Nor is there a writing of the folds, but rather a luminosity and transparency of the cloth which lets the flesh show. The point of view is more human: the cloth will represent a knowable world and, like for the Dogon, language rather than the Logos. This evolution is announced by a fresco of Giotto where the cloth spread on the ground lightens the whole painting and is again like a painting within a painting (see plate 24).

The fact that this cloth is offered to St. Francis is charged with meaning: for just as Cusa learned that ignorance is the secret to a deeper understanding, the Franciscan Order asserted that vowed poverty is the secret to heaven's invisible wealth. In Giotto's image, the poor man of Assisi is promised a great destiny and, invisibly and symbolically, the world—presented as a cloth—is displayed at his feet. St. Francis is also known for speaking to the birds, which is a way of saying that he knows all the tongues "of men and angels" and thus that he can listen to the voice of silence. Just as pure white light can correspond to an all-seeing—a seeing of all things simultaneously—and to a sort of fusion of all aspects of the void, silence can correspond to the simultaneous hearing of all possible voices. The cloth, which on the painting looks like water, is also a symbol of language or of the sea of signifiers. As he walks on it without confusion and without sinking, he acts like Christ walking on water, he keeps in touch with the Logos. The fact that St. Francis can hear the voice of silence is corroborated by the story which tells how, as he was praying in front of an icon of the Italo-Byzantine style representing the crucifixion, he heard it speaking to him and say: "Go Francis, and repair my church which, as you see, is falling into ruin."

A   B

Fig 34.1

*(A) An image of Christ from the church of Thuret, Puy de dôme, France. The fold of the vestment recalls
the curves and circles on the shrine of Gavrinis. (B) The Lamentation. The cloth or shroud is knotted
somehow like the cross of life, the ankh, in contrast with the corpse of Christ and the image of death.*

But this last story also indicates that he understood the old symbolism of icons, the connection between images and words, and that he could experience or live it. The cloth on which he will walk and leave the imprint of his feet is also a symbol of the shroud on which the image of Christ, the image of the Logos, is imprinted—the shroud being the prototype of all icons. Thus as he walks on it, St. Francis recreates an icon, an eloquent icon. As his feet join different regions of the cloth, the step becomes equivalent to an elocution reaching "coincidences." He starts to incarnate the goddess of speech who, as Virgil said, is recognized by her step.

All these detours bring us nearer to our purpose, as the image painted by Sasseta is somehow the reverse of the one painted by Giotto. Instead of being presented to St. Francis, the cloth or coat is now given by him to a beggar, a destitute knight who suffers from poverty instead of vowing to it. The painting seems to say that only the poor can give efficiently, and thus the question arises: from what kind of poverty does the beggar really suffer? As the cloth represents language, one could answer that it is from the ignorance of language and its proper use. The beggar represents, then, all of us. Francis does not exchange with him the gift of the gab, but the use of a language that, like the first word of the Dogon genie, "covers the nakedness of the earth" and creates a world, a language that gives back to the beggar his humanity.

Instead of being spread and rested on the ground, the cloth is now stirred or shaken. Moreover, the arm of St. Francis is still caught in the cloth, indicating that it is turned inside out, as if to show its lining or reverse side. One is led to ask: What could be the reverse of language? Perhaps silence—the pregnant silence of the void. And thus, if the gift of Francis is that of language with its double, or reverse, then perhaps it is also a way to design elocution as an art of echoing with words a pregnancy of silence.

There is something else which is odd in the execution of the painting: the coat is sky blue, a complementary color to the yellow sky of the landscape. In this way, it represents the sky that can really envelop and protect the earth of the beggar. But on a good reproduction of this image one can see that on the middle left side of the coat there is an area stained in a color similar to that of the undercoat of St. Francis. It is not exactly a shadow because the lower left side of the coat is still blue. It is as if Sasseta used the law of successive color contrast and represented the ghost of a preceding color, but the color of what? The contrast of what? Perhaps of what was in the coat: the body and soul of St. Francis. In a language more appropriate to the quattrocento, it is better to assume that since the coat is reversed, there is also a reversal of the halo or aura of St. Francis that stays within the coat and somehow shines through. This can explain his strange attitude when, as well as taking off his coat, he seems to pour something into a bag through a funnel. He even seems to be copulating with the coat or with his anima inside. Or perhaps the anima belongs to the beggar and the color is a reflection of him. This sort of suggestion is not too farfetched because Sasseta was a master of such visual tropes, which he was able to use without being accused of sacrilege, as in *The Temptation of Saint Anthony*, where he dared to daub the faces, buttocks, and genitalia of the tormenting devils with the gold reserved for the halo of saints, thus suggesting a connection between wealth and evil (or even more subtly, a connection between the glory of God and a reciprocal negative force).

With the gift of elocution, the beggar is also given a new ethereal body. This body can hear, sense, and feel silence as well as speech. The coat can transform his body or, more exactly, his relation to his body. The somersault of the coat (or of the aura caught in

it) occurring between St. Francis and the beggar becomes complementary to the somersault of the Cretan vaulting of the bull, also a symbol of transformation. One could also put in the mouth of the beggar the same words proffered by the destitute son (in the hymn of the pearl, previously applied to the apocryphal acts of St. Thomas), who receives a robe, representing the celestial counterpart of his human soul, from an angel in disguise:

> *Suddenly, when I saw it over against me,*
> *the robe became like me, as my reflection in a mirror*
> *I saw it wholly in me,*
> *And in it I saw myself apart from myself,*
> *So that we were two in distinction*
> *And again one in a form*

The horse in plate 25 recalls the gesture of St. Martin who, still riding, cut his coat in half in order to share it with a beggar (St. Martin being, perhaps, a transposition of the good "Samaritan" once one moves the "i"). One could ask how a coat cut in half would still be useful and if there is a proper way to cut the coat efficiently. Certainly, the coat was a sort of cape which, in order to be worn properly, demanded a certain skill in folding and strapping or knotting. So it is then somehow this folding or knotting gesture that was also cut in half. There is, again, some topology here.*

Thus there is a correspondence between the sharing and shearing of the coat in the story of St. Martin and the gift of the coat in Sasseta's painting. In the painting, however, the shape of the coat indicates that a cutting, or rather a tailoring, already took place, one that transformed the cape into a coat. Moreover, instead of being halved, the coat is represented doubled with a lining (and this strange equivalence corresponds, again, to the division of a knot being obtained through

---

*The cutting is also symbolic. One is reminded of other stories mentioning a cutting in half, such as that of the Gordian knot by Alexander or the menace of a child being split in the judgment by Salomon. All are related and brought into perspective by the division of the knot into a torus knot and by the geometry of the labyrinth.

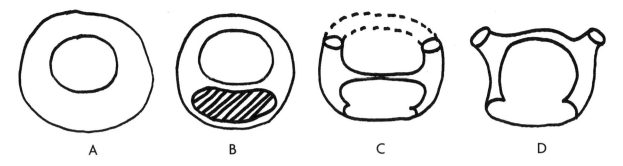

Fig. 34.2. The torus transformed into a coat
Starting with a simple torus (A) one moves to a single cut, resulting in a torus with one hole (B).
The central circle of the torus can then be pulled through the hole and reversed (C), resulting in a coat (D).

a doubling of the string in the geometry of the labyrinth). The coat also looks a bit like the dragon that St. George pierced, as if St. Francis is taking St. George's place. We have already seen that the dragon can evoke a labyrinth as well as the mutation of symbols. This dragon could also be similar to the Egyptian primeval snake from which, when it is slain, all life surges.

However, it is mostly the strange shape of a swirl presented by the stirred coat brings us back to topology. We have already considered how objects such as a Möbius strip can represent something more primordial than the knot. As figure 34.2 shows, with the coat we already have a torus cut twice and partially turned inside out.

As for the torus knot, we do not have to see it, we can imagine that it is there as a fibrillation of the tore, hidden inside and included in the brocade of the cloth. To transform the torus knot into a labyrinth path, a hole must be cut into the tore, through which the inside is pulled, and then a second cut must be made to disjoin the beginning and end of the labyrinth path, as we have seen in figure 34.2. All of this is already accomplished in Sasseta's painting, which would explain the concentrated look on St. Francis' face as he applies himself to a complex geometric transformation. St. Francis pulls out his arm as if he pulls out the self axis only to leave the invaginated matrix of the path of the labyrinth within the membrane of the coat. The stirring of the coat can suggest the construction of a labyrinth center or, from another point of view, the elocution of Nicholas of Cusa.

The different parts of the cloth of language brought in contact with each other are like the blitz of elocution reaching the coincidence of contraries.

The gift of St. Francis' coat can thus represent the creation and offering of a labyrinth center. And since this center is equivalent to the original place of creation, the creation of all things from one thing, meaning the creation of the tree of life and not of the tree of knowledge, then the picture potentially contains that tree. Thus the Egyptian fresco of the cutting of the primordial snake (see plate 26), becomes complementary to the painting of Sasseta. The first one shows a tree and a knife which are hidden in the second one. With the two pictures compared in such a way, they coincide, and a cycle is closed. The Egyptian snake represents the first topology of manifolds preceding the appearance of knots—a topology that occurred at the beginning of time. The folding of the cloth represented in the second picture could represent the last topology of manifold, occurring at the end of a long learning process. It produces the center of the labyrinth—the source of all things including the tree of life—but a center now defined in this world instead of undefined in the original chaos.

One could object that this imagined center located somewhere within the coat is still undefined or extremely temporary, since the stirred coat will immediately fall back, unanimated. Not necessarily so! In addition to the arts of knotting or knitting, or of folding cat's cradles, or origami, there is also the art of staining patterns by knotting textiles (found in batik or ikat, for example) or the popular Chinese art form of producing intricate designs by cutting out material folded in a complex way. One can easily imagine, when noticing St. Francis' concentrated attitude, that to persuade the doubting beggar he is like a shrewd magician hiding a pair of scissors in his coat; as he folds the coat he is cutting out of the unseen cloth, and not the lining that hides the procedure. The result of his endeavors will be a labyrinth or a tree of life that he will pull out at the last minute. The knife and the tree seen in the Egyptian picture in plate 26 are hidden inside St. Francis' coat in plate 25. However, as is illustrated by the Egyptian fresco that shows the knife being replaced by a feather, all of these gestures are purely symbolic and no real cut is necessary.

Of course, this divagation, or collage, or ripping of palimpsests, can seem deranged and cannot be accepted as an interpretation of the painting by Sasseta. It is rather the interpretation of a sensation obtained in a flash, in front of the painting, which made me return to it. It is the interpretation of the image as if it appeared in a dream, a lucid, waking dream. Actually, the image is only half of the original painting which is, itself, half of a diptych. The other half shows St. Francis in bed, strangely wrapped in his sheets as if in a wave. He dreams he is given the direction of an army, and misinterprets the dream, thinking he will become a great warrior. This misinterpretation of an image in a dream by St. Francis could mean that we can also misinterpret the second side of the painting. Furthermore, on the other side of the diptych we see Francis being received naked by the church after having abandoned all his clothes. Beside him, his father is collecting the heap of clothes in anger—as if he was trying to recover the reassuring conventional use of language and interpretation.

All things considered, my interpretation is not even like that of a dream because there is nothing personal in it. It is, rather, an interpretation imposed by tradition, or by an evolution of tradition that was bound to continue after Sasseta painted the picture. Thus, in a way, it is an interpretation of Sasseta's dream or hidden prophecy given through signs, inflections, gestures, or a visual elocution evoking a *locus solus*, a central place of the sun as the source of spiritual light. From this point of view, it can be considered as a valid interpretation of Sasseta's painting. The interpretation seems to say that the elocution of learned ignorance was not so much used for the sake of argument or influence, but for sharing a grace.

The work in this book addresses itself first and foremost to the enigma of the labyrinth, but at the same time, since the labyrinth presents a pathway, a reversal, and a reunion, it cannot help but suggest the necessity or the inevitability of changes or the necessity of becoming aware of a direction indicated by changes taking place. It initiates and solicits an action, an exchange, and a dialogue.

Fig. 34.3. Cretan seals
On the left: the hypostasis of the sacred knot through the form of the double ax.
On the right: the personification of the axis within a shrine.

6
Myth and Meaning

35

Meaning and the Mythic Path

The world is an overflow of the abyss.
—FRONTO

We have indicated how the structure of the labyrinth appears to be the one that structuralism was looking for. But to reach this structure starting from the material offered by myth, we needed a basic method, which we borrowed from structuralism. In order to resolve the problems posed by the labyrinth, we have had to extend or revise this method. In part 6 we shall examine the way in which this has been done.

Myth has no author. Like the Vedas, the Koran, or the Bible, myth can be considered as revelation, yet we have no way of knowing who collected or transmitted this revelation. We are thus unable to assume an intention behind myth or examine it in a rational manner. By establishing that myth has its roots in the unconscious, Jung, after Freud, clearly faced this issue when he noted, "In general, a meaning of myth that suits us is suspect, because the point of view of the unconscious is complementary or compensatory to that of the conscious and surprisingly different."[1]

One can easily accept that myth addresses itself to the unconscious. However, to elaborate a theoretical model of myth that would coincide with that of the ancient mentality it is preferable to postulate that the source of myth can be found in the depths of the unconscious—or divine principle mentioned by Zimmer in his discussion of tantrism—rather than in

a subconscious that remains a vague and relativist modern concept. But there is also a complementarity between the unconscious and the deep unconscious, which raises the question: What sort of complementarity do these two terms present with consciousness? Or what kind of relationship exists between the unconscious and ordinary consciousness? As soon as a third term is introduced, the notion of complementarity, with its axes and symmetry, becomes problematic. It is around this question that the interpretation of myth is knotted. Myth has several dimensions. An illustration of this problem follows from the study or questioning of primitive architecture. One man finds that the Stonehenge is aligned with certain planets and stars, and another man discovers that its placement corresponds to a maze of underground water currents. We certainly cannot conclude, however, that the underground water currents obey astrology, but perhaps there exists some common denominator between the two, or some mediating force.

By assuming that myth has its source in the depths of the unconscious, we obtain a particular view of myth. The deep unconscious may possess another truth, whether it be Self-knowledge or knowledge of the Logos. It is true consciousness. But just like the unconscious or the oracle at Delphi, it cannot express a truth accessible to ordinary consciousness. This is the crux of the problem—namely, that as long as man is stratified, divided, and forbidden access to a totality, there is only relative and no absolute truth. The unconscious can only indicate its own existence by suggesting a center, a topos, or a place where it can be found and from where it has a point of view, a spatio-temporal perspective in a primeval light. It suggests and locates this center in the myth by describing the terrain where it is situated, a world that surges forth and envelops it, a universe as tropos (a reversal) and a cosmos as life of the Logos. Thus the myth indirectly reveals a path emanating from this center, a middle path where "middle" (*milieu*) is taken to mean both center and environment. This path can be called Tao, Dharma, Logos, or something else, but these names that designate something toward which we yearn remain incomprehensible for ordinary consciousness—"The Tao that can be named is not the Tao."

From the point of view of ordinary, superficial consciousness, this center is something that no longer exists, like the place or the original sound of the big bang. It is a scattered or filled emptiness, a buried memory that, once projected into this world, becomes an absurdity or a void. In a reversal, the original center becomes an invisible or menacing black hole, which becomes in turn the symbol of our ultimate destination. With the disappearance of its origin, the essence of myth has become dissipated and the map dissociated from the territory. The "way" becomes the sinuous and branching path of the maze. From the creative impulse there remains only a momentum and an opposing reaction.

This process of the myth's emergence that we have obviously crudely sketched and described in an awkward manner corresponds to the Hebrew doctrine of the Tzimtzum. This doctrine describes the creator retiring into language to emancipate his creation. We cannot dismiss this doctrine too easily, inasmuch as it corresponds to the one described by the myths themselves. Ptah, creator of language and of Tatanen, "the surging earth," is absorbed by the matter he has created, immobilized like a living mummy within his cre-

ation. He thus does the "labor of those who are in their caves"—that is, he emanates. Merlin, whose magic creates the world of the Round Table, is also imprisoned by the power of the incantations he taught his disciple Vivian; he thus retires into the power that constitutes him, or that is his "Self." His knowledge returns to the silence of the abyss, and he once more fuses with the skein of the world and the forest of the unconscious, where he must again be discovered and reassembled. In a certain sense, the same is true of Daedalus, who is sealed within the labyrinth by Minos after Theseus slays the Minotaur and must escape by way of the sky, as if volatizing into thin air.

The truth of myth lies in its path, a path describing a transformation, but this path is hidden and veiled. The study of myth therefore reveals itself as the search for what appears as a vacancy or a rupture, a black space, an emptiness that can resemble the eye of a needle or of a shuttle with which the myth is woven. Of the truth that has the face of a lie, as Dante said, there remains only a mask, an apparently absurd message from the unconscious, similar to that of dreams.

If there is a quest that myth proposes and to which ritual disposes, it is precisely that of finding and re-creating a center, a center from which the myth can perpetuate itself, not as an invented fiction, but as the story/history of the eternal Logos.

To accept the existence of this mythic path, it is not even necessary to believe in the existence of a divine principle or in a deeper unconscious; the meaning of these notions will always fluctuate.

> The definition of what counts as an essence or as substance has a lot to do with this question of maintaining a constant through transformations. It is fair to say that, in our scientific cultures, we cannot entertain any alternative notion of what is a substance, except as what is maintained through successive transformations. . . . What is kept constant from one representation to the next is morphed, quite naturally, into the *thing itself* to which, thanks to "accurate

information," we gain access. But in this little shift from information by transformation to information as a mere transfer without any transformation, the word "reference" changes its meaning and instead of being what is carried through the media and the successives inscriptions, it becomes what the thing is, unaltered, unmediated, uncorrupted, inaccessible. This, then, is the ultimate paradox of a historical mediation that provides access to what is then seen as an inaccessible, ahistorical, and unmediated essence.[2]

We cannot look immediately for a metaphysical answer; we must first examine the nature of the mediated message. It is not a question of belief, but one of paradigm and method. What is important is noticing that myths present a source and a path that are irreducible to any particular interpretation and that most often the accessible material is expressed in terms of divine sources. It is a question of examining what can be transmitted by this language rather than what it communicates in a given context. If, for example, we base ourselves solely on a theory of the unconscious or the subconscious to understand myth, we reach an even less complete interpretation and

encounter the defects denounced by Freud and Lévi-Strauss, who wrote, "It is not my purpose here to replace sexual symbolism with a symbolism of a linguistic or philosophical nature; that would bring us dangerously close to Jung, who, as Freud rightly pointed out, 'attempted to give to the facts of analysis a fresh interpretation of an abstract, impersonal, and ahistorical character.'"[3]

The hypothesis of a mythic path presents the advantage of being homologous to those other paths suggested directly or indirectly in the myth:

1. A path corresponding to the human quest that describes both a psychic transformation and a transformation of the world.

2. A language path by which the myth delivers an implicit message.

3. A geometric path presented in the rites that corresponds to the profound structure of the world described in the myth.

These three aspects are inseparable and are defined by referring to each other. Each finds its true meaning only in a whole, and only the symbol can link such apparently disparate aspects.

Fig. 35.1. Cretan seals
Inner space in a silphium seed, the difference between open and closed space?

36

The Crossing of Codes Evokes Space

The buzzing of the Talmud escapes from a hive of silence.
—EMMANUEL LEVINAS

The path of language in myth, which constitutes myth's structure and substance, is what can lead us to the other aspects. But if we can speak of myth as a language, of equations solved by the myth, and even of a mythic path, it is no doubt in thanks to the structural study of myth and principally to the work of Lévi-Strauss, who is responsible for much of the progress in the formal study of myth. The first of Lévi-Strauss's discoveries that I wish to explore is that each myth constitutes a variant or a transformation of another myth, and thus all myths are linked. This is what makes it possible to discover, in a sometimes astounding way, a latent or "nonspoken" message obtained by a sort of counterpoint between myths and the establishment of new relations between themes. But what is the nature of this message that reaches us indirectly or through the subconscious?

Every myth confronts a problem, and it deals with it by showing how it is analogous to other problems, or else it deals with several problems simultaneously and shows that they are analogous to one another. No real object corresponds to this set of images, which *mirror each other*. More exactly, the object draws its substance from the *invariant properties* that mythic thought manages to identify when it sets a number of statements side by side. To simplify matters considerably, we could say that a myth is a system of logical operations defined by the "it's when . . ." or "it's like . . ." method. . . .

Thus mythic reflection's originality is to operate with *several codes*. Each extracts latent properties from a domain of experience, permitting us to compare it with other domains or to translate them into each other. . . .

A myth appears like a system of equations in which the symbols, never clearly perceived, are approximated by means of concrete values chosen to give the illusion that the underlying equations are solvable. Such choices are guided by an unconscious finality, but they are made among arbitrary and contingent elements, the products of history, so that the initial choice remains as impossible to explain as the choice of the set of phonemes that comes to make up a particular language . . .

There is more. Each code constitutes a sort of deciphering grid applied to empirical data; but the myth, which always uses several codes at once, keeps only parts of each grid, and, combining these with parts taken from other grids, it creates a kind of *metacode* that becomes its distinctive tool.[1]

This text seems to confirm one of the points of view we have adopted, or instead it is what inspired us to adopt it: A particular interpretation of myth is not wrong; it is simply incomplete and thus is unable to grasp the essence of the myth. The astrological code pierced by Max Müller, the psychological or sexual code, the linguistic or philosophical code, all help to penetrate the opacity of myth, but not what is most essential, what Lévi-Strauss calls an invariant, or "a primitive apprehension of a total structure of meaning." What is more, in the finale of *The Raw and the Cooked,* Lévi-Strauss concludes: "The unique answer that this book suggests is that . . . myths signify the mind that elaborated them by means of the world of which it is itself a part."[2]

It thus seems that we have entirely followed the hypothesis first put forward by Lévi-Strauss. But, according to him, as the myth's equations lead to illusory solutions and to no real object, the mind/spirit or the itinerary leading to it remains indefinable or unreal. Instead of leading us out of myth, structuralism examines myth as a closed system. The meaning of a sign or a story is thus exhausted by studying its relations with other myths in the mythic corpus. The formal structuralist method can only discover an immanent meaning that is enclosed in myth, and the subject is decomposed "like a spider dissolving itself in the constructive secretions of its web."[3]

The myth can present false solutions exactly because at a more profound level, it copies the mental process that constructs a maze, but it does this in order to pull apart this process and deconstruct it, and in order to lead to what is more fundamental—that is, to the center of the labyrinth and to the unspoiled nature of the spirit/mind, the access to which is barred by the mental. It is finally this entire process of construction and deconstruction of this pathway that can signify the mind and the passage from mental activity to natural mind or spirit, because no formula can describe the thing or spirit or mind in itself, no "open sesame" can reveal its entrance in an intelligible manner.

If, on the other hand, we consider the myth as an open system, it is the unknown matrix at the origin of its structure that becomes the essential foundation and the source of meaning. The structure of myths is the product of the assembling and ever-renewed combining of concrete elements in this matrix. Neither the nurturing womb nor the fruit can alone lead to the reconstitution of the matrix, no more than the spectacle of the world can, without mathematics, reveal a map of creation.

But let us examine further how Lévi-Strauss considers the signification of myths:

In a book about Sophocles, J. Lacarrière suggests that the Greeks may have sought to discover "the secret laws that reveal the tragic itself," that is, a tragic approach about which "we can wonder if it is not an attempt to find, in the fate of men, the same symmetry as the one that Greek science and philosophy found in the cosmic order" (Lacarriére 1960: 103, 108).

What is this scheme (or order or symmetry)? . . . [I]t consists in a set of rules aimed at bringing coherence to elements that are at first presented as incompatible or even contradictory. We have an initial set and a final one, both made up of terms [the characters] and relations [the functions attributed to them in the plot]; various operations—superposition, substitution, translation, rotation, inversion—will result in establishing a correspondence between the two sets so that each element in one will be an image of one element in the other; each operation in one direction is compensated by its counterpart in the other, so that the final set is also a *closed system.* . . .

In sum, the intellectual pleasure derived from such exercises lies in the fact that they make the presence of invariance felt beneath the most improbable transformations. . . .

We will not attempt to find the *"true" signification* of myths or dreams. Myths, and perhaps also dreams, bring a variety of symbols into play, none of which signifies anything by itself. They acquire a signification only to the degree that relations are established among them. Their signification is not absolute; it hinges on their position.[4]

According to Lévi-Strauss, there is in myth no "true signification," just as there is no "real object." But the notions of truth, reality, and meaning are precisely those that the study of myth puts into question. They correspond to that of a Logos that is inaccessible to rational understanding. "The last function of myth is to signify signification."[5] With topology (the science of position and situation) the signification does not only hinge on the position of the symbol, but also finds, after its transmigration, its absolute or ultimate harbor.

In quantum physics, there is also no real object behind symbols, no tangible electron turning around a nucleus like a planet around the sun. "The identity of a particle is inherent to the way it interacts."[6] The object is defined by its relation. In addition, it is defined by a point of view, as when, for example, with the introduction of a fractal space-time in quantum physics, the elementary particles become new objects: "The concept of particle would no longer concern an object 'possessing' a spin, a mass, or a charge, but would be reduced to the geometric structures of fractal geodesics of a non-differentiable space-time. . . . A group of several particles does not identify itself with a collection of individual objects in the classic sense: it is a new object, a network of geodesics possessing its own geometric properties."[7]

In physics, symbols also correspond to a combination of different codes, and yet this physics leads to perfectly correct predictions concerning real phenomena.

When codes are crossed in myth, meanings proliferate and cancel themselves out. Certain information loses its absolute value, other information springs forth, creating new possibilities for investigation. This is precisely the way Michel Serres sees a science of sciences that functions like a maze or a knot.

> If, in effect, each region is a complexion, and connects multiple liaisons within itself, arriving from the periphery of the encyclopedia, or going toward this periphery, it is, *quodammodo* [in some measure], a science of sciences; it tends to become a point of view on the encyclopedic world. . . . If each region is an intersection, a knot of interrelations, it ends up containing, at least blindly, an interpretation of all the

domains it mobilizes, from one bias or another. . . . We no longer speak of the science from the outside but from the point of view and in the language of each region.[8]

In the myth, the crossing of codes would be a way to bar or deny the absolute value of each particular code in order to reveal and affirm the primacy and primordiality of a matrix and reveal its nature. The crossing of codes reveals the primacy of the space between different worlds, the space without which they could not be embedded within each other and woven together. Space is an emptiness that embraces everything, but it is also the foundation of all existence and the nourishing ground of being. Like the spirit/mind, space as an emptiness, as an invisible and intangible ether, can be described or qualified only by the relation between things and by the crossing of codes. As L. E. Sullivan has established, this notion is prevalent in mythic thought:

> The multiplicity of world-planes and of qualities of space indicates the richness of manifested being. . . . More important than that, this multiplicity proves that space itself is, in its essence, a manifestation of the meaning of existence in whatever form.
>
> The disjunct planes of being are systematically associated with one another in such a way as to constitute a whole. At root complete systematization is possible because all spaces were, in primordial times, inherently related. Then unity of being is revealed most clearly at the time of their origin. Systematization of the spacial universe becomes a way of thinking about being's essential integrity, as revealed in myth. Examination of the systemic processes of connection and separation among levels of space clarifies the very nature of disjunction and conjunction, concepts essential to the formation of the separate categories used in thought.[9]

With the transition leading from things to space, we pass from existence to being, and from relative values to absolute values. This change of point of view is clearly expressed in the *Tao te Ching:*

Heaven and Earth are impartial;
They see ten thousand things as straw dogs. . . .
The space between heaven and earth is like a bellows
The shape changes but not the form.[10]

In his essay "Experience," Emerson wrote about the relation between void, language, and being: "'I fully understand language' [said Mencius] 'and nourish well my vast-flowing vigor'—'I beg to ask you what you call vast flowing vigor?' said his companion. 'The explanation,' replied Mencius, 'is difficult. This vigor is supremely great, and in the highest degree unbending. Nourish it correctly, and do it no injury, and it will fill up the vacancy between heaven and earth.'"[11]

In ancient Egypt, space was also seen as uniting all things. As can be seen in the frescoes, space, Shu, maintains the correct distance and the right relation between sky and earth (see fig. 16.14C), and the soul of Shu is described as the universal spirit/mind, which expresses itself in the following way: "In the flesh of the one who creates himself, it is I who am edified, for my coming forth is his being. . . . I am the dweller within the million beings. . . . I establish the lord 'This' to exalt the self-creator and reveal the sky as his inherent power and the unity of all creative laws. . . ."[12]

The primordial, original, indefinable element of space can also be identified by light, by sound, or even by the wind representing both a movement of space and the breath of the spirit. In Celtic texts, the wind is perceived as the solution of an enigma proposed by the child Taliesin:

Discover what it is
The powerful creature from before the flood
With neither flesh nor bones

With neither veins nor blood
With neither head nor foot . . .
It is as large
As the surface of the earth
And it is not born
Nor can it be seen.[13]

In the Buddhist tradition that remains attached to myth, the experience of emptiness, *sunyata*, also becomes a necessary condition for obtaining a right view and for perceiving reality. It can ultimately lead to the union of emptiness and clarity. Emptiness represents the original, fundamental nature of mind. Myth also speaks to us of space and emptiness, but like in Buddhism of an emptiness that has no inherent nature.

> If something existed that was not empty, then something empty would also exist
>
> If nonemptiness does not exist, how could emptiness then do so?
>
> The conquerors said that vacuity erases all wrong views
>
> Those who reached enlightenment (or vacuity as existing in and of itself) were declared incurable.[14]

Like emptiness, space does not exist in itself and cannot be described or conceived by itself. Even if, like some modern physicists, we imagine space as curved or crumpled so that each ray of light would follow a multiplicity of paths and deliver to us multiple images of stars and galaxies and thus a universe much bigger than it really is, this crumpled space would still exist somewhere, in some kind of outer or inner space that we cannot fathom.

Fig. 36.1. Cretan seals
Transition from a bucrane to a vase or from what has been emptied of life to what can be filled—
or a representation of what must be emptied to be filled anew?

37

Physics, Anthropology, and the Continuous Whole

It is the theory that decides what can be observed.
—Einstein

Lévi-Strauss observed an even stranger phenomenon having to do with counterpoint and complementarity in myth. Often, when a myth evolves and changes, another myth belonging to another culture or another system is also modified in a complementary way, as if all myths were connected by a strange system of cords and pulleys and formed a continuous whole with a global symmetry.

Returning to the image of the labyrinth, we can note that, curiously, by completing the circles sketched by the path of the labyrinth or by juxtaposing the paths of two symmetric labyrinths, one presenting itself as the reflection of the other, we can obtain the image of a system of wheels or of spheres connected as if by belts (see fig. 37.1). One finds here an indication about another way to transform a group of circles into a labyrinth.

One can find many examples of mosaic or pavements producing such belts—for example, the pavement of St. Mark's Basilica at Venice (see fig. 37.2), which depicts three belts joining nine circles or spheres or wheels and two small belts in the center. It is a maze because the design is exactly like a *kolam* in which the *bindus* or points marking the spaces are replaced by concentric circles. It is as if the *bindus*

propagated through space like waves. It is a Western version of the Indian *kolam* and we have seen that the *kolams* are mazes.

The phenomenon described by Lévi-Strauss is comparable to the Einstein-Podolski-Rosen experiment in physics that Gary Zukav calls the Pandora's box of modern physics. A brief description of this experiment will suffice here. If a particle is split in half and one of the subparticles is then deviated, for example, by a magnet, we discover that the other subparticle has also deviated, as if the two subparticles were communicating by telepathy. This led to Bell's theorem, which holds that "separate parts are connected in an immediate and intimate way" and that the principle of "local causes" is incompatible with the quantum theory. Henry Pierce Stapp, who calls Bell's theorem science's most profound discovery, gives the following commentary:

> The important thing about Bell's theorem is that it puts the dilemma posed by quantum phenomena clearly into the realm of macroscopic phenomena. . . . [It] shows that our ordinary ideas about the world are somehow profoundly deficient even on the macroscopic level. . . .

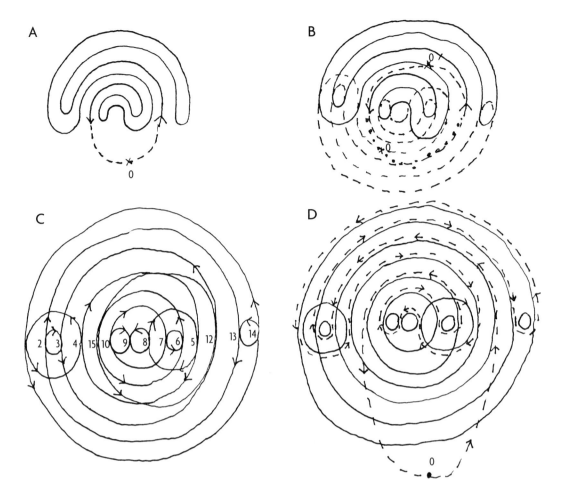

Fig. 37.1. The labyrinth as an array of wheels
(A) The path in this labyrinth is composed of semicircles that can be completed, as in illustration B. (B) Full circles are also obtained by juxtaposing two symmetrically opposed paths of the labyrinth. (C) A system of wheels or gears turning simultaneously at different speeds is depicted. (D) The path in the labyrinth can also appear as a belt connecting the wheels. This sort of diagram suggests the motion of celestial spheres and can be compared to any number of other medieval designs that also depict a sort of belt circulating around spheres.

Quantum phenomena provide *prima facie* evidence that information gets around in ways that do not conform to classical ideas. Thus the idea that information is transferred superluminally is, *a priori* not unreasonable.

Everything we know about nature is in accord with the idea that the fundamental process of nature lies outside space-time . . . but generates events that can be located in space-time.[1]

This leads to four principle hypotheses that deny the fundamental principles of classic physics. These are:

1. Unbroken wholeness, defined by David Bohm

in the following way: "Parts are seen to be in an immediate connection within which their dynamic relations depend, in an irreducible way, on the state of the whole system . . . one is led to a new notion of *unbroken wholeness* that denies the classical idea of analyzability of the world into separately and independently existence parts."[2]

2. The second hypothesis presupposes *super-determinism*. According to superdeterminism, "No matter what we are doing, at any given moment, it is the only thing that *ever* was possible for us to be doing at that moment."[3]

3. The third is the *many worlds* theory. According to this interpretation, "[W]henever a choice is made in the universe between one possible event and another, the universe splits into several branches."[4]

4. The fourth is the *no models option*, which acknowledges "that it might not ever be possible to build a model of reality . . . it is a recognition of the difference between knowledge and wisdom."[5]

Our ordinary ideas about the world are profoundly deficient because we cannot easily accept that familiar objects obey quantum laws, yet the myth presents such quantum phenomena as objects and beings transforming, dividing, and leaping from one state and from one place to another. In the myth, things are transformed and split because consciousness itself is divided and transformed. The hypotheses that science follows strangely resemble the fundamental themes raised by myth, and the phenomenon discovered by Lévi-Strauss leads to conclusions that are similar to Bell's theorem.

How can we speak about a mentality and an information engendering the myth that seems to communicate by telepathy? Does the fundamental process of the mind reside outside of space-time to generate concepts about space-time? Isn't what we call creativity or genius perfectly predetermined by a complete balance between the actual and the potential, the real and the virtual, the manifest and the invisible, consciousness and the unconscious? As it is suggested by myths, could the laws governing the genesis and the maintenance of the universe be the same as those that govern their description? Is there a continuous whole that includes both nature and culture? Does the myth present a model to describe the coexistence of several worlds?

If Lévi-Strauss can be called the Einstein of anthropology for having discovered "reciprocal perspectives" and a relativity of meaning in primitive thought, it is tempting to seek a unified theory in this domain as well, a theory of everything and of the whole. The problem with the notion of symmetry and complementarity between myths, fundamental to the structuralist method, is that it depends in a large part

A

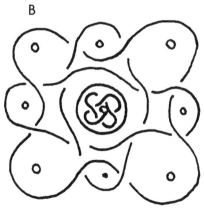

Fig. 37.2
(A) Pavement at St. Mark's basilica in Venice representing three belts uniting nine circles or wheels, plus two extra belts in the center forming a torus knot. (B) Here we see that it is like a Hindu Kolam.

on a system of preestablished categories that arise from a dualistic mentality (which opposes, for example, the raw and the cooked, honey and ashes, top and bottom, sky and earth, content and container); thus it introduces a logico-combinatory structure at too early a stage and engenders a premature interpretation. We can first attempt to discover a complementarity not only in the limited realm of myth but also in a more complete system and within a whole including along with myth, rites, iconography, choreography, social structures, and so on, a complementarity indicated by the available material itself.

If a connection exists, on the one hand between all myths, and on the other hand between all patterns and images of ancient or primitive art, there also exists a transverse one that rejoins the visual and the spoken. Parallel to the transformation of myths, we can discover a geometry governing the transformation of symbolic patterns. In exchange, this geometry, testimony to ancient science, can redefine more dynamic aspects of complementarity and of symmetry that are pertinent to the myths.

Associated with the problem of defining new criteria of complementarity is the one of how to define the field in which the notion of complementarity is applied. Similar and neighboring myths present meaningful differences and resemblances once again leading to other stranger and more distant myths. These myths are like the links in a chain that can be indefinitely extended. But we can also directly discover more distant and disparate myths that seem obviously opposed to each other. Finally, all myths correspond, but the way to connect them appears subjective and dependent upon the skill and intuition of the decoder. The complete map of the network of correspondences seems as impossible to attain as that of the maze described in the myth, so much so that Lévi-Strauss himself refused to make a distinction between legitimate myths and others that are seemingly not so: "We cannot insist enough on the fact that all available variants must be taken into account. If Freudian com-

mentaries on the Oedipus complex are part of the myth of Oedipus, then . . . there is not one true version that all the others are copies and distortions of. All the versions belong to the myth."[6] By following this principle we can thus enlarge the domain of investigation beyond myths to forms of gnosis, doctrines, canons, sutras, and cosmologies belonging to philosophical and religious systems, which are all linked to myth in a more or less direct way. These cannot be confused with the myths but they present yet another complementary version that must be decoded. They correspond to an interpretation of myths and rites and of their connection as well as to a transformation and a reversal in which organized ideas take the place of the concrete logic of myth. This transformation is part of the movement animating the continuous whole (the diffused meaning takes a dominating position while the concrete logic that connected different images becomes an autonomous science separate from myth, a logic that gave birth to modern science). This transformation can also correspond to a change of mentality of consciousness accompanying the rupture of the bicameral brain.[7] While in the past, the inspired voice was a manifestation of the spirit and a witness to reality, it has gradually been supplanted by the idea, which has become the means of defining reality and transforming language.

The meaning embedded in the myth is extracted and translated by a mentality that uses it as a theory leading to an experience. As Einstein stated, "It is the theory that decides what can be observed." The meaning that this new mentality offers can be seen as corresponding to the theoretical aspect replacing the description given in the myth of things as they are lived within experience. Myths describe experience from the inside, gnosis and science from the outside.

This inclusion of ancient tradition and modern mentality alongside myth is the method we have followed from the start, and it is what has allowed us to follow simultaneously the trace of several meanings corresponding to Ariadne's thread. Finally there is also a connection between ancient and modern science and their two different ways of observing and talking about the world. As Bohr himself realized, science only discovers what we can say about the world. All these strategies have already been indicated by Lévi-Strauss, but with different emphases and in different combinations. We are not trying to abandon the formal structuralist method and know-how for an ancient hermeneutic, but rather to weld these two methods together and find their deeper connections in order to consider a complete network in which semantic, semiologic, and semiotic structures correspond. Besides simultaneously investigating how myths, ritual patterns, and gnosis become science, we must try to discover their relation and how different processes, paradigms, and mentalities are transformed into new ones giving priority to either so-called conscious or unconscious aspects.

The interpretation of a myth's meaning poses the same problem as the one encountered when interpreting theories of quantum physics: "To interpret, what does this mean? On one level it is to harmoniously reconcile formalism with the experimental concrete. It must also be to say how pure chance and determinism can be reconciled in the same world. And finally, it is the perspective on the horizon to found, beyond previous philosophical principles, the process that we call understanding."[8]

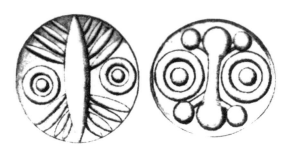

Fig. 37.3. Cretan seals
Why not different faces of knowledge?

38

Circumambulation and Revelation

Mantra is a path of return through the maze of the Sakti world.
—HARVEY ALPER

The three systems or forms of gnosis found in alchemy, tantrism, and the fragments of Heraclitus have led us to discover diverse possible meanings for Ariadne's thread. We have seen that these meanings are all intimately linked. We shall now try to show more directly how the three systems correspond and how they represent three approaches that use different codes to describe the same whole and the same unity from different points of view.

First of all, the metallurgical jargon employed in alchemy is a privileged code chosen only because the blacksmiths were the guardians of secret traditions. The alchemical code is the translation of other codes. Thus the applications of alchemical symbolism are undefined. "Symbolic notions correspond to mythical constellations." "Observing that 'everything observable is symbolic,' alchemy affirms that 'everything symbolic is observable' and that in consequence, the supreme symbol of symbols, which is to say unity, is observable and that 'real man can contemplate the incarnation of Logos in matter.'"[1]

We again encounter the Logos of Heraclitus in alchemy, but we also encounter language because, according to René Alleau, when the Great Work presents itself in three successive steps—*prima materia, mercury,* and *sulfur*—the sulfur's influence on the mercury represents the influence of myth and Logos on the world of reason and language. *The Forsaken Word,* the title of an alchemical work, reminds us of this aspect.

Alchemy, like tantric yoga, deals first and foremost with the transformation of the consciousness of the operator, which is inseparable from that of matter. It deals with rediscovering the creative Word hidden in matter, the light in the shadows, or a vital energy that can manifest itself as a vibration and produce forms. It is about making perceptible and regenerating what was at the beginning, as revealed in the Gospel of John: "In the beginning *[in principe]* was the Word [logos] and the Word was with God, and the Word was God. . . . All things were made by him; and without him was not anything made that was made" (1:1, 3) and, "The Word was made flesh, and dwelt among us" (1:14).

In alchemy, everything is spoken of in terms of matter, while in tantrism it is in terms of deities, but it is always a question of the same whole and the same unity. "The gods of a given culture constitute a pattern of interpretation that allows the great diversity of everyday experience to refer itself to the action of a restrained number of types of forces."[2] The forces discovered by physics also operate in man and manifest themselves through him in particular ways. They can thus be described or evoked in an anthropomorphic manner as gods or deities.

Even Heraclitus suggests a sort of yoga or alchemy when speaking of the Logos. If, according to him, the eternal Logos can be heard only by "paying attention," this logos or spirit must itself become observable. The attention and the observation he mentions are not those used in ordinary circumstances; they are the same as those acquired by the alchemist and the yogi.

It remains that for the noninitiated, the way Logos becomes observable is incomprehensible. The question is one of a total transformation due to an alchemical circumambulation. We do not understand how this circumambulation operates because the process leading from language to Logos, and thus to a deeper understanding, itself corresponds to a circumambulation. The problem of understanding what is meant by circumambulation does not so much consist in decoding a text to find a precise method, but rather of using the text itself as material in an appropriate action, in a circumambulation, and this in order to extract from it the Word or the spirit that created it. We need to practice in order to understand the description of the practice. We thus need a guide and a method to lead us through the text, or rather to teach us how to use and transform the text.

Circumambulation can thus be seen as a generic term embracing a group of diverse processes. It can describe alchemical or tantric processes; it can describe a process of transformation like that of the churning of the ocean to produce soma, as well as the conduct recommended by Peter, of the apostles: "Unless you make the things of the right hand as those of the left and those of the left as those of the right, and those that are behind as those that are before, ye shall not have knowledge of the kingdom." But circumambulation also corresponds to an operation applied to the revealed Word in order to liberate a meaning that can direct a line of conduct or liberate a creative and efficient word. It is this last operation that will help us to understand in a practical way what can be meant by Logos.

In Midrashic interpretation, the Kabbalah uses a similar procedure in its exegesis of the Bible (or the Torah). It "strides up and down the text" in all directions, animating it by correspondences and echoes (a labyrinthine procedure). It "skims the meaning" (a churning procedure) by reversing and transforming words by anagram and numerology. "It does not only subvert words by auscultation and by dislocation. It penetrates by breaking in . . . like an intruder it lodges one or several vowels that make possible the displacement of meaning and the deviation of a word from its initial meaning."[3] This is possible because of the fact that in Hebrew, only consonants are written. The letters constitute the corporeity of God, and the consonants and the vowels are considered as male and female, respectively, and as interpenetrating. Some techniques of calligraphy where the letters are intertwined, tangled, or jumbled can also produce multiple possible readings of a text (see plates 27, 28, 29, and 30). "The science of combination of letters is the science of the superior interior logic."

Midrash not only interprets the text of the Bible through this "science of combination of letters," but it also can interpret in its turn interpretations of the Torah by the rabbis. "And Rabbi Hayim concludes: even if their words seem simple and narrow-minded, in reality, under the force of the hammer, they are disseminated. As the more we triturate and the more we meticulously examine these words, the more our eyes are illumined by the luster of their bright light, the more we will find an unsuspected content, as our master says (Avot 5, 22): 'Turn and return it for everything is there.'"[4]

Finally, "the meanings have nothing to cling to in the text, if it isn't an infinite number of questions that we can ask about the context." The process does not consist so much in an interpretation leading to a particular knowledge, as that of a solicitation, a "modality of reading that consists in disturbing with a disturbance that has to do with the whole."[5] It is about rediscovering what is at the origin of a given word and how that can scatter or generate a multitude of different words depending on the circumstances. Thus interpreted, the Midrashic method can lead to the undoing of knots described by Abulafia, and according to him to prophecy.

An explanation of the reason for this deconstruction of sacred texts is indirectly suggested by Bruno Latour:

> What we have to retrieve is the carrying of a movement that uses the message to produce the enunciators of this message. Since this is obviously impossible, the only way it can be done is to render the message unable to do the job of information transfer, in order to force attention away. But this "away" is not the "beyond" of belief, and here again, the path falsely indicated by the message has to be broken, shattered, and interrupted, so as to redirect the sight away from the invisible and unalterable substance of the spiritual world. *Always away, but not beyond.* Yet neither is the direction, the depth of an individual soul, moved by the beauty of a message that is addressed to the ego, *hic, nunc.* Again, to cancel out this third possible reading and escape in the right direction, "the message has to be split, cracked, shaken and redirected away. *Away, but not down* toward the feelings of psychology or even deeper in the dark unconscious. And so on in a circulation, a spiral, which provides meaning not only for a painting but for the whole setting—theological, institutional, cultural—in which the mediators are gathered, reshuffled, and assembled."[6]

The extremely elaborate and codified techniques created to memorize the Vedas also consist in "taking apart, in disarticulating the text, in such a way as to sever all logical links, to sever the continuity of the text and its coherence. Thus, one begins by learning a text or a part of a text in order, then one learns it backwards, then by inverting the stanzas or the members of the stanza *disposed in braids*, etc. . . ."[7] It is no longer a question of an interpretation but rather of following instructions, as the Veda contains its own mode of interpretation. "The Veda is constituted, on the one hand, of a central nucleus made of prayers or hymns, and on the other, of a periphery, also revealed, also sacred, that indicates the way to use the central nucleus of the word. . . . It is a question of the correct and very codified use of this fixated speech that constantly speaks of a speech that passes from possibility to actuality. . . . Thinking about the contents would harm the fidelity of the literal transmission and its efficacy."[8] Brahmans and Vedists must learn to cut up the text in order to connect it to melodies, ritual gestures, and the silent unfolding of the ritual that "invigorates" the word. Its purpose, by a verbal alchemy, is to make prayer efficient and to reach the gods who "are in their names."

Moreover, the fixed word is a means of attaining a more complete word, since for Vedic thinkers the perceptible word is but a quarter of the whole word. "There is a creative word that takes refuge in all sorts of sonorous elements that are not necessarily part of articulated language, but which can be put into relation with the development of sacrificial operations."[9]

The goal is thus finally to return to the source of the revealed word. In fact the Vedic text itself explicitly mentions those who have grasped the creative word concretized in the Veda: "Although their power is defined as superior to that of the gods, they are men called *rishis*, which is to say seers. . . . The essential paradox is as follows. The Veda is a sonorous mass and yet the *rishis* saw it. And their role was to fix and unfold in articulated and stable words what was word only in potency."[10] The name of the mythic author of the Mahabharata, "Vyasa," means he who unfolds or distributes.

Alongside the *rishis*, the Veda speaks to us of jousters "who put their improvisational talent into play, in other words their aptitude to grasp the word, and find a reply to counter the speech of a rival improviser."[11] They are, in a certain sense, linguists who have continued the work of the *rishis*, and who have bent and knotted the word after its unfolding in order to use it and move from a word in potency to an actual one. Thus the origin of the word as it is finally presented in the Veda is double.

This complementarity between linguists and seers can be found in many civilizations.

In the Caucasus, the shaman (*kadag*) is the receptacle of the word of the gods and he gains access to this knowledge by an apprenticeship. He hears the gods speaking their language, or else speaking through his own mouth during a trance, but the language and what it signifies remain obscure. Beside him there is also a standard-bearer who sees the god and can converse with him, but one does not know in which language. It is a kind of pilgrim who "follows invisible tracks, invisible limits, invisible paths that the gods have traced." There is a collaboration or even sometimes an exchange between the two roles when, for example, the standard-bearer loses himself. When the trail is lost, it is the linguist who enters a trance. "The god then speaks to say 'it is not there, it is here' and the limits are retraced, but always in the mind."[12]

The Cunas of Panama are also guided by two partners: The medicine man who speaks "the language of great trees," who knows and sings therapeutic songs, is accompanied by the "Nele," who sees. In certain songs the latter is called "he who forms things by his gaze, he who gives birth to things through his gaze."

> During a vision, the seer can thus enter into contact with the vegetable spirits. These latter reveal for example the origin of an illness or the identity of an animal spirit who has attacked someone, the place of his residence in the other world, and the correct path to get there. . . . It is thus always the seer who establishes the diagnostic of an individual illness, and it is from these indications that 'the shaman who speaks' sings the appropriate song.[13]

The Nele sees and follows a path; for example, he sees in the jungle the path of the sky jaguar, a path of sound indicated by the cries of other animals through whom the jaguar speaks. "Another case must be mentioned where the two roles are inverted. There exists a singer-shaman specialized in the orientation of the Nele's soul when it leaves his body to seek the spirits who have attacked the entire community. It is

in this case that an offering is given to the gods: it is the ashes of the furnace that is lit during all ritual recitation. In this case, it is the seer who gives, by this act, the health back to the community, while the singer-shaman, by the enunciation of his song, makes the diagnosis."[14]

There is still another subtle relationship between the singer and the Nele because the apprenticeship of the singer culminates

> with the transmission of a crucial part of the song. . . . This part is called the "invisible part of the path" or the "soul" of the song itself, *purpa* in Cuna, which is now called the *secreto* of the song in Spanish. Once this secret part of the song is known the singer becomes "he who knows." . . . It comprises knowing the origin of certain spirits, and this in sexual terms . . . A *secreto* must never be pronounced: it must be hinted at in silence. . . . We have here a very strong performative aspect, because this text is directly addressed to the spirit responsible for the sickness, or even, depending on the case, to its enemy, who must intervene to achieve the therapy.[15]

Thus the song not only is a path of sound, but it also contains an invisible path that corresponds to the one the seer sees. Perhaps we could say, since it is still about untangling what is knotted, that the secret path is also that of the Logos and the labyrinth, rediscovered into a maze. It is also perhaps the one described in the *molas*.

Most of the time there is, on the one hand, a seer who speaks to the god, sees a path, and sees in the path a speech and a message, and on the other hand, a linguist who uses speech to communicate with the gods, who untangles what is tangled, and who liberates a powerful word. Sometimes, though rarely, both can be present in a single person.

The language of the gods is not fundamentally different from our own. It is similar to ours but used specifically to describe and reveal a network, a path, and a reversal. In this language, speech itself becomes the goddess of that same name but paradoxically "words become gods only through taking hold of a man, they become gods only by tearing themselves away from the lips of the priest, the possessed or crazy or simply ill man. It is the language of the gods that has the virtue of producing the gods."[16] Somehow it seems that it is by producing gods by giving a form and a figure to forces and energies that language can lead back to Logos.

This vision-word relation can implicitly be found in alchemy, in tantrism, in the sayings of Heraclitus, as well as in Vedism. The essence of a revelation unveils itself by bringing to the surface a dimension of vision proper to the primordial nature of the mind. This is also—according to this study—what the labyrinth strives to achieve since it also represents a path for the word.

The labyrinth is a precise image of circumambulation, and the geometry reveals that it explains its process. The difference between circumambulation and deconstruction is just as important as the one between iconophile and iconoclast. Circumambulation rediscovers the power of the word, a word that can perform, that becomes present to us and makes us present. "The meaning of the message (of the revelation) is in a presence that becomes absent through the displacement of the mediation itself."[17] The circumambulation transforms again the mediation and brings back the presence. "I am" also means that an "I" is present to me, an "I" that is one; thus I become complete. A spirit or a god, which is a guide, an impartial observer, but also a mediator, becomes present to what "I" become in his presence.

It is then not sufficient that the interpretation of a revealed text disclose the content of the message,

Such is not at all the way messages order themselves along religious paths. They are not about messages at all; no matter how abstract, pious, reasonable, or gnostic, they are about messengers. And they are not about having access to a superior reality beyond, but about designating the speaker as the one who receives the gift of life anew, and suddenly starts to understand what those messages finally—but always provisionally—meant. Messengers, not messages; persons here and now, not substance there and above or below.[18]

Deconstruction, on the other hand, produces a multiplicity of meanings; it transforms the world into an archipelago instead of uniting it with all possible worlds and thus eliminating the beyond. As mentioned previously, deconstruction probably stems from the kabbalistic tradition, but one distorted or incompletely understood. Midrashic interpretation transforms the text in accordance with the context in order to reveal a specific situation and the nature of an interpersonal relation that itself determines the context and the nature of a person. Like the *I Ching,* it produces relevant images and judgments. With deconstruction, the legitimacy of the messenger and the law conformity of the message are denied.

In other respects, in a materialistic world disconnected from the symbolic realm, the circumambulation becomes ineffectual, but the labyrinth of life can transform a pilgrim into a mediator who can create or reveal new symbols.

Fig. 38.1. Cretan seals
Are these sound or circles or glory becoming a face, spirit, or goblin?

39

Cretan Seals and the
Unique Kind of Whole

Have you taught the dawn to grasp the fringes of the earth . . .
To bring up the horizon in relief as clay under a seal,
Until all things stand out like the folds of a cloak . . .

—JOB (38:13, 14)

The art of Cretan seals, examples of which are scattered through these pages, is difficult to evaluate for many reasons, the first being that the meaning of the figures is difficult to interpret. Its idiom or the structure of its visual language remains completely foreign to us. Sometimes we recognize scenes or objects represented in a realistic or schematic manner, but often we encounter purely geometric drawings or mysterious symbolic patterns. The figures seem to include a representation of all possible things, all of them linked by what appears to be a continuous transformative process, each image a provisional frame for a series of transformation.[1]

No seals are identical, but when comparing two similar ones, it is always possible to find a third that suggests a transition. The figures seem to have been extracted from multiple versions of a cartoon. They constitute a whole and cannot be correctly interpreted in isolation.

Representations of plants, for example, appear doubled, folded, or unfolded, and they transmute themselves to liberate or define an inner space that itself engenders new images, such as lion masks (fig. 39.1). The space is sometimes enclosed, but at other times seems to reverse itself and to extend beyond the scope of the seal, while new, barely sketched

Fig. 39.1. Three-sided seal with lion mask

Fig. 39.2. Dislocation? Or transformation of a well ordered composition?

motifs surface, lending a new significance to the originals (fig. 39.2). But where or how this continually regenerating process began we cannot say.

Circles or crescents that may represent heavenly bodies become rings or replace eyes, nostrils, mouths, or articulations; or else, breaking apart, they form horns, handles, crab or octopus arms, or even waves, eddies, or furrows. Images of bucrania are transformed into those of vases or cuttlefish. Bars that first appear as light rays become beams or joists used to portray an architecture that in turn seems to collapse into a chaotic heap of debris. Sometimes they can also suggest the formation of crystals or resemble the intersecting threads of weaving, or, when the visual field is broadened, of cords being knotted or unknotted.

The variety of styles is also disconcerting! Though some figures are traced with refinement, others seem to have been roughly cut out, not as a result of clumsiness but as if a rough effect was intentionally sought. Similar figures appear decomposed in a cubist or surrealist manner, or elsewhere integrated into a movement as in futurist painting. Sometimes, when bucrania are represented, the figures appear desiccated, torn in shreds, as if this image of death had been unearthed in order to discover in it an opening leading to another world.

Do these images constitute symbols? One cannot be certain; it seems that, as with myths, we can speak only of a symbolic approximation. The images can best be understood as an art describing the genesis, transformation, and destruction of symbols, or even the interaction of the symbolic and the concrete.

Yet one does not find only figurative or abstract images. We also encounter talismanic signs and groupings of hieroglyphs that correspond to pictographic or Linear A script (as yet undeciphered) and thus represent a syllabic sound (fig. 39.3). Do they represent mantras, formulas, or proper names? No one is sure. The hieroglyphs are often arranged in clusters, allowing them to be read in different ways and for plays on words. Moreover, as there is little difference between the elements of image and of hieroglyph, all sets of seals can suggest, in a certain sense, a jumbled fluctuation of sounds, or the partition of an aleatory music that is more elemental than concrete.

The seals are created by incisions reminiscent of

Fig. 39.3. Three-sided seal with hieroglyphs corresponding to sounds or syllables

cuneiform writing, and the images are almost illegible. It is only when they are stamped that the details become perfectly clear. Color thus seems to play no role. But as the designs are cut into rare or precious stones of various hues, some transparent or translucent, others streaked or spotted with colors, they nonetheless are submerged in the colorful atmosphere reflected on the edges of the imprint. The motifs, like insects imprisoned in amber, appear as the well-protected vestiges of an ancient world. We can thus think of painting and evoke a sort of archetype of color represented by the precious stones—as does the nineteenth-century sheikh Kirmani who compares the relationship of color and light with that of body and soul.

The geometry of the labyrinth can once again help us. As we have seen, it is that which enables symbols to be created and transformed from the representation of concrete objects. This geometry does not constitute a separate science—as it does today—but rather a way of perceiving. It can thus be applied not only to a knot, but also to all kinds of objects and to everything implicitly contained within the knot, understood as symbol of the whole. We are thus better prepared to understand how the art of the seals connects a representation of the object to a multitude of aspects that we encountered in the geometry, most notably torus knots but also all sorts of doublings. As there is a transformation of the knot into a labyrinth, there is simultaneously a transformation of all that is potentially or virtually contained in the knot. As the knot is transformed into a labyrinth and the pilgrim advances on his path toward a more complete experience of reality, he crosses from a concrete or imaginary world to a symbolic world. He goes through different stages or levels of development accompanied by diverse experiences and impressions or visions. These impressions can be represented by the seals, while the labyrinth containing them is transformed into a sort of mandala. However, the seals ought not to be visualized as if displayed precisely along the path as in a game of snakes and ladders, for

if the labyrinth contains all things, it is in the same way that a window or a mirror contains a landscape. Like the relaxed knot, it is a roofless architecture and thus completely open. Along those lines, I understand better what I described in the very first chapter, how as I ran through the labyrinth of Götland and contemplated the surrounding country, different views of the landscape merged together to produce new and suggestive images.

To understand the complex process suggested by the path in the labyrinth of life and how it can bring the pilgrim through different stages of development accompanied by diverse visions, it must be understood as the synthesis of several other symbolic processes, such as the ascent of a Jacob's ladder, for example, which could be a rope ladder capable of moving somehow like a flying carpet; or the peeling of an onion revealing the emptiness of its essential core; or the growth of the tree of life that was often represented juxtaposed with the labyrinth. All these processes are indirectly connected to the labyrinth through myths and legends.

Now, why are these views or visions uniquely represented on seals and not, for example, on frescoes or on vases? What is the special meaning of the seal? As they served to mark goods in commerce, they were thought to be emblems used as trademarks—that is, emblems, not symbols. This is possible, but this interpretation is not sufficient and does not take into account the important interpenetration between religion and the system of exchange that was itself endowed with symbolic meaning.

An indication of the symbolic meaning of seals can be found in the Sanskrit term *mahamudra*, which means Reality in its highest sense, or as Herbert Guenther says, reality as "the enlightened realization of the value sphere."[2]* It could be literally translated as "great sign," for mudras constitute a kind of prayer sign language that can have the significance of seals.

*The information that follows is inspired by the works of Guenther, and I am solely responsible for the way I understand his ideas and the use I make of them.

Seal has the double meaning of "imprinting" and "not going beyond" while *great* means that "nothing superior is possible." One cannot go beyond the stamped seal because one cannot go beyond Reality. This Reality that is fused with the divine cannot be known as such but it can reveal itself in a moving experience through symbols. It is certainly not considered to be a thing, but rather an immediate and ultimate experience that corresponds to a process by which one gets rid of illusions created by fundamental ignorance. It thus presents itself as a stamp that marks a vision with an experience of nothingness and lucidity that, joined together, render the vision comprehensible. "Nothingness is sealed by appearance and appearance by nothingness."[3]

But what is the nature or the source of these visions? How are they created? In Dzogchen, a Tibetan system that has roots in shamanism, creation holds a very particular place: "Man/human is not created by a god or demiurge, but evolves out of the potential that he/she/it is and that in its dynamics express itself in symbols of its own making, 'epiphanies of (its) mystery' that are understood in the immediacy of their experiencing them prior to their shaping them in distinct patterns of meaning and/or images by the omnipotent experiencer's consciousness."[4] This dynamic has a name that Guenther translates as "pure intensity" or "individualized energy."

We discover that by means of contemplation, the tantric or Dzogchen practitioner can have a direct experience of what he calls the whole united in a single point, or as Guenther translates it, "a unique kind of whole." This unique kind of whole is equivalent to unity because it is recognized as coming from a unique source, an infinite space that is the basis of all things and which becomes present or concentrated in a point. The whole is united with this space to constitute reality. This experience is thus in accordance with the all-encompassing and penetrating view obtained at the center of the labyrinth.

But this immediate experience of Reality divides itself into an experience of pure presence that is the source of bliss and a pure creativity that manifests itself in an endless variety of forms perceived by the contemplator. As the contemplation progresses, perception melts into pure sensation and corresponds to a lucid and discriminating consciousness, an intuition that allows Reality to be understood both as immutable and as continually developing. The forms and the movement perceived can be seen as the recording of both reality and the process of creativity. It is as if the united whole becomes signified by every one of its parts, as if each impression in the labyrinth announced and virtually contained the overview of all things contained at the center. Since in this experience the proliferation of conceptual propositions is completely interrupted, there is a loosening and a self-dissipation of the conventional, disunited whole that corresponded to associative thoughts. The whole becomes a developing fluctuation, a vortex bringing mystic visions. The contemplator moves in a continuum that can, at each moment, take on the role of symbol or else slide into the concrete. Thus, in a certain sense, contemplation liberates a symbolic geometry that is spontaneously self-activated. In the same way as the circumambulation of a revealed text allows one to recover the creative word, the circumambulation of the visible allows one to recover a creative vision. The two processes are linked.

"Various names are given to different visions. For example, 'the fish of rays in movement' refers to the movement of visions and describes them as moving like a fish swimming in waves. The text explains that we should try 'to capture the fish of rays in movement in the net of darkness' and describes the state of presence as an arrow that must reach the target, the fish. The vision is the fish and the arrow, presence and the instrument by which it is obtained."[5]

If the images and symbols appear to be uniquely visual, they represent a form of energy, and they correspond as well to certain mantras, or as Guenther translates the Tibetan, to "mystery spells." They represent the language of *dakinis:* "It is like a mother speaking to her child by means of reasoned certitude."[6]

At first, the visions are supposed to appear like crossed colored lines or roughly woven textiles, then as chains made of knots "like those found on a horse's tail, then as rosaries or garlands made of pearls or flowers, then appear as *tigles* or seed syllables surrounded as by rainbows and colored circles." All these images can remind us of topology. At a more advanced stage the visions become like apparitions of peaceful or wrathful guardians or deities, or of syllables and objects as emblems of a deity, or of stupas, mandalas, or yantras, which are like the house or the body of a deity. At the final stage they dissolve, leaving us with the certitude that all perceptions are projections of our mind and have no inherent truth. These visions that, taken together, constitute a dissipative structure are thus used to destroy the illusion created by our ordinary perceptions in order to stabilize the sense of a truer reality. The aesthetic sensibility thus developed becomes a means of discovering and evaluating ethical values linked to integrity.

The Cretan seals can correspond to an ancient Mediterranean version of this unique kind of whole. The art of these seals would then constitute the bridge uniting the diverse geometric and figurative designs of primitive and ancient art. We find here a new concept of art with therapeutic properties and a kind of description of the experiences to which the labyrinth could lead. If the knot represents the whole and the labyrinth the One, the seals function as the "betwixt and between." The visions or seals showing the nature of reality "as a mother to a child" are then the complement of a more virile language that, because of our condition, is unable to bring us to a true reality. The images are again the Other of the text.

We can find an understanding similar to one in Islam according to a known Hadith:

> The first thing that God created was the Pen [which here signifies the first-created Logos], then he told it: "Write!" "What shall I write," asked the Pen. "That which is and that which will be until the day of the resurrection." And the Pen wrote. Then God put a seal over the mouth of the Pen and, having written it, did not declare the hidden meaning.[7]

But today the real is recognized only in the concrete and in the passions—in other words, in the ephemeral. This art has thus become mute. Mechanical or conventional perception, indissolubly linked to a system of categories and constructions that have become instinctual and organic, keeps us from perceiving a truth or reality always and everywhere present. When we consider reality like a bone full of marrow we become somewhat like dogs—"*Cave canem*," beware of the dog. It seems that in the history of art, as with that of cultures, there is always a confrontation and an alternation between a creative vision leading to a symbolic language that can become petrified or reductionist and a meaningful and vitalist rediscovery of realism that also demands lucidity, but becomes easily vulgarized. The ultimate goal would be to make them coincide or communicate harmoniously. In Cretan art we find a coherent exchange between both. With the art of frescoes, the decoration of pottery, and the carving of seals, we find three different art forms that together teach us how to read the movement of images, what Bruno Latour calls *iconophylie* (something quite different from the images of movement)—how to see more fully, and how to conquer space.

Fig. 39.4. Three-sided Cretan seal: with talisman, serpent, and fish. A "fish of rays in movement"?

Notes

Preface

1. See, for example, Fritjof Capra, *The Tao of Physics* (New York: Bantam, 1979); Gary Zukav, *The Dancing Wu Li Masters* (New York: Bantam Books, 1979); or Douglas Hofstadter, *Gödel, Escher, Bach* (Boston: Shambhala, 1975).

Chapter 1

1. Charles F. Herberger, *The Thread of Ariadne* (New York: Philosophical Library, 1972).

2. Steven Odin, *Process Metaphysics and Hua-yen Buddhism* (Albany, N.Y.: State University of New York Press, 1982).

3. Robert M. Pirsig, *Zen and the Art of Motorcycle Maintenance* (New York: Bantam, 1979), 14–15.

4. Jean François Lyotard, *La condition postmoderne: rapport sur le savoir* (Paris: Éditions de Minuit, 1979). See English version, *The Postmodern: A Report on Knowledge*, trans. Geoff Bennington and Brian Massumi (Minneapolis, Minn.: University of Minnesota Press, 1984).

5. Rudy Rucker, *The 57th Franz Kafka* (New York: Ace Books, 1983).

6. Michel Serres, *L'Interférence* (Paris: Éditions de Minuit, 1972).

Chapter 4

1. Roland Barthes, *Roland Barthes* (New York: Hill and Wang, 1977).

2. Geoffrey of Monmouth, *The History of the Kings of England* (New York: Penguin, 1966).

3. C. G. Jung and C. Kerenyi, *Essays on a Science of Mythology*, trans. R. F. C. Hull (New York: Harper and Row, 1963).

4. Fulcanelli, pseud., *Le Mystère des Cathédrales*, trans. Mary Sworder (London: Neville Spearman, 1971).

5. Antoine-Joseph Pernety, *An Alchemical Treatise on the Great Art* (York Beach, Maine: Samuel Weiser, 1995).

6. Nicolaus Moronus, *Tractatus Aureus* (Venetijs: Apud Damianum Zenarum, 1574).

9. Fragment 64, Heraclitus, *Ancilla to the Pre-Socratic Philosophers*, ed. and trans. Kathleen Freeman (Cambridge: Harvard University Press, 1948), 29.

10. R. A. Schwaller de Lubicz, *Sacred Science*, trans. Andre VandenBroek (Rochester, Vt.: Inner Traditions, 1989).

11. Fragments 1 and 2, *Heraclitus Seminar*, ed. Martin Heidegger and Eugen Fink, (Tuscaloosa, Ala.: University of Alabama Press, 1979).

12. Fragment 45, Ibid.

13. René Alleau, *Aspects de l'alchimie traditionelle* (Paris: Éditions de Minuit, 1953), 130.

14. Gregory Bateson, *Angels Fear* (New York: Bantam Books, 1988), 146.

Chapter 5

1. Bertrand Vergely, *Peinture et spiritualité*, (Paris: Édition Noésis, 1998) [Quote translated by Patrick Conty].

2. Ibid.

Chapter 6

1. Ananda Coomaraswamy, *Time and Eternity* (Bangalore, India: Select Books, 1989).

2. Ananda Coomaraswamy, "L'Iconographie des núuds de Dürer et des concaténations de Leonard de Vincy" [from French version of the Detroit Institute of Art's] *Art Quarterly* 7, no. 2 (1944).

3. Yannic Mellier, *Gravitational Lensing* (proceedings of workshop held in Toulouse, France, 13–15 September 1989).

4. Brian Greene, *The Elegant Universe* (New York: Vintage, 1999), 18.

5. *Discover*, June 1983.

6. *New York Times*, 21 February 1989.

7. Keith Devin, *New Scientist*, 10 November 2001, 42.

8. Paul Davies, *The Cosmic Blueprint* (New York: Simon and Schuster, 1989).

9. Giorgio de Santillana and Hertha von Dechend, *Hamlet's Mill: An Essay Investigating the Origins of Human Knowledge and Its Transmission through Myth* (Boston: David R. Godine, 1977).

10. Claude Lévi-Strauss, *The Story of Lynx*, trans. Catherine Tihanyi (Chicago: University of Chicago Press, 1991).

11. Niels Bohr, quoted in *Inventing Reality: Physics as Language*, by Bruce Gregory (New York: Wiley Science Editions, 1988).

12. Bruno Latour, quoted in *Picturing Science, Producing Art*, ed. Caroline A. Jones and Peter Louis Galison (London: Routledge, 1998).

Chapter 7

1. Moshe Idel, *L'Experience mystique d'Abraham Aboulafia* (Paris: Éditions du Cerf, 1989).

2. Michel Foucault, *The Order of Things* (London: Tavistock, 1970).

3. Jacques Derrida, *Of Grammatology* (Baltimore, Md.: Johns Hopkins University Press, 1976).

4. Italo Calvino, *Invisible Cities* (New York: Harcourt Brace Jovanovich, 1974).

Chapter 8

1. Heinrich Zimmer, *The King and the Corpse* (New York: Pantheon Books, 1957).

2. Jackson Knight, *Journal of the Royal Anthropological Institute* 64 (1934).

3. Ibid.

4. See Gertrude Rachel Levy, *The Gate of Horn: A Study of the Religious Conceptions of the Stone Age, and Their Influence upon European Thought* (London: Faber and Faber, 1948).

5. Jackson Knight, *Journal of the Royal Anthropological Institute*. Recorded by A. B. Deacon in the Semiang district of Malaysia.

Chapter 9

1. Heraclitus, *Ancilla to the Pre-Socratic Philosophers*, ed. and trans. Kathleen Freeman (Cambridge: Harvard University Press, 1948).

2. Lawrence E. Sullivan, *Icanchu's Drum: An Orientation to Meaning in South American Religions* (New York: Macmillan, 1987).

Chapter 10

1. Olivier Clément, *Trois priéres* (Paris: Desclée de Brower, 1993).

2. Homer, *The Odyssey*, trans. Robert Fogles (New York: Penguin, 1977) 19.179.

3. Friedrich Nietzsche, *Thus Spake Zarathustra*, trans. Thomas Common (Mineola, N.Y.: Dover Publications, 1999).

Chapter 11

1. Carlos Castaneda, *The Art of Dreaming* (New York: HarperCollins, 1993).

2. Ibid.

3. Ibid.

Chapter 12

1. Herodotus, *The Famous History of Herodotus*, trans. B. R., anno 1584 (New York: AMS Press, 1967).

2. Trismegistus Hermes, from the *Asclepius*, in *Corpus Hermeticum*, trans. A. J. Festugière (Paris: Société d'Èdition "Les Belles Lettres," 1945) [trans. from French to English, Patrick Conty].

3. Isha Schwaller de Lubicz, *Her-Bak: Egyptian Initiate*, trans. Ronald Fraser (London: Hodder and Stoughton, 1967).

4. M. Griaule and G. Dieterlen, *Le Renard pâle* (Paris: Institut d'ethnologie, 1965) [in English, *The Pale Fox*].

5. Gertrude Rachel Levy, *The Gate of Horn: A Study of the Religious Conceptions of the Stone Age, and Their Influence upon European Thought* (London: Faber and Faber, 1948).

6. Ibid.

Chapter 13

1. Isha Schwaller de Lubicz, *Her-Bak: Egyptian Initiate*, trans. Ronald Fraser (London: Hodder and Stoughton, 1967), 349.

2. R. A. Schwaller de Lubicz, *Sacred Science*, trans. Andre VandenBroek (Rochester, Vt.: Inner Traditions, 1989), 150.

3. R. A. Schwaller de Lubicz, *Sacred Science*, 237–238.

4. Janet Gyatso, *Apparitions of the Self* (Princeton: Princeton University Press, 1998).

5. Moshe Idel, *L'experience mystique d'Abraham Aboulafia* (Paris: Cerf, 1989), 165.

6. Ibid., 166.

7. Ibid., 129.

8. Ibid., 136.

9. Ibid., 136.

10. Isha Schwaller de Lubicz, *Her-Bak: Egyptian Initiate*, 220.

11. Rundle Clark, *Myth and Symbols of Ancient Egypt* (New York: Thames and Hudson, 1978).

12. Gilles Deleuze, *La Logique des sens* (Paris: Union générale d'éditions, 1973).

13. Bhartrhari, *Vakyapadiya Brahmakanda*, trans. in Madeleine Biardeau, *Theorie de la parole dans le brahmanisme classique* (Paris: Boccard, 1964).

14. Ibid., 118.

Chapter 14

1. M. Griaule and G. Dieterlen, *Le Renard pâle* (Paris: Institut d'ethnologie, 1965).

2. M. Griaule, *Dieu d'eau* (Paris: Fayard, 1975).

3. Ibid.

4. Ibid.

5. Ibid.

6. Ibid.

7. Ibid.

8. G. Meurant, *Shoowa Designs* (Thames and Hudson, 1986).

9. Michel Perrin, *Tableaux Kuna* (Paris: Arthaud, 1998).

10. Henri Stierlin, *Nazca: la clé du mystére* (Paris: Albin Michel, 1983).

11. Ibid.

12. Ananda Coomaraswamy, "L'Iconographie des núuds de Dürer et des concaténations de Leonard de Vincy" [from French version of the Detroit Institute of Art's] *Art Quarterly* 7, no. 2 (1944).

13. Michel Serres, *Passage du nord ouest* (Paris: Éditions de Minuit, 1980).

14. Walter Benjamin, "On Language As Such and on the Language of Man," *Reflections* (New York: Schocken Books, 1986).

Chapter 15

1. *New York Times*, 8 July 1996.

2. Michel Serres, *L'Interférence* (Paris: Éditions de Minuit, 1972).

3. Monika Langer, *Merleau-Ponty's Phenomenology of Perception: A guide and commentary* (Tallahassee: Florida State University Press, 1989).

4. Jeanne Granon-Lafont, *La topologic ordinaire de Jacques Lacan* (Paris: Point hors ligne, 1988).

5. Paul Ricoeur, *Hermeneutique and the human sciences* (Paris: Maison des sciences de l'homme, 1981).

6. Jacques Lacan, *Ecrits* (Paris: Seuil, 1966).

Chapter 16

1. Jorge Luis Borges, *Labyrinths: Selected Stories and Other Writings*, trans. Donald A. Yates (New York: New Directions, 1964), 86–87.

2. Giorgio de Santillana and Hertha von Dechend, *Hamlet's Mill: An Essay on Myth and the Frame of Time* (Boston: Gambit, 1969), 58, 61–62.

3. Charles F. Herberger, *The Thread of Ariadne* (New York: Philosophical Library, 1972).

4. Bellamy and Allan, *The Calendar of Tiahuanaco* (London: Faber and Faber, 1956).

5. Bika Reed, *Rebel in the Soul* (Rochester, Vt. Inner Traditions, 1997), 94.

6. Lawrence Eugene Sullivan, *Icanchu's Drum* (New York: Macmillan, 1988), 133–4.

7. Ibid.

8. Ibid.

9. Ibid.

Chapter 17

1. Lawrence Eugene Sullivan, *Icanchu's Drum* (New York: Macmillan, 1988).

Chapter 18

1. Ananda Coomaraswamy, *Time and Eternity* (Bangalore, India: Select Books, 1989).

2. Ibid.

3. Ibid.

4. Ibid.

5. W. M. Urban, *The Intelligible World* (New York: AMS Press, 1978), 260.

6. Stephen Hawking, *The Universe in a Nutshell* (New York: Bantam Books, 2001).

7. Coomaraswamy, *Time and Eternity*.

8. Ibid., 52.

9. Ibid., 51.

10. Nicholas of Cusa, "De visione dei" in *Complete Philosophical and Theological Treatises of Nicholas Cusa*, trans. Jasper Hopkins (Minneapolis, Minn.: A. J. Banning Press, 2001).

11. Coomaraswamy, *Time and Eternity*, 48.

12. Ibid.

13. Plato, "Philebus," in Coomaraswamy, *Time and Eternity*.

14. Plato, "Cratylus," in Coomaraswamy, *Time and Eternity*, 47.

15. Coomaraswamy, *Time and Eternity*, 63.

16. Aristotle, "Physics," in Coomaraswamy, *Time and Eternity*.

17. Rundle Clark, *Myth and Symbols of Ancient Egypt* (New York: Thames and Hudson, 1978), 227.

18. Lucy Lamy, *Egyptian Mysteries* (New York: Crossroad Publishing, 1981), 16.

19. Ibid.

20. "Knots, Chains, and Video" in *Science*, February 1994.

21. Jean Yves Leloup, *The Gospel of Mary Magdalene*, trans. Joseph Rowe (Rochester, Vt.: Inner Traditions, 2002).

22. Alwyn Rees and Brinley Rees, *Celtic Heritage: Ancient Tradition in Ireland and Wales* (London: Thames and Hudson, 1961), 346.

23. Martin Heidegger, *What Is a Thing?* (Chicago: H. Regnery Co., 1968).

24. Bruno Latour, "How to Be Iconophilic in Art, Science and Religion," in *Iconoclash: Beyond the Image Wars in Science, Religion, and Art*, ed. Bruno Latour and Peter Weibel (Cambridge, Mass.: MIT Press, 2002), 45.

25. Jeremiah Ostriker and Paul Steinhardt, "The Fifth Cosmic Element," *Scientific American,* March 2001 [translated from the French edition], 44.

26. Henry Corbin, *Temps cyclique et gnose ismaâelienne* (Paris: Berg International: 1982).

27. Ibid.

28. Ibid.

29. Ibid.

30. Ibid.

31. Ibid.

32. Basarab Nicolescu, *Science, Meaning and Evolution: The Cosmology of Jacob Boehme* (New York: Parabola, 1991).

33. Marcel Griaule, *Masques Dogons* (Paris: Institut d'ethnologie, 1983).

Chapter 19

1. R. A. Schwaller de Lubicz, *Symbol and the Symbolic,* trans. Robert Lawlor and Deborah Lawlor (New York: Inner Traditions International, 1981).

2. Ibid.

3. R. A. Schwaller de Lubicz, *The Temple in Man: Sacred Architecture and the Perfect Man,* ed. Robert Lawlor and Deborah Lawlor (Rochester, Vt.: Inner Traditions, 1988).

4. Alwyn D. Rees, *Celtic Heritage* (New York: Grove Press, 1961), 146.

Chapter 20

1. Frank Waters, *The Book of the Hopi* (New York: Penguin Books, 1977).

Chapter 22

1. René Thom, *Modèles mathématiques de la morphogénèse* (Paris: Union général d'éditions, 1981).

2. Lawrence Sullivan, *Icanchu's Drum,* (New York: Macmillan, 1988).

3. Gary Zukav, *The Dancing Wu-Li Masters* (New York: Bantam Books, 1979), 83–4.

Chapter 23

1. Seyyed Hossein Nasr, foreword to *Islamic Patterns* by Keith Critchlow (Rochester, Vt.: Inner Traditions, 1999), 6–7.

Chapter 24

1. Henri Atlan, *Entre le cristal et la fumée* (Paris: Éditions Seuil, 1979).

Chapter 25

1. Albert Ducrocq, *L'Esprit et la neuroscience* (Paris: J.C. Lattés, 1999).

2. Jean-Pierre Dieny, *Le symbolisme du dragon dans la chine antique* (Paris, College de France, 1994).

Chapter 27

1. Maurice Merleau-Ponty, *The Visible and the Invisible* (Evanston, Ill.: Northwestern University Press, 1968).

2. Mircea Eliade, *Images et symboles* (Paris: Gallimad, 1952).

Chapter 28

1. Jacques Brosse, *Maître Dôgen: Moine zen, philosopher et poète, 1200–1253* (Paris: Albin Michel, 1998).

2. Maurice Merlau Ponty, *Phenomenology of Perception,* trans. Colin Smith (London: Routledge, 1962).

3. Ibid.

4. Ibid.

5. Bhartrhari, *Vakyapadiya Brahmakanda,* trans. in Madeleine Biardeau, *Theorie de la parole dans le brahmanisme classique* (Paris: Boccard, 1964), 30, 37.

Chapter 29

1. Maurice Merleau-Ponty, *The Visible and the Invisible* (Evanston, Ill.: Northwestern University Press, 1968).

2. Albert Ducrocq, *L'Esprit et la neuroscience,* (Paris: J. C. Lattés, 1999), 84, 87.

3. Nietzsche, *Beyond Good and Evil,* trans. by Walter Kaufman (New York: Vintage Books, 1966).

4. Merleau-Ponty, *The Visible and the Invisible.*

Chapter 31

1. Bhartrhari, *Vakyapadiya Brahmakanda,* trans. in Madeleine Biardeau, *Theorie de la parole dans le brahmanisme classique* (Paris: Boccard, 1964).

2. Henri Michaux, *Darkness Moves: An Henri Michaux Anthology 1927–1984,* trans. David Ball (Berkeley: University of California Press, 1997).

3. H. Michaux, *Tate: The Art Magazine* (Spring 1999).

4. Paul Gauguin, *Oviri ecrits d'un sauvage* (Paris: Gallimard, 1998).

5. Bruno Latour, "How to Be Iconophilic in Art, Science and Religion," in *Iconoclash: Beyond the Image Wars in Science, Religion, and Art,* ed. Bruno Latour and Peter Weibel (Cambridge, Mass.: MIT Press, 2002).

6. Brian Greene quoted in Bertrand Vergely, "A Singular Image: The Icon, Transfigured Knowledge"

in *Peinture et spiritualité* (Paris: Édition Noésis, 2002).

7. Maurice Blanchot, *La livre à venir* (Paris: Gallimard, 1959).

8. Brian Greene quoted in Bertrand Vergely, "A Singular Image: The Icon, Transfigured Knowledge" in *Peinture et spiritualité* (Paris: Édition Noésis, 2002).

9. Ibid.

10. Roland Omnés, "Une nouvelle interpretation de la Mechanique quantique," *Recherches* 280 (October 1995).

11. Murray Gell-Mann, *The Quark and the Jaguar* (New York: W. H. Freeman, 1994).

12. Mircea Eliade, *Images et symboles* (Paris: Gallimard, 1952).

Chapter 32

1. *Kularnava Tantra* in *Theorie de la parole dans le brahmanisme classique* by Madeline Biardeau (Paris: Boccard, 1964).

2. Bruno Latour, "How to Be Iconophilic in Art, Science and Religion," in *Iconoclash: Beyond the Image Wars in Science, Religion, and Art,* ed. Bruno Latour and Peter Weibel (Cambridge, Mass.: MIT Press, 2002).

Chapter 33

1. Gurdjieff, *All und alles* [All and Everything] (Innsbruck, Austria: Verlag der Palme, 1950).

2. Gilles Deleuze, *A Quoi Reconnait-on le structuralisme,* in *Histoire de la Philosophie* (Paris: Hachette, 1973).

3. J. Petitot-Concordat, *La morphogénèse du sens* (Paris: Presses Universitaires de France, 1985).

4. Deleuze, *A Quoi Reconnait-on le structuralisme.*

5. Claude Lévi-Strauss, *Histoire du lynx* (Paris: Hachette, 1972).

6. Petitot-Concordat, *La Morphogénèse du sen.*

7. Ibid.

8. Deleuze, *Logique du sens* (Paris: Union générale d'éditions, 1973).

9. Deleuze, *The Logic of Sense,* trans. Mark Lester and Charles Stivale, ed. Constantin V. Boundas (New York: Columbia University Press, 1990).

10. Ibid.

Chapter 34

1. Umberto Eco, *The Island of the Day Before*, trans. William Weaver (New York: Harcourt Brace, 1995).

2. Herbert Guenther, *From Reductionism to Creativity* (Boston: Shambala, 1989).

3. Hourya Sinaceur, *Jean Cavaillès: Philosophie, Mathematique* (Paris: P.U.F., 1994).

4. Michel de Certeau, "The Gaze. . . Nicolas de Cusa," *Diacritics* (Fall, 1987).

5. Ibid.

6. Ibid.

7. Ibid.

8. Ibid.

9. Ibid.

10. Ibid.

Chapter 35

1. C. G. Jung and C. Kerényi, *Essays on a Science of Mythology*, trans. R. F. C. Hull (Princeton, N.J.: Princeton University Press, 1969).

2. Bruno Latour, "How to Be Iconophilic in Art, Science and Religion," in *Iconoclash: Beyond the Image Wars in Science, Religion, and Art,* ed. Bruno Latour and Peter Weibel (Cambridge, Mass.: MIT Press, 2002)

3. Claude Lévi-Strauss, *The Jealous Potter* (Chicago: University of Chicago Press, 1988), 197.

4. Michel de Ceerteau, "In the Gaze: Nicholas of Cusa," *Diacritics* (Fall 1987).

5. Ibid.

6. Ibid.

7. Ibid.

8. Ibid.

9. Ibid.

Chapter 36

1. Claude Lévi-Strauss, *The Jealous Potter* (Chicago: University of Chicago Press, 1988)*,* 171–72.

2. Claude Lévi-Strauss, *Le cru et le cuit* (Paris: Plon, 1964).

3. Roland Barthes, *Le Plaisir du texte* (Paris: Éditions du Seuil, 1973).

4. Lévi-Strauss, *The Jealous Potter,* 197.

5. Umberto Eco, *La Structure Absente* (Paris: Hermès, 1972).

7. Laurent Nottale, "L'espace-temps fractal," *Pour la science* (1995).

8. Michel Serres, *L'Interférence* (Paris: Éditions de Minuit, 1972).

9. Lawrence E. Sullivan, *Icanchu's Drum: An Orientation to Meaning in South American Religions* (New York: Macmillan, 1987).

10. Lao-tzu, trans. Gia-fu Feng and Jane English (New York: Vintage Books, 1989), 7.

11. R. W. Emerson, in *Essays and Lectures* (New York: Library of America, 1983), 485–6.

12. Bika Reed, *The Field of Transformations* (Rochester, Vt.: Inner Traditions, 1986), 145–6.

13. Taliesin, *The Poems of Taliesin*, ed. Sir Ifor Williams (Dublin Institute for Advanced Studies, 1968).

14. Nagarjuna, *The Fundamental Wisdom of the Middle Way*, trans. Jay L. Garfield (Oxford: Oxford University Press, 1995).

Chapter 37

1. Gary Zukav, *The Dancing Wu Li Masters* (New York: Bantam Books, 1979), 290, 295.

2. Ibid., 300.

3. Ibid., 304.

4. Ibid.

5. Ibid., 306–7.

6. Claude Lévi-Strauss, *L'Étude structurale des mythes* (New York: Basic Books, 2000).

7. Julian Jaynes, *The Origin of Consciousness in the Breakdown of the Bicameral Mind* (New York: Houghton Mifflin, 2000).

8. Roland Omnés, "Une nouvelle interpretation de la Mechanique quantique," *Recherches* 280 (October 1995).

Chapter 38

1. René Alleau, *Aspects de l'alchimie traditionelle* (Paris: Éditions de Minuit: 1953).

2. Robin Horton quoted in *La lecture infinie,* by David Banon (Paris: Éditions du Seuil, 1987).

3. David Banon, *La lecture infinie.*

4. "Nefesh Hahaim,"[Soul of Life], *La lecture Infinie.*

5. Ibid.

6. Bruno Latour, "How to Be Iconophilic in Art, Science and Religion," in *Iconoclash: Beyond the Image Wars in Science, Religion, and Art,* ed. Bruno Latour and Peter Weibel (Cambridge, Mass.: MIT Press, 2002).

7. All the quotes about the Veda are extracted from *La Déese Parole,* a film directed by M. Detienne and G. Hamonic.

8. Ibid.

9. Ibid.

10. Ibid.

11. Ibid.

12. Mircea Eliade, *Shamanism: archaic techniques of ecstasy,* trans. Willard Trask (London: Arkana, 1989).

13. Michel Perrin, *Tableaux Kuna* (Paris: Arthaud, 1998).

14. Ibid.

15. Ibid.

16. Bruno Latour, "How to Be Iconophilic in Art, Science and Religion," in *Iconoclash: Beyond the Image Wars in Science, Religion, and Art.*

17. Ibid.

18. Ibid.

Chapter 39

1. Bruno Latour, "How to Be Iconophilic in Art, Science and Religion," in *Iconoclash: Beyond the Image Wars in Science, Religion, and Art,* ed. Bruno Latour and Peter Weibel (Cambridge, Mass.: MIT Press, 2002).

2. Herbert Guenther, *Tibetan Buddhism in Western Perspective* (Berkeley, Calif.: Dharma Publishing, 1989).

3. Ibid.

4. Guenther, *The Teachings of Padma Sambhava* (Kinderhook, N.Y.: Brill Academic Publishers, 1996).

5. Tenzin Wangyal, *Wonders of the Natural Mind* (Berkeley, Calif.: Snow Lion Publishers, 2000).

6. Guenther, *Tibetan Buddhism.*

7. Henry Corbin, *Temple and Contemplation,* trans. Philip Sherrard with the assistance of Liadain Sherrard (London: KPI in association with Islamic Publications, 1986).

Bibliography

Alleau, René. *Aspects de l'alchimie traditionelle*. Paris: Éditions de Minuit: 1953.

Atlan, Henri. *Entre le cristal et la fumée*. Paris: Éditions Seuil, 1979.

Banon, David. In *La lecture infinie*. Paris: Éditions Seuil, 1987.

Barthes, Roland. *Le plaisir du texte*. Paris: Éditions du Seuil, 1973.

———. *Roland Barthes*. New York: Hill and Wang, 1977.

Bateson, Gregory. *Angels Fear*. New York: Bantam Books, 1988.

Bellamy and Allan. *The Calendar of Tiahuanaco*. London: Faber and Faber, 1956.

Benjamin, Walter. "On Language as Such and on the Language of Man," in *Reflections*. New York: Schocken Books, 1986.

Biardeau, Madeleine. *Theorie de la parole dans le brahmanisme classique*. Paris: Boccard, 1964.

Blanchot, Maurice. *La livre à venir*. Paris: Gallimard, 1959.

Borges, Jorge Luis. *Labyrinths: Selected Stories and Other Writings*. Tr. Donald A. Yates. New York: New Directions, 1964.

Brosse, Jacques. *Maître Dôgen: Moine zen, philosopher et poète, 1200–1253*. Paris: Albin Michel, 1998.

Calvino, Italo. *Invisible Cities*. New York: Harcourt Brace Jovanovich, 1974.

Castaneda, Carlos. *The Art of Dreaming*. New York: HarperCollins, 1993.

Clark, Rundle. *Myth and Symbols of Ancient Egypt*. New York: Thames and Hudson, 1978.

Clément, Olivier. *Trois priéres*. Paris: Desclée de Brower, 1993.

Coomaraswamy, Ananda. "L'Iconographie des núuds de Dürer et des concaténations de Leonard de Vincy." From French version of the Detroit Institute of Art's *Art Quarterly* 7, no. 2, 1944.

———. *Time and Eternity*. Bangalore, India: Select Books, 1989.

Corbin, Henry. *Temple and Contemplation*. Tr. Philip Sherrard with the assistance of Liadain Sherrard. London: KPI in association with Islamic Publications, 1986.

———. *Temps cyclique et gnose ismaêlienne*. Paris: Berg International, 1982.

Critchlow, Keith. *Islamic Patterns*. Rochester, Vt.: Inner Traditions, 1999.

Davies, Paul. *The Cosmic Blueprint*. New York: Simon and Schuster, 1989.

de Certeau, Michel. "In the Gaze. . . Nicholas de Cusa." *Diacritics*, Fall 1987.

de Santillana, Giorgio and Hertha von Dechend. *Hamlet's Mill: An Essay on Myth and the Frame of Time*. Boston: Gambit, 1969.

Deleuze, Gilles. "A quoi reconnait-on le structuralisme," *Histoire de la philosophie*. Paris: Hachette.

———. *La logique des sens*. Paris: Unrongénérale d'éditions, 1973.

———. *The Logic of Sense*. Tr. Mark Lester and Charles Stivale, ed. Constantin D. V. Boundas. New York: Columbia University Press, 1990.

Derrida, Jacques. *Of Grammatology*. Baltimore, Md.: Johns Hopkins University Press, 1976.

Devin, Keith. *New Scientist*. 10 November 2001, 42.

Ducrocq, Albert. *L'Esprit et la neuroscience*. Paris: J.C. Lattés, 1999.

Eco, Umberto. *La structure absente*. Paris: Hermès, 1972.

———. *The Island of the Day Before*. Tr. William Weaver. New York: Harcourt Brace, 1995.

Eliade, Mircea. *Images et symboles*. Paris: Gallimad, 1952.

Emerson, R. W. in *Essays and Lectures*. New York: Library of America, 1983.

Foucault, Michel. *The Order of Things*. London: Tavistock, 1970.

Fulcanelli, pseud. *Le mystère des cathédrales*. Tr. Mary Sworder. London: Neville Spearman, 1971.

Gauguin, Paul. *Oviri ecrits d'un sauvage*. Paris: Gallimard, 1998.

Geoffrey of Monmouth. *The History of the Kings of England*. New York: Penguin, 1966.

Granon-Lafont, Jeanne. *La topologic ordinaire de Jacques Lacan*. Paris: Point hors ligne, 1988.

Greene, Brian. *The Elegant Universe*. New York: Vintage, 1999.

Gregory, Bruce. *Inventing Reality: Physics as Language*. New York: Wiley Science Editions, 1988.

Griaule, Marcel. *Dieu d'eau*. Paris: Fayard, 1975.

———. *Masques Dogons*. Paris: Institut d'ethnologie, 1983.

———, and G. Dieterlen. *Le Renard pâle* [*The Pale Fox*].
Paris: Institut d'ethnologie, 1965.

Guenther, Herbert. *From Reductionism to Creativity.*
Boston: Shambhala, 1989.

———. *Tibetan Buddhism in Western Perspective.* Berkeley,
Calif.: Dharma Publishing, 1989.

———.*The Teachings of Padma Sambhava.* Kinderhook,
N.Y.: Brill Academic Publishers, 1996.

Gurdjieff. *All und alles* [All and Everything]. Innsbruck,
Austria: Verlag der Palme, 1950.

Gyatso, Janet. *Apparitions of the Self.* Princeton:
Princeton University Press, 1998.

Heidegger, Martin. *What Is a Thing?* Chicago: H. Regnery
Co., 1968.

———, and Eugen Fink. *Heraclitus Seminar, 1966/67.*
Tr. Charles H. Seibert. Tuscaloosa, Ala.: University
of Alabama Press, 1979.

Heraclitus. *Ancilla to the Pre-Socratic Philosophers.* Ed. and
tr. Kathleen Freeman. Cambridge: Harvard University Press, 1948.

Herberger, Charles F. *The Thread of Ariadne.* New York:
Philosophical Library, 1972.

Hermes, Trismegistus. *Corpus Hermeticum.* Tr. A. J.
Festugière. Paris: Société d'édition "Les Belles
Lettres," 1945.

Herodotus. *The Famous History of Herodotus.* Tr. B. R.,
anno 1584. New York: AMS Press, 1967.

Homer. *The Odyssey.* Tr. Robert Fogles. New York:
Penguin, 1977.

Idel, Moshe. *L'experience mystique d'Abraham Aboulafia.*
Paris: Cerf, 1989.

Jaynes, Julian. *The Origin of Consciousness in the Breakdown of the Bicameral Mind.* New York: Houghton
Mifflin, 2000.

Jones, Caroline A. and Peter Louis Galison, editors.
Picturing Science, Producing Art. London: Routledge,
1998.

Jung, C. G. and C. Kerényi. *Essays on a Science of
Mythology.* Tr. R. F. C. Hull. Princeton, N.J.:
Princeton University Press, 1969.

Knight, Jackson. *Journal of the Royal Anthropological
Institute,* 64, 1934.

"Knots, Chains, and Video," *Science,* February 1994.

Lacan, Jacques. *Ecrits.* Paris: Seuil, 1966.

Lamy, Lucy. *Egyptian Mysteries.* New York: Crossroad
Publishing, 1981.

Lao-tzu. Tr. Gia-fu Feng and Jane English. New York:
Vintage Books, 1989.

Latour, Bruno. "How to Be Iconophilic in Art, Science
and Religion," in *Iconoclash: Beyond the Image Wars
in Science, Religion, and Art.* Ed. Bruno Latour and
Peter Weibel. Cambridge, Mass.: MIT Press, 2002.

Leloup, Jean-Yves. *The Gospel of Mary Madgalene.*
Tr. Joseph Rowe. Rochester, Vt.: Inner Traditions,
2002.

Lévi-Strauss, Claude. *Le cru et le cuit.* Paris: Plon, 1964.

———. *L'Ètude structurale des mythes.* New York: Basic
Books, 2000.

———. *Histoire du lynx.* Paris: Hachette, 1972.

———. *The Jealous Potter.* Chicago: University of
Chicago Press, 1988.

———. *The Story of Lynx.* Tr. Catherine Tihanyi.
Chicago: University of Chicago Press, 1991.

Levy, Gertrude Rachel. *The Gate of Horn: A Study of the
Religious Conceptions of the Stone Age, and Their
Influence upon European Thought.* London: Faber and
Faber, 1948.

Lyotard, Jean François. *La condition postmoderne: rapport
sur le savoir.* Paris: Éditions de Minuit, 1979. See
English version, *The Postmodern: A Report on
Knowledge.* Tr. Geoff Bennington and Brian
Massumi. Minneapolis, Minn.: University of
Minnesota Press, 1984.

Merlau Ponty, Maurice. *Phenomenology of Perception.*
Tr. Colin Smith. London: Routledge, 1962.

———. *The Visible and the Invisible.* Evanston, Ill.:
Northwestern University Press, 1968.

Meurant, G. *Shoowa Designs.* Thames and Hudson, 1986.

Michaux, Henri. *Darkness Moves: A Henri Michaux
Anthology, 1927-1984.* Tr. David Ball. Berkeley:
University of California Press, 1997.

———. *Tate: The Art Magazine,* Spring 1999.

Moronus, Nicolaus. *Tractatus Aureus.* Venetijs: Apud
Damianum Zenarum, 1574.

"Nefesh Hahaim," [Soul of Life]. *La lecture Infinie.* Paris:
Éditions Seuil, 1987.

Nicholas of Cusa. "De visione dei," *Complete Philosophi-
cal and Theological Treatises of Nicholas Cusa.*
Tr. Jasper Hopkins. Minneapolis, Minn.:
A. J. Banning Press, 2001.

Nicolescu, Basarab. *Science, Meaning and Evolution: The
Cosmology of Jacob Boehme.* New York: Parabola,
1991.

Nietzsche, Friedrich. *Beyond Good and Evil.* Tr. Walter
Kaufman. New York: Vintage Books, 1966.

———. *Thus Spake Zarathustra.* Tr. Thomas Common.
Mineola, N.Y.: Dover Publications, 1999.

Nottale, Laurent. "L'espace-temps fractal," *Pour la
science,* 1995.

Odin, Steven. *Process Metaphysics and Hua-yen Buddhism.* Albany, N.Y.: State University of New York Press, 1982.

Omnés, Roland. "Une nouvelle interpretation de la mechanique quantique," *Recherches,* 280 October 1995.

Ostriker, Jeremiah and Paul Steinhardt. "The Fifth Cosmic Element," *Scientific American,* March 2001.

Pernety, Antoine-Joseph. *An Alchemical Treatise on the Great Art.* York Beach, Maine: Samuel Weiser, 1995.

Perrin, Michel. *Tableaux Kuna.* Paris: Arthaud, 1998.

Petitot-Concordat, J. *La morphogénèse du sens.* Paris: Presses Universitaires de France, 1985.

Pirsig, Robert M. *Zen and the Art of Motorcycle Maintenance.* New York: Bantam, 1979.

Reed, Bika. *The Field of Transformations.* Rochester, Vt.: Inner Traditions, 1986.

————. *Rebel in the Soul.* Rochester, Vt.: Inner Traditions, 1997.

Rees, Alwyn D. *Celtic Heritage.* New York: Grove Press, 1961.

————, and Brinley Rees. *Celtic Heritage: Ancient Tradition in Ireland and Wales.* London: Thames and Hudson, 1961.

Ricoeur, Paul. *Hermeneutique and the human sciences.* Paris: Maison des sciences de l'homme, 1981.

Rucker, Rudy. *The 57th Franz Kafka.* New York: Ace Books, 1983.

Schwaller de Lubicz, Isha. *Her-Bak: Egyptian Initiate.* Tr. Ronald Fraser London: Hodder and Stoughton, 1967.

Schwaller de Lubicz, R. A. *Sacred Science.* Tr. Andre VandenBroek. Rochester, Vt.: Inner Traditions, 1989.

————. *Symbol and the Symbolic.* Tr. Robert Lawlor and Deborah Lawlor. New York: Inner Traditions International, 1981.

————. *The Temple in Man: Sacred Architecture and the Perfect Man.* Tr. Robert Lawlor and Deborah Lawlor. Rochester, Vt.: Inner Traditions, 1988.

Serres, Michel. *L'Interférence.* Paris: Éditions de Minuit, 1972.

————. *Passage du nord ouest.* Paris: Éditions de Minuit, 1980.

Sinaceur, Hourya. *Jean Cavaillés: Philosophie, Mathematique.* Paris: P.U.F., 1994.

Stierlin, Henri. *Nazca: la clé du mystère.* Paris: Albin Michel, c1983.

Sullivan, Lawrence E. *Icanchu's Drum: An Orientation to Meaning in South American Religions.* New York: Macmillan, 1987.

Thom, René. *Modèles mathématiques de la morphogénèse.* Paris: Union général d'éditions, 1981.

Urban, W. M. *The Intelligible World.* New York: AMS Press, 1978.

Vergely, Bertrand. "A Singular Image: The Icon, Transfigured Knowledge," *Peinture et spiritualite.* Paris: Édition Noésis, 2002.

Wangyal, Tenzin. *Wonders of the Natural Mind.* Berkeley, Calif.: Snow Lion Publishers, 2000.

Waters, Frank. *The Book of the Hopi.* New York: Penguin Books, 1977.

Zimmer, Heinrich. *The King and the Corpse.* New York: Pantheon Books, 1957.

Zukav, Gary. *The Dancing Wu Li Masters.* New York: Bantam Books, 1979.

Index

Note: Page numbers in bold-italics indicate illustrations. When a page or page range contains both text and illustrations for the topic, bold-italics is not used.

superdeterminism, 266
superstrings, 29–30, 31–32, 62, 98
Suzhou, *plate 6*
symbolon, 141, 158, 223
symbols
   in alchemy, 270
   algebra of, 164–65
   broken rings and, 141, 158–59
   form and, 211
   in physics, 263
   reversal of relation to, 223–24
   structuralism and, 245, 246–47
   yantra function of, 249–50

tai chi postures, **128,** 129
tankas, 188, 217, *plate 8*
tantrism, 20–21, 209, 240
Tao
   path of the labyrinth as, 259
   sign of, 117, **118,** 128–29, 215, 216, *plate 5*
   the way and the, 245
Tao te Ching, 263–64
Tara, as center of Ireland, 167
Temple in Man, The, 163
Temptation of Saint Anthony, The, 254
tennis ball, 215–18, 219
textiles
   Cuna, **90–91,** 92, 95
   Shoowa, 89, **90–91,** 92, 95, *plates 1–2*
   weaving in Dogon myth, 88, 89
Theseus myth
   Aeneid and, 45–47
   Ariadne's thread in, 4, 56
   labyrinth transformed in, 56, 57, 59
   Oedipus myth and, 47
   ring of Minos in, 125–26
   shell threaded by Theseus, 55–56, 109
   transformation of Theseus, 56–58
   See also Ariadne's thread; Cretan labyrinth
Thom, René, 98, 99, 181–82
Thomson, William, 236
Thuret, church of, **253**
Thus Spake Zarathustra, 59
tie knot
   enneagram obtained from, 240, **241,** 242
   path of Cretan labyrinth and, 112–13, **114, 115**
Tilla Kari mosque, *plate 29*
Tilopa, 243, 244

time
   alchemical transformation and, 146–47
   cyclical, system of rings and, 156–59
   Egyptian iconography for, 147, **148**
   eternal, as emptiness, 145–46
   "form" of, 147
   in Hindu philosophy, 145
   in-between experience and, 153–56
   labyrinth as representing, 147
   Logos and, 149
   reversal of, 148
tombs
   designs representing, **189**
   Gavr'innis, 208–9, 252, **253**
topology
   ancient vs. modern, 223
   in children's art, 101
   of crystals, 188
   knot theory, 29–31, 89, 97–101, 153
   linguistics and, 25, 99
   logic and, 99–100
   morphogenesis and, 246
   psychology and, 100–101
   science and, 33
   as study of relation, 211
torus, transformation into coat, 255
torus knots
   with circular axis, **105,** 106
   circulation and mapping of, 199, **200–201**
   coat and, 255
   on Cretan seals, **113**
   enneagram and, 240, **241**
   as leap between two reversed knots, 135, **137**
   maze and mapping of, 174–75, **177**
   Möbius strip and, **123,** 124
   movement of knot and, 107
   obtained by leap within the knot, 138, **139**
   tie knot, 112–13, **114, 115**
   triangular, 106
   twist of self axis in, 112–13, **115**
Tower of Babel, 223
Tractatus Aureus, 19
Transfiguration, The, 252, *plate 21*
tree
   cat's cradle representing, **39,** 227–28
   of life, 256, *plate 26*
trigrams, Taoist, 128–29
Trungpa, Chögyam, 20, 26
Tzimtzum doctrine, 259

Uisiang, Ocean Seal of, 6, 7, 52
Uisnech, as center of Ireland, 167
umbilical cord, 49, 104, 169
unconscious
   becoming conscious, 59
   doubling of the cord and, 109
   labyrinth representing, 46–47
   myth and, 258–59, 260
   structured like language, 65
Under the Volcano, **231**
unified theory, 30–31
Universal History of the Creation, manuscript page, **131**
universality of the labyrinth, 15
Unknown Masterpiece, The, 226

van Gogh, Vincent, 226
Varuna's rope, 69, 107
Vedic deconstruction, 272
vibration, of superstrings, 29
void. *See* emptiness
Voltovo fresco, 152, *plate 15*

walls of the labyrinth
   axis of the knot as, 160, **161**
   polarity with path, 164
Waters, Frank, 168–69
Western interpretation, 6, 8–10, 16
wheels, labyrinth as array of, 265, **266**
whole
   fourfold sphere of wholeness, 190, **191,** 192
   knot as symbol of, 82, 193
   maze as symbol of, 22, 23, 178
   unbroken wholeness, 266
will, 162–63
Williams, William Carlos, 26
Wittgenstein, Ludwig, 193
world, maze as symbol of, 20, 22, 23, 178
world knot, 82
worm holes, 30

yantra, 20, 240, 249–50
yoga, as loosening of knots, 75
Yourcenar, Marguerite, 17

Zen and the Art of Motorcycle Maintenance, 8
Zeus's golden cord, 28–29, 36, 65, 69, 149, 237
Zimmer, Heinrich, 20
Zukav, Gary, 265
Zulu labyrinth, **12**